Defending
"A Christian Country"

Defending
"A Christian Country"

**Churchmen and Society in New South Wales
in the 1880s and after**

Walter Phillips

University of Queensland Press

Typeset by Press Etching Pty Ltd, Brisbane
Printed and bound by Silex Enterprise & Printing Co., Hong Kong

Distributed in the United Kingdom, Europe, the Middle East, Africa,
and the Caribbean by Prentice-Hall International, International Book
Distributors Ltd, 66 Wood Lane End, Hemel Hempstead, Herts.,
England.

National Library of Australia
Cataloguing-in-Publication data

Phillips, Walter, 1931-
    Defending a Christian country.

    Index
    Bibliography
    ISBN 0 7022 1539 2

    1. Australia — Church history. 2. Church and social problems —
Australia. I. Title.

261.1'0994

FOR TRICIA

Contents

Illustrations

Tables

Preface

Religion and its representatives in Australia have not been regarded as of much importance in the history of this country until recently. Some still seem to doubt whether the subject is worth exploring. In 1976 a reviewer of the sixth volume of the *Australian Dictionary of Biography* complained at the number of clerics it included, questioning whether Australian history in the second half of the nineteenth century would have been "so very different without most of these clerics and their generally forgotten squabbles?" (*Age,* 30 October 1976). This book presupposes that churchmen, that is the clerics and their lay stalwarts of all denominations (not only members of the Church of England, as English historians use the term) are significant in Australian history. Their "squabbles" and their confrontation with society in the later nineteenth century helped to shape the future; whether always for the good is another question.

This book is mainly about the conflict between churchmen and their society in New South Wales in the 1880s; it also describes a confrontation not confined to New South Wales, but seen in boldest outlines in that Australian colony during that decade. There were some differences between the various colonies, although the proceedings of general synods, general conferences and other intercolonial gatherings show that the similarities between churchmen in Australia, and the issues they faced, were much greater than any differences. This is illustrated by comparison here and there to parallel movements in other colonies, especially in Victoria.

Throughout Australia churchmen in the late nineteenth century were concerned about carrying out their mission in growing cities and reaching those out of touch with organized religion, especially the urban working classes. In varying degrees they also faced a challenge to the credibility, relevance, and authority of Christianity in their society. Everywhere they were trying to advance their cause and to extend the influence of religion.

Above all they saw themselves engaged in a great battle against secularism. They fought to defend Australia as "a Christian country". Even their "aggressive" tactics in church extension and evangelism were seen as part of this overall strategy, to combat secularism. Their warfare made them intransigent on issues that called for compromise, such as Sunday observance and divorce law reform. They looked for an ally in the State, which they expected to uphold religious values in law and in the public recognition of Almighty God.

The front line in this defence of Christianity was in New South Wales. Decisions made there during this decade influenced churchmen in other colonies. The first Central Methodist Mission was established in New South Wales in the 1880s to attract the working classes. In 1889 the first Council of Churches was organized, principally to defend the Christian Sunday and to combat gambling. The campaign for the recognition of God in the Australian Constitution may be traced back to the movement for a religious celebration of the centenary of Australia in 1888. Thus the reactions of churchmen in New South Wales greatly influenced the course of events in the next decade and later.

This is not to say that churchmen in other colonies slavishly followed the example of New South Wales. No colony ever recognized the superiority of another. But churchmen in other parts of Australia recognized their own battles in the conflict between religion and secularism in New South Wales, especially in the defence of Sunday and the campaign for the recognition of God. Victorian churchmen were close to their brethren in New South Wales in these matters. In South Australia they were less concerned about desecration of the Sabbath, for there was less of it; but they were more concerned about gambling in South Australia because the totalizator was introduced there in the 1880s. Gambling became a greater concern in New South Wales early in the twentieth century for much the same reason. But temperance reform was the prominent concern of churchmen in all colonies in the late nineteenth century, and determined their response to social questions. The reactions of churchmen to the challenges facing them in the 1880s and the policies they framed in the period influenced their relationship to society for the next eighty years. Only within the last fifteen years have those policies and attitudes been abandoned by the successors of these militant churchmen.

Acknowledgments

This book has been a long time in the making, and I have benefited from helpful criticism and advice from a growing number of people; in the first place from Professor K.S. Inglis of the Australian National University, who helped me chart my course, and from Dr F.B. Smith who guided me wisely to the completion of a thesis. The late Douglas Pike, who directed my first venture in historical research at the University of Adelaide, and his colleague in the *Australian Dictionary of Biography*, Mr Bede Nairn, also encouraged this enterprise. In the task of turning the thesis into a book I have been particularly indebted to my colleagues at La Trobe University, Professor J.S. Gregory and Dr John Barrett, both of whom read the manuscript and gave me warm encouragement as well as helpful criticism. My thanks are due as well to Dr J.B. Hirst of La Trobe University and to Dr Bruce Mitchell of New England University, Armidale, for their good advice.

I have also received courteous assistance from the librarians in the Australian National Library; the Menzies Library, Australian National University; St Mark's College Library, Canberra; the Mitchell Library, Sydney; officers of the New South Wales State Archives and more recently the La Trobe Library, State Library of Victoria and the La Trobe University Library. Officers and archivists of the various religious denominations have also assisted me generously, especially Monsignor C.J. Duffy of St Mary's Cathedral Archives, Sydney; the Reverend W. Tredennick, secretary of the former Australasian Methodist Historical Society; the Reverend E.G. Clancy of the Church Records and Historical Society of the Uniting Church in New South Wales; Mrs Norma Hart, librarian of the Presbyterian Church of New South Wales and Miss Mary Rusden, former librarian of Trinity College, Melbourne. I also wish to thank Mr Lindsay Howe of La Trobe University Library Reprography for technical assistance with illustrations, Mrs Shirley Gordon of the History Department, La Trobe University, who typed the final draft so efficiently and cheerfully, and Miss Margaret Kennedy for her skilful editing of the manuscript. Most of all I thank my wife, Tricia, not only for translating my scrawl into legible type, but above all for her support and encouragement, and my family for their tolerance of the book and its author.

Material included in chapters 5 and 7 has appeared previously in the *Journal of Religious History*.

Part One

Churches and the People

1

The Churches in a Challenging Decade

When the Australian colonies federated in 1901 they envisaged a Christian nation. The preamble to the Constitution Act spoke of "humbly relying on the blessing of Almighty God" and at the inauguration of the Commonwealth the Anglican primate, on behalf of the Protestant churches, invoked Divine favour upon the new nation. The first federal Parliament opened with the singing of the "Old Hundredth":

> All people that on earth do dwell,
> Sing to the Lord with cheerful voice;
> Him serve with fear, his praise forth tell;
> Come ye before Him and rejoice.

The governor general then read prayers for King and people, asking especially that God would direct and prosper the Parliament's consultations to the advancement of his glory and the welfare of the Australian people.[1] Within a few weeks of the new Parliament's life both Houses adopted the practice of daily prayers. Australians today accept this as customary even if they set little store by it. Few probably realize that the inauguration of the Commonwealth gave more recognition to religion than had any of the formal proceedings of the colonies which formed it. Daily prayers are observed in all the state Parliaments today, but at federation the practice obtained only in the Victorian Legislative Council and in the Parliaments of Queensland and Western Australia. Churchmen in New South Wales failed to win this recognition of religion in their own Parliament in the 1880s, thus they had little ground to hope that a federated Australia would give any official recognition to religion at all.

In New South Wales, following the pattern set by South Australia and Victoria, Parliament seemed to be driving a wedge firmly and deeply between church and state. State aid to churches as such had been abolished in the colony as early as 1862, but in 1880 stronger measures were taken by Parliament. Legislation was passed to withdraw state aid to denominational schools and to dedicate the revenues of the Church and Schools Estate, enjoyed by the Anglican, Catholic, Presbyterian and Wesleyan Methodist Churches since 1845, to state education. That same year Parliament resolved, against the wishes of the premier, Sir Henry Parkes, that grants of crown lands for religious purposes should cease.[2]

Anglicans and Catholics stood to lose most from these measures. Their bishops and clergy opposed them forcefully but to no avail, even though the combined denominational strength represented around 70 per cent of the population. To the Catholic Archbishop, Roger Bede Vaughan, they were signs of an advancing secularism which threatened to overthrow all religion. Anglicans took a less portentous view of the legislation, but certainly saw it as a sign that the Anglican Church lacked the political influence to which they believed it entitled.

The other main recipients of state aid, the Presbyterian and Wesleyan Methodist Churches, were more complacent. Mostly willing to accept state funds themselves, they nevertheless recognized that their larger competitors fared better under the scheme. The Methodists, in particular, preferred to go without themselves rather than subsidize Anglicanism or Popery.[3] Moreover, Methodists and Presbyterians would feel the loss of revenues from the Church and Schools Estate only slightly. Their day schools had declined to such a degree that they were hardly worth fighting for. Assurances that there would be continuing provision for religious teaching in government schools were sufficient to win the support of these two denominations for Parkes's public instruction bill in 1879.

The smaller Protestant churches, especially the Baptists and Congregationalists, were principled voluntaryists* adamantly opposed to all forms of state aid to religion. They had agitated for "free, compulsory and secular education" in the 1870s and for the diversion of revenue from the Church and Schools Estate to public education. Convinced that state aid gave an unfair advantage to the larger denominations, they expected to do better in open competition. But by 1880 the boast was a little hollow for, compared with the larger denominations, Baptists and Congregationalists had not made very remarkable progress since the abolition of state aid to religion in 1862. And even while they rejoiced in the triumph of voluntaryism, they were becoming anxious over newer trends towards secularism in colonial society.

In March 1878 Parliament had voted to open the Sydney museum and public library on Sunday afternoons, despite strong opposition from the churches. Trains, trams, harbour steamers and a good climate made Sunday picnics and other outings both possible and

---

* Voluntaryists held that the churches should be independent of the state, supported entirely from the voluntary contributions of their members.

appealing. At the same time spiritualist and secularist lecturers were hiring halls and theatres for Sunday night lectures on the alleged fallacies of orthodox religion. The number of these lectures increased early in the 1880s and Sunday afternoon and evening concerts were soon to follow. The churches thought competition with each other healthy enough, but to be forced to compete with secular diversions on Sundays or with programmes "pointedly opposed to our common Christianity"[4] was quite another thing in a supposedly Christian society. In October 1880 Protestants, including Anglican Evangelicals, revived the Lord's Day Observance Society, defunct since the 1860s, to combat the movement for freer Sunday observance and in 1889 the major Protestant denominations formed a Council of Churches, with the same intention. Protestant churchmen also united to oppose divorce law reform and to preserve and reinforce the religious provisions of state education. They formed the Christian Evidence Society to defend religion against the attacks of freethought lecturers and at the end of the decade they also established a branch of the Evangelical Alliance to strengthen Christian influence in public and social life.[5] Industrial unrest, and particularly the growing enthusiasm for socialist theories offering worldly salvation to men, also disturbed Protestants. Their preachers attempted to show that Christianity ultimately held the answer to the social and economic conflicts of the age.

The defence of Christianity, and especially of the status of New South Wales as a Christian country, largely devolved upon Protestantism in the 1880s. This was not altogether surprising since, like other Australian colonies, New South Wales was overwhelmingly Protestant, with the nominal membership, at least, of about 70 per cent of the population at that time (see Table 1).[6] While this proportion was on the increase, the proportion of Catholics in the population declined during the decade. Unlike other colonies, about two-thirds of Protestants in New South Wales were Anglicans although in 1880 they numbered only a third of regular churchgoers in the colony, and by 1890 they were little more than a quarter. Presbyterians and Wesleyan Methodists formed the majority of non-Anglican Protestants. The smaller Methodist Churches, particularly the Primitive Methodists, grew threefold during the decade, so that by 1891 combined Methodist strength was slightly greater than Presbyterian. Congregationalists and Baptists were around 2 per cent and 1 per cent of the population respectively, but, like the Methodists, Congregationalists in the 1880s were about twice as numerous among churchgoers as they were in the community at large. Presbyterians and Baptists maintained about the same strength among churchgoers as their average in the population. The increase in the

Table 1. The principal denominations in New South Wales as percentages of the population, 1851-1901.

	1851	1861	1871	1881	1891	1901
Church of England	49.7*	45.6	45.5	45.6	44.7	46.0
Presbyterian	9.7	9.9	9.8	9.6	9.7	9.8
Wesleyan Methodist	5.3	6.7	7.2	7.6	7.8	10.2
"Other Methodist"			0.6	1.0	2.2	
Congregationalist		1.5	1.8	1.9	2.1	1.8
Baptist	3.5	2.8	0.8	1.0	1.2	1.1
Other Protestant			1.6	2.1	2.6	2.4
Total Protestant	68.2	66.5	67.3	68.8	70.3	71.3
Roman Catholic†	30.4	28.3	29.3	27.6	25.6	25.7
Total Christian	98.6	94.8	96.6	96.4	95.9	97.0

Source: Census of NSW, 1851-1901

All figures rounded to nearest decimal point

* Unspecified Protestants included with Anglicans in 1851

† Roman Catholic figures for 1891 and 1901 include Greek Orthodox (0.02 per cent in 1891 and 0.04 per cent in 1901)

small number of other Protestants was largely due to the advent of the Salvation Army in 1882; it claimed just under 1 per cent of the population by 1891. These smaller denominations, however, played virtually no part in the campaigns for the defence of Christianity in the 1880s.

Despite a consensus among most Protestant denominations about the interrelationship between religion and society, and concerted efforts in defence of Christianity, there did exist a degree of denominated rivalry and even friction. Most churches cherished a great pride in their own traditions and were anxious to advance their respective causes in competition with others. Considerable social prestige attached to the Church of England; God had given to many Anglicans the "wealth, power and influence to do good beyond others", said the Dean of Sydney, William Macquarie Cowper, in 1881.[7] Although there was no state church in the colony, Anglicans did not forget that they represented the established Church of England and Wales, and the precedence accorded their bishops on state occasions rankled with Catholics and other Protestants alike.

Cowper expected the Church of England to be at the forefront of every evangelistic effort and reforming movement, but colonial Anglicanism, especially in the diocese of Sydney, was divided by rival schools of churchmanship. The evangelical majority maintained the Protestant and reformed character of the Church, while the high church minority upheld its Catholic heritage. In 1880 the Bishop of Sydney, Frederic Barker, was a pronounced Evangelical. His more liberal successor, Alfred Barry, Bishop of Sydney (1884-89), justified Anglicanism as both Catholic and Protestant, without the extremes of either; it stood between Rome's "system of absolutism" on the one hand and the "theory of Congregational disintegration" on the other. Bishops were also frustrated by the constitutional limits placed on episcopal authority, so much so that Josiah Pearson, Bishop of Newcastle (1880-89), branded the synodical system as Presbyterian. Parochialism, sometimes perjoratively called "congregationalism", helped to hinder effective organization in the diocese as did "diocesanism" in the province.[8] There was sometimes obvious disagreement between Anglican laity and clergy, particularly on issues such as state aid and divorce law reform. But in spite of this divisiveness the Church of England retained its position as the leading denomination.

Presbyterians in the colony mostly belonged to the Presbyterian Church of New South Wales, formed by the union of several Presbyterian synods in 1865. The Presbyterian Church of Eastern Australia was formed by Free Presbyterians, many Gaelic-speaking Highlanders among them, who refused to join the union in 1865. A dissident and declining group, they split into rival synods in the 1880s. The Presbyterian Church of New South Wales accounted for 98 per cent of all Presbyterians and around 10 per cent of the total population. Although smaller than the Anglican Church, it could still boast of some wealth and influence among its members, especially on the North Coast, in the New England district and the Riverina. It was claimed that nearly all the squatters in the Riverina were Presbyterians and a partisan visitor to New England in 1882 was proud to find that "the Presbyterian Church occupied a position of power and influence equalled by no other in the district". He remarked that the wealthy squatters and merchants had ranged themselves "under the blue banner of the covenant" and that the new Presbyterian church in Armidale, "a cathedral in all but name", surpassed in dignity the Anglican and Catholic cathedrals close by.[9]

Presbyterians proudly claimed to represent "the National Reformed Church of Scotland", although there were some who regretted that Presbyterianism was generally regarded as a church for Scots and Northern Irishmen. They deeply resented being called

Frederic Barker, Second Anglican Bishop of Sydney (1854-82). (From *The Episcopate of the Right Reverend Frederic Barker D.D.* edited by W.M. Cowper [Sydney: Angus and Robertson, 1888]. Photo courtesy of Baillieu Library, Melbourne.)

Dissenters, a term applied to them by High Anglicans in particular, and equally shunned the label of Nonconformists, as did the representatives of English Nonconformity in the colony, especially the Congregationalists.[10] In Australia, these Protestants preferred to call themselves the "Evangelical Churches", and took this to include the Presbyterians as well. There was good justification for this since by 1880 former Free Presbyterians dominated the Presbyterian ministry; their evangelical theology and spirit brought them close to these other non-episcopal Protestants.

Of the Methodists in the colony, 80 per cent were Wesleyan Methodists. Primitive Methodists, around 2 per cent of the total population in 1891, were the largest of the minority Methodist groups, which included the Bible Christians and the United Methodist Free Church. These smaller denominations united with the Wesleyans to form the Methodist Church of Australasia in 1902. The Primitive Methodist Church was stronger in the country, especially in the mining districts around Newcastle and at Broken Hill, where Methodist miners migrated in large numbers from South Australia. Compared with the Wesleyan Church, it played a minor part in the concert of Protestant denominations.

Wesleyan strength was vested largely in the lower middle classes,[11] although there were Methodists who, by industry, frugality and sobriety, rose from humble beginnings to positions of wealth and eminence — a proof of the promise that "Godliness is profitable unto all things...".[12] Conscious also of an ecclesiastical progress more impressive than the larger denominations, the Wesleyans took great pride in their connexional system and its itinerant ministry, which extended Methodism throughout the colony. Methodism, said the President of the Wesleyan Conference in 1885, was the safest polity he knew, midway between Anglicanism and Congregationalism — "between tyranny and lawlessness". Wesleyans in New South Wales viewed the smaller Methodist denominations somewhat smugly and in the 1880s were largely indifferent to moves originating in South Australia and Victoria towards the union of the Methodist Churches. Primitive Methodism, commented the *Weekly Advocate* in 1881 was "about the cheapest Methodism we know". The Wesleyans made bold claims for the influence of Methodism; Methodist preaching, they asserted, had saved England from revolution at the end of the eighteenth century and it was claimed that Methodism had made a large contribution to the development of the colony.[13] Although they were confident that Methodism would become an even stronger religious force in Australia, it was apparent that Methodist church discipline was weakening. Throughout the 1880s Wesleyans debated

Richard Sellors, President of the Wesleyan Methodist Conference of New South Wales (1886-87). (From *The Methodist Jubilee Conference Album, 1855-1905* [Sydney: Mark Blow (The Crown Studies), 1905]. Photo courtesy of La Trobe University Library, Melbourne.)

whether attendance at the weekly class meeting should remain obligatory. By 1890 the majority of Australian Wesleyans had decided that the progress of Methodism depended on the abandonment of this rule.

The Congregationalists, the most bourgeois of the Protestant denominations, were largely confined to the metropolitan area and a few of the larger towns nearer Sydney. An influential minority, they too displayed considerable confidence in their potential progress around 1880. The withdrawal of state aid and other secularizing legislation made it appear that their voluntary principles were triumphing. Their Chairman in 1880 predicted that Congregationalism would be the system of the future. But at the Intercolonial Congregational Conference in 1883 the chairman, James Jefferis, minister of Pitt Street Congregational Church, reflected soberly that Congregationalism in the colonies, where everything appeared to be in its favour, had not "laid that hold upon the population" to which he thought it "entitled". Congregationalists had failed to overcome the problem of extension in country New South Wales where numbers were lost to more enterprising denominations, such as the Wesleyans. Nevertheless, they took some comfort in the progress of "congregationalism" in other denominations: wherever church polity seemed to become more democratic or congregations more independent, Congregationalists rejoiced in the supremacy of their principles.[14]

The Baptists shared a similar anxiety over church extension in the country and even contemplated a union with the Congregationalists to represent the "congregational order" in the interior. It had been tried with little success in South Australia,[15] but prospects for cooperation in New South Wales were poor largely because Baptists there were notably narrow and rigid in their beliefs. They were almost all Particular Baptists, holding to Calvinist theology with its doctrines of predestination and election in contrast to the Baptists in the other colonies who were mostly General Baptists, upholding the Arminian belief in the unlimited offer of salvation. Even so, the Baptist Union of New South Wales was often regarded as a body of General Baptists, by a minority which formed a Baptist Association. The latter were strict and particular Baptists, led by Pastor Daniel Allen, a militant Orangeman.[16]

During the 1880s members of the Baptist Union were disturbed over the loss of followers to other denominations and some also lamented the failure of Baptist churches to attract non-Baptists around them. In the hope of winning broader support for new Baptist causes, a few advocated "open churches", which admitted persons not baptized as adults or on profession of faith. Open churches were the rule in Victoria but remained the exception in New South Wales because the majority would not compromise on a fundamental principle. As to Baptists worshipping with other denominations, one minister declared that if they were true to their principles either the churches they were with would become Baptist or the Baptists in them would leave. Baptists, then, remained more exclusivist than other Protestant denominations in the colony, and they were not destined for the decline which later befell the more liberal Congregationalists. The Baptist Union of New South Wales was largely to set the pattern for the denomination in Australia.[17]

Although there was a marked degree of denominational self-consciousness and competition among the Protestant denominations, this rivalry did not prevent the churches from achieving a fair degree of cooperation in common causes. The High Churchmen were an exception; they held "Dissenters" in disdain and would have preferred an alliance with Catholics to secure the restoration of state aid. But the great majority of Anglicans and other Protestants were heirs of the British evangelical tradition and they accepted each other as standing within a "common Christianity", despite their differences. There was some liberalizing of Protestant theology in the 1880s especially on questions of biblical inspiration and Darwinism, which modified this older evangelicalism somewhat, without eclipsing it. Although this liberalism did cause some tension within denominations, it boosted interdenominational cooperation because the liberal churchmen were more ecumenical than the conservative Evangelicals; and the defence of religion in society was a broad platform on which men of different schools of theology could stand.

The degree of unity achieved, especially between Anglicans and other Protestants, was due in no small part to the Right Reverend Alfred Barry. Third Anglican Bishop of Sydney and former principal of King's College, London, Barry was a man of "fine presence" and "sonorous voice"; if he seemed "donnish",[18] his conciliatory spirit and broad vision were the more remarkable. Although these attributes were not always strong enough to heal the divisions within his own diocese, they did win him the trust and admiration of the many non-episcopal Protestants who came to regard him affectionately as "our Bishop". The Catholic press also held him in high regard.[19]

Barry, considered a Broad Churchman* by many in the 1880s,

---

*   A Broad Churchman was one of a diverse group of liberal Anglican clergymen whose attempts to restate Christian theology led them from the paths of strict orthodoxy. The Bishop of Melbourne, James Moorhouse (1877-86), who refused to pray for rain because it was contrary to the scientific understanding, was a more typical Broad Churchman than Bishop Barry.

Alfred Barry, Third Anglican Bishop of Sydney (1884-89). (From *Sydney Quarterly Magazine*, vol. 5 (1888). Photo courtesy of Mitchell Library, Sydney.)

claimed to belong to no party within the Church. Not as radical in theology as some Broad Churchmen, he remained orthodox but without the narrowness of the Evangelicals. Reared and trained in the Established Church, he esteemed the union of Church and State, but did not hanker for it as did some Anglicans. In accepting the different situation of the Church of England in the colony, he recognized soon after his arrival in April 1884 that the separation of Church and State might give "more and freer scope to the power of intrinsic religious influence". The issue for him was not one form of churchmanship against another but the greater conflict between Christianity and secularism. Declaring that Christianity had suffered most from sectarian rivalry, Barry was prepared to work with all who professed a "common Christianity", for the sake of humanity and "the higher life of the colony".[20] His offer was to Catholics as well as to Protestants, but Protestants only were to rally behind him.

Even the militant voluntaryist, James Jefferis, minister of Pitt Street Congregational Church, found Barry's appeal irresistible. Jefferis came to Sydney in 1877 after a distinguished ministry in Adelaide. Ever a champion of religious liberty, he arrived in the colony in time to take part in the last stages of the education campaign and the agitation over the Church and Schools Estate. Barry's imminent arrival was one reason he gave for refusing an invitation to visit Adelaide early in 1884. Imagining that the new bishop might claim some special privilege or status for the Church of England in the colony, he wrote to a friend in Adelaide that he would be "watching & *possibly* breaking a lance with him [Barry], if he waves any objectionable banner". But Barry's conciliatory stand disarmed him and he sounded a new note on the old controversy between Anglican and voluntaryist. Voluntaryists still opposed the establishment of any particular denomination as the State Church, Jefferis explained; but at the same time they looked for a "vital union between religion and the state". He admitted that the battle against "the national establishment" of the Church of England had "for a while weakened the sanctions of Christianity", but declared that he was now ready to work with others to restore those sanctions "with more than their old authority".[21]

Congregationalists in New South Wales tacitly accepted Jefferis's view; at least there seems to have been no dissent then or later in 1886 when he referred to "the true God-made union between Church and State". The South Australian correspondent to the *New South Wales Independent* in 1884 hailed Jefferis's distinction between state aid through legislative support to religion and morals as "masterly, true and telling". The Victorian Congregationalist, the Reverend Alexander Gosman, also restated his denomination's position on the relation of the State to religion.[22] Between them, Jefferis and Gosman resolved the dilemma for Congregationalists, particularly after 1880. As convinced as others that New South Wales was a Christian country, they had also begun to look for a secular arm to uphold religious institutions when it appeared that the Christian character of the colony was threatened.

The Presbyterian and Wesleyan Methodist Churches, both former recipients of state aid, were not troubled by the same conflict of principles. Presbyterians were inclined to some form of union between Church and State and at least some public recognition of religion (see Chapter 9). The Presbyterian General Assembly petitioned Parliament in 1887 to introduce daily prayers and in 1888 the Moderator, John Auld, disclosed his dream that a united Protestantism would one day form a national Australian Church.[23] Expediency rather than principles determined the Methodists' attitude to Church-State relationships, especially the question of state aid. However, when the chief justice, Sir James Martin, stated from the bench in 1884 that "Christianity in its broadest sense" was part of the common law of England and of the colony, the *Weekly Advocate* was thankful that there were judges "brave enough to uphold the essentially Christian foundation of our Commonwealth".[24] The Primitive Methodists, more sect-like in their attitude towards the State, nevertheless cooperated with the other Protestant denominations. The Baptists were more suspicious of political activity on behalf of religion, and although they sometimes withheld their support, they did join the other denominations in forming the Council of Churches and the Evangelical Alliance in 1889.

The religious equality achieved in the Australian colonies, ecclesiastical precedence on official occasions excepted, facilitated cooperation among the churches. As well as this, the social differences found in England between the Anglican parson and the Dissenting minister hardly existed in Australia. The Anglican clergy in the colonies were "as a class inferior to their English brethren" and the ex-Nonconformists had become "a superior class of men as a whole to those in the old country", according to one observer in the 1880s, Richard Twopeny.[25] Thus the antithesis between church and sect, already blurred in England, was even less relevant in Australia, where the metamorphosis of Protestants from church to denomination on the one hand and from sect to denomination on the other was virtually complete.[26]

Many of the issues on which Protestants took a united stand were of concern to the Roman Catholic Church as well. But the Catholics always declined to join in the concerted efforts of the Protestants and to some extent they waged a separate campaign. The clerical hierarchy in Australia denied that any other denomination had made "any serious attempt to dispute the ascendency of secularism".[27] Catholic efforts were largely directed towards protecting the faithful from anti-religious influences, although Archbishop Vaughan was an enthusiastic apologist who defended Christianity in general, as well as Catholicism, against its detractors. For this reason he attracted Protestants as well as Catholics to his lectures, but under his successor, Cardinal P.F. Moran, apologetics became more sectarian. However Moran was also concerned with upholding the influence of religion in colonial society. The principal work of the First Plenary Council which he convened in 1885 was "precisely to combat those evils which threaten to undermine the social fabric", and one of his main objectives as a candidate for the Federal Convention in 1897 was to ensure that the religious foundation of Australian society was recognized in the proposed federation.[28] But this concern did not bring him any closer to Protestants. The *Sydney Morning Herald* in 1888 noted his aloofness in comparison with Bishop Barry, and it could not see why Moran should not appear on public platforms with other clergymen, as Cardinal Manning did in England.[29] Moran justified himself in his lecture on "The Reunion of Christendom" in 1895. He argued that while there were some areas where Protestants and Catholics might cooperate profitably in the defence of religion in society, the anti-Catholicism of Protestants precluded such cooperation; the same line of argument had been taken in the *Freeman's Journal* in 1884. Yet in an interview in 1894 Moran had described Protestants and Catholics in Australia as "most peacefully united", except for the Orangemen whom he considered to be "very few" in number; and the Pastoral Letter of the Second Plenary Council in 1895 had remarked on the friendly disposition of the Australian people towards the Catholic Church.[30]

There was sectarian bigotry on the part of both Catholics and Protestants alike. A Catholic layman, a youth in the 1890s, later recalled: "On one side, the Orange Lodges kept noisily proclaiming some secret viciousness of the Scarlet Woman, and on the other side an excited Irish priest was constantly belching forth a windy hatred".[31] Cardinal Moran, himself, could provoke Protestant ire; in 1895 when he was upbraiding Protestants for their anti-Catholicism, he saw fit to repeat scandalous but false charges that Protestant missionaries plied natives in the South Pacific with "grog".[32] Besides, the Catholic hierarchy cultivated an exclusiveness among Catholics which was in no way conducive to closer relations with Protestants. Overprotective of the faith of their flock, they banned the faithful from attending Protestant services and strenuously discouraged marriages between Catholic and Protestant, with a warning to parents not to allow courtship relationships to develop between their children and non-Catholics. Protestants sometimes spoke out against Protestant-Catholic marriages, but the Catholic aversion to them was more general. The policy of separate schools for Catholics also helped to foster Catholic mistrust of Protestants; one hymn in the *Australian Catholic Hymn Book* taught children to regard state schools as places which sought "To snare poor Catholic youth",[33] while Protestants generally regarded the Catholic Church's insistence on separate schools with suspicion or contempt. The intemperate denunciations by which Archbishop Vaughan attempted in 1879 to frighten Catholics out of state schools did little to enlist Protestant sympathy for Catholic education.[34] On the other hand, the refusal of Protestants to concede Catholic claims for state aid to their schools only strengthened the Catholics' conviction that they were a persecuted minority under a Protestant ascendancy.

Apart from ecclesiastical policy, there were also national and social differences between Catholics and Protestants in the colony. Overwhelmingly Irish by birth or descent, most Catholics were deeply committed to Ireland's struggle for home rule which enlisted little support among Protestants. Conversely, Catholics did not show much enthusiasm for Protestant patriotism towards throne and empire. Nor were they, overall, as prosperous as their Protestant contemporaries. The Catholic Bishop of Brisbane, Dr Robert Dunne, painted the social situation of Australian Catholics in rather gloomy terms in a letter to Moran in 1884: "Our people unhappily run into the crowds of unskilled labour, — irregular occupations; viz: publicans, police-men, cabdrivers, wharf-labourers, pick-and-shovel men."[35] Dunne's words exhibited a general tendency to exaggerate the extent of poverty and lowly occupations among colonial Catholics.[36] Nevertheless, while Catholics could be found in every walk of life the tables of religion and occupation in the census of 1901 provide solid evidence that Catholics were found in relatively higher proportions than Protestants in the above occupations mentioned by Dunne. Twenty-five per cent of Catholic male breadwinners were engaged in the supply of board and lodging (including publicans and their employees), domestic service, transport (including railway and tramway employees and cab-drivers) or in unskilled labour. The same occupations absorbed 20 per cent of Anglicans, 17 per cent of Presbyterians and only 8 per cent of Methodists. To put it another way, a third of the men engaged in board and lodging (and 39 per cent of females in this area), were Catholic, and, within the unskilled category, 40 per cent of road and railway workers or navvies and 40 per cent of those engaged in the disposal of refuse were Catholic. The proportion of Catholics in the police force is not clear, but 26 per cent of government employees in the broad field of law and order were Catholic, which is only slightly higher than the average of Catholics (24 per cent) in the male work force. On the other hand, Catholics were proportionally underrepresented in commerce, especially banking and finance, where they registered only 8 per cent compared with Anglicans who comprised 60 per cent, Presbyterians 14 per cent and Methodists 5.5 per cent. That 30 per cent of Catholic men were engaged in primary pursuits is not surprising since Catholic strength lay largely in rural areas particularly in the Southern Tableland and the South Western Slope regions where they formed about 35 per cent in 1891. But they were more likely to be found among struggling free selectors than among wealthy pastoralists, while in the towns and cities Catholics were above average among the unemployed.[37]

That some Catholics believed there was a sinister discrimination against them in employment was revealed by an incident in 1889. The young politician, B.R. Wise, in an ill-natured attack on Irish Catholics asserted that they were best suited to lowly and unskilled work. The militant Irish nationalist, F.B. Freehill, retorted that there was a Protestant conspiracy to exclude Catholics from better positions, especially in the public service, while the *Freeman's Journal* asserted that the Masonic Lodge was the gateway to the higher levels of the public service and the Orange Lodge the door to the lower levels.[38] Regarding themselves as a persecuted minority, Catholics perhaps exaggerated such discrimination as there may have been. Admittedly, they had less than their share of wealth, power and influence, but their bishops seemed to think that the cause lay mainly in Catholics themselves. Bishop Dunne thought there were too few "pushing" parents, and the hierarchy generally thought that intemperance and improvidence were rife in the Catholic community. The Pastoral Letter issued by the Plenary Council in 1885 exhorted Catholics to improve their social and economic position by adopting a more sober, industrious and stable way of life and by binding their children to some respectable trade or profession, for "God never meant the Irish Catholic to be the wanderer that he is over the face of the earth."[39]

Of course there were some Catholics who did prosper and rise to eminence, such as Herbert Moran, a Catholic surgeon. His father arrived in the colony from Ireland in 1876 with little money and no trade, but after three years in the country he had saved enough to invest in a small bakery in Sydney which was to become a large and prosperous business. Herbert Moran studied medicine at Sydney University, took his fellowship in surgery at Edinburgh and returned to practise in Australia. Among other Catholics who distinguished themselves in New South Wales in the 1880s were Sir Patrick Jennings (premier, 1886) and Mr Justice Faucett on the bench. On the eve of Cardinal Moran's departure for Rome in 1888, he could rejoice that the "gifted sons" of the Catholic Church held an honoured place in the foremost ranks of Australian society.[40] But perhaps most notable was William Bede Dalley, son of convict parents, who was eminent as a barrister as well as in politics. Such Catholics generally dissociated themselves from the more exclusivist attitudes of their Church and from militant Irish nationalism. They were thus less abrasive in their relations with Protestants, as the poet Kendall testified of Dalley:

> Firm to the Church by which his fathers stood,
>   But tolerant to every form of creed,
> He longs for universal brotherhood,
>   And is a Christian gentleman indeed.[41]

By the same token, Protestants within the same social circle were generally more liberal in their attitude towards Catholics and disdained the bitter anti-Catholicism of the Orangemen. Protestants of this kind were probably those who gave generously to the building of St Mary's Cathedral and to Catholic charitable institutions, as Archbishop Vaughan and Cardinal Moran freely acknowledged. Unmoved by the taunts of Evangelicals that they were "weak-kneed Protestants", their liberality serves as a reminder that there was also a brighter side to Catholic-Protestant relations in the 1880s. In general, it is reasonable to assume that there must have been more friendly social intercourse between Catholics and Protestants than the policy of exclusivism might suggest. A substantial number of Catholic parents continued to send their children to public schools despite the strictness of the Church's policy and the denunciation of such parents by priests as "bad Catholics"; and mixed marriages, particularly of Catholic women to Protestant partners, were frequent enough, whatever the priest might say.

Anti-Catholicism was the excuse rather than the reason for the Catholic Church's refusal to cooperate with Protestants in the 1880s. Such cooperation would have compromised its dogmatic claims and undermined its pastoral discipline. In June 1884, two weeks after the *Freeman's Journal* had explained that anti-Catholicism made impossible cooperation with Bishop Barry's movement to strengthen religious teaching in public schools, "Presbuteros" wrote in the same weekly: "Were she [the Catholic Church] to recognize the teaching of Protestantism in the slightest degree, she would fail in her divine mission as the sole teacher of Christianity on earth."[42] To have joined with Protestants in their campaigns would have implied that Roman Catholicism was but another expression of a "common Christianity". And to admit that religious teaching could be carried out in public schools would have undercut the Catholic educational effort. The attitude of the Catholic Church today, especially since the Second Vatican Council, is very different, but in the 1880s and for some time afterwards, although Catholics hoped for Protestant goodwill, the hierarchy officially maintained that Catholics could not cooperate with Protestants in religious movements. Some Catholic laymen did work with Protestants in opposition to divorce law reform in the 1880s, but they lacked official recognition from their Church.

Although Catholic clergy in Australia echoed the Vatican's warning against secularism and infidelity, the solidarity the Australian Catholic Church enjoyed, largely through its Irish composition, and the achievements of the Church, especially under Cardinal Moran, gave it a sense of well-being. Compared with Catholicism in Continental Europe, Australian Catholicism was doing well, and colonial Catholics thought that they were doing rather better than Protestants. In 1881 the *Freeman's Journal* complacently observed that Protestantism was fast drifting into that paganism which Christianity once conquered.[43] But this confidence was not entirely well founded for in the 1880s only a third of those in the colony who called themselves Catholics appeared to be regular attenders at Mass. This fraction was higher than the proportion of Anglicans who worshipped regularly, but Table 2 shows that it was only slightly better than the Presbyterian record and below that of other Protestants. Statistics aside, it was the sense of spiritual progress and prosperity that confirmed the Catholic resolve to stand alone.

Table 2. Average church attendance as a percentage of total adherents in each denomination, 1880, 1890.

	Church of England	Presbyterian	Methodist*	Congregationalist	Baptist[+]	Roman Catholic
1880	21.5	29.6	71.3	55.9	28.8	33.4
1890	16.1	29.7	49.1	54.0	35.4	32.5

Source: Statistical Register, NSW and *Census of NSW*, 1881 and 1891

* Includes "Other Methodists"
+ There may have been some deficiency in Baptist returns in 1880 and 1890; the figures for 1870 and 1900 were 52.1 and 54.5 per cent respectively, about the same as the Congregationalists.

Protestant churchmen were not so complacent. They found evidence of religious decline around them, especially when judging by the standards of an older Protestant piety. Protestant church discipline seemed weak. Earlier in the century the Protestant churches had expelled, suspended or rebuked members for a variety of trifling as well as serious offences; in 1830, for example, a schoolmaster was deposed from his position as a leader of a Wesleyan class meeting for employing a dancing teacher in his school.[44] Later in the century any member censured for such peccadilloes by one of the strictest churches or congregations would probably soon find a home in a rival, more liberal denomination, or even in another, less strict congregation within the same denomination. The Wesleyans were finding it hard enough in the 1880s to get their members to attend the class meeting, without being seen to uphold its old disciplinary function. There were also frequent complaints of small attendances at weeknight prayer meetings in other denominations. Protestant ministers generally believed the custom of family prayers to be waning and the *Presbyterian* saw the trend to more recreational Sunday afternoons as the cause of the widely recognized decline in evening church attendances in the 1880s. There were few like the Reverend Dr Thomas Roseby, who stated at a discussion by Congregationalists on the spiritual condition of the age, that there was too much "laudation of older times".[45] Pessimism was endemic among the clergy and many could not see the signs of spiritual progress which encouraged Roseby to view the future more hopefully. Not only did the majority find the spiritual climate of their churches tepid, but also they believed there was a falling away from religion altogether.

Reports of unofficial surveys of church attendances in some large English provincial cities taken in 1881 were not encouraging; they showed a significant decline since 1851.[46] These overseas reports rather than the published Australian religious statistics confirmed the opinion of some colonial churchmen that religion was declining. There was indeed substantial local evidence of a decline in church-going in the annual returns of attendances for New South Wales during the 1870s and 1880s, but few churchmen at the time seemed to have studied them seriously. One exception was the Reverend Warlow Davies, Chairman of the Congregational Union in 1881, who quoted figures from the ecclesiastical returns for 1880 in his address to the union. Davies was concerned not so much to prove a decline as to show that many people were out of touch with the churches and that church accommodation was inadequate for the population. Although average attendances in 1880 represented 30 per cent of the total population, Davies estimated, and with probable accuracy, that 50-60 per cent of the population attended services at one time or another. The churches could only accommodate 29 per cent of the population at once, and, except for Catholic churches, this accommodation was not used fully each Sunday.[47] Had Davies looked further back he might have noticed that this represented a decrease since 1870, when there was accommodation for 36 per cent of the population. Church attendances also fell from the high point of 35 per cent of the population in 1870 to 27 per cent in 1890. Sunday school attendances, however, increased a little during the 1880s.[48]

It would be rash to conclude from these figures that there was a uniform loss of faith or even of religious habits throughout the colony. Closer examination of the ecclesiastical returns shows that the decline took place more in the city than in the country. City church attendances dropped from 40 per cent of the metropolitan population in 1870 to 31 per cent in 1880; by 1890 they had fallen to 25 per cent. At the same time the metropolitan population was increasing rapidly; from a little more than a quarter of the colony's total population in 1871 to just over a third in 1891 (see Table 3). The

Table 3. Distribution of the population of New South Wales, 1871-91.

	1871	%	1881	%	1891	%
Sydney and suburbs	137,586	27.4	224,939	30.1	383,283	34.3
Country	363,993	72.6	523,302	69.9	734,967	65.7
Total population	501,579		748,241		1,118,250	

Aborigines and Lord Howe Islanders have been excluded from the figures for 1891 and "Shipping" from the figures for each census.

Source: Census of NSW, 1891, p. 730.

real decline in city attendances was probably accelerated to a large extent by immigrants, chiefly of the English working class, who helped to swell the metropolitan population, especially in the 1880s. The English working class was not noted for its churchgoers, and of those who were, many would have found it easy to break the habit in a new land. The *Presbyterian* drily observed that thousands of immigrants had lost all their religion at sea.[49] It is not surprising, then, that the growing city and its religious problems should occupy the attention of churchmen so much during this decade.

Up to 1880 country church extension had absorbed much of the churches' thought and energies. The larger denominations in particular endeavoured to keep up with the expanding settlement of the interior as pastoral lands were opened to selection. While provision was being made for these areas, the significant increase in the metropolitan population in the 1870s was largely overlooked. As a result there was church accommodation in the city for 40 per cent of the metropolitan population in 1870 and for only 30 per cent in 1880. Accommodation in the country also decreased comparatively in the period but not as drastically; 33 per cent of the rural population could be seated in 1870, and 29 per cent in 1880, slightly less than the accommodation available in the city. As the wrangling over education began to subside by 1880, the churches became more conscious of mushrooming suburban growth in the city. There they saw areas of neglect largely unnoticed before and new spheres for home mission endeavour. Although they did not forget the country and its needs, most denominations attempted vigorously to make up leeway in the city.

The city became the front line in the encounter between religion and society for other reasons also. Intellectual ferment, such as there was in Australia, was largely a phenomenon of city life and the evidence of secularization and religious indifference seemed more obvious there. It was principally in the city that freethought lecturers assailed Christianity. In the city where there were more facilities for recreational and cultural enjoyment on Sundays and more people to enjoy them, "Sabbath-breaking" was more obvious. Inevitably, the churches' campaigns in opposition to these movements and trends took place in the city where they hoped to influence the colony's legislators. The problems of church life which disturbed so many churchmen, such as poor attendances at weeknight meetings and Sunday evening services, were the problems of city and suburban churches and those of larger towns rather than of the widely scattered parishes and circuits of the country where there might be only one service fortnightly, or even monthly. In the city, churchmen were also aware of the large numbers indifferent to organized religion; and the coming of the Salvation Army to the colony in 1882 made acutely apparent the needs of the unevangelized poor in their midst.

In response to these challenges, as well as their campaign against secularism, the churches competed with each other in building new churches in the metropolitan area and at the same time cooperated in evangelistic campaigns to reach the people. There was a new emphasis on clubs and societies to attract and hold people to the churches. There was also much discussion of the problem of the absent working classes and some innovatory attempts to reach them. This decade gave birth to the first Central Methodist Mission in Australia and similar missions in other denominations, all attempting to reach the outsiders.

The peril which many churchmen thought faced religion and society gave greater urgency to their efforts in religious extension. In this way, the dual preoccupations of the Protestant churches in the 1880s, the defence and extension of religion, were complementary objectives. In 1885 Bishop Barry, in an appeal for more vigorous church extension by Anglicans, told the Sydney Church Society that they were witnessing a conflict between the old civilization "impregnated with the principles of Christianity, and the new civilizations, on secular bases, which were offered in its room".[50] Alexander Gosman made the same point more luridly in 1883 when he told the Intercolonial Congregational Conference in Sydney that they must Christianize and evangelize for secularism was "lifting its ugly head in every land, shaking from its terrible locks everything that is detrimental to the welfare of humanity".[51] Barry and Gosman each thought their own denomination best suited to the peculiar challenges of the age. But both agreed that church extension and evangelization were crucial weapons in the battle against secularism.

2

An Honourable Rivalry

The challenge presented by secularism encouraged the churches to work strenuously at church extension in the 1880s. At stake, it was believed, was not only the future of Christianity but the future of society itself. As churchmen constantly asserted, religion was the necessary cement for a sound social order in which moral and spiritual purity would foster intellectual and material progress. To this end, Bishop Barry maintained that Christianity should be "an ally to civil power", rather than its "rival or enemy".[1]

Only a tiny minority of militant secularists was prepared to challenge Bishop Barry's assumption in the 1880s, and there was not much exaggeration in his claim in 1888 that the government was "almost clamorous for their [the churches'] religious work". The premier, Sir Henry Parkes, had asserted in Parliament in 1882, in connection with Sunday observance, that the churches deserved protection because they helped the progress of civilization and promoted sound morality. Mr Justice Owen used a similar argument in support of church extension at the annual meeting of the Sydney Anglican Church Society in 1888. He observed, with some disdain, that political power was passing into the hands of the masses with the result that secular influences were controlling the life of the community. The churches were to make good the spiritual imbalance by providing "that moral and religious teaching which alone could make good citizens". People without moral and religious nurture would make "lopsided and dangerous citizens", warned the *Presbyterian* in 1880, while the Wesleyan *Weekly Advocate* argued that religious provisions must be extended, not only "for the salvation of the *individual* man", but also because Christianity provided "the unique remedial and directive energy for our civic and municipal life". That existing provisions were grossly inadequate was pointed out by Warlow Davies in his jeremiad on "The State of the Colony in Regard to Religion", delivered to the Congregational Union Assembly in 1881. "Enough, more than enough" had been said from the ecclesiastical returns on the one hand, and statistics of crime, drunkenness and reports of larrikinism on the other, he thought, to show that the "moral and religious condition" of many was "full of peril, not only to themselves but to the safety, and strength, and well-being of the colony".[2]

These arguments were intended to impress church members with the importance of a work which depended largely on their financial support. But there were pastoral motives behind church extension programmes as well. Churchmen, working in a Christian colony as the census returns suggested, believed that the churches should follow the people wherever they went to provide religious facilities. Each denomination was hopeful, but not overconfident, of support from its adherents for the churches as they were established. They knew well enough that a substantial number of the population did not attend church services, but they also knew that there was insufficient accommodation in churches. Increased accommodation seemed necessary for increased support. Although not all the available accommodation was taken each Sunday, the Presbyterian Statistics Committee argued plausibly that the provision should not be measured by the number of vacant pews, but by the amount of accommodation provided "at a reasonable distance". It was realized that churchmen would have to accept whatever distance the potential churchgoers considered to be reasonable if they were to be persuaded to attend. The primary task of the denomination, declared the Moderator in 1890, T.E. Clouston, was to place "a church and minister within easy access of every Presbyterian in the land". According to W.J. Green, secretary to the Congregational Church Extension Society, congregations mostly came from within a mile of a church building. He explained that as the climate was too hot for long walks in summer, children usually attended the closest Sunday school, whatever its denomination, and that if there was not a church of the parents' persuasion within a mile they would end up going to the church of another denomination.[3]

Determined thus to retain their hold on their followers and not to be outdone by others, church leaders kept a watchful eye on the progress of their competitors in church extension. In 1885 Bishop Barry exhorted Anglicans to take the lead in "the honourable rivalry" of extending religion in opposition to sin and unbelief. He thought the generous support for church extension by Catholics on one side and Congregationalists on the other put Anglicans to shame. The *Presbyterian* also urged its denomination not to rest on its oars, but to take part in the "healthy rivalry", while hoping that "the higher considerations of the glory of God and the salvation of souls, even more than a desire not to be outdone by any other Church [would] ever . . . be the grand motive power." Proper sentiments indeed! But the competition of the denominations with one another was at least as powerful a motive as disinterested evangelical zeal. This competitiveness was also evident in other colonies, notably Victoria, and as much in Britain and North America as well, especially as the differences between the various Protestant denominations became blurred.[4]

Competition was noticeable in New South Wales before 1880, particularly in the creation of rural dioceses by the Anglican and Catholic Churches. Each church established new dioceses in the same areas around the same time. When Catholic Archbishop, Dr Polding, got wind of Bishop Barker's intention of creating two new dioceses in 1862, he wrote to Bishop Goold in Melbourne arguing that Catholics should try and "gain the valuable prestige of giving the first and real Bishops" to the northern and southern districts of New South Wales. And Barker cannily used knowledge of Catholic plans in his campaign to establish a new diocese in Bathurst.[5]

In the 1880s the competition was keenest in Sydney where large scale immigration was increasing the population rapidly and pushing development out into new suburbs. Dean Cowper warned the synod of Sydney in 1881 that Anglicans must keep pace with expanding suburban population, or members of the Church of England would be absorbed into other denominations. Not surprisingly then, most of the energies of the Sydney Diocesan Church Society were directed towards the religious needs of the metropolis in the 1880s. Other denominations also responded to the challenge in the city. In 1879 the Wesleyans formed the Sydney and Suburban Wesleyan Methodist Sites Fund to assist church extension in the city. In an appeal to Scotland in 1877 the Presbyterian Church Extension Committee designated the interior of the colony as the most needy area, but by 1879 the Presbytery of Sydney began to take metropolitan church extension seriously, although its attempts to make up leeway there were at first abortive. Land donated by laymen for church buildings in several places remained vacant for some time while it was strongly disputed whether the Presbyterian Church Extension Fund could be used in Sydney or if the funds were for rural extension only. The General Assembly resolved the matter after some bitter wrangling in March 1883. Persuaded at least of the need to prevent losses to other denominations, it authorized the Church Extension Committee to work in Sydney on the same terms as in the rural presbyteries. The assembly defined Sydney and the Riverina, where census returns indicated a relative strength of Presbyterians, as the most important areas for church extension. In 1887 the Baptists, somewhat tardily, formed the Sydney and Suburban Baptist Association, among other things to foster church extension in the metropolitan area. There were similar developments in Melbourne in the 1880s as the denominations sought to cope with that expanding metropolis.[6]

The work of the Congregational Church Extension Society had mostly been in the city, and in 1882 the secretary of the Colonial Missionary Society in Britain, while complimenting the Church Extension Society on its work in the metropolitan area, suggested that Congregationalists should also stimulate church extension in the country. However a symposium on Congregationalism in New South Wales earlier that year and the debate on church extension at the Intercolonial Conference in 1883 revealed that Congregationalists lacked either the will or the conviction to tackle the problem of rural extension. Some held that Congregationalism was peculiarly suited to large centres of population, and those who advocated more general rural extension admitted that Congregational polity had some limitations in a sparsely settled country; they proposed the grafting of some aspects of Methodism on to Congregationalism to facilitate extension in the interior. But few Congregationalists were willing to sacrifice the autonomy of the local church to any degree, even for the sake of the growth of the denomination.[7] Baptists largely shared this dilemma of country church extension.

The maintenance of religion in the country was thereby undertaken almost entirely by the larger denominations. There were some among them who feared that attention to the city might lead to neglect of the country. The Anglican Bishop of Melbourne, Dr Moorhouse, thought it necessary to admonish the Sydney Church Society in 1883 not to leave religious provisions in the interior to other denominations, for that would be a stigma on the Church of England.[8] But the remoter parts of the colony were the responsibility of the rural dioceses rather than the Sydney Church Society. About three decades earlier, church societies had been founded in the dioceses of Newcastle in 1851 and Sydney in 1856 to cope with the extension of religious provisions in the country; but soon after the dioceses of Goulburn, Bathurst and their joint offspring, the diocese of Riverina were founded, they established their own church societies to cater for regional needs, although there was no Church Extension Fund for Grafton and Armidale until 1899.

As well as subsidizing clergymen's stipends and church building, the church societies provided religious services for itinerant populations in road and railway workers' camps, distributed Bibles and religious literature and supported some missionary work among Aborigines.[9] The functions of the Newcastle Church Society were taken over by the diocesan synod in 1868. But Bishop Pearson thought additional efforts necessary and in 1885 he launched the Diocesan Church Extension Fund in an attempt to overtake the problem of religious provision in the diocese.[10] Between their metropolitan and rural dioceses the Anglican Church carried out a programme of church extension throughout the whole colony. The same was true of the Catholic Church. The Presbyterians and the Wesleyans also did not neglect church extension in the country as they sought to overcome the needs of the city.

Financing Church Extension

Church extension placed heavy financial demands on the denominations, which by 1880 were almost entirely dependent on voluntary support. State aid in the form of payments to clergy and subsidies for buildings, enjoyed by the larger denominations, had been abolished in 1862, although clergy in receipt of state grants up to that time continued to receive the money for the duration of their ministry in the colony. In 1880 41 of the 212 Anglican ministers and 25 of the 182 Catholic priests were still receiving state subsidies; slightly more than half of the Anglican grantees received £200 a year and about the same proportion of Catholic grantees received £150 a year. Eleven of the 80 Presbyterian and 9 of the 93 Wesleyan ministers in the colony were also receiving grants, mostly of £150 a year. The heads of the three colleges affiliated with the University of Sydney, St Paul's, St John's and St Andrew's, were well provided with salaries of £500 a year. Not many clergymen received that handsome sum, even with a state grant. As the financial burden on the parish was lightened if its clergyman was in receipt of a grant, the Anglican diocese of Newcastle attempted in 1881 to maximize this benefit. Its Stipend and General Fund provided all clergymen with a subsidy of £100 instead of £200 only to those on the state list.[11] This sensible arrangement depended on the cooperation of the endowed clergy and could only last as long as they remained in the diocese. But death slowly removed the recipients and so the subsidies diminished with the passing years, as Table 4 shows.

Table 4. Government subsidies paid to clergy since the passing of the Abolition Act.

	Church of England	Roman Catholic	Presbyterian	Wesleyan Methodist
	£	£	£	£
1870	12,386	6,583	2,180	1,572
1880	7,739	3,893	1,702	1,716
1890	5,591	2,600	702	900

Source: Statistical Register, NSW.

The grant of £800 to the Catholic Archbishop ceased in 1877 on the death of Dr Polding and the state guarantee of an income of £2,000 a year to the Anglican Bishop of Sydney ended with the death of Bishop Barker on 6 April 1882; by this time anyway, the Bishopsthorpe Estate was returning an adequate income. [12]

However income received from the Church and Schools Estate, originally an endowment for the benefit of the Church of England but enjoyed by the four larger denominations from 1845, increased until 1883, when the last payment was made (see Table 5).

Table 5. Income to denominations from the Church and Schools Estate.

	Church of England	Roman Catholic	Presbyterian	Wesleyan Methodist
	£	£	£	£
1870	1,576	1,024	326	180
1880	3,283	1,822	581	320
1883	3,290	2,362	581	320

Source: Statistical Register, NSW

This useful source of additional income was disbursed to assist individual clergy and churches and it relieved the pressure on local fund raising. The Catholic priest at Moruya, for example, spent £114 of the £116 he received from this source in 1879 on maintenance of and repairs to church and presbytery. Bishop Thomas wrote to Bishop Barker to say that the struggling clergy in the diocese of Goulburn were dependent upon aid from the Church and Schools Estate to keep their heads above water; he forecast divine judgment upon the government if it deprived the Church of these revenues.[13] Nevertheless, in 1880 Parliament passed legislation to divert the income of the Church and Schools Estate to public education. Parliament's termination on 11 May 1880 of grants of crown land for religious purposes also deprived the churches of valuable assistance in church extension.[14]

Anglican and Catholic clergy, in particular, disliking too much dependence on their parishioners, preferred state aid to the voluntary system, but there was no hope of its renewal in the 1880s. State aid to religion was "something worse than murder or sacrilege in this place", sneered Bishop Barry at a meeting of the Sydney Church Society in 1888. This prompted one lay member to point out that the voluntary system had advantages for the laity, particularly the power of the purse, a fact which the clergy knew only too well. On a different plane Mr Justice Owen observed that the Church was better free from state endowment and control. But some bishops sought parochial endowments in place of state aid to allow the clergy some independence from their parishioners. Bishop Pearson suggested that if some wealthy families endowed parishes for their sons, as in England, it would relieve the financial difficulty and the problem of ministerial supply as well. This idea did not catch on, but in 1884 John Campbell, MLC, wealthy pastoralist of "Duntroon" and chancellor of the diocese of Goulburn, provided an endowment of £10,000 for the newly established diocese of Riverina. Bishop Tyrrell, Pearson's predecessor, had bequeathed certain sheep and cattle stations worth £250,000 to the diocese of Newcastle. Tyrrell expected these properties to provide an annual income of £25,000, but during the 1880s, due mainly to bad seasons, this grand endowment did little to relieve the financial anxiety which harassed Pearson and ultimately caused his chronic ill health.[15]

It was never envisaged that state grants would be the only source of church income. The Church Act of 1836 assumed that churches would receive income from pew rents, a custom that was almost universal in churches until 1880. But the churches had taken other measures to supplement income well before the abolition of state aid. In the 1840s Anglican bishops revived the custom of an offertory during the communion service to supplement church income, rather than to fund charitable works as the *Prayer Book* intended. There was some strong opposition to a measure regarded by Evangelicals as an Anglo-Catholic innovation, but the offertory soon became fairly general in the colony,[16] and by 1880 it was the most important source of church income. In addition there were often retiring collections for special purposes, such as missions and church extension. But the weekly offering was not as well supported as Anglican and Catholic bishops thought it should be. According to Bishop Pearson, some pew-holders considered their pew-rent alone to be a fair contribution to the Church and in 1882 Dean Cowper estimated gloomily that only about one quarter of the congregations in Anglican churches contributed to the offertory. The excuse Bishop Barry heard frequently, that Anglicans had not been educated to give, provoked him to retort that if such were the case they had failed to grasp "the plainest teaching" of individual Christian responsibility. The Catholic Bishope Dunne included the question of giving in his suggestions for the agenda of the Plenary Council in 1885. He considered that less than 10 per cent of Catholics contributed to the financial support of public worship; but many more Catholics were paying for the religious education of their children. Pleas for more generous and systematic giving were frequent enough from Presbyterian and Wesleyan clergy while the *Independent* complained about "systematic withholding" among Congregationalists. By 1880 most Congregational churches had substituted weekly freewill offering envelopes for the old pew-rent system. The Wesleyans, who retained pew-rents, also adopted the envelope system during the 1880s, notwithstanding opposition from those who despised such worldliness in the Lord's business.[17]

A variety of other fund-raising activities were used to supplement church income. Women in the churches collected money for special causes and organized bazaars, fetes, fancy dress balls and other entertainments. Easter 1882 witnessed a remarkable example of fund-raising enterprise and denominational competition. Inspired by the success of a similar venture in Melbourne in 1881, Anglicans from the North Sydney churches of St Thomas and Christ Church, St Leonard's, held Ye Olde Englyshe Fayre in the Garden Palace to pay off their building debts. The "fayre", patronized well by the Sydney establishment, was an attempt to reproduce "Merrie England", as it was "in the days of Good Queen Bess", so Lieutenant Governor Sir Alfred Stephen put it when he opened the fair on Easter Monday. The northern hall was transformed into a typical street in an Elizabethan town, flanked by facades of timbered houses, with a Chelsea bun house at the end. The fair also featured a gaily decorated maypole, maypole dancers, morris dancing, tournaments and dramatic and musical presentations. The coarser or grosser aspects of Elizabethan England, which could have been "calculated in any way to offend the fine, nice taste of this fastidious nineteenth century" were omitted, the rector of St Thomas's, S.H. Childe, declared at the opening.[18] But enough was retained, apparently, to arouse the indignation of the Evangelicals' puritan conscience, and an unsuccessful attempt to have the fair condemned almost split the synod in May.

That same Easter, Archbishop Vaughan opened Ye Fayre of Ye Olden Tyme in the unconsecrated shell of St Mary's Cathedral. He claimed that he had a precedent for the venture and venue in a fair held in the uncompleted St Patrick's Cathedral, New York, although Vaughan sought to reproduce not Old Ireland, but England before the Reformation, when, according to him, bishops controlled the business and pleasure of the people as well as religion. (To this, the

Grand fund-raising — artist's impression of Ye Olde Englyshe Fayre. (From *Illustrated Sydney News*, 8 April 1882. Photo courtesy of Mitchell Library, Sydney.)

Sydney Morning Herald retorted: "The men and women of today breathe a new atmosphere and live in a new world.")[19] Ye Fayre of Ye Olden Tyme had most of the features of Ye Olde Englyshe Fayre, but with the addition of a liquor licence, although the committee decided at the last minute that liquor would not be sold. A special attraction was a May Queen procession that was "headed by a pretty baby Queen".

The Anglican fair ran for just over a fortnight and the fair at St Mary's for four weeks. The competition between them was friendly enough and during the first week the Anglican ladies paid a courtesy visit to the Catholic fair and the following week ladies from St Mary's returned the visit. Both fairs attracted large crowds as well as abundant Protestant criticism, especially of the Anglican enterprise. One Anglican clergyman dubbed the ladies who ran the fair the "daughters of Moab" and the Congregational *Independent* sneered that "Vanity Fair" built churches for Anglicans, who had never tried "pure voluntaryism". This taunt was accurate enough to embarrass the evangelical Dean Cowper, who commended the voluntary principle when he presided over the stormy sessions in synod that May. At the same time, he also exonerated the Anglican Church by instancing a number of churches built on voluntary support. But the Anglican organizers defended the propriety of their venture, which cleared some £4,000. Vaughan certainly was not one to be troubled by Protestant criticisms and thought a profit of £6,000 a creditable effort for Catholics.[20]

The Catholics continued to hold fairs of all descriptions, including Irish, Shakespearian, and French ones, while the Anglicans held many bazaars and a variety of fund-raising entertainments. It was easier to condemn them than to stop them, which the Reverend Henry Latimer Jackson, the distinguished incumbent of St James's Church, found out in 1887. He sought to have the synod condemn "Bazaars, Flower Shows, Exhibitions" as well as some forms of gambling as "wrong in principle" and "unworthy of professing Christians". The synod would not countenance raffles and art unions, but the other methods, although far from ideal, did after all provide necessary supplements to church income. Some clergy did regret this fact. "We are so much occupied with the finances and the mere external scaffolding of the Church", lamented Bishop Thomas, "that our minds are too much turned aside from the living spiritual power of the Gospel. . . ." According to Canon Arthur Selwyn, Vicar General of the diocese of Newcastle during Pearson's long illness, the clergy were often stigmatized as "inveterate beggars"; and the *Presbyterian* went so far as to say that some people were alienated from the Church because it seemed to them "a mere money-gathering institution". But fund raising had other positive benefits apart from the money it put in church treasuries; it did help to promote the social coherence of the congregation, but that some clergy apparently recognized this with too much enthusiasm moved Warlow Davies to complain that they believed "Churches would not be kept alive unless they were compelled to pay off debts".[21] Whatever the critics said, money had to be found to make religious ends meet, and especially for church extension in the growing colony and the expanding metropolis.

During the 1880s the various denominations found occasions for launching special appeals for church extension or other wider denominational objectives. At the Intercolonial Congregational Conference in Sydney in 1883 a Jubilee Fund was opened to mark the denomination's first fifty years in the colony and Australia. In New South Wales they aimed to raise £25,000, principally to establish a ministers' retiring fund and pay off church debts. Before the fund was even officially launched, £13,022 had been subscribed and by 1886 it had reached nearly £39,000, of which £30,000 went o church debts and extension. It was the only fund in the 1880s to exceed its target. In 1886 the Presbyterians opened a Majority Fund — it was twenty-one years after their union — with a goal of £50,000 to fund the building of manses and churches. At the end of the first year nearly £14,000 was promised and when the fund closed in 1892 £35,680 was promised and £25,489 subscribed. Although it fell far short of its target, it helped to reduce the accumulated deficit of the Church Extension Fund. To celebrate their golden jubilee in 1886 the Baptist Churches also launched a Jubilee Home Mission Fund with a modest target of £5,000. Only a little less than half was promised initially, and many promises remained unfulfilled.[22]

The centenary of the colony in 1888 gave the Anglicans and Wesleyans their occasion to open special appeals, and Catholics adopted W.B. Dalley's proposal to complete the chancel and a portion of the central tower of St Mary's Cathedral as a centenary memorial. Through a Centennial Thanksgiving Fund, the Wesleyans hoped to raise £50,000 in five years for a theological institution, a site for a girls' college, for church extension in the city and country and to liquidate trust debts. At its opening in January 1888 £10,967 was promised, but the fund was never fully subscribed even though it remained open for eleven years. Between £2,000 and £4,000 was raised annually in the first five years and by 1895 total receipts amounted to around £13,000. Donations trickled in until 1899 when the fund was officially closed to make way for the Twentieth Century Commemoration Fund. Two-fifths of the proceeds of the Thanksgiving Fund went to the theological institution and one-fifth to church extension; Methodist Ladies' College received 10 per cent and the remainder went to local ends such as the liquidation of debts.[23]

Anglicans established the Centennial Church Extension Fund for the Province of New South Wales with a target of £200,000. The fund received £4,950 at its inception and by February 1889 £38,515 was promised and £15,000 received within the diocese of Sydney. Bishop Barry claimed in 1888 that the contributions had come mainly from a few wealthy Anglicans and appealed to the diocese to rise above party spirit and parochialism. It was, he said, the Church's fund, not his; for Barry had fallen foul of Evangelicals in 1887 over the installation of a reredos in St Andrew's Cathedral depicting the Crucifixion and then displeased High Churchmen by agreeing to substitute a scene of the Transfiguration. Party rivalry among Anglicans was sometimes bitter and hindered the Church's efforts in extension and other common enterprises. The refusal of the wealthy parish of St Mary's, West Maitland, a stronghold of evangelicalism in the diocese of Newcastle, to contribute to diocesan funds in the late 1880s was mainly influenced by party principle. But there was still solid support for the Centennial fund in the Newcastle diocese, which was responsible for almost half the £23,800 promised by the rural dioceses. Contributions began to decline from 1892 and many promises were not fulfilled, so that by 1897 the total amount subscribed was only £29,383, the greater part from the diocese of Sydney.[24] The fund was invested and its income subsidized stipends, new church buildings and home mission work, mostly within the diocese of Sydney — after all, the response from most of the rural dioceses to the Centennial Fund had been poor. Dr Camidge, second Bishop of Bathurst, apologized to his synod in 1890 for having consented to the provincial scheme. He was sure that Bathurst would have raised more money if the fund had been a diocesan venture. Indeed, after the fund was launched the board had agreed to include contributions for special and more local purposes and in 1889 each diocese was given control of the amounts promised and collected within its jurisdiction. But this made little difference in the rural dioceses and Camidge may have done better to recall the complaint of his predecessor, Bishop Marsden, that little of the wealth from the stock and wool sales found its way "into the treasury of the Lord".[25]

There were abundant complaints from the clergy of most denominations about the niggardliness of their people. Anglican clergy in all dioceses deplored the parochialism of wealthier parishes which made ungenerous contributions to denominational funds designed to help poorer parishes and establish new causes. It was a tendency to "congregationalism", explained Canon White to the Newcastle Synod in 1886, that led the older parishes to protest that because they were meeting the financial demands of their own parishes well, they should not have to burden themselves with the poorer parishes of the diocese.[26] Confident that this was substantially the case, Bishop Pearson recommended increasing the number of parishes in the diocese of Newcastle. To allay the anxiety of those who feared the financial consequences of the proposed subdivision, he argued that people would support a regular, attentive pastor better than they would an itinerant minister, so that "within reasonable limits, the more the workers the more liberally will each worker be supported". Pearson's successor, Bishop Stanton, seemed to share the same opinion when he concluded that the voluntary system was "practically payment by results".[27]

These views were understandable, for the church for many people was principally their own local church. They had little appreciation of wider church work and its financial needs, except perhaps missions to the heathen, which had a certain romantic appeal. So the failure of denominational funds to reach their objectives did not necessarily mean that people were loath to give to religious causes in the 1880s. It was easier to raise money for local objectives and in the 1880s considerable sums of money were spent on the extension and renovation of old church buildings or installing pipe organs in several large city churches. Like the bystanders at Bethany, there were a few who protested at extravagance which diverted money from charity and missions.[28]

While the people were not as responsive to wider appeals as the clergy had hoped, nevertheless denominational funds did receive substantial support in the early 1880s. There was a significant response to Bishop Barry's appeal for money for church extension. Contributions to the Sydney Church Society nearly doubled during his first year in 1884 and continued to rise in 1885 giving the society an income of £8,947. The decline of this income, particularly after 1887, can be offset to some extent by the contributions made to the Centennial Church Extension Fund in that diocese. The annual income of the Goulburn Church Society for the period 1864 to 1905 reached its peak early in the 1880s when it was between £10,000 and £12,000; by 1890 it had fallen to £5,000. This fall was due partly to the formation of the diocese of Riverina in 1884, but also to drought and depression which probably affected collections elsewhere. Bishop Pearson's Church Extension Fund established in 1885 raised £1,900 in its first year which at least tided the diocese over a period of financial difficulty.[29]

St Andrew's Cathedral, Sydney and the Town Hall, c.1880. (Photo courtesy of Mitchell Library, Sydney.)

An English visitor to the colonies in 1887, the prominent Non-conformist minister, Dr R.W. Dale, found "remarkable proofs of religious energy and liberality".[30] The number of churches built by all denominations in New South Wales in the 1880s testified to this. According to the *Statistical Register,* church buildings in New South Wales increased by 784 in the 1880s compared with an increase of 434 in the 1870s and 294 in the 1890s. Although an independent calculation based on denominational sources, where available, suggests a lower figure of about 700 new church buildings in the 1880s, church extension for the decade was still considerable. A similar pattern occurred in Victoria where, according to the *Statistical Register,* 685 new church buildings were erected in the 1880s compared with 429 in the 1870s and 373 in the 1890s.[31]

In New South Wales the number of Anglican church buildings increased in the 1880s by about 170; a third of these were erected in the diocese of Sydney, the greater number (39) being in the metropolitan area. The Catholic Church in the colony built about 100 new churches during the decade, nearly a quarter of them in the archdiocese of Sydney and most of these in the metropolis.[32] Unlike Protestants, who had to place churches "at a reasonable distance", Catholics could count more on the loyalty of their people and did not need to build quite as many churches to cope with the expansion of settlement in the country or in the suburbs. Not only could the faithful be expected to travel further to Mass than Protestants might to church, but churches in the city and larger towns were used several times on a Sunday.

Among the other denominations, the Presbyterian Church more than doubled its strength during the decade. In 1880 it had 70 charges and 328 preaching centres, including 113 church buildings; in 1890 there were 141 charges with 773 preaching centres of which about 250 were church buildings. Both J.M. Ross, General Agent of the Presbyterian Church, and Robert Collie, Moderator in 1891, saw the 1880s as a new era in church extension focused on Sydney and suburbs, where church buildings increased from 18 to 33. There had obviously been considerable extension of Presbyterianism in the country in the 1880s, proportionately more than in the city. Even so, they had not overtaken the problem in the country for in 1890 it was reported that the Riverina, where Presbyterian adherents were relatively strong, was without a Presbyterian minister or home missioner. And Presbyterianism was left relatively weak at the centre compared with the Congregationalists, who increased their metropolitan churches from 22 to 35 by 1890, and the Wesleyans, who raised their number from 35 to 51 in the decade.[33]

Wesleyan Methodists also expanded more in the country than in the city. They built 100 new churches between 1880 and 1890, less than the Presbyterians, but the Wesleyans did not have as much leeway to make up. By 1890 they had 387 church buildings compared with some 250 for the Presbyterians. In addition to churches, their preaching centres, almost all in the country, rose from 374 in 1880 to 433 by 1890. During the 1880s, despite the emphasis on church extension in the city, there were Methodists who argued that rural extension be given priority if Methodism was to retain "its proud pre-eminence as an organisation peculiarly adapted to carry the Gospel to all sorts of men and to every corner of the continent". It seems that their view prevailed, for only 16 of the new churches built in the 1880s were in the metropolitan area.

Methodism did have some advantages over other denominations when it came to church extension in the country; its stationing system, the use of probationary ministers, usually unmarried, and of local preachers enabled it to supply some areas before other denominations could maintain a permanent ministry there. The outback town of Bourke is a case in point. The Presbyterians had established a church in the town but failed to provide an adequate follow-up of ministers. The Wesleyans had also been interested in Bourke for some time and in 1885 the Wesleyan Conference decided to station a minister there. It was pointed out that although there were few Wesleyans at Bourke there was also little sectarianism and one of their best young men would be sure to get a good following.[34] However gains from other denominations were not always permanent, as J.E. Carruthers found at Wagga Wagga when he went there in 1877; the Presbyterians placed an able man there at the same time and the Wesleyan Church lost a third of its congregation "including some excellent and substantial Presbyterians"! But the Wesleyans also drew some adherents of the "Other Methodist" Churches into their fold by coming first on the scene, as in South Australia where Bible Christian Missionaries were sometimes told by former followers: "You did not come soon enough."[35]

These smaller Methodist denominations, more sect-like than the Wesleyans, were less likely to attract people from other churches. Their growth in the 1880s was mostly through migration of Methodists to mining districts in New South Wales. This explains why the greater proportion of their churches were in the country. The number increased from around 70 to 105 during the decade; the majority were Primitive Methodist churches, 65 in 1880 and 81 in 1890, of which 61 were in the country.[36] Among the remainder were some United Methodist Free Churches and a few Bible Christian Churches as well as two "Lay Methodist" chapels. Some of these "Other Methodists", especially the Bible Christians, were significantly stronger in Victoria and South Australia, but the Wesleyans were generally the dominant group of Methodists in Australia.

Of the smaller Protestant denominations, the Congregationalists built 17 new churches in the colony in the 1880s, 4 of them in the country, making a total of 55 churches in 1890. However the denomination was evidently losing ground in the country as the number of rural preaching stations dropped from 31 in 1880 to 16 in 1890. Only in South Australia did Congregationalists succeed to any degree in rural church extension, where they were assisted by the endowment of the Parkin Mission. The Baptists fared better in country New South Wales. Of their 20 new churches built in the 1880s 13 were in the country, making a total of 33 churches in all in the colony. Even so, the Baptists also found rural church extension a great difficulty and some were prepared virtually to abandon it. In 1881 the *Baptist* argued that church extension should be mainly in the city. Educated ministers, it maintained, could not be supported by small communities. The Baptist Union in 1887 could offer Baptists in the country only its moral support, although the same year it advocated union churches in country areas between Baptists and Congregationalists. But the Congregational *Independent* was not enthusiastic about this proposal; it preferred comity instead of competition among Protestants in the country. It thought that the best idea would be to set up "free and evangelical churches" in the sparsely settled parts of the colony and, by agreement, leave some areas to the denomination with the best claim. Comity was an established principle among Protestants in overseas missions, but there was little support for it in the home mission in the 1880s. The Wesleyans had sought and largely achieved "a proud pre-eminence", although in 1891 there was a marked change in their policy; influenced perhaps by less prosperous times, the conference passed a resolution advocating comity in church extension in the country.[37] But it was the competitive spirit that still stimulated the growth of the larger Protestant denominations; the Congregationalists more or less left the country to them, although the Baptists slowly improved their strength in the rural areas.

There were other smaller denominations in the colony, including the Salvation Army; it won a considerable following soon after its establishment in New South Wales in 1882 and by 1890 it had 99 meeting places, 25 of them in the city. Church building by other smaller denominations and sects increased from around 32 premises in 1880 to 67 in 1890.

The church building programmes of the 1880s are more remarkable when measured by the amount of accommodation available in churches in a decade when the population was increasing rapidly

(refer Table 1.3, p. 22). The churches largely reversed the downward trend of accommodation of the 1870s; there was accommodation for only 29 per cent of the population in 1880 compared to 36 per cent of the population in 1870. By 1890 there was room in the churches for 40 per cent of the colony's population, and this proportion was maintained to the end of the century. This was considerably below church accommodation in South Australia, where there was room for 60 per cent of the population, and in Victoria where places in churches increased from a capacity for 49 per cent of the population in 1880 to 59 per cent by 1900.[38] Although most denominations in New South Wales made much of church extension in the city, the greatest overall gains were in the country where accommodation available for 29 per cent rose to cater for 42 per cent of the rural population. When the necessarily large number of preaching centres in rural areas is taken into account it becomes apparent that the country fared relatively well for accommodation. The improvement in the city, where capacity for 30 per cent of the metropolitan population rose to 37 per cent, was still substantial, even if a little short of the proportion in 1870 when city churches could have seated 40 per cent of the metropolitan population at once.

The achievements of church extension in the city are the more impressive in that the churches built there were usually more stately and more costly than those erected in the country. Competition also operated in the choice of architectural styles. Anglicans built their churches and cathedrals in Gothic Revival style after English medieval models and Catholics, seeking to outbuild the Church of England, did the same. As the new St Mary's Cathedral progressed in Sydney, the *Freeman's Journal* boasted that its splendour and prominence would daily remind the world that "it represents the Christianity of New South Wales", clearly marking "the contrast between the sects and the Church".[39]

While the Catholic Church thought that Gothic magnificence would emphasize distinction, the smaller Protestant denominations adopted the style to minimize any outward appearance of difference between themselves and their biggest competitor, the Church of England. In this they were following a pattern already set by Nonconformists in Britain since the mid-nineteenth century.[40] Thus from around 1870 non-episcopal Protestants in Australia began to erect substantial Gothic buildings in the new suburbs of their cities and in some larger country towns. These buildings testify to the wealth of their congregations; the *Presbyterian* thought them in keeping with "the improved dwelling houses of the worshippers". Wesleyans agreed that it was necessary to make their churches com-

St Stephen's Presbyterian Church, Phillip Street, Sydney (since demolished). (From *Centenary History of the Presbyterian Church in New South Wales* by J. Cameron [Sydney: Angus and Robertson, 1905]. Photo courtesy of La Trobe University Library, Melbourne.)

fortable and attractive; a Victorian Methodist contended in 1867 that ecclesiastical buildings ought not to be confused with post offices or banks, a criticism which might have been aimed at churches with classical lines such as York Street Wesleyan or Pitt Street Congregational Churches in Sydney. Even the Baptists were affected by this trend; the Reverend Charles Bright exhorted them, in terms reminiscent of the arguments of English Nonconformists, to build churches that men would "not be ashamed of attending". Such an emphasis on outward appearance occasionally disturbed the evangelical conscience, but the Reverend Dr Kinross sought to calm it when he spoke at the laying of the foundation stone of a new Presbyterian Church at Ashfield, to cost between £6,000 and £7,000, in 1885: "A beautiful church would not convert a sinner," he admitted, "but neither would an ugly one"; a beautiful church, however, showed the attachment of its people to their God.[41]

This aestheticism also influenced standards of music in worship. It was "pre-eminently a musical age", the *Presbyterian* observed in 1881. Every home, it exaggerated, had a piano or harmonium and singing was taught in schools; to play a musical instrument was the "*sine qua non*" in every young lady's education. Colonial youth were "generally fond of aesthetics", asserted a correspondent in the same weekly. It was argued that music in worship should be of the highest quality. So there was a trend away from hearty evangelical singing to more formality and grandeur in music, including the chanting of the psalms led by the choir, which assumed greater importance. Appointments in the new churches and alterations carried out at considerable cost in a number of older churches gave greater physical prominence to the choir, in the centre front in most non-Anglican churches, and this added an air of performance to the service. These arrangements or renovations generally included the installation of a pipe organ costing £500-1,000, although the organ placed in St Andrew's Cathedral in 1868 cost more than £2,000. Similar developments took place in Melbourne among most denominations. The former Free Presbyterians overcame their objections to the organ; the historian of Victorian Presbyterianism, the Reverend Robert Sutherland explained in 1877 that not only did an organ assist the singing, but as other denominatons used organs, Presbyterians were constrained to adopt them "to preserve their people from going to other churches".[42]

Sutherland claimed that the only opponents of organs were "a few small sects in Scotland", but he might also have mentioned the continuing Free Presbyterians in Australia who kept the organ out of their churches. Some in other smaller denominations also attempted to resist the new musical trends. A Baptist minister in New South

Wales who disapproved particularly of the innovations in Victorian Baptist Churches quipped that they might as well introduce the bag-pipes. Yet the Bathurst Street Baptist Church in Sydney installed a pipe organ, "providing additional interest to their Sunday services and increased attractiveness to our Denominational home". Members of Crown Street Primitive Methodist Church stood firm against the stream and in 1893 they dismissed the choir master and resolved that "the choir shall exist for the purposes of Congregational singing only, and that it shall be under the charge of the minister".[43]

It was the hope of most churches, however, that good choirs and pipe organs would attract better congregations, but some loftier reasons were offered to justify these developments. Music was "the handmaid of religion", said Bishop Barry at the dedication in 1884 of a new pipe organ worth about £550 in St John the Baptist's Church, Ashfield. High class music could add vitality to worship, the Bishop continued, and there was "a duty" to cultivate it "so long as true devotion was not sacrificed to aestheticism". Consistent with this, Barry attempted during his short episcopate to make St Andrew's Cathedral a model of worship "in frequency and beauty" for the whole diocese. In 1885 daily choral services were introduced and a school primarily for choristers commenced, thanks to a generous donation which also provided for two additional clergymen to the cathedral staff. When funds ran out three years later, the daily cathedral services were reduced to choral evensong.[44] The large sums of money lavished on churches, especially in the metropolitan area, in addition to providing places for an expanding population, also helped to inhibit losses to other denominations and even to attract members from other local and possibly less ostentatious churches. It was, after all, "a fair and open field".

Preachers for the Pulpits

New churches needed pastors, which meant that the supply of clergy was an important part of any church extension programme. The church societies and other denominational sustentation and extension funds subsidized clerical stipends. They were also used to fund the passage of ministers to Australia from Britain. Every denomination depended to a lesser or larger extent on recruits from the British Isles to man the pulpits and altars in the colonies, even though the churches did have some facilities for training their own clergy. Early attempts to establish theological education in Australia failed, but in the second half of the nineteenth century most denominations set up permanent colleges to train candidates for their respective ministries. The first of these was Moore College, established by the Church of England at Liverpool in 1856; in 1891 it moved to Newtown, where it was close to Sydney University. Although several diocesan seminaries had been set up by the Catholic Church, it was left without any institution for theological training by 1870. A national theological seminary in Sydney was mooted by Vaughan but it was in Bathurst, in 1876, that Bishop Matthew Quinn opened St Charles Borromeo Seminary. The training of an Australian priesthood was one of Cardinal Moran's priorities and he established St Patrick's College, Manly, which opened in 1889. St Charles Borromeo Seminary closed soon after and St Patrick's functioned as a national Catholic seminary until 1922 when Rome recommended the establishment of provincial or diocesan seminaries.[45]

Presbyterians opened a theological hall in Victoria in 1866 and in St Andrew's College in Sydney in 1873. During the 1860s the Wesleyan Methodists set up theological training in conjunction with their denominational schools, Wesley College in Melbourne and Newington College in Sydney, and the Congregationalists established Camden College in Sydney in 1864. Baptists in New South Wales, who were unsuccessful in their attempts to establish theological education in the 1870s, arranged for their students to train at Camden College in the 1880s. From 1895 until 1915, when a Baptist college opened in New South Wales, theological students studied in Victoria, where a college had opened in 1891. There was a unique attempt at united theological education in South Australia. In 1872 Baptists, Congregationalists and Presbyterians there established Union College to provide both advanced secular and theological education. Through the initiative of the council of the college, the University of Adelaide was founded soon after. In 1873 Union College gave up secular instruction and provided theological education for the three denominations and the Bible Christians until 1886, when it was dissolved; the partners in the enterprise had set their hearts on denominational colleges. As these were established, schemes of cooperation developed among them and the formation of the Melbourne College of Divinity in 1910 was a product of this cooperative spirit.[46]

The theological halls, however, were far from full in the 1880s and there were frequent pleas for recruits from colonial families. Dean Cowper warned Anglicans in 1881 that England would not be an unlimited source of supply for the colonial churches. In 1882 the *Presbyterian* ventured the opinion that the best ministers were "sons of the soil" and Cardinal Moran stated that no church was "on a permanent footing until it enlists clergy from among the ranks of its own faithful children". But that combination of patriotism and piety

Joseph Horner Fletcher, Principal of Newington College and President of the Wesleyan Methodist Theological Training Institution. Taken in Sydney in 1874. (From *The Illustrated History of Methodism* by J. Colwell [Sydney: William Brooks and Co., 1904]. Photo courtesy of La Trobe University Library, Melbourne.)

which Bishop Stanton of Newcastle thought desirable in colonial youth was rare.[47]

There were many explanations for the dearth of recruits to the ministry. Some Protestants blamed worldliness and the lack of spirituality in the churches and homes of the people. They pointed to the materialism of their age and the attractiveness of other professions. A few thought the ministry was not challenging enough for colonial lads with their love of adventurous life, and others that Australian youth lacked the necessary literary tastes to take it on. There were those who thought that the challenges to religious belief discouraged youth from considering the ministry. This had some point in the 1880s for intellectual difficulties had led two prominent Protestant ministers, the Baptist James Greenwood, a founder of the Public Schools League, and John Osborne, a minister of York Street Wesleyan Church, to leave the ministry early in the decade. Moreover, Jackson of St James's Anglican Church, typically for a Broad Churchman, thought the theological difficulties serious enough to introduce a motion in the Sydney synod in 1887 asking for a relaxation of doctrinal standards. Judge Wilkinson supported Jackson, but such a move had little hope of success among the evangelical majority and Jackson soon withdrew the motion. Yet not all liberal Anglicans viewed the theological difficulties so seriously. Bishop Pearson pointed out that there was also theological unsettlement in Britain, but that the Church in England did not suffer the colony's shortage of clergy. He blamed voluntaryism which, by "the power of the purse", made the clergyman too dependent on his congregation.[48]

Most blamed the financial insecurity of the ministry for the shortage of candidates. In a rare editorial on the problem in May 1888 the *Sydney Morning Herald* expressed the opinion that the financial arrangements of the churches were degrading and deterred many good men from joining the ministry. An Anglican layman agreed: little wonder, he thought, that Moore College wanted for students when Anglicans treated their ministers so meanly. With some exaggeration and a little bitterness, he pictured the aged clergyman seeking refuge in the Benevolent Asylum while the Church provided homes for fallen women.[49] Certainly there were better prospects for educated or studiously inclined youth in other professions, but there were also rewards in the churches for a few exceptional men. Pitt Street Congregational Church was prepared to pay £1,000 a year to bring James Jefferis, a co-founder of Union College, Adelaide, from South Australia to its pulpit and Llewellyn Bevan received an annual stipend of £1,450 at Collins Street Independent Church in Melbourne. A few Anglicans also enjoyed substantial salaries for the times; the Bishop of Sydney received £2,000, the Dean £600 and Jackson's annual stipend at St James's in 1886 was £700. a number of city ministers received between £400 and £500 per annum, but the churches generally regarded £300 a year with a house as a reasonable stipend. This was a comfortable salary in the 1880s, well above the average annual earnings of tradesmen and labourers, who received from £100 to £150 a year. Even the lowest paid ministers received more than that; however when churchmen (and the *Sydney Morning Herald*) blamed low stipends for difficulties in recruiting candidates for the ministry, they were not comparing themselves with the working classes, but with medical practitioners, lawyers and senior school teachers.[50] The churches may have made the problem of recruitment more difficult in the 1880s by an emphasis on a better educated ministry. An "increasing intelligence . . . among all classes" demanded that men be possessed of both spiritual zeal and "a rounded and full-orbed culture", argued the Reverend George Martin in his retiring presidential address to the Wesleyan Conference in January 1883. Two years later the conference's Pastoral Address stated that "a cultured ministry is a *sine qua non* if we would reach all classes in the community". The letter also mentioned that Methodists could not ignore the "strenuous efforts" being made by other denominations "to raise up a cultured ministry".[51]

Neither could they ignore the lay preacher on whom the Methodist system depended so much. Baptists and Congregationalists also looked for better educated lay preachers. The schoolmaster had been abroad since the days of Wesley and Whitfield, Alfred Allen told his fellow lay preachers at a Congregational conference late in 1879. Congregations could no longer be expected to endure uncouth manners from barely literate preachers. The Wesleyans, in an attempt to raise standards, prescribed a course of reading for local preachers on trial, and in 1886 a Local Preachers Mutual Improvement Society was formed in the Sydney district. But these endeavours to improve the quality of their local preachers were frustrated by the Public Service Board's regulation which forbade state school teachers from engaging in such religious activities, thereby excluding the better educated layman from the pulpit.[52]

Anglicans and Presbyterians had always subscribed to the ideal of a learned ministry. Late in the 1870s Bishop Barker stated his aim that candidates for the ministry should graduate before proceeding to Moore College, and in 1884 Bishop Barry announced that he intended to appoint only clergy with university degrees to the principal city and suburban churches.[53] But a few Anglicans did not esteem theological college education very highly at all. The proposal to bring Moore College to Sydney provoked Jackson to say that candidates for the ministry would be better trained under tutors at St Paul's College, affiliated with Sydney University. Bishop Moorhouse had adopted such a scheme in Trinity College in Melbourne. Archbishop Vaughan also hoped for a time to give Catholic clergy "a good university course" through St John's College.[54] Presbyterians in New South Wales established their theological hall in their university college, St Andrew's, and the theological hall in Victoria moved to Ormond College in 1888. Methodists in New South Wales had no university college in the nineteenth century. Despite its concern for higher standards the conference turned down an offer from a young English Methodist scholar, Edward Holdsworth Sugden, to undertake special educational work in the colony. In 1889 Sugden became master of the new Methodist college at Melbourne University, Queen's College, and in that year Victoria's candidates for the Methodist ministry came under his instruction. For nearly twenty years Queen's was a central theological college for Australian Methodism, except New South Wales, which continued to rely on Newington until it set up its own theological seminary, Leigh College, away from the university in 1914.[55]

If theological college education was not ideal, it was better than none at all, as Bishop Pearson recognized in 1886. He wanted men for his diocese with at least this much training, but he preferred them to be graduates in both arts and theology. Pearson denied that the need for a cultured ministry was due to the higher educational standards of the age; he disparaged contemporary culture as shallow anyway. The need was rather because of the nature of the ministerial office itself. Sound enough sentiments, but perhaps more compelling was the other belief that better-educated congregations demanded better-educated ministers. This was certainly the view the *Presbyterian* took in 1881 when it argued that the intellectual challenges of the day demanded men competent if not distinguished in a variety of disciplines. The Presbyterian General Assembly had already set a requirement that from 1878 all its students should take arts and theology. James Jefferis showed that he largely shared these ideals in his appeal for candidates for Camden College in 1877. Similarly, Alexander Gosman, principal of the Victorian Congregational College, told Australian Congregationalists at their jubilee conference in Sydney in 1883 that they should aim for university trained men wherever possible and that at least candidates should have matriculated.[56]

A mostly graduate ministry, however, was far from attainable for all denominations and probably not desirable. The Presbyterian General Assembly seemed to recognize this when it set the requirement of arts and theology for its students but reserved the right "to make special provisions". Actually the Presbyterians progressed a long way towards their goal and in their letter to Scotland in 1877 they boasted that the Presbyterian Church of New South Wales had a higher proportion of graduates and men with honorary degrees than any other denomination. Approximately 45 per cent of Presbyterian ministers in the colony were graduates in the late 1870s, although the proportion was to drop later; it was 43 per cent in 1890 and 36 per cent in 1898. In that year, when the *Presbyterian* again compared the academic qualifications of the ministers of the various denominations, it was found that the Presbyterians still had more graduate ministers than the others. It was the same in Victoria where 47 per cent of Presbyterian ministers had university degrees in 1900. At the same time, about 25 per cent of Anglican clergy were graduates in both New South Wales and Victoria (in the diocese of Melbourne), although the proportion had been higher in the older colony in the mid eighties. The proportion of graduates in the diocese of Newcastle in 1885 was 33 per cent, for Sydney and Grafton and Armidale dioceses 30 per cent and in the two larger rural dioceses, Bathurst and Goulburn, it was 20 per cent. But by 1890 the proportion of graduates in the metropolitan diocese had fallen to 25 per cent, despite Bishop Barry's efforts to recruit graduates for city churches. Like other bishops, Barry had to accept men from theological colleges in Britain as well as the colony, and some theological students passed through university colleges, such as Trinity College, Melbourne, without obtaining a degree. Congregationalists fared no better, with only 25 per cent of their ministers graduates, and, there were fewer graduates among Methodists and Baptists. Wesleyans in Victoria had a few more graduates in their ministry than there were in New South Wales in 1889 (nine as against four) when the first *Methodist Ministerial Index* was published. The situation had not changed much by 1898 when the *Presbyterian* reported that 4.5 per cent of Wesleyan ministers were graduates. Only one Baptist minister was a graduate in New South Wales in 1890.[57]

So the churches had to be satisfied with men mostly trained in theological colleges, and some with not even that training. A few affected to despise any formal preparation for the ministry. College men were "too conceited", asserted George Hurst in 1884, a self-taught Wesleyan minister, who claimed that more valuable work had been done by untrained Methodist ministers. Some thought that as few academic obstacles as possible should be placed in the way of candidates for the ministry. In 1879, for example, the church-wardens of the Adelong district in the diocese of Goulburn asked Bishop Thomas to ordain their popular deacon, W.M. White, without an examination. Thomas told them that while this could not be done, he thought that he and the examining clergy might "take a lenient method of examination" with White. In some instances licensed catechists or home missionaries found their way into the ministry. Despite a preference for graduates, Bishop Moorhouse found it expedient to ordain lay readers to the ministry in Victoria. Bishop Pearson disapproved of this entry into the ministry by the back door, and especially the notion that catechists might acquire the necessary theological training from the clergy under whom they were working.[58] But principles had to bend to pressing demands, although under-trained parsons were mostly found in the remote rural districts.

Other denominations also found that a higher educational standard was a luxury they could not always afford. When Gosman advocated matriculation as an entrance requirement to Congregational theological colleges, Josiah Mullens, chairman of the Sydney Stock Exchange and treasurer of Camden College, warned that there would be very few recruits for the ministry if this were enforced. He wanted to see the time of training shortened, not lengthened. Wesleyans in New South Wales, for all their rhetoric about higher standards, decided in 1885 that students for the ministry could not be spared for a three year course. However at least the conference accepted a minimum of two years in college, and probationers were expected to complete additional studies before ordination. Wesleyans in Victoria were faced with problems when theological training was connected with Queen's College, because most of the candidates for the ministry had not matriculated, which was a requirement of entry. As separate theological education avoided this problem, it is of little wonder that in other states Methodists eventually broke with Queen's to establish their own theological colleges.[59]

That not many well-educated young men were attracted to the ministry was probably because they saw that it was not a highly esteemed profession in Australia, and that it offered limited scope for men of talent and ambition. Colonial youths who contemplated this calling might also have observed that the colonial-trained parson was not as highly regarded as those trained "at home", as an Anglican report implied in 1887. The "plums" seemed to fall into the hands of Englishmen like Jackson and Jefferis; and all the Anglican bishops were English. After Vaughan, the last English archbishop in the Catholic Church, the Irish born and Irish trained dominated the episcopate and priesthood. Scotsmen occupied the leading pulpits and positions in the Presbyterian Church. A correspondent to the *Presbyterian* in 1882 probably spoke for many in the churches when he disagreed with that weekly's advocacy of "sons of the soil". He extolled the strengths of the men from "home" in education and understanding human nature compared with the more limited experience of the colonial born. But were all migrant ministers so superior? In 1883 the secretary of the Colonial Missionary Society told Green of the Congregational Church Extension Society that he could send dozens of men, some unmarried, to New South Wales, "but you would not thank us for them" — "every student worth anything, and popular in style" had been engaged to settle before the college term had ended.[60]

Some exceptional men did come out, but for every one of these there were probably many of mediocre ability who were less talented than some of the colonial-born clergy. In the diocese of Sydney, for example, among the Anglicans there were Dean Cowper, Archdeacons W.J. Gunther and R.L. King and the Reverend Dr J.C. Corlette, although all of them went to England for their education. Canon A.E. Selwyn, the administrator of the diocese of Newcastle for the greater part of the 1880s, although born in England, was trained and ordained in the colony. Some of the outstanding Australian-born ministers in other denominations were Dr J.E. Carruthers, Wesleyan, Dr A.J. Gilchrist, Presbyterian, and Dr Thomas Roseby, F.R.A.S., and George Clarke, F.R.S., of Tasmania, both Congregationalists. The latter two were examples of clergymen who distinguished themselves in science and other academic pursuits as well as in religion.[61] And there were enough of them to show that the "sons of the soil" were not necessarily inferior to the men from "home". But whatever the quality of colonial-born ministers, their numbers fell far short of the churches' needs in the nineteenth century.

The dependence on supply from the British Isles did not trouble the Catholic Bishop of Maitland, James Murray. With a touch of pride he told the congregation at the consecration of Bishop Dunne of Brisbane in June 1882, that they could look to no other place to provide clergy for the colonies except that "little land" of theirs, Catholic Ireland. Apart from Cardinal Moran and perhaps Matthew Quinn of Bathurst, it seems that the bishops had little intention of seeing what the colony could offer. By 1914 Manly Seminary had trained only 160 of the 800 priests in Australia, the rest of whom nearly all came from Ireland.[62]

The Anglicans continued to rely on clergy from England although by the 1880s a little more than half the clergy in the diocese of Sydney had been trained locally, mostly at Moore College, and the majority of the clergy in the diocese of Bathurst at the same time had been born in the colonies. There were more Englishmen in some of the newer dioceses, and, overall, colonial-born clergy made up about a third of New South Wales ministers.[63]

In 1877 the Presbyterians made a special appeal to Scotland to send ministers to New South Wales, and during the 1880s a steady stream flowed into the colony, some of them sent at the Scottish churches' expense; eighty-seven came from the British Isles, mostly from Scotland and Ireland, thirty-three from other colonies or countries (including two Chinese pastors), fifteen from other denominations, a few of them from the Presbyterian Church of Eastern Australia and only eight were recruited and trained in the colony, at least five of whom were born there. In 1890 the Church Extension Committee confessed that the "mother country" was still the main source of supply for ministers, but the situation changed in the 1890s when the number of new ministers trained in the colony increased and the supply from Britain fell by half.[64]

The Wesleyans also requested assistance from Britain, but the British Wesleyan Conference refused to send eight ministers in 1884 due to the need in Britain. In any case, the proportion of colonial-born clergy was improving; by 1890, they formed about a third of the Church's ministry compared with a little more than a quarter in 1880; this was not as high as in Victoria where they were in the majority as early as the 1880s. The Congregationalists drew heavily on Britain for ministerial supply, with only ten of the sixty-four ordained ministers in New South Wales in 1890 trained at Camden College. The goal of the principal of Camden, J.G. Fraser — "an Australian ministry for Australian churches" — seemed far off. The Baptists, likewise, were almost entirely dependent on England for their ministers during the nineteenth century.[65]

Discouraging though it was to try to recruit ministers in Australia or to obtain men from overseas, the provision of clergy in New South Wales not only kept pace with the demands, but overall, improved a little (see Table 6). In achieving this, the number of

Table 6. Ratio of clergy to population for New South Wales and Victoria, 1880, 1890.

State	1880	1890
New South Wales	1:1,110	1:1,050
Victoria	1:1,170	1:750

All numbers are rounded to nearest ten.

Sources: Number of clergy registered to conduct marriages as given annually in *Statistical Register, NSW* and *Victorian Year Book.*

clergy rose from 671 in 1880 to 1,063 in 1890. Table 6 shows the improvement in Victoria over the decade to have been even more remarkable. This was due mainly to the increase in the number of Catholic priests, which nearly doubled, and also to the influx both of Salvation Army officers and ministers of other small sects.

The changes in clerical provision for the main denominations are listed in Table 7, which also presents the corresponding figures for Victoria. The larger denominations in New South Wales, Anglican, Catholic and Presbyterian, all managed to improve the provision of their clergy relative to their congregations, which was a considerable feat when the population had increased so dramatically over the decade. The ratio of Wesleyan pastors to their people remained roughly constant, but the "Other Methodist" Churches in the colony fared less well, unlike their co-religionists in Victoria. The migration of their adherents to the mining districts of Broken Hill and Newcastle outstripped the provision of ministers there. Baptists and Congregationalists both had an enviable supply of pastors throughout the period, but their adherents increased at a greater rate than their ministers. In Victoria the churches' efforts to provide

Table 7. Ratio of clergy to adherents by denomination, New South Wales and Victoria, 1880, 1890.

Denomination	New South Wales		Victoria	
	1880	1890	1880	1890
Anglican	1:1,160	1:1,550	1:1,740	1:1,730
Catholic	1:1,140	1:1,020	1:2,190	1:1,380
Presbyterian	1:790	1:700	1:820	1:760
Wesleyan*	1:610	1:600	1:870	1:880
Other Methodist	1:480	1:700	1:330	1:200
Baptist	1:300	1:400	1:430	1:560
Congregationalist	1:340	1:390	1:400	1:410

All numbers are rounded to nearest ten.

* Wesleyan ministers were not distinguished from "Other Methodist" ministers in the *Victorian Year Book*. The number is taken from the stationing lists in *Minutes, Victoria and Tasmania Annual Conference of the Australasian Wesleyan Methodist Church*, 1880 and 1890, excluding ministers stationed in Tasmania and home missionaries.

Sources: Statistical Register, NSW; Victorian Year Book; Census, New South Wales and Victoria, 1881, 1891.

ministers for the increasing population were not as productive as in New South Wales, with the already-mentioned exception of the Catholic Church.

The city was by and large well provided with clergy, despite the gloomy claim made by Dean Cowper in 1890 that there was only one clergyman to every 5,000 or more people in the large centres of population.[66] About a third of the clergy in New South Wales in 1890 were in the metropolitan area where the same proportion of the population was living. But people in the country still did not fare as well as the city congregations, either in regularity of pastoral care or in quality of ministry. Both colonial-trained and migrant ministers generally preferred and sought city and suburban charges; the better-educated and more able men usually obtained them. The Wesleyans had less of a problem here as they could station men in the country as need required, but the denominations that worked by invitation found it harder to get good men into rural churches. They often had to rely on unsuspecting recruits from England, who were not always prepared for the rough conditions of Australian country life. According to Robert Kay, the colonial-trained Presbyterian minister at Glenn Innes, some of them had never been on a horse in their lives. John Fraser, MLC, thought it unkind to send a newly arrived minister to the bush after only a week in Sydney, but the colonial parson was hardly likely to give up his city charge for the sake of the migrant. If Englishmen could not be found, catechists and unordained home missionaries often had to be used to minister to the religious needs of country districts. The New South Wales Bush Missionary Society, an interdenominational agency founded in the 1850s, was chiefly run by laymen but it received little recognition or encouragement from the churches. In the 1880s it supported some four missionaries who travelled the outback selling Bibles, distributing tracts, delivering addresses and praying with people. But by the end of the decade there were only two missionaries at work. The Anglican Bush Brotherhood did not begin work in New South Wales until 1903.[67]

The religious provision in Australia at the end of the 1880s, and at the end of the century, might be considered inadequate for a professedly Christian country, especially in New South Wales where there was room for only 40 per cent of the population in the churches of the colony in 1900. But the efforts in church extension should not be underrated. The churches had arrested the trend of the 1870s, when the religious provision in New South Wales was declining. By and large, they had met the challenge of the expanding metropolis and at the same time improved the provision in the country, although the remoter parts were not as adequately supplied.

Yet, judged from the actual support the churches received, the religious provision was sufficient. Allowing for the use of other than church buildings in the country, there was room for the regular churchgoers with some empty pews in almost every church.

Far from being in a weaker position at the end of the nineteenth century, the churches in Australia seem to have been at the peak of their prosperity and achievement, and there was a little self-congratulation. In a review of the religious bodies of New South Wales on the occasion of the colony's centenary, the *Sydney Morning Herald* observed that voluntaryism had proved "equal to the occasion". The former Presbyterian Free Churchman, George Grimm, went even further in his *Concise History of Australia* (1891) in which he smugly claimed that the churches had prospered more under voluntaryism than under state aid to religion.[68]

The remarkable programme of church extension in the 1880s testifies not only to the effectiveness of voluntaryism. It also demonstrates the powerful impulse of competition among the churches, for it was largely through the initiative of denominational agencies rather than local efforts that new causes were begun. Of course local support was essential, especially in raising funds, but in the initial stages new causes were often assisted from central funds. Each Protestant denomination knew that adherents would be lost to other churches if places of worship were not built within easy reach of people in new areas and men provided to minister in them. The smaller denominations tended to lose out in this competition, especially in the country, and the Wesleyan Methodists mostly gained at their expense. But the larger denominations generally kept pace with one another's expansion into new places.

This competitiveness tends to overshadow other motives that underlay church extension. The belief that religion was essential to social well-being, common to all churchmen of the period, also meant that it was important to provide churches and pastors within reach of people everywhere. They could not leave a community without the redeeming influence of religion. It was both the fight against secularism and the desire not to lose out to others that motivated the vigorous programmes of church extension. But how to fill the empty pews in churches in new and old areas was another question. Evangelism as well as extension was necessary, but in this there was more cooperation than competition.

3

Waves of Revival

Australia has never experienced a religious revival like the Evangelical Revival in eighteenth century Britain or the Great Awakening in North America, and it has produced no indigenous evangelical movements or sects, such as emerged in the United States in the early nineteenth century. Australian Christianity lived largely in the afterglow of the eighteenth century revivals. Most of the Protestant clergy in the nineteenth century were evangelical, but the colonies produced no evangelists of the stature of John Wesley, George Whitfield or Jonathan Edwards, or of the distinction of Dwight L. Moody or Charles Haddon Spurgeon. Nevertheless, Australian churchmen hoped and prayed for a revival of religion, especially in the late nineteenth century, confronted as they were by the indifference of many and the hostility of a few outside the churches, and the lukewarm spirituality of many within. Their hopes were quickened by glowing but exaggerated reports of the success of the Moody and Sankey mission in Britain in 1873-75. A Presbyterian minister, John Walker, recorded his delight at finding on his arrival in New South Wales in 1875 "what an impetus and new energy" had been given to religious life in the colony "by the happy tidings of the great spiritual revival in Scotland and England".[1] The colonies were clearly ready to receive an evangelist who would preach revival in Australia, and counter the influence of the missioners of secularism.

They did not have to wait long. In 1877 the Reverend Dr Alexander Somerville, a Scottish evangelist, came to Australia. Somerville had considerable experience in evangelism, including campaigns in Spain, India and Canada. He had also been closely associated with Moody during the Glasgow mission in 1874. In December 1876, aged nearly sixty-four, he gave up his pastorate in Anderston Free Church, Glasgow, and accepted "the call" of the Glasgow United Evangelistic Association to "go wherever the English language is spoken". More than that, he made the world his parish, and for the next twelve years conducted campaigns in North America, Europe, including Italy and Russia, South Africa, Greece and Asia Minor, and a mission to the Jews in Eastern Europe. But he

Alexander Somerville, Minister of the Free Presbyterian Church of Scotland and itinerant ev:
gelist. Presumably taken in Glasgow in the 1880s. (From *A Modern Apostle* by G. Sm:
[London: 1890]. Photo courtesy of Mitchell Library, Sydney.)

chose Australia as the starting place for his new career, conducting missions in cities and country towns in Victoria, New South Wales, Queensland, Tasmania and New Zealand as well.[2]

Dr Somerville was not the first visiting evangelist to come to Australia. William "California" Taylor, an American, had toured the eastern colonies twice in the 1860s, preaching in Wesleyan churches.[3] But Somerville was the first of a succession of evangelists who visited Australia after Moody's great mission to Britain. The organization of Somerville's campaign in Australia bore some marked similarities to Moody's British mission, especially in its interdenominational support. In Melbourne and Sydney a United Evangelistic Committee, formed from representatives of the main Protestant churches and the Young Men's Christian Association, prepared the way of the Lord's messenger beforehand. And Somerville himself had adopted some of Moody's methods. He came with his own song leader — his youngest son, W.E. Somerville — and the singing was from *Sacred Songs and Solos,* the collection of Moody's song leader, Ira D. Sankey. A United Evangelistic Choir, made up of various city church choirs also assisted. Other features that probably came from Moody were the daily midday prayer meetings held during the mission and the children's service; and, as had happened in Moody's missions, ministers of the various denominations sat on the platform behind the preacher. Such features make Somerville's mission the first modern evangelistic campaign in Australia.[4]

After a successful mission in Melbourne, Somerville came to Sydney in September 1877. He came to an expectant city; for some weeks beforehand there had been prayer meetings and "services of preparation". The mission began on Sunday 9 September in the Exhibition Building in Prince Alfred Park. Designed to accommodate some four thousand people, the building was packed on this occasion with about five thousand. Some who could not hear Somerville attempted to leave the meeting, but were restrained by the organizers. This created quite a hubbub at the rear while the preacher continued unperturbed at the front. A venerable figure with his locks of white hair, Somerville had the energy and enthusiasm of a much younger man. He possessed a great gift for picturesque illustration and, it was said, a fervour and eloquence "calculated to impress even an apathetic Australian audience".[5] Despite the poor acoustics (an attempt was made to improve them with a sounding board), his audiences continued to fill the Exhibition Building for three weeks.

Somerville conducted several special meetings as well as the nightly mission service. About four thousand children and a thousand adults attended his afternoon children's service on Saturday

15 September to hear about "The Way to Heaven". On Monday night, 24 September, he delivered what was to become his most famous sermon, "The Fiery Furnace", to a meeting of young men. It was a vindication of "scriptural Christianity", in which he exhorted youth not to bow down to the idols of the modern world and to resist all its allurements and temptations, especially the temptation to deny the faith. Like Moody and most itinerant evangelists who came to Australia in the later nineteenth century, Somerville was conservative in theology and confident before the challenges to belief from modern science and higher criticism. While freethought lecturers were exposing the contradictions of the Bible, he assured his Sydney audience in another lecture that the Scriptures were free from all error and inconsistency; in them was the only infallible authority on earth. Here was reassurance for many, but a few, disappointed at this obscurantism, left the meeting.[6]

At one meeting time was set aside to answer questions dealing with the conduct of the Christian in society. Somerville warned his questioners against various secular entertainments and novels, and above all against opera and dancing — especially the waltz and the galop which were "not fit for young people of the different sexes to join in". It was even worse "for a man to be waltzing with another man's wife". There was a meeting for "men only" on Friday 28 September when some six thousand heard Somerville warn against sexual licence — the dangers being "forcibly portrayed with striking and appropriate illustrations".[7]

During the fourth week Somerville conducted special meetings for country folk, for church women and another for young men in which he pressed the claims of the YMCA, a movement he did much to promote throughout Australia. He also had a meeting with "fallen women" of Sydney brought in by city missioners for tea, refreshments and words of comfort from the venerable evangelist. On Friday 5 October, at the end of the mission, he addressed a large meeting of "converts" and "enquirers" in the Exhibition Building.[8] The number of converts was not published, and in any case they were generally much less than the hundreds of enquirers who went forward at these meetings.

Somerville's mission did not noticeably affect the trend of declining church attendances in the city, but it did make a lasting impact on the churches of Sydney; the United Evangelistic Committee continued to hold prayer and other religious meetings for some time afterwards. In the long term, Somerville's mission largely set the pattern for future evangelistic campaigns in Australia.

The YMCA, then more interested in religion than in recreation

David Walker, Presbyterian layman and Secretary of the YMCA. Presumably taken in Sydney about 1890. (From *Centenary History of the Presbyterian Church in New South Wales* by J. Cameron [Sydney: Angus and Robertson, 1905]. Photo courtesy of La Trobe University Library, Melbourne.)

and closer to the churches than today, received particular stimulus from Somerville's visit. It was reorganized in 1877 along the lines of Somerville's advice in this regard, and benefited from his public commendation. One of the aims of its revised platform was "to reach especially the careless and neglected portions of the community which lie outside the Churches. . ." YMCA leaders stated at the laying of the foundation stone of the association's new hall in 1883, that "only one-tenth of our young men are in the Churches and Sunday Schools".[9] This was probably too low an estimate, but youth at a loose end on Sundays apparently seemed numerous enough in Sydney for the YMCA to begin evangelistic services in the Victoria Theatre late in 1877, not long after Somerville's mission.

This work expanded in 1879 when the Ladies Evangelistic Association presented the YMCA with a "gospel tent" which it used as a venue for meetings around the city. In 1882 it leased the Opera House in King Street on Sunday evenings for three months to conduct services for young men in the city. YMCA members went into the streets before the service and invited wandering youth, but not the larrikins of the city, to come to the meeting. The venture proved such a success that the YMCA took a longer lease on the Opera House. Attendances averaged around five hundred young men, aged chiefly between eighteen and twenty-five. Although it might have appeared a competitor with regular church services, the denominations generally approved this interdenominational venture. When the Opera House services began, the *Presbyterian* assured its readers that the service was not likely to affect church attendances too much, while the Wesleyan *Weekly Advocate* observed that it was reaching a class not touched by the churches. It even suggested somewhat sweepingly that the colony had no need of the Salvation Army while these services were held, and that the merchants who made all the money out of these young men ought to contribute to the cost of the services. [10] The Opera House meetings continued to the end of October 1885 when they were transferred to the newly opened YMCA Hall. Services were also held in a hall in Haymarket.

The Opera House service was a layman's meeting led by the Presbyterian, David Walker, general secretary of the YMCA. The service was short and simple, the addresses direct but fervently evangelical. Speakers appealed to young men to accept Jesus Christ as their Saviour and each year it was reported that about two thousand or more enquirers waited at the close of the services for counsel from the YMCA workers. Temperance was also a keynote of the addresses given and many were induced to sign the pledge of total abstinence. [11] As well as these regular services for young men the YMCA sponsored the visit of several itinerant evangelists in the 1880s. Mrs Margaret Hampson, a middle-aged matron, was one of the more notable of these visitors.

Margaret Hampson had been engaged in evangelistic work in Liverpool for some twenty years, assisted by her husband, a prosperous Liverpool business man. In 1881, by then a widow, she left England for New Zealand to recover her health, where she resumed her evangelistic work. She came to Sydney in September 1883 after attracting large crowds in Melbourne and Adelaide. In both cities people besieged the gates of the Town Hall an hour before the meeting and at the final meeting of her ten-day mission in Adelaide hundreds were turned away. Churchgoers made up the over-whelming proportion of Hampson's audiences, and it was her unavailing plea to church folk in Adelaide that they stay home and let non-churchgoers fill the hall. So great was her impact on the Adelaide religious community that the presiding minister at her farewell tea attributed the repeal of the Totalizator Act, virtually accomplished that day in Parliament, in large part to her.[12]

As with Dr Somerville's mission, Hampson's campaign had inter-denominational support and was preceded by weeks of preparation. The Sydney churches organized house to house visitations to invite people to the services. About five thousand people attended the Exhibition Building on Sunday 16 September 1883 for the first meeting of what was to be an eight-day mission. Nearly seven thousand, it was claimed, were there the next Sunday afternoon. The mission was extended several times and lasted five weeks in all, with crowds at each meeting, mostly of religious folk.[13]

A woman evangelist was indeed something of a novelty, but this fact alone hardly explains Margaret Hampson's success. The *Sydney Morning Herald* thought her medium height, stout build and plea-sant, homely face made her "a good representative of the English matron". Her voice was "marvellously strong" and with the audito-rium draped to improve the acoustics, her "admirably distinct enunciation" enabled the whole audience to "hear almost every syllable". She was a woman "possessing strength and purpose" and abundant self-assurance. One critic went so far as to suggest that "faith in Mrs Hampson" was "one of the chief elements in any just explanation of her power."[14]

Margaret Hampson's success lay more in the similarity of her style to that of other evangelists than in any womanly differences. She promoted much the same view of religious faith and conduct and delivered the same defence of the Bible against its critics. She conducted the same kind of services; as well as the nightly public meetings, she addressed about five thousand children at an after-noon service on Saturday 22 September, at which W.G. Taylor, a local Wesleyan minister, and John Vaughan, an Anglican clergy-man, assisted her. Two hundred or more young people between ten and eighteen years signed cards professing to have "received good" at this service and 150 younger children were "counselled" by another Anglican minister, the Reverend T.B. Tress. Undaunted by her sex, Mrs Hampson also addressed a meeting for men (to which admission was by ticket) at the YMCA service in the Opera House on Sunday 21 October. What this doughty woman said to the young men on this occasion does not seem to have been reported, but pre-sumably she counselled them on moral purity. She was also a strong

Margaret Hampson, itinerant English evangelist. (From *Illustrated Australian News*, 11 Ju
Photo courtesy of La Trobe Library, State Library of Victoria.)

advocate of temperance and encouraged her converts to sign the
total abstinence pledge; she pinned the blue ribbon on those who
had signed at the final service in Adelaide. Her last meeting in
Sydney was held in Pitt Street Congregational Church, which was
filled to overflowing. At the conclusion she presented New Testaments to the converts — 800 of them, it was claimed. She had also

formed Women's Prayer Unions in the various cities. The Sydney Women's Prayer Union continued for some years after her departure and was one of the main pressure groups for stricter Sunday observance and moral purity.[15]

A number of other evangelists came to Australia after Mrs Hampson, including George Williams, a Welshman and associate of Moody, who came to the colony primarily for health reasons in 1885. He conducted missions in St Stephen's Presbyterian Church and elsewhere. An English evangelist couple, the Reverend J. Mountain and his wife, conducted their campaigns in Congregational churches during 1885 and 1886 and two of Charles Haddon Spurgeon's evangelists, Messrs Mateer and Parker, campaigned in New South Wales in 1886. In 1888 John J. Lewis came from New Zealand to crusade against gambling, intemperance and impurity and the same year the YMCA brought George Clarke, an advocate of muscular Christianity, to Sydney. There were others, and they mostly visited Victoria and other colonies as well. But their campaigns did not make the same impact on the public as the Somerville and Hampson missions, because they were generally on a smaller scale. Nevertheless, the number of them indicates the intensity of evangelistic effort during the decade. Mateer and Parker left Australia because there was too much competition from other evangelists.[16] As well as these, several temperance evangelists crusaded around the colonies in the 1880s.

Temperance Evangelists

Evangelists like Dr Somerville and Mrs Hampson generally encouraged temperance in their campaigns; Hampson, in particular, made much of it, and in her campaign in Australia she commended the Blue Ribbon Gospel Temperance Movement. There had been some religious objection to the temperance movement earlier in the nineteenth century, largely because it seemed to emphasize human will and endeavour rather than dependence on divine grace, thus, in effect, making temperance the agent of man's redemption. Moody held that conversion, not the pledge, saved a man from drink. Mrs Hampson seemed to have these objections in mind when she said that "Gospel temperance" brought "the spiritual into the world of total abstinence".[17] There was a religious atmosphere in the meetings of most of the temperance missioners who came to Australia in the 1880s, but evangelism seemed to rank second place with them, although some protested otherwise.

Temperance was "the handmaid of the Church", the American

temperance missioner, Eli Johnson, claimed when he came to Australia in 1882. He had conducted campaigns in England and Sweden and carried commendations from the distinguished American preachers, Henry Ward Beecher and De Witt Talmage as well as United States ex-President Hayes. Two powerful agencies were working for the degradation of mankind, Johnson told his Sydney audience — infidelity and intemperance. Eve, he pointed out, fell from grace through unbelief, but Noah fell through drunkenness — in Johnson's view the crime of crimes. His main object, therefore, was to "expose the deleterious character of the drinks" sold as wines, spirits and malted liquors. So religious language was used to justify what was largely the old campaign against drink. As well as winning people to total abstinence, Johnson and his wife assisted in the formation of branches of the Woman's Christian Temperance Union in Australia.[18]

The YMCA brought R.T. Booth, another American temperance missioner, to the colony in May 1884. A Yankee veteran of the Civil War, Booth was a reformed drunkard himself. The message of his preaching, shaded by personal experience, was the ruin of individual lives caused by drink. There was, he declared, no place in the intensely competitive modern world for the man who drank spirits and liquors — they clouded his brain and enfeebled his powers. He sought to persuade his audience to commit themselves to total abstinence by signing the pledge or, if they were already teetotallers, to wear the blue ribbon as a public testimony. Leading churchmen and politicians patronized Booth's "Gospel Temperance Mission", including some who took a very different view of temperance, among them Bishop Barry. Barry presided at Booth's meeting on 12 May and, significantly for this occasion, Booth was persuaded to change the title of his lecture from "Moderate Drinking", which he denounced, to "Personal Responsibility". During his Sydney mission Booth persuaded 12,798 people to don the blue ribbon and 6,452 to sign the pledge. He remained in New South Wales until December 1886 preaching temperance throughout the land. Before his departure he was entertained at a banquet at which Sir Henry Parkes, no teetotaller but a support of temperance, presided.[19]

William Noble, an English temperance missioner, came in July 1886, like Booth also under the auspices of the YMCA; he saw himself primarily as an evangelist — "the Gospel first and temperance next". But his preaching was almost entirely about drink and its devastations, even though he sometimes made an evangelical appeal to save the soul as well as the body in concluding his lecture. He preached temperance as "the *true* reform" — virtually as a panacea for all social ills, and wanted to get at working men to show them that drink was a greater evil than over-production! But Noble found he was preaching largely to the converted, when, at his first meeting, he asked the large audience to stand and then told the total abstainers to sit down. About twenty people were left standing before the scornful or pitying gaze of the audience, and, needless to say, pledge cards were soon provided for them.[20]

Matthew Burnett, known as "the Temperance Advocate of the Southern Colonies", came to Sydney in July 1889 after preaching in "nearly every town, village and hamlet" in New South Wales over a period of two years. An English Wesleyan, Burnett began his Australian career in Victoria in the 1860s and since the mid 1870s he had been employed by the Wesleyan Home Mission Committee. He launched himself on a wider campaign in Adelaide in April 1880 with a series of temperance meetings on Saturday nights in the Adelaide Town Hall. He owed his reputation as much to his sensational methods as to his enthusiastic advocacy of temperance. As in Victoria, torchlight processions and open air meetings preceded his Adelaide meetings, and in Sydney in 1889 the combined Salvation Army bands led the procession to the Centenary Hall.[21]

In Adelaide Burnett declared that the preaching of the gospel was his "higher mission"; for several weeks he conducted open air evangelistic meetings in Light Square, Adelaide, on Sunday evenings and preached afterwards in Pirie Street Wesleyan Church. His temperance mission was also organized like an evangelistic campaign and enjoyed interdenominational support. People in Sydney were invited to bring Sankey's hymns, but there was also some secular music at his meetings such as solo renditions of "The Englishman" and "The Bonnie Hills of Scotland". In Adelaide the choir sang "Men of Harlech" while people came down to take the pledge. Yet evangelism was not as prominent in his Sydney mission as in Adelaide, although he preached in some Sydney churches. It was temperance which seemed to have become his "higher mission", as the *Sydney Morning Herald* noted: "He cared not for sect, creed or party, and so long as he could lessen the evil of intemperance he accomplished his mission." This "purely humanitarian" work, Burnett owned, was for the social, moral and religious elevation of the masses of the people". He claimed to have administered the pledge to 140,000 people over twenty-five years in Australia, apart from the soldiers and sailors he had won to total abstinence.[22]

In most places Burnett enjoyed the support of distinguished citizens. Chief Justice Sir Samuel Way, and Sir Henry Ayers were among those who presided at his Town Hall meetings in Adelaide. They were not teetotallers, but others were, like Mr Justice "Water Jug" Foster, who presided at Burnett's farewell meeting in Sydney.

Non-drinkers made up most of his Sydney audience and a resound-
ing "Yes" greeted Alexander Hutchison, MLA, when at one of
Burnett's meetings he asked the members of the audience if they
were ready to close the public houses. Amid such enthusiasm, the
uncommitted were easily persuaded to take the pledge.[23]

Booth, Noble and Burnett were foremost among the temperance
prophets who came to the colony in the 1880s and after. They
mostly preached to sympathetic audiences of abstinent church folk.
While there were undoubtedly some victims of drink induced to
sign the pledge, if not the thousands claimed for Burnett, it is probable that many of them soon lapsed. By and large, the preaching of
the temperance evangelists bore most fruit among the younger
generation of churchgoers whom they confirmed in total abstinence.
They helped to form the opinion that total abstinence was syn-
onymous with being a Christian. Although there were still some in
the churches, clergy and laymen, for whom temperance meant
moderation, the moderate drinker was beginning to feel lonely
among the growing number of teetotallers. At the annual festival of
the Church of England Temperance Society on 30 May 1884,
shortly after Booth's Sydney mission, Bishop Barry protested at the
unbrotherly attitude of the teetotallers towards the moderate
drinkers, whom they regarded as worse than open drunkards. At the
same meeting Sir William Manning, a moderate drinker, complained that a teetotaller had declared him unworthy to call himself a
Christian,[24] supporter of temperance though he was. But the
increasing number of temperance enthusiasts among churchmen
recognized no want of charity here for intemperance was even ahead
of infidelity (see Chapter 5) and impurity in the trinity of heinous
evils.

Evangelists and Social Purity

Other evangelists had treated the topic of impurity, but Dr Harry
Grattan Guinness gave it central place in his mission to men only,
which began on Sunday 27 June 1886. Guinness bore the names of
his evangelist father, founder of the East London Training Institute
at Harley House. The younger Guinness had intended becoming
a medical missionary; he had studied at London Hospital,
Whitechapel, and graduated in January 1886. Yet this ambition was
not fulfilled. Guinness began evangelistic preaching at the age of
eighteen and was much influenced during his student days by
Moody in his second London campaign in 1883. After graduation
Guinness devoted himself to evangelism and succeeded his father as

director of Harley House in 1887. The year before, he came to Australia to visit family friends in Tasmania, and the YMCA soon enlisted his services as a missioner in South Australia and the eastern colonies.

Guinness's style was easy and informal. He was armed with a ready supply of anecdotes to illustrate his addresses and occasionally ridiculed the "follies" of freethought. The YMCA hall in Sydney was crowded nightly during the mission and many had to be turned away from the last meeting on Sunday 4 July, when, incidentally, ladies were admitted to the gallery. Large numbers of young men went to the "enquiry room" after the services, where Guinness won "conversions" — 753 in all during his Australian mission.[25] In the daytime he saw youths who sought his advice on spiritual and medical questions, the latter being raised no doubt by his attack on impurity. The highlight of his Sydney mission was the "medical meeting" on Wednesday 30 June.

"Where drink has slain its thousands, lust slays its ten thousands", Guinness wildly avowed. Drawing on his medical experience, as well as the fund of bogus information given out by crusaders against sexual licence, he warned of the dire consequences, especially venereal disease, of giving in to "youthful lusts". He aimed to persuade or frighten youth into abstinence from all forms of sexual gratification outside marriage and to practise extreme abstemiousness within marriage itself. Guinness's medical lecture, which took nearly two hours to deliver, produced such an effect that at some meetings young men were carried out fainting. In his Sydney meeting seventy-six young men stood to ask for special prayers in their struggle against the flesh, and almost the whole audience signed the social purity pledge — to observe the strictest standards of sexual purity and maintain the honour and virtue of womankind. The lecture was so well received by church leaders in Sydney that they invited Guinness to repeat it under the chairmanship of Bishop Barry, himself a strong supporter of the social purity campaign. Guinness's campaign gave a lift to the Social Purity Society and two days after his mission the society formed a deputation to the premier to seek better protection for women and young girls in particular; foremost in their proposals was the raising of the age of consent from fourteen to sixteen, as had been done in Britain the previous year.[26]

Other evangelists inveighed heavily against sexual immorality, but none so vehemently as Henry Varley at the end of the eighties. Varley, son of a Lincolnshire brewer, came to Victoria in 1854 at the age of nineteen to seek his fortune on the goldfields. He returned to England three years later and became a butcher in London and part-time preacher at the Free Tabernacle, Notting Hill. In 1869 he took up evangelism, visiting North America and Australia. He was in Australia at the same time as Somerville but did not make as much impact then as the venerable Scottish preacher. However Varley migrated to Victoria in 1887 and made Melbourne his base for further missions to the Australian colonies and also to India, South Africa, Britain and the United States. He came to Sydney for his second visit in August 1889.[27]

Varley had a commanding presence redolent of moral as well as physical strength — "not a man to be trifled with", as one journal observed.[28] He adopted an easy conversational style but could rise to heights of glowing oratory in denunciation of sin or in calling sinners to accept their Saviour. Varley's mission, which began on Sunday 18 August 1889, soon attracted overflowing audiences, although the New Masonic Hall could not have held the crowds that thronged the Exhibition Building for the Somerville and Hampson missions. During September he conducted campaigns in the suburbs and Saturday night meetings in Sydney for men only. On Sunday afternoons he went to the Domain to speak on social questions. Some two thousand men crowded into the Protestant Hall for his last lecture at which he dealt specifically with the question of sexual morality.

Varley had no time for the prudish parson who dared not speak forthrightly about sexual morals. He warned against the "self-pollution" of masturbation, as well as fornication, the seduction of innocent girls and consorting with harlots. At the same time he spread much false information on sexual matters. He told his audience that it was essential to retain "the seed of life" to sustain mental and physical vigour, and claimed that many men in their early twenties were "mentally imbecile and physically broken up by the twin curses of self-pollution and fornication". No wonder some young men swooned at such lectures! Needless to say, the claim was hardly borne out by the statistics on insanity.[29] He also used case histories of sufferers of venereal disease, those victims "slain by lust", to scare the young into virtue. Sexual intercourse was an "animal function" to be tolerated but strictly controlled within marriage only. Its end was procreation and he denounced contraception in all circumstances. Conception, too, could be denounced if it resulted from animal passion, for children so begotten were likely to grow up licentious themselves. Varley placed women on a pedestal: the pure woman was not carried away by passion as were men. Like Guinness, he gave plenty of advice on how to control the lusts of the flesh. He enjoined youth to abstain from drink, which incited to lust, to avoid evil companions and lewd conversation, and also to shun the theatre, novels, and anything visual that might arouse passion.

Above all young men should avoid idleness, and to this end, healthy exercise, mental and physical, and a good hobby were generally prescribed. Varley had delivered the lecture many times already; with dramatic effects thus well rehearsed, he so stirred his male audience in Sydney that at the end the crowd rose to cheer the evangelist and to pledge themselves to stand for God and purity.[30] Varley had also accompanied a deputation to Premier Parkes seeking the suppression of a weekly, *The Dead Bird,* which had been banned as immoral by the Victorian Post Office. Afterwards, with an Anglican clergyman, J.D. Langley, he harangued a crowd of two thousand on the evils of immoral literature, at such an appropriate site as Queen Victoria's statue.[31]

Gambling and the desecration of the Sabbath also came under heavy fire from Varley, and he warned his audiences of "the sin of unbelief" — as serious in his book as blasphemy or adultery. He looked for unquestioning acceptance of the Bible as the infallible book. Like most fundamentalist evangelists, he was also an ardent millenarian, and his addresses on the Second Coming proved as attractive as most of his lectures. At the end of his mission Varley was entertained at a breakfast where seventy ministers and forty laymen invited him to return to Sydney; they appointed a committee to assist in arranging his next visit.[32] Varley returned to New South Wales in October of the same year, 1889, and conducted missions in Parramatta and Newcastle before holding another fortnight's mission in Sydney.[33]

Prior to leaving Sydney after his first mission Varley took part in an all-day united conference in Pitt Street Congregational Church where he thundered at the iniquities of Sydney — "Satan has his seat in this city", he declared — and at the lethargy of the churches which he urged to unite in a common front against the forces of evil. Such a front was already forming; in June 1889 the Protestant denominations had set up a Council of Churches to safeguard the Sabbath, and the Sydney Ministers' Union, probably under inspiration from Varley, had also set in motion plans for another united body. These plans came to fruition during Varley's second mission to Sydney. On Tuesday 26 November representatives of the main Protestant denominations, at least the leading evangelical clergymen and laymen among them, met in the YMCA hall, under the chairmanship of John Harris, Mayor of Sydney, to constitute a local branch of the Evangelical Alliance, founded in Britain in 1846 by Protestants of Europe, North America and the British Isles. The object of this combination of "the vital Christianity of the country" was to make Christian influence and principles "more strongly felt in moulding the public as well as the social life of the community".[34]

These principles were those upheld by the succession of visiting evangelists from Somerville to Varley and those who came after them. The alliance's theological basis was conservative, lagging behind the thought of some of Sydney's more prominent church-men, and its social concerns were essentially "wowserish". Its basis was too narrow for some Anglicans, especially in so far as it might be against "Popery" and "Puseyism", as the liberal *Church of England Guardian* pointed out.[35] How the alliance would seek to achieve its aims was not clear, but its formation was a gesture by the more con-servative churchmen to affirm that doctrine and morality which they thought, with some justification, to be under threat. Such church-men were grateful to the evangelists whose campaigns had upheld that evangelical faith and morality.

The Denominations and Evangelism

Evangelistic activity in the 1880s was not confined to the YMCA and the missions of itinerant evangelists. From the beginning of the decade there was a growing demand within most denominations for special evangelists to conduct missions in local churches and parishes. At a clerical conference in Goulburn in 1881 Canon A.D. Soares proposed eight-day parochial missions, with shorter liturgical services and an evangelistic address on weeknights, and a meeting for working men in the Sunday school hall on the Saturday night. Persuaded that no denomination was better fitted to minister both to the cultured and refined and to the illiterate poor than the Church of England, he asserted that there would have been no Methodist Church and no Salvation Army had the Anglican Church done the work of the evangelist.[36] Missions of the kind Soares advocated were occasionally conducted by Anglicans and Presbyterians, and especially by Methodists, who believed that theirs was "a revival church". Each year the Wesleyan Conference designated a week of prayer for revival in conjunction with special evangelistic services.

The demand for organized evangelism grew more insistent from around 1880, although it did not win an immediate response. The Wesleyan Conference rejected a proposal in 1880 that it should appoint a conference evangelist, for evangelism was supposedly the task of every preacher. But the demand persisted and, finally, in January 1885 the conference appointed J.A. Bowring, one of its younger ministers, to the position. The recommendation of the Presbyterian Religion and Morals Committee in 1884 that the General Assembly should appoint evangelistic deputies to conduct missions in Presbyterian Churches was taken up at once.[37]

Two factors, in particular, seem to have led to these decisions in the mid 1880s. By this time the churches were feeling the challenge of the freethinkers quite keenly, but more significant was the impact of the Salvation Army in the colony from late 1882. The Army's novel and sensational methods made a strong impression on the city; crowds turned out to follow the bands with their martial music or to watch with curiosity or contempt the tambourine-beating Hallelujah Lasses singing the Lord's songs to the Devil's tunes. The processions led to services in hired halls until the Salvation Army Barracks were opened early in 1885. On occasions the crowds were too great for all to get in to the meetings; but many were accommodated and some converted.

Churchmen could hardly ignore the presence of the Salvation Army, but attitudes towards it varied. Some Protestants found the Army's methods extremely distasteful. Jefferis, who had observed its operations closely in Bristol in 1881, confided to the Congregational assembly the next year, shortly before the Salvationists' trumpets sounded in Sydney, his fear that the Army would do more harm than good, despite the sincerity of its leaders.[38] In Methodism, from which General Booth had come, there were some who took a rather jaundiced view of the Army. When it raised its standard in Sydney the *Weekly Advocate* recognized it as an aggressive form of Methodism, but contended that Wesleyans did not need to take a leaf from the Army's book; they had only to make their own evangelistic machinery work. But the Salvationists' meetings were apparently attracting some Methodists, so much so that Dr Richard Sellors, President of the Wesleyan Conference in 1886-87, deplored the fact that people should forsake churches "in which the Gospel was faithfully and intelligently preached . . . for services which were marked by so much that was foreign to the spirit of Christianity and in the highest sense emotional". Some Methodists were less critical. A predecessor of Sellors, J.H. Fletcher, told the conference in 1885 that the Salvation Army had hewn for itself a new path and deserved sympathy and encouragement, provided it did not proselytize among the denominations. (He also could have added that it should not disturb church services with its bands and open air meetings for such disruption occasionally strained Protestant tolerance.) There were some also who would imitate the Army. A Wesleyan layman stated in 1883 that its methods were simply "the old Methodist plan", which Wesleyans should not be too respectable to follow. John Austin was one Methodist evangelist who was willing to take a lead from the Army. In the mission he conducted at Singleton in 1884 he organized a procession with banners and a band of singers to march through the town before the mission service to attract out-

How the *Bulletin* saw the Salvation Army in 1882. (From *Bulletin*, 30 September 1882. Photo courtesy of State Library of South Australia.)

siders and did the same again, with illuminations, in Paddington in 1889.[39]

A few wealthy laymen of the larger denominations, Sir Alfred Stephen among them, thought the Salvation Army was performing a useful function "doing work the Churches did not, would not or could not undertake" in raising the fallen and reforming the drunkards. Some of them contributed to the cost of building the new barracks. Few church leaders, however, were prepared to abandon any section of society to this novel form of evangelism. Among Anglicans and Presbyterians, as well as Methodists, there were many who recognized that the Salvation Army presented the churches with a challenge. The Presbyterian Moderator, Roger Mackinnon, told the General Assembly in 1885 that the Army was filling a gap which the churches had left empty, even though he would have preferred to see the gap filled by other than "the burlesque and fantastic tricks of the Salvation Army".[40] The Army's campaign did force the churches to look more critically at their efforts to reach the working classes (see Chapter 4), and its activity also highlighted the need for more energetic evangelism on the part of the Protestant denominations. Not surprisingly then, the middle of the decade saw the most intense evangelistic activity among the churches.

Bishop Barry launched a special mission throughout metropolitan Sydney in June 1885. This mission aimed at both the conversion of "the careless and unbelieving" and "spiritual refreshment and revival" among Christians. There were to be services of preparation beforehand and special services conducted by visiting clergy in city churches during the week of the mission. (Suburban churches did not conduct their missions until September and in some cases November.) The week-night services at St Andrew's Cathedral, at which Barry was the speaker, were for men only. His addresses were not obviously evangelical, but more instructive on points of religion and morality. One of his lectures was on "Love and Purity" and another on "Work and Amusement". Barry also took part with H.L. Jackson in a series of fairly well attended, short midday services for businessmen in St James's Church. The bishop's addresses on these occasions were preceded by brief worship which evoked "a heartiness not characteristic of Sunday services". In these services Barry was more concerned to explain than to convert, his addresses being apologetic rather than evangelistic. In his lecture "The Bible: What it is and what it is not" he espoused views on inspiration quite different from the fundamentalism of the professional evangelist, and for that matter of the ordinary evangelical parson. The style of preaching would have been different in the other churches where so many of the visiting missioners were evangelicals. But these received little publicity, although Barry was pleased with what he heard of them, and reported to the synod in July, shortly after the city campaign, that the mission had been "a token of spiritual progress".[41]

Nevertheless, Barry apparently experienced some frustration in this area, as he suggested in his statement to the General Synod in 1886, that the Anglican Church, was "better fitted for pastoral edification than for evangelism".[42] It was certainly true that Barry himself was a better pastor and an even better teacher than evangelist, but he was flexible enough to adopt new methods, such as his attempt to introduce the Church Army to Australia. His licensing in May 1886 of Thomas Wales, formerly of the Evangelisation Society in England, as an evangelist connected with the parish of Pyrmont and Ultimo[43] is also evidence of his recognition that in some areas a local approach to evangelism was needed.

Barry's comment on his own denomination might have been applied equally well to others, especially the Presbyterian Church. One Presbyterian ventured to suggest in 1886 that his denomination could do with a "little of the fervour and force of the Methodists", and the evangelistic deputies who conducted missions in Presbyterian churches in 1885 thought it best to depart from the austere dignity of the reformed tradition. They conducted informal services and substituted Sankey's *Sacred Songs and Solos* for the Scottish Psalter. One of them, David Smith, told how he abandoned the lofty pulpit and addressed the people from the floor of the church, looking them straight in the face and speaking directly "in colloquial Saxon-English". Not all Presbyterians welcomed this imitation of the professional evangelist. In 1886 some ministers voiced criticism of the way evangelists conducted the special missions. John Auld, brought up "in the school of Jonathan Edwards not in that of John Wesley", thought the whole approach superficial. He considered the good results of missions to be often inflated, and the advice to anxious enquirers, as he had witnessed it, shallow and even misleading. Support for special missions throughout the denomination was not wholehearted, for by 1887 the Evangelistic Deputies Fund was insolvent. But the General Assembly continued to recommend that eight-day missions should be held annually and there were still ministers ready to serve the churches as missioners.[44]

One of these was John MacNeil, an experienced evangelist who had come to Sydney from South Australia in 1885. He became the convenor of the Religion and Morals Committee and gave considerable time to evangelism. It was he who had borne the brunt of Auld's criticism of evangelists in 1886. In 1887-88 he took extended leave from his parish at Waverley to conduct missions but soon left for Victoria, after only three years in the colony. The Religion and Morals Committee continued to offer help to churches that conducted missions but in 1888 none sought its aid, although a few churches here and there held missions on their own.[45]

The office of conference evangelist, set up by the Wesleyans, lapsed in 1887 when J.A. Bowring was sent to the York Street church, which had become a centre for city evangelism and was known unofficially as the Central Methodist Mission. For two years Bowring had conducted missions in Wesleyan churches throughout the colony. He kindled no great revival but his campaigns produced "a gracious awakening" in some places. He persuaded "encouraging numbers" to seek salvation and even more to sign the pledge. It is not clear why the appointment lapsed, although some might have thought that Bowring's services were not being used strategically enough, as the *Weekly Advocate* feared might happen when he was appointed in 1885. That journal thought that he should be sent to centres with large non-churchgoing populations rather than be used as an evangelist in Methodist circuits.[46]

The camp meeting was also adopted as an evangelistic technique by the Wesleyans in 1885. American in origin, camp meetings had been introduced to England in 1807 by the Primitive Methodists, at first with the disapproval of the Wesleyans. They were regular features of Primitive Methodist church life in Australia. A camp meeting was held at Newcastle overlooking the harbour each Easter.[47] A few Wesleyans, J.E. Carruthers in particular, had experimented with the idea before January 1885, when a "Grand Conference Camp Meeting" was held on the Sydney Domain on Anniversary (now Australia) Day. It was an occasion for family picnics as well as for spiritual renewal, but it was seen also as an attempt to preach the gospel to the masses of the city population. However, rain forced the crowd to disperse early and an open-air service outside the Town Hall in the evening was abandoned. The day concluded with services in York Street Church where a few converts were won.[48] From around this time smaller camp meetings were held increasingly often, especially on Good Fridays. The *Weekly Advocate* encouraged the movement, and there was another large scale camp meeting — a Methodist "Field Day" — on the Domain in November 1889. There were some variations on the earlier event, partly influenced by Salvation Army methods. A procession led by the Central Methodist Mission Band marched from the new Centenary Hall, York Street, to a marquee on the Domain. The morning meeting was held in the marquee and crowds attended the open-air meeting in the afternoon. The day concluded with services in the

Centenary Hall and once more the organizers were rewarded with some conversions.[49] The camp meeting idea was not confined to Methodism. It was also taken up by the Baptists, who boasted in 1889 that their Good Friday meeting at Plattsburg, near Newcastle, quite a stronghold of Methodism, outshone anything that Methodists or the Salvation Army had done in the district.[50]

One other special feature of Methodist revivalism in the 1880s was the holiness convention. In 1880 the Wesleyan Conference reaffirmed that it was Methodism's mission to "spread Scriptural Holiness through the land". But did Methodists still experience the "new birth" through "entire sanctification", of which John Wesley had made so much?[51] The President of the Wesleyan Conference in 1885, the conservative J.A. Nolan, did not think so. He pictured the ordinary church member as someone once converted, and since then a regular churchgoer of acknowledged good character:

> But when you come to the matter of his religious experience, ah! then is the rub. Being an honest Christian man, he will be himself the first to tell you that his religion does not give him much delight. The motive of his religious life is a sense of duty rather than an impulse of love.[52]

This ordinary church member might as well have been found in the pews of churches of the other denominations. It was hoped that special missions would kindle more spiritual warmth in him. Generally, the Wesleyan Conference also seemed to think that an annual evangelistic campaign was more or less adequate, but the more zealous Methodists looked for a clearer and direct promotion of holiness, and American evangelists were at hand to help.

One of these was the Reverend J. Inskip, who, with his wife and the Reverend W. Gardiner, conducted a holiness mission at York Street Church in May 1881. Members of other denominations as well as Methodists came to the mission which evoked great religious fervour and ecstasy. Gardiner and Mrs Inskip "did some effective singing", and Inskip preached. He used the fear of death and eternal punishment to coerce his congregations, including children, whom he warned not to defer their conversion until it was "too late, too late". To some the mission exceeded expectations; for John Austin, for example, it was "another Pentecost". To others it must have seemed like Babel, with a class leader praying loudly, while the missioner appeared to be trying to drown him out. At the same time, there were twenty or more people below the pulpit speaking audibly, "the whole thing partaking of excitement, instead of Christians quietly showing to enquirers THE WAY from God's word".[53] The mission's defenders considered that the spiritual good achieved excused any excesses, but its critics thought that the proceedings brought discredit upon religion. With such division of opinion, the conference was not likely to give much encouragement to further holiness missions, but a president of conference might lend the dignity of his office to a holiness convention, as Nolan did in 1885.

The United Methodist Holiness Convention of 1885 owed much to the organization and energy of W.G. Taylor, of the Central Methodist Mission, one of the more innovative and certainly one of the more "evangelical" Methodist ministers. Influenced by the holiness conventions of Canadian Methodism and, more particularly, by a convention held at Southport in England in June 1885, Taylor determined to organize such a convention in Sydney. He invited Primitive Methodists and United Free Methodists to a camp meeting with Wesleyans at Lane Cove on 9 November 1885 where about twelve hundred supported plans for a holiness convention to be held at York Street Church in December. Modelled on the Southport convention, it was an attempt to recapture the "old spirit of Methodism". The programme consisted of addressed on holiness, including one from Bowring, the conference evangelist, and testimonies from those who had experienced "entire sanctification". The proceedings seem to have been largely free of the emotionalism which marked the Inskip mission, but many, it was claimed, came forward to seek divine forgiveness and blessing or to profess that they would "rest on Christ for full salvation".[54]

For some the holiness convention recaptured the old glow of fervent Methodism and it boosted the confidence of those who thought that the effectiveness of the church in that age depended not on change but on greater faithfulness to the old ways or, at least, the old-fashioned doctrine of Methodism. Still basking in its religious warmth, one Wesleyan minister, M. Maddern, claimed enthusiastically that if every church took " 'Holiness unto the Lord' " as its motto for 1886 it would hasten the coming of the millennium.[55] One immediate result of the convention was the formation of the United Methodist Holiness Association, embracing Primitive Methodists and the more conservative Wesleyans. The association published a monthly paper, *Glad Tidings,* and held successive conventions on a small scale,[56] but it remained a minority movement. The spiritual fervour it sought to generate might have injected new life into the languishing class meeting, but there was to be no revival there. In any case, other voices in Methodism were clamouring to depart from some of the old ways and the General Conference of 1890, in fact, abandoned the rule that members of Wesleyan Methodist churches should attend the weekly class meeting.

Holiness conventions apart, there was an impressive amount of evangelistic activity in the 1880s, both through the campaigns of visiting evangelists, of whom only the more prominent have been discussed, and through the special arrangements made by the denominations in the mid 1880s. The Baptists and Congregationalists were also caught up in the evangelistic movement, and there were a number of interdenominational missions held in local churches in city and country, mainly through the cooperation of Wesleyans, Presbyterians and Congregationalists.[57]

It is perhaps not too fanciful to suggest that the presence of the Salvation Army and the frequent missions held by the Protestant denominations affected the Roman Catholic Church as well. Whether this be so or not, the bishops in their Pastoral Letter from the First Plenary Council in 1885 exhorted the clergy to arrange "opportune missions" and visits of "extraordinary confessors" to restore to the fold those who might have been away long from penance and communion, and found it difficult to return through confession to the local priest. Catholic missions were conducted by members of various religious orders and their style departed to some extent from the conventional preaching of the secular clergy, although it was also quite different from that of the Protestant evangelist. It was, for example, the custom of the Redemptorists to preach from a large platform erected in front of the sanctuary with a great crucifix at the side. It became the rule in the archdiocese of Sydney to hold missions "conducted by approved Religious", biennially in city parishes and triennially in country districts.[58]

Catholic and Protestant missions had this much in common: in each case they sought to reawaken religious devotion, according to their respective spiritual ideals, in those of their members who had grown cold or indifferent. But Protestants also clearly aimed at the conversion of the unbeliever. They talked hopefully of reaching the ungodly masses living in neglect of religion.

Not all enquirers who came forward at missions became "converts". Although at every mission conversions were claimed, statistics were not often given, and neither was it clear how many of those were converts from among those outside the churches. Austin claimed to have converted several non-churchgoers at Singleton in 1884 and here and there one finds instances of a freethinker converted to evangelical Protestantism. Carruthers told of a railway man at Armidale, an avowed sceptic and profaner of religion, who was converted during a revival sparked off by the Salvation Army and later became an earnest lay preacher. Taylor also claimed to have converted a freethinker and Austin a young Jew at Parkes.[59] But these were exceptional instances; a critical observer of evangelistic missions in the mid 1880s claimed that three-quarters of the people usually attending them were "already evangelised".[60] This contemporary impression corresponds with investigations of more recent evangelistic campaigns.[61] Audiences then, as now, seem to have consisted largely of churchgoers, and "converts" mostly seem to have come from among them.

These were, by and large, the younger members of the congregations, even children. Austin's accounts of his missions indicate this. At Windsor, where the number of converts was disappointing, "there were still four or five good cases of adults, besides a number of children brought in that Sunday", and at Paddington he mentioned that 100 children professed conversion. It is significant also that he should find it necessary at the conference in January 1882 to exhort Methodists to look for the conversion of their "older hearers" as well as of their young people.[62] A report on the Mountain couple's mission at Kew in Victoria in 1886 admitted that it had, "with few exceptions, not reached the unawakened outside"; but as was generally the case in mission services, "the young enquirer, halting between two opinions", had been led "to take the final step and boldly come out on Christ's side".[63] Modern scholarship suggests that this mostly has been true for the twentieth century as well — the majority of so-called conversions occurring among the ten- to twenty-year-olds. "Conversion" in these cases, Michael Argyle argues, is really a misnomer: the decision is rather an expression of "heightened commitment" to Christianity by those brought up in its beliefs and practice,[64] even if the decision is made under an induced conviction of sin. Moody had no qualms about it: he held that "there is no child too young to be brought to Jesus".[65] Most evangelists, it seems, agreed.

Churches in the nineteenth century certainly did not despise the conversion of the young. Indeed, they looked to youth as an important source of church members and regarded Sunday Schools as "feeders to the churches". It was more important to prepare Sunday school children for church membership than to wait for adult conversions, James Jefferis told Congregationalists in 1883. Similarly, the Presbyterian Sabbath Schools Committee reminded the General Assembly in 1880 that the Catholic Church knew the importance of training the lambs of the flock, and that it would ill become Protestants to neglect this field.[66] The emphasis here was on training and Christian nurture rather than conversion, although that was not ruled out, especially by the Methodists.

Wesleyans as well as "Other Methodists" regarded an evangelical conversion as an important, indeed a necessary, step in this process. The rules of Wesleyan Sunday schools instructed teachers to look for the conversion of their scholars and in 1876 the conference ruled that an annual sermon should be preached to the young, warning them of "the danger and guilt of religious indecision and the duty and privilege of uniting themselves" with the Church through membership. The conference went further in 1881 when it recommended selective classes to secure the conversion of older Sunday school youth.[67] Those in other denominations who were not so insistent on conversion were still grateful to evangelists who could clinch the religious decision of the young, who might then be drawn into church membership.

Generally converts filled in cards which were passed on to local pastors to follow up. How many of the converts did become church members is almost impossible to say, but the evidence there is suggests that the intense evangelistic campaigns of the 1880s did not make much difference at all to church attendances or to church membership. Indeed, church attendances declined slightly in the 1880s and church members remained very much a minority of churchgoers to the end of the century. Given that Sunday school attendances increased during the decade, it would seem that many of the children in Sunday schools were not gathered into church congregations as they became older, let alone membership. Those that were, one suspects, probably came from churchgoing families.[68] Many of the adult converts were apparently already churchgoers, perhaps even communicant members, so that their numbers would hardly have affected ecclesiastical statistics at all. There would seem to have been no numerical gain to the churches through their investment in evangelism, although it could be argued that there might have been greater losses if the denominations had put less effort in this direction.

Some churchmen in the 1880s, as has been suggested, were sceptical as to the gains that might be made through evangelism, especially from the campaigns of the typical itinerant evangelist. In 1881 the Wesleyan *Weekly Advocate* observed that even people in sympathy with Moody and Sankey were saying that the enduring results of their campaign were very few. Scepticism about the professional evangelists was perhaps more widespread among Congregationalists and Presbyterians; but the liberal James Hill asked his fellow Congregationalists in 1884 of what consequence it was that Moody's meetings were largely made up of churchgoers, which was not to suggest that they were of little use. It was after all something to get good church people stirred up and set to work. Similarly, the *Presbyterian* in 1887, apropos of John MacNeil's mission, sought to allay the misgivings of those offended by the crude theology and sensational methods of some evangelists. It admitted that excesses occurred too often in the campaigns of some missioners "whose zeal sometimes outruns their discretion"; but, it asked, "is it not better to bear with an occasional irregularity than to lie benumbed in spiritual torpor?"[69]

Even if evangelistic campaigns were, by and large, not reaching the unconverted, here was one important reason many churchmen found to support evangelism — to lift their churches out of spiritual torpor. Too frequent excesses were passed off as occasional irregularities. If there were converts to count they rejoiced in them, but where there were few or none they consoled themselves, as John Austin did at Windsor, with the belief that the mission "did more for the uplifting of the church . . . than double the number of conversions would have done". By the same token, Alexander Osborne, one of the Presbyterian evangelistic deputies in 1885, affirmed that missions always did some good to congregations even if the wave of enthusiasm and revival receded after the mission; it "left its mark higher on the beach", bearing fruit "in a more sincere belief, and in a more hearty worship".[70]

As was happening in the rest of the Anglo-Saxon world in the later nineteenth century, so in Australia churchmen were coming to depend more on professional evangelists.[71] The special efforts made by the various denominations in the middle of the decade did not endure, partly because of a growing conviction that other approaches were needed to reach non-churchgoers especially in the city, where the Methodists in particular were developing new techniques. But, as the *Australian Christian World* replied to a critic of the itinerant "expert", it was also partly that too few ministers could do, or would do, the work of an evangelist.[72]

The reasons for this are not obscure. There was a significant liberalizing of Protestant theology in the 1880s, and the more liberal parson would not have found the role of evangelist a congenial one. The liberal Protestant did not share the professional revivalist's view of biblical inspiration, and since he had rejected the doctrine of eternal punishment, he would not invoke the fear of death or the threat of hell-fire. But he would welcome the evangelist who could arouse people from spiritual lethargy to religious commitment, hoping afterwards to lead them to "the fuller faith" he cherished. Dr Roseby is a case in point. One of the more advanced religious thinkers of his day, he liked to think of himself as belonging to an ecumenical extension of "the Board Church school". Yet he was an advocate of evangelistic missions and on one occasion he took his intelligent young daughter to a visiting evangelist's meeting. On the way home he apologized constantly for the evangelist and gave the revivalist's sermon his own liberal reinterpretation.[73] Of course not all supporters of the professional itinerant were liberal theologians.

The more conservative Evangelical would have supported revivalism with less compunction, although he might sometimes have winced at flamboyance and vulgarity in the service of Christ. He might have done the work of the evangelist in his own parish, and many did; but the local evangelist, like the prophet, was often "without honour in his own country". An outsider could speak with an authority and directness that was not always easy in the pastoral situation. And for the conservative Protestant the evangelist's preaching was generally a reinforcement of his own doctrine. Thus both conservative and liberal Protestants came to see evangelism as less the work of the pastor than of the professional itinerant.

In a way it might be said that the professional evangelist had become to Protestantism what to some extent certain religious orders were to the Catholic Church — specialists who might be called in to induce spiritual awakening. The revivalist enjoyed something like apostolic status. A visitor to Sydney during the 1894 mission of John McNeill (the "Scottish Spurgeon", not John MacNeil of South Australia) observed the adulation which that evangelist received in the city bookshops on posters and in cheap editions of his life-story. McNeill also drew crowds, mostly of churchgoers according to this witness, to the Exhibition Building. They left "in a high state of spiritual exaltation", after hearing the Scotsman castigate the vices of colonial society.[74]

In 1891 Protestant churchmen invited the prince of revivalist preachers, Moody himself, to come to Australia, but he disappointed them. However his evangelistic apostles followed. Reuben A. Torrey, superintendent of Moody's Bible Institute in Chicago, conducted an evangelistic campaign in Australia in 1902, accompanied by Charles M. Alexander, his song leader. Alexander returned to Australia again in 1909, this time in company with Dr J. Wilbur Chapman, whom Moody had dubbed in 1895, "the greatest evangelist" in the United States.[75] Chapman's Simultaneous Evangelistic Campaign was a new strategy: teams of evangelists led missions in local centres while Chapman and Alexander conducted a meeting at a large central auditorium. The method was new, but the message was old and the results much the same as in previous missions. The crowds came and were thrilled and uplifted, both in 1909 and in the second visit of this pair in 1912.[76] That was the last big evangelistic mission in Australia, until the Billy Graham Crusade in 1959. In the interim other evangelists came, causing ripples rather than waves. But none of them had shown how to reach the masses with religion.

4

Worship for the Working Classes

During the 1880s Australian churchmen became increasingly aware of the large number of people outside the churches, especially in the cities. In a comment on church attendances in May 1888 the *Sydney Morning Herald* estimated that, when all such allowances as age and infirmity had been made, "something like one-half of the population of large cities consists of people who are never found within the church doors from one end of the year to the other". This was true for Sydney where church attendances had been declining since the 1870s and continued to fall in the 1880s: regular churchgoers were around 50 per cent of the adult population in the metropolitan area in 1880 and 40 per cent in 1890.[1] But many of the rest were not completely cut off from religion. According to the *New South Wales Independent,* they still had their children baptized, their dead given Chris.ian burials and their marriages celebrated by ministers of religion; but they did not attend church or take any personal interest in religion. Yet, the journal continued, "thousands of these send their children to the Sunday School, and have a dim conception that this is the proper thing to do".[2] Who were they, and why did they not attend church regularly? What could be done to attract them? Churchmen asked themselves these questions increasingly often in the 1880s.

A variety of reasons why many people did not go to church were offered in a spate of correspondence to the *Sydney Morning Herald* in May 1888, following the publication of church attendance figures for 1886. In that year only attendances at the "principal service" of the day were counted, making the decline in churchgoing look worse than it was, especially for the Anglican Church, on which the correspondence focused.

Some of these correspondents blamed dull preaching, long sermons and dreary services for the absence of many. Others found fault with church music: it was either too ambitious and difficult to sing, or of low standard and badly sung. A few criticized the theology preached: an Irish Protestant condemned the "Romanist" teaching of the high church party while another correspondent abhorred the outdated theology of the Evangelicals. Some argued for the revision of the *Book of Common Prayer* and others that it should be followed more closely.[3] Despite these complaints, there had been significant changes in Protestant church services during the third quarter of the nineteenth century. Generally, they had become shorter, although Anglicans in New South Wales had only recently taken advantage of the Shortened Services Act of 1872.[4] There had also been improvements in church architecture and music which might have attracted or held those with an eye for beauty and ceremony.

The non-churchgoers generally came from a different section of the population. "It is pretty well agreed", wrote one of the correspondents in May 1888, "that the majority of working-men in Sydney do not go to church". Another thought that they mainly stayed away from Anglican churches, but in fact the absence of the working classes was a problem common to all the Protestant denominations, in Australia and England alike.[5] The Catholic *Freeman's Journal,* commenting on the letters to the *Sydney Morning Herald,* was not surprised that the working classes generally made bad Protestants. It argued that the Protestants had lost the poor largely because of the affectation and worldliness of their preachers. Protestants conceded that the Catholic Church kept the working classes, at least in Australia and Britain, but few thought that they could learn anything from the authoritarian Church of Rome, as they saw it.[6]

The working classes (as distinct from the working class) was a term which covered a wide range of people engaged in manual labour, from the ambitious tradesman who might own a cottage and live according to the standards of bourgeois respectability, to the unskilled labourers and the impoverished who lived in the depressed parts of the city.[7] But Warlow Davies admitted to Congregationalists in Sydney in 1881 that it was rare enough to find even a respectable working man in church, let alone the very poor. Dr Jefferis differed slightly when he tackled the theme in one of his Sunday evening lectures in November 1889. He claimed that there were working men and their families in the congregation that evening but they were inconspicuous, because in colonial society there was no "remarkable difference . . . between the [Sunday] dress of a well-to-do mechanic or artisan or even the labourer and those engaged in commercial or trading pursuits". True though that might be, Jefferis conceded that congregations were composed "mainly of the respectable burgher class". He considered that, unlike their great Master, whom "the common people heard . . . gladly", the churches of the nineteenth century had "lost much of their hold" on those who lived "by hand labour".[8] Whether the churches indeed had "lost" the support of the working classes is a debatable question, but Australian churchmen in the late nineteenth century believed that they had, and they looked for reasons.

According to the *Presbyterian* in 1889, the alienation of the working classes was due to the same factor as the alienation of some people of other classes from religion — "the enmity of the carnal mind to the things of God". In a similar vein, the *Weekly Advocate* on one occasion put hostility to religion down to dissolute living which made many rail at all authority, "human and divine".[9] These diagnoses presupposed that evangelical conversion was the simple solution to the problem. But the correspondents to the *Sydney Morning Herald* in May 1888 clearly thought that the fault might lie more squarely with the churches than with the working classes themselves.

One of the most interesting letters came from H. Tennent Donaldson, an auctioneer and an Anglican, who claimed that the reason working men did not attend church was not that they had "ceased to believe the great truths of Christianity, but because in most of our city and suburban churches the largest portion of the sittings are let off to the monied classes". In contrast, Donaldson pointed to the amount of space allocated to the working classes in city theatres. Why, then, should churches not be "free and open to all", and working men be encouraged to hold office of one kind or another, instead of the undemocratic way in which Anglican church affairs were managed? Donaldson also advocated shorter, brighter services to attract the working classes to worship. But his main plea was for the abolition of pew-renting.[10]

The Campaign against Pew-renting

The renting of pews was a custom brought from England which was common in Protestant churches in Australia and in some of the larger Catholic churches. Bourke's Church Act of 1836 presupposed pew-renting, but stipulated that at least one-sixth of the seats in a church should be free for the poor; seats so designated were usually backless benches "in some obscure corner or side aisle". Voting in parish affairs was tied to the paying system. The English Church Temporalities Act of 1837 (known to Anglicans as the Church Act, and under which their parishes were governed) gave the franchise for the election of churchwardens to seat-holders (people renting single places) and pew-holders (the heads of families). These latter might have up to six votes at the Easter vestry meeting, while "the working man who cannot afford to rent a portion of his parish church is disenfranchised", Donaldson protested.[11] There were several free and open churches, but no legal provision for elections in them.

Pew-rents might not have been beyond the reach of some working men. The annual rate ranged from ten shillings per sitting (or individual place) in some churches to thirty shillings in the wealthy parish of St John's, Darlinghurst, with the average at one pound per sitting. So a man with three or four children could expect to pay around five or six pounds a year for a family pew. (Older sons in large families usually found a place at the back of the church.) No one expected poor people to pay these rents when there were free seats in the church, but they were not too prohibitive for a skilled workman who wished to attend church regularly, although in addition there was the cost of cushions, hymnals and prayer books. Pew-holders were expected to provide their own and churches rarely supplied prayer books for the poor or strangers, as casual visitors were called. Nor were cushions or kneeling pads provided in the free seating, and sometimes the rows were too close for kneeling, about which Bishop Pearson complained. He had also been distressed to see so many visitors without books in churches where he had preached. The provision of a few books for the use of visitors, he told his synod, would be "an inexpensive courtesy". It was the same in churches of other denominations. A visitor to Pitt Street Congregational Church in May 1890 observed "much want of attention to the comfort of visitors", many of whom were without books throughout the service.[12]

It was easy, then, for a visitor to feel unwelcome in a colonial church. Churches mostly had cedar box pews with doors (many of which have since disappeared or have at least lost their doors) and pew-holders sometimes guarded their rights jealously. "Now and then someone, distrustful of his fellow-worshippers, had a lock and key on that door", Dame Mary Gilmore recalled from her childhood. If a pew-holder came late to find that a church officer had seated a visitor in his pew, the rightful occupant usually insisted, not always politely, that the visitor move out. In one country Methodist church, it was reported, a pew-holder, determined to teach strangers a lesson, stuffed his cushion with thorns and stayed away purposely so that visitors might use it! In most cases these visitors were not working-class folk but churchgoers from other places. One of these, a Methodist local preacher, did not mind being asked to move when the claimant arrived, but he wondered how much treatment would affect outsiders, especially the working classes.[13] Jefferis deplored this conduct and blamed pew-renting as one reason for the alienation of the working classes. A number of Anglican clergy and laymen saw the system in the same light.

The *Australian Churchman,* a high church weekly, took up the cause for free and open churches in 1880, when a dispute occurred among parishioners of All Saints, Petersham, over seating in their new church. The majority wanted free seating, but a strong minority stood out for rented sittings. Bishop Barker recommended a compromise which would obviate some of the more pernicious aspects of the system. He suggested that half the seats be free and half rented at one pound per sitting, with alternate free and rented pews. He also advised that the church wardens fill all vacant places after the bell had stopped ringing. Apart from this occasion, Barker does not seem to have been very concerned about the question of pew-rents. Bishop Marsden of Bathurst did not like the system and looked forward to the day when offerings would be large enough to dispense with pew-rents.[14] Until then, and like many, he accepted them as a necessary evil.

Churchmen who had some experience of the movement for free and open churches in Britain saw it differently. The colonial-born parson, J.C. Corlette, was influenced by the English campaign as a student at Oxford, and protested against pew-rents on his return to New South Wales in 1863.[15] In those days he was a voice crying in the wilderness. But in the 1880s others spoke out against the system, especially Bishop Pearson. Before coming to Newcastle, he had been in charge of a church in England which became free during his incumbency. As bishop of Newcastle he frequently attacked pew-renting, especially in his addresses to synod. He argued that it discouraged generosity, as people tended to consider their financial obligation to the church discharged when they had paid their rent. More than that, he condemned the system as contrary to the Bible, catholic usage and English common law. It was "unseemly", he declared, in reference to the difference between rented and free accommodation in churches, "that the distinction between the furniture of the rich man's home and the poor man's home should be extended to the House of Common Prayer".[16]

Bishop Barry, while not as outspoken on the matter as Pearson, agreed with his fellow bishop, commending the free and open principle. Pew-renting, he stated, was "a thing unknown to ancient church practice, and to the old law of the Church of England". Persistent opposition to the system was to come from H.L. Jackson, rector of St James's Church, Sydney. In 1886 he moved in synod "to assert the Democratic character of the Church by making the House of God in every parish free and open to all". There was no hope of such a resolution being passed. The synod would not even accept an amendment to the effect that free seating should be available in positions equally as good as the rented seats occupied; moreover, it formally declined to express an opinion on the matter. Jackson, convinced that there would be no proper church life in the colony until the churches were entirely free and open, did not give up his campaign. He failed to persuade both the diocese and his own parish to adopt the free and open system, but the proportion of rented pews in St James's fell from 50 per cent in 1886 (when the number of free and rented sittings were first included in the returns) to 15 per cent in 1891.[17]

Why were so many churchmen loath to abolish the custom of pew-renting, if only as a gesture to make their churches appear less exclusive to the outsider? According to Pearson, the system was defended on the grounds of personal convenience (for a few) and financial advantage.[18] Certainly many regarded pew-rents as a financial necessity. "Liberal and systematic giving [was] a grace apparently hard to cultivate", said a Presbyterian report in justification of pew-renting, and the Wesleyan Conference made the collection of pew-rents as well as weekly offerings a condition of financial assistance to circuits.[19] Not too well informed on the diocese of Newcastle, that "Episcopalian paradise of New South Wales", the *Weekly Advocate,* thought it ill became Bishop Pearson to inveigh against pew-rents; they were a "godsend and a happy solution" to churches which would face "insuperable" financial difficulties without them. Austin apparently thought so, for during the depression in 1891 he increased the pew-rents in Bourke Street Wesleyan Church to alleviate the circuit's financial problems. But most churches derived the greater part of their income from offertories rather than pew-rents, and Anglican opponents of pew-renting argued that church finances would not suffer, but might even improve, if the practice were abolished. St Luke's, Scone, provided a good example. This parish made its new building a free and open church (with provision for kneeling throughout); and Pearson was able to report triumphantly that its offertories and collections provided a larger income than had previously been raised "by offertories, collections and pew-rents".[20]

But few were willing to discard the crutch. The churchwardens at St John's, Ashfield, feared the financial consequences when Dr Corlette proposed the abolition of pew-rents at the Easter vestry meeting in 1884. There were legal difficulties, too. The churchwardens found the Church Temporalities Act of 1837 to be an insuperable obstacle to a "free-seat" system. Such appeals to the Act irritated Bishop Pearson, who demanded to know what was "so specially bright and promising in the condition of the Church of England" in 1837 "that we should be forbidden all development from that date, and all return to the methods of an earlier time?"[21]

Pearson was not alone in regarding this Act of 1837 as less than divinely inspired. In Bishop Barry's first address to the Provincial Synod in October 1884, he suggested that at least some amendment to the Act was necessary. The prominence it gave to pew-renting was one of the reasons he advanced. The Act not only presupposed state aid to religion, Barry told the next Provincial Synod but it made no provision for free and open churches and left the qualification of those other than pew-holders "dangerously vague". The *Church of England Guardian* thought the provisions of the Act, which gave one man six votes because he was a pew-holder and another, a regular attendant and contributor to the offertory, but not a pew-holder, no vote at all, "a strange anomoly, and a standing disgrace to the Church".[22]

Discontent with the Temporalities Act did not arise solely from opposition to pew-renting. There had been some discussion of "a safe and useful substitution" for the Act in the early 1870s, particularly to remove certain ambiguities concerning church property and to provide for the election of churchwardens where there were no pew-holders.[23] But no misgivings about pew-renting at that stage appeared to lie behind the moves. The matter seemed to have lapsed by 1879 when the dioceses of Bathurst and of Grafton and Armidale applied independently to Parliament for legislation to deal with property in their respective dioceses. But the diocese of Sydney revived the question of repeal in the 1880s. The synod clearly wished to make proper provision for free and open churches but without prejudicing the position of parishes with rented seating. In 1885, for instance, it rejected a motion which would have recommended the repeal of all references to pew-holders and subscribers.

Bishop Barry continued to advertise the defects to Provincial Synod and in 1887 it set up a committee to prepare a scheme for its repeal.[24] But Barry, somewhat uncertain that an ordinance agreeable to all dioceses in the province could be devised, had the Sydney synod pass a provisional church ordinance for that diocese. Its interpretation of an "Occupier of a Seat" embraced both a pew-holder of at least twelve months' standing or a person having regularly attended divine service for at least three months preceding the time of elections. The ordinance for parochial government in the province passed in 1892 incorporated this definition.[25] These ordinances thereby legalized elections in free and open churches and also enfranchised the non-renters in other churches. The new rulings excluded women, for occupiers of seats were taken to mean male members of the Church of England over twenty-one; in 1904, the Provincial Synod agreed to include married women in the definition. The provincial church ordinance recognized the question of free or rented seating as a matter of local preference, but it did specify that at least one-third of the seats in a church were to be free. This was a fairly safe provision as by the 1880s or 1890s few churches were able to rent more than two-thirds of their sittings anyway. In 1895 the Provincial Synod finally approved an ordinance seeking the repeal of the Temporalities Act and in 1897 Parliament passed the necessary legislation.[26]

While these measures removed certain unfortunate anomalies in colonial Anglicanism, they must have left the opponents of pew-renting in some measure disappointed, for the custom remained fairly well entrenched. The Sydney synod had attempted to qualify the unprescribed rights of pew-holders in 1889 when it agreed to the principle that all seats in churches should be considered free after the service had begun — something Pearson had previously dismissed as a palliative rather than a real remedy.[27] But it was a difficult principle to enforce and many late pew-holders were still impolite when they found strangers in their seats.

The custom remained almost as firmly established in other denominations, at least nominally. Figures for the Presbyterian Church in 1900 showed a marked increase in appropriated seating, although, apparently, pews were commonly allocated without rental. This was becoming the custom in Congregational churches also. "The great event of the year has been the introduction of the purely voluntary system", stated Jefferis proudly in his pastoral report for the Pitt Street Congregational Church in 1880. But pew-renting was still the general rule among Congregationalists when they held their Intercolonial Conference in Sydney in May 1883. During a discussion on "Reaching Those Who Live in Neglect of Christian Worship" there were suggestions of throwing the churches open occasionally, and allowing unrestricted use of books and cushions, as was done in some of the larger churches in South Australia. In support of this someone mentioned Spurgeon's custom in England of setting apart one Sunday a month for the working classes, when the regular members of the congregation "generously gave up their seats and went elsewhere". When a minister from Victoria suggested that they should resolve to make the churches wholly free, Jefferis, the chairman of the conference, pointed out that any such motion would convey the impression that their churches were not free and open all the time. They had to show that the church was not for the rich or the middle classes, "but a house of God for all people". So the matter was left unresolved.[28]

Nevertheless, most Congregational churches in Sydney followed Pitt Street in abolishing pew-renting but the practice of allocating pews to families continued, and each head of family was supplied with weekly "freewill" offering envelopes. It amounted to the pew-holder setting his own rent, although seats unoccupied after the commencement of the service were usually considered free. The officers of one church even stated that as the church existed for the public worship of God, not private convenience, occupants of pews had no exclusive claim on them. But the Congregational and Presbyterian Churches had modified rather than abolished the pew-renting system. Wesleyans in Victoria also changed the system a little in 1891 by making their churches open to all for the evening service, which was not well attended anyway.[29] However a visitor to any of the churches of these denominations would not have noticed much difference from those that retained the old system. The names of regular worshippers could still be found attached to the pews, and people were just as proprietorial in their attitudes to "their" family pew as under the old system.

The reasons for the persistence of this custom were not solely financial, as the practice of allocating pews without rent in Congregational and Presbyterian churches suggests. The other reason Pearson offered for the popularity of the custom was personal convenience. The regular churchgoer liked to enjoy a reserved place, furnished for his own comfort, each Sunday; and a certain amount of sentiment attached to "the family pew". To hold a pew in a church was also some evidence of respectability, even if one were not in it every Sunday. Pew-renting was also a way of choosing one's company in church, and for those who were hard of hearing, of ensuring a position from which the sermon could be heard, an important consideration before the days of public address systems.

So pew-renting, or at least the allocation of family pews, lingered on well into the twentieth century; as recently as October 1979 the Melbourne Anglican synod took steps to abolish the custom completely.[30] But some of the worst features of the system were removed in New South Wales by 1895. Yet was pew-renting as important a reason for the alienation of the working classes as Jackson, Pearson, Tennent Donaldson and others seemed to think? Probably very few working men came near enough to a church to be aware of this invidious custom. In any case there were free and open churches in the inner city — St Barnabas', Glebe, St Luke's, Sussex Street, St Peter's, Woolloomooloo, Ss Simon and Jude, Campbell Street — but the working classes did not flock to them, or to St Andrew's Cathedral which was practically free. Pew-renting then was not the chief cause of their alienation from the churches, although the campaign against it should not be dismissed complacently as "a fad and no more", as Dr Zachary Barry termed it in his letter to the *Sydney Morning Herald* in May 1888. Pew-renting was an expression of the middle class exclusiveness of the churches, and as such quite a formidable obstacle in the way of attracting the working classes.[31] But some churchmen never thought they would get the working classes into ordinary churches, with or without pew-rents. Like the Salvation Army, they considered class divisions "too broad for any bridge".[32]

Missions for the Poor

Mission rooms were necessary to reach "the tens of thousands" who were indifferent to the claims of Christianity and unaccustomed to conventional worship, Dean Cowper told the Sydney Anglican synod in 1881.[33] Cowper represented a large group of churchmen who were not interested in the controversy over pew-renting. They thought not of bringing the working classes into the churches, but of taking religion to them. There had been developments in this direction since the mid nineteenth century, as Sydney became more populated and its poor began to cluster together. From this time the churches began to make separate arrangements for them. In 1849 Pitt Street Congregational Church appointed Samuel Goold, formerly a city missioner in London, to work among the poorer classes in Sydney. Goold began by visiting houses, distributing religious tracts and organizing prayer meetings and religious services. He also established a free-school to teach reading and writing, using Sunday School Union books for the purpose.[34] Nathaniel Pidgeon, a cabinetmaker and Methodist lay preacher, became a full-time city missionary under the Wesleyan Church in 1850. Ten years later he set up as an Independent Methodist and his supporters built a brick chapel in Sussex Street. In 1868 the mission became a non-sectarian establishment. Unconventional in outlook and preaching style, Pidgeon continued to minister to the poor of the city until sickness overtook him in 1875. He died in 1879 and in 1880 Pitt Street Congregational Church bought the property from Pidgeon's trustees as a base for "its evangelical efforts among the neglected poor". The little congregation flourished under its pastor, George Lewis, and by 1886, it had transformed its buildings from "an ugly mass of brickwork to a well-proportioned and pleasing Gothic edifice".[35]

Most important among these early endeavours to reach the inhabitants of the heart of the city was the Sydney City Mission, founded in 1862. Benjamin Short, the first insurance canvasser for the Australian Mutual Provident Society, was the moving spirit in the formation of the mission. Short had been associated with the London City Mission and he brought his ideas to Australia in 1860.

Protestants united to set up the mission and to support its work. Its missioners spent most of their time making house to house visitations, handing out tracts, reading the Bible and praying with people, especially the sick and dying. They induced a few to sign the pledge, prevailed upon some to attend church services, perhaps at Pidgeon's mission chapel, and also persuaded some parents to send their children to school, as well as providing various forms of social service and relief.[36] Two similar missions were set up in Melbourne in 1856 and in Adelaide in 1867, both modelled on the London City Mission.

Among other agencies at work in the city was the Ladies' Evangelistic Association, which conducted a "cab mission" to cabmen, bus drivers and draymen, sought to reclaim drunkards and distributed charitable relief to poor households. The Pitt Street Christian Instruction Society of Jefferis's church also maintained a mission to the poor. This company of young men conducted Sunday schools for the children of the hovels and rookeries in the darker parts of Sydney and preached to the patrons of the City Night Refuge and Soup Kitchen and the Female Refuge. Dean Cowper also supervised evangelistic efforts among the poor within the vicinity of St Andrew's Cathedral.

With these various missions existing before 1880, the religious welfare of the poor of the inner city was not entirely neglected. But the churches began to pay more attention to this part of the population in the 1880s, particularly as the expansion of the metropolis and the migration of the middle classes to the new suburbs left some city churches with depleted congregations. This was especially the case with York Street Wesleyan Church; many Methodist families had moved away from the city leaving the old church surrounded by heathenism of the worst form, as one minister described the remaining population to the annual conference in 1883.[37] Another factor which focused the churches' attention on the unevangelized masses of the city was the arrival of the Salvation Army in Australia.

The *Presbyterian* reported on a Salvation Army meeting in the Protestant Hall soon after the Army began its work in Sydney. While critical of the shallowness of much that was witnessed, the columnist acknowledged the heartiness and enthusiasm of the meeting. The proceedings were an entertainment for some of the audience, but most entered into the religious spirit of the occasion. The report conceded that the Army would attract "a certain class untouched by the Churches", but doubted whether it could hold them. Still, it thought that numbers in churches of the existing denominations might receive a boost from the Army's activity;[38] although how its converts might move into the conventional churches was not explained, and General Booth's policy of setting the converts or recruits to work certainly did not encourage a casual attitude to his organization. Wesleyans could not view the Salvation Army with such complacency in view of the tendency of some Methodists to see the Army as old-fashioned Methodism. A few Wesleyan ministers, determined to show that Methodism had not lost its evangelical fervour, were willing to adopt some of the Army's methods. Foremost among them was the Reverend W.G. Taylor, founder of the Central Methodist Mission. There were Anglicans also prepared to follow Booth's strategy, and Bishop Barry was one of them.

The Church Army

Barry admired some aspects of the Army, especially in the way in which it set its recruits to work at once. What the Church of England could do with such a lay agency, Prebendary Wilson Carlile attempted to show. In 1882 he founded the Church Army, an agency which "frankly copied the methods of the Salvation Army".[39] When Barry spoke to his synod in July 1885 about the need for mission work in the more densely populated parts of the city, he suggested that the Church Army might provide the means of doing it. It was "rough and homely work" which could probably be best done by "rough and homely hands". The synod initiated no action, although some Evangelicals were well disposed to the idea. The *Church of England Record* had in fact proposed that the Church Army be used in inner city areas the previous year.[40] Soon after the synod in July 1885, it seems, a group of enthusiasts formed a committee and attempted, without the sanction of synod but with Barry's approval, to set up a branch of the Church Army in the inner suburb of Ultimo. The newly-formed corps, led by Captain W.M. Briggs, formerly of the Salvation Army, made its first public appearance at the laying of the foundation stone of the Church of England Mission Hall at Ultimo on 24 October 1885. It had marched to a band from St Bartholomew's Church, Pyrmont, to the site in Harris Street, Ultimo, bearing a banner which read: Church Army — No Cross, No Crown — Pyrmont and Ultimo Corps". Barry, flanked by evangelical clergy, presided at the ceremony and declared that the Church Army had his heartiest commendation in the work it would do.[41] It seemed that the Salvation Army was now to face an Anglican competitor.

But Barry had not sought the support of all the clergy for this new enterprise and he did not count on the opposition of some High Churchmen, especially C.F. Garnsey of Christ Church, St

Bishop Barry and his merry band. A comment on brighter church services. (From *Bulletin*, 14 June 1884. Photo courtesy of La Trobe Library, State Library of Victoria.)

Laurence, in the neighbourhood. Within days of the ceremony at Ultimo the columns of the *Australian Churchman,* voice of the high church party, featured letters strongly critical of the Church Army. One correspondent thought it made a mockery of Anglican worship and another alleged that Briggs was a fanatic, a rejected Salvation Army officer, who had caused a great deal of trouble to the Anglican priest at Maitland when he was leading the Salvation Army there. The *Churchman* declared the Church Army unsuitable to the Ultimo district, where, it claimed, the inhabitants were mostly tradespeople, with a minority of "mechanics" earning about three pounds a week who were as independent as the richest squatter. In any case, it thought that there must be better ways of reaching the indifferent masses than by parading the streets at five in the morning with "braying trumpets and trombones . . . disturbing the rest, not only of the ungodly, but of the righteous also". Its recommendation was the introduction of sisterhoods, Anglican nuns, as used in the slums of London.[42] But this proposal was likely to receive even less support in Sydney than the Church Army. Although Barry thought there was a place for both sisterhoods and deaconesses as well as the Church Army in the Church's ministry to the poor,[43] few took so comprehensive a view.

The question of the Church Army and the proposed rules for its operation came before the Sydney clergy at a retreat on 18 December 1885. It was hardly a topic conducive to meditation, with the Army's defenders and opponents divided mostly on party lines. But no decision was reached until early January 1886, when the city clergy agreed to form a Church of England Missionary Society, having rejected the Church Army as a way of reaching the poorer classes of the city.[44] Not all Evangelicals, it seems, were convinced of its propriety and the experiment at Ultimo, perhaps lacking stable leadership, had not gone well; by the end of 1885, apparently, it had folded up.

Barry admitted his disappointment at the next synod that the diocese had not adopted the Church Army. He confessed that he was not ashamed to acknowledge that the Church of England could learn some lessons from the Salvation Army and at the same time improve on it with the "sounder doctrine and more varied organisation" of Anglicanism. He pleaded for a flexible approach to the task of reaching the working classes. As far as he was concerned, parishes were still free to adopt the Church Army in name or method, but none did. At least the clergy had agreed to an agency to carry out the mission to the poorer classes and at the 1886 synod Barry reported that lay agencies were operating in several city parishes; these were St Peter's, Woolloomooloo, St Bartholomew's, Pyrmont and Christ

Church, St Laurence, and a beginning had been made at the cathedral and St Stephen's, Newtown. Barry had also licensed Thomas Wales of the Evangelisation Society in England to do special work in the Pyrmont and Ultimo area, where the Church Army had failed. Nearby at Darling Harbour C.F. Garnsey, a strong opponent of the Church Army, had in 1884 opened a mission room to carry out practical and evangelizing work among the poor and neglected in the slums of his parish. It lasted about eleven years, providing a variety of clubs and social activities as well as religious services.[45] Even if the Anglican Church had not adopted the Church Army, the challenge of the Salvation Army had stimulated new endeavours in its attempts to reach the urban poor. There was also an unsuccessful attempt to establish the Church Army in Victoria in 1904. Not until 1934 was it permanently introduced in Australia, and then only on a small scale.[46]

The Central Methodist Mission

The Methodists, prompted by the plight of their central church, also tried new ways of reaching the poorer people of the city. Old York Street, as the Centenary Wesleyan Chapel was best known, was built as a monument to Methodism in Australia, commemorating the centenary of John Wesley's ordination to the ministry in 1839. A dignified building of classical proportions, it was opened in 1844 and for some thirty years it accommodated a respectable congregation of middle-class Methodists. The morning service there was quite formal by colonial standards; it was the only Methodist church in New South Wales to use Wesley's abbreviation of the Anglican service, the *Book of Offices*. By 1880, with the exodus to the suburbs, "it was left high and dry upon the sands of desolation with its banner, still waving, bearing the word *Ichabod*" — that is, its glory had departed.[47.]

Methodists debated what was to be done with York Street at their conferences in the early 1880s, especially in January 1882. Some suggested that it should be sold and the proceeds used to build new churches in the suburbs and mission rooms in the city. Others argued for the appointment of a popular preacher who might compete with the freethought lecturers, or an earnest evangelical preacher who might convert the poor. But the conference adopted the proposal to appoint a second minister to York Street specifically for "home mission work . . . among the large masses not reached by . . . ordinary means", hoping in this way to fill the empty pews with the kind of people the church had previously overlooked. For a

year the younger second minister, C.W. Graham, worked among the poorer classes of the city to bring them into the church, and with some success. All the seating in the church was made free for the less formal Sunday evening service at which there was plenty of hearty singing. The evening congregations increased, but the regular morning congregations, which provided most of the church's income, continued to decline, so much so that it was reported at the next annual conference that the church could no longer afford two married ministers.[48]

In 1883 the conference decided to try another suggestion and appointed John Osborne, one of the younger colonial-born ministers, with a probationer to assist him. Popular in style and liberal in outlook, Osborne aimed to attract artisans rather than the poorer people among whom Graham had worked. He launched a series of Sunday evening lectures for working men, thus competing with the freethought lecturers, who spoke to audiences composed mainly of artisans in the theatres on Sunday nights. The music at Osborne's services was more refined than hearty. Like Jefferis, he dealt with social and political topics as well as religious themes, but he was mostly concerned to justify Christianity to sceptics. His liberal approach to theological questions attracted a following, but it also aroused suspicion of his orthodoxy among the fathers of his denomination. However it was to be his fulsome flattery of Dr Vaughan, the Roman Catholic Archbishop, which brought him to trial. Acquitted of departure from Methodist standards but cautioned, Osborne forestalled any further action against him by resigning from the Methodist ministry to take up journalism and also to lecture on the Free Christian Platform. Most of those he had attracted to York Street, including the organist and choirmaster, left with him. A former opponent of the freethought lecturers, he turned his guns on orthodox Christianity, and within two years announced himself a secularist.

When the next conference met, York Street was once again without a minister and with a depleted congregation. Again there were proposals to sell the place, but this brought a strong protest from a veteran of the conference, George Hurst, who appealed for the appointment of an evangelist "of the old school". William George Taylor, born in Yorkshire and three years younger than Osborne, was nominated. "Converted" at twelve years and unspoiled by his college training, Taylor began his ministry in Australia in 1871. Around the time of the 1884 conference he had been conducting an evangelistic campaign in Glebe. His nomination for York Street surprised him, and although he produced medical advice against his accepting the appointment, the conference was set on him. It gave him a "free hand to do what 'grace, grit or gumption' might suggest". "Let him kick down the old pulpit — anything to make the place go", exclaimed an ex-president of the conference.[49]

Like General Booth, Taylor believed in militant evangelism. To attract a congregation to York Street he and his assistant, F.C. Boyer, went out with his custom-built "gospel chariot", equipped with a small organ, to conduct an open-air service on the Town Hall corner. Some Wesleyan ministers thought his methods vulgar and sensational and criticized them strongly at monthly preachers' meetings. He also had to contend with a great deal of heckling from the followers of the freethought lecturers. On one occasion, Taylor recalled in his autobiography, "a drunken sundowner in the crowd staggered to the front to champion our cause" and a fight broke out between this spirited advocate and a secularist opponent. Unable to preach with the scuffle going on before him, Taylor broke into a hymn which attracted a much larger crowd.[50] By this street preaching Taylor drew increasing numbers to Old York Street which he had renamed the Central Methodist Mission. It was to take five years for the conference to accept the name and the concept behind it, although Taylor's idea of the mission was to change in that time too.

Taylor's success created its own problems. In twelve months he had filled the building to overflowing and the next annual conference had to consider not the sale but the demolition of Old York Street to make way for a larger, more suitable building. Developments in British Methodism helped to direct colonial Wesleyans in this direction. In 1885 the British Wesleyan Conference espoused the idea of a central mission put forward by Hugh Price Hughes, leader of the Forward Movement. Missions were established in East and Central London and in Manchester, and in 1887 Hughes became superintendent of the West London Mission. In Manchester the old Wesleyan chapel was demolished in 1883 and replaced by the Central Hall, opened in 1887, and in Piccadilly, London, Hughes built St James's Hall. These halls dispensed with traditional church furnishing such as pews and the high pulpit. The services conducted in them were simple, with bright music to attract the working classes; social and educational entertainments were also held there on weeknights. Not without some difficulty, Hughes had persuaded the conference to free the superintendents of these missions from the itinerancy rule, which required Methodist ministers to move every two or three years, and from responsibility to circuit and synod.[51]

In New South Wales the conference, rejecting any proposals for alterations to York Street, decided instead in 1886 to demolish the

The Centenary Hall, York Street, headquarters of the Central Methodist Mission. (From *The Methodist Jubilee Conference Album, 1855-1905* [Sydney: Mark Blow (The Crown Studies), 1905]. Photo courtesy of La Trobe University Library, Melbourne.)

William George Taylor. (
*The Illustrated History of M
dism* by J. Colwell [Sy
William Brooks and Co., 1!
Photo courtesy of La Trobe
versity Library, Melbourne.)

Centenary Hall decorated for a Harvest Festival. (From *The Methodist Jubilee Conferen
Album, 1855-1905* [Sydney: Mark Blow (The Crown Studies), 1905]. Photo courtesy of L
Trobe University Library, Melbourne.)

building and replace it with a hall and denominational offices. The moving "farewell service" before demolition commenced was held on Monday 15 November 1886. While building was under way a remnant of the great congregation met in a temporary room holding 200 people, under the care of J.A. Bowring, the erstwhile conference evangelist. The Centenary Hall, built at a cost of £30,000 to accommodate 1,750 people was dedicated on Friday 19 October 1888.[52] But its status was still in doubt. Was it a circuit church or a "mission"?

The conference had deferred this question in 1886, although Taylor continued to call York Street the Central Methodist Mission. But after the closure of the old building the conference had sent Taylor to England to restore his health and to enable him to study the Forward Movement there at first hand. He visited both the Central Mission in Manchester and Hughes's West End Mission in London and both greatly impressed him.[53] But he had to wait before he could begin to apply his lessons because on his return he found himself appointed to William Street, Woolloomooloo; and in 1888 the conference was still debating the question of mission or circuit.

Some opposition came from the more conservative Methodists who believed that no changes in techniques or organization were needed; all that was required was the earnest, spiritual soul-saving preaching of old-fashioned Methodism. There were some also who regarded the circuit and itinerancy as essential to Methodism. During the debate on York Street in 1888 George Brown, general secretary of Foreign Missions and a former missionary, criticized the whole idea of a mission to the working classes in the area because there were also men of culture in the vicinity; they wanted good preaching and something better than Sankey's hymns and brass bands. A layman retored that "the souls of men in fustian" were as valuable as those of the rich. Carruthers, maintaining with some grounds that the conference was in fact committed to the idea of a mission, attempted to pacify both sides by pointing out that if they followed Hughes's pattern in London they could cater for the cultured in the morning, for working men in the afternoon, and have evangelistic services with brass bands at night.[54] But this conference rose with the status of the Centenary Hall still in doubt.

Support for the idea of a special mission was growing and the *Weekly Advocate* encouraged the idea. While it thought that most in the working classes were outside the churches because of dissolute living, it conceded that there were some victims of "honest poverty" who could hardly be expected to leave the slums and "flock to fine churches in respectable neighbourhoods". For them, it argued, "we must open cheap and comfortable halls in the poorest neighbourhoods" and "go down to them and endeavour to brighten their lives with innocent and instructive recreation", and with charitable relief as well as preaching the gospel "in its most elementary forms".[55]

By January 1889 the majority was apparently persuaded of the need for a different approach to the working classes; the conference finally recognized York Street as the Sydney Central Mission and exempted it from circuit and itinerancy rules. Taylor was appointed superintendent of the mission, which was also to include Princes Street church, but the Centenary Hall, built like the English mission halls in a deliberately non-ecclesiastical style, was the centre of operations. Yet the conference did not intend it to become exclusively a working-class "church". The morning services were to follow, as much as they could in such a setting, the traditional pattern, to attract the more cultured and better educated. To this end the conference in 1889 designated two of Methodism's most distinguished ministers, Principal J.H. Fletcher and Dr William Kelynack, a gifted orator, as the morning preachers. The next year Charles Prescott, principal of the Wesleyan Ladies' College, was appointed another morning preacher, in place of Fletcher who had since died.[56]

Evangelism remained foremost among Taylor's aims; and now he had the opportunity to apply the lessons learned in England in 1887. He soon established a Seaman's Mission and, with the support of a wealthy Methodist philanthropist, Ebenezer Vickery, an Evangelists' Training Institute. This institute sent teams of young men to visit homes in the slums and hospitals, to go out among wharf labourers and cabmen and to hold meetings in factories. At night these young men took part in outdoor evangelism in the city or in meetings at the mission. Taylor also introduced the Sisters of the People, modelled on Hughes's sisterhood in London (and nothing like the sisterhoods of Rome, the *Weekly Advocate* assured its readers). These women were dedicated to a ministry of comfort and redemption among the poor and degraded in the city's slums.[57]

Much of this programme was an extension of the kind of work done by other missions and interdenominational agencies among the depressed classes of the city, although with better organization and more resources. It was hoped that the mission's less conventional style of worship in the Centenary Hall on Sunday nights would attract working-class folk. In addition, early in the 1890s Taylor introduced to Australia the "Pleasant Sunday Afternoon", an institution developed by English Nonconformists in an attempt to reach the more thoughtful working men. The Pleasant Sunday Afternoon combined musical entertainment with an address on religious and social topics. It was to develop into a platform for the airing of Christian social concern, particularly under Taylor's successor, W. Woolls Rutledge.[58]

Taylor had both coined the name and initiated the idea of a central mission for Sydney. But the programme it offered after its official inception in 1889 owed much to the influence upon Taylor of Hugh Price Hughes. From his visit to England in 1887 Taylor had come to see that evangelism alone was not enough, and so during the 1890s the Central Mission developed social and philanthropic agencies alongside its evangelistic programme. It established a Literary and Debating Society, a free reading room, and ran a Boys Institute and a Girls Brigade as well as a gymnasium and several other clubs for social and physical recreation. "Whether wisely or unwisely," wrote Taylor in his autobiography, "this Mission has sought to provide healthy entertainment for non-churchgoing people, and with the best results."[59]

Taylor set the pattern for Australian Methodism. In Victoria the Wesleyans began to look seriously at the problems of reaching the city population in 1887. But Victoria did not follow New South Wales directly. In 1891 a Victorian minister, A.R. Edgar, also visited Hugh Price Hughes in London and the next year the Victorian and Tasmanian Conference made Wesley Church the Central Methodist Mission. Yet Melbourne did not follow Sydney's example by demolishing its "cathedral church" to replace it with a hall, as some had proposed. In 1901 Methodists in Adelaide established a central mission and similar institutions were set up in other capitals as well as in some large towns.[60]

Other denominations were also influenced by this new trend. The Primitive Methodists, following the example of their denomination in England rather than of Wesleyans in Australia, set up a mission under an evangelist in Glebe in 1888. The Burton Street Baptist Tabernacle became the Central Evangelistic Mission in 1889. Its minister, A.J. Clarke, continued to conduct conventional morning services in the Tabernacle in the morning, but on Sunday afternoons he attempted to reach outsiders on the Domain; at night he held a less conventional service in the New Masonic Hall.[61]

Taylor's example seems to have impressed Dr Jefferis, who sought unsuccessfully to persuade his church to sell the Pitt Street property and use the proceeds to build a new church in the suburbs, where his congregation came from anyway, and also a "Memorial Hall" both for denominational meetings and as a central mission for work among the poorer city population. The church was apparently satisfied with its existing mission work and hopeful that with improved transport people would continue to come in from the suburbs.[62]

Overall, the churches made strenuous efforts to reach the working classes in the city. But their missions were no more than dikes against a sea of indifference — they did not turn the tide. Taylor's Central Methodist Mission gave the Wesleyan's city cause a new lease of life and provided a model for the institutional church, catering for social and recreational activity as well as religious needs. Undoubtedly the Central Methodist Mission and others touched some of the working-class people living in the inner city, probably more women and children than men. There was a tendency for lower middle-class folk used to churchgoing to support these innovations. They appreciated the brighter, informal services more than the "aesthetic improvements" introduced into most suburban churches during the 1880s. Some of them were attracted to the Salvation Army as well. Both Jefferis, during his visit to Bristol in 1881, and a Presbyterian observer in Sydney in 1883 claimed that respectably dressed "church people" predominated at the Salvation Army meetings. Richard Sellors, a Wesleyan minister, disturbed that Methodists were attending the Army meetings warned that intelligent members of the working classes would be revolted by these "caricatures" of Christianity. Bishop Barry had also recognized that a different approach would be needed with thoughtful working men who had difficulties with the Christian faith.[6] The Pleasant Sunday Afternoon was intended to cater for them, but it seems that the audiences were largely middle class.[64] That many working men who had difficulties with the Christian faith.[63] That many working men were attending the theatres on Sunday nights during the 1880s to listen to freethought lecturers refute religious belief did not disturb Taylor; he held that converted and regenerated lives were "Christianity's unanswerable argument".[65] Others thought they had to try and show the reasonableness of Christianity, and its relevance to the social questions which concerned intelligent working men.

Part Two

Christianity and Contemporary Intellectual and Social Questions

5

Defending the Faith

Christianity came under open attack in Australia from around 1870, particularly in Melbourne, but the campaign against religious belief was at its height in the 1880s, both in Melbourne and Sydney. The attack came from freethinkers, spiritualists and secularists; one of the leading freethought lecturers in Sydney, Thomas Walker, who began as a spiritualist trance lecturer, became a strict secularist in 1882.[1] These opponents of Christianity focused mainly on the alleged incompatibility between science and religion; they relied heavily on popular interpretations of the findings of geology and, more especially, of Darwin's theory of evolution. In reply to a lecture by Archbishop Vaughan in 1879 repudiating the theory of evolution, the prominent freethought lecturer, Charles Bright (not the Baptist minister of the same name), warned that theology would suffer if it opposed the facts of science; but "religion" would not suffer "for all that is vital and not idolatrous in it necessarily conforms itself to Science".[2] The case was not always stated as reasonably as that, as may be gathered from an advertisement in 1886 for a lecture by an American freethinker, "Dr York".

Saved, saved, saved, from hell and the Devil, by Dr York.
Are you saved? If not attend Dr York's lecture.
Glory be to science.[3]

Most of the antagonists of orthodox Christianity came from an evangelical Protestant background: some had been Sunday school teachers and lay preachers, like Thomas Walker, or even ordained ministers, as were Joseph Symes, the leading Victorian secularist, and John Tyerman, who was active in both Victoria and New South Wales. They were offended by the apparent immorality of the Old Testament as well as inconsistencies in the Bible. They also revolted against the harsh penal substitutionary theory of the Atonement — that is, that Christ had suffered by divine decree, the punishment for the sin of all mankind, and against the doctrine of eternal punishment — that is, that the souls of the unredeemed would endure endless torment in hell. Annie Bright, wife of Charles Bright, gave a personal testimony of the fear of hell at her husband's meeting on Sunday 21 October 1883, when Margaret Hampson was preaching in Sydney. Mrs Bright, who had been a Sunday school teacher, recalled that as a child she used to lie awake "shuddering with fear, lest that night the dreadful Christ should come and cast into the fire all who were not saved". Anxious for her mother's salvation as well as her own, she resolved that she would rather go to hell with her than be separated from her. She went through "another prolonged crisis of mental agony" in adolescence, sparked off by an evangelical preacher, before she finally "got rid of the terrors of religion" at the age of eighteen. No longer believing in any book that told of "endless fire", Mrs Bright became a Unitarian, and then a formidable spiritualist and feminist.[4]

It was rare for the daily press to report anything that was said at a freethought lecture and the space given to Mrs Bright's simple, straightforward and moving story was most unusual. But the newspapers did print advertisements for freethought lectures. Each lecturer promised a variety of musical entertainment as well as an interesting address usually under sensational titles. "Horses and Monkeys, and their Influence on Religion", and "Heaven and Hell; or, A Night with the Devil" were two of Thomas Walker's titles in October 1883. Charles Bright's so-called Sunday Lectures for Rationalists in the Gaiety Theatre offered "Lord's Days and Man's Days; or, the Art of Superstition", and " 'Pious Larrikinism', and What It Portends", and during Mrs Hampson's mission, "Christian Missions and Omissions; or, Revivals and Survivals". At the Theatre Royal a certain Dr H.P.W. Hughes conducted the Freethought Platform, from which he lectured on "The Biblical Fable of Creation; or, Science versus Moses"; "Christianity, Insanity and Humanity"; "Bible Pap for Bible Sucklings"; or, more alarmingly, this: "The Genuine Gospel of Jesus Christ is not delivered in any Christian Church. There is not a true Christian in Christendom."[5]

The daily press preferred to report Sunday sermons rather than offend its readers with summaries of the secularist attacks on Christianity. The professed freethinker was something of a pariah in late nineteenth century colonial society, but Mrs Bright affirmed that there was "no social prize" that she would exchange for her "position as an emancipated believer". Even the Sydney *Bulletin* found the freethinkers too much in 1880. "The persistent vituperation of every revered tradition sanctified by the growth of ages, the ruthless violation of every hallowed sentiment, and the vulgar blasphemy of every sacred doctrine" formed the precepts of the colonial freethinker's gospel. The freethinker, professing "a lofty contempt for those who differ from him", displayed "all the rancour and prejudice of bigotry in its most repulsive form". Always seeking notoriety, he obtruded "his crude opinions on one's notice, irrespective of time or place".[6] The *Sydney Morning Herald* could hardly have put it more strongly, although the *Bulletin* later showed more sympathy with the secularists.

Needless to say, "respectable" people were not often among the crowds who heard the freethought lectures. The majority of the audiences were working men who found the ridicule of orthodox religion amusing if not instructive. But churchmen were not amused at what they heard of the freethought lectures. They disturbed Archbishop Vaughan; in his lecture, "Hidden Springs" in 1876 he sounded the alarm against that materialism which he luridly portrayed as bent on "Deicide" and the extirpation of all religion, even "to the most scantily clad Deism". In 1881 he warned that freethought lecturers in Sydney and other large cities were "striking at the very heart of Christianity".[7] It was partly his purpose to persuade the population, Catholics in particular, of the importance of religion in education. Protestants were also alarmed at this "systematic propagandism" of the secularists. In a pastoral report in 1880 Jefferis asserted that the freethinkers were maintaining principles akin to those which flourished in Paris during the French Revolution.[8] Both Jefferis and Vaughan saw freethought and secularism as a threat to society, as well as to religion.

In face of the freethought attack, Archbishop Vaughan took it on himself to defend Christianity. As well as warning against "infidelity" in Pastoral Letters, he attempted to refute the case against religious belief in various Lenten lectures. His series of "Arguments for Christianity", delivered in 1879, were prompted, he acknowledged, "by the painful fact that infidelity is making its power felt in Australia, and especially in the great towns like Sydney". This course of lectures was concerned with "the shallowness of infidelity on the one hand, and the reasonableness of Christianity on the other". Vaughan was one of the more learned clerics in Australia and he had been acclaimed for his two-volume work on Thomas Aquinas. Although not an original thinker, he was an eloquent lecturer who attracted Protestants as well as Catholics. In his "Arguments" he maintained that religion and science were not in conflict. Modern science, he claimed, pointed steadily to the teachings of religion. But he made no concessions to Darwin. He dismissed evolution and the alleged descent of man from the animal kingdom as unproved and untenable. He used the traditional philosophical arguments for the existence of God, but also appealed to the universality of religious belief, as attested by recent studies of primitive religion, as a proof of its validity. Unbelief, he warned, led to intellectual imbecility, moral depravity and spiritual death. In 1882 the Archbishop defended the divinity of Christ against John

Roger William Bede Vaughan, Second Catholic Archbishop of Sydney (1877-83). Taken in Sydney probably around 1877 when he succeeded to the Archbishopric. (Photo courtesy of St Mary's Cathedral Archives.)

Stuart Mill's humanist view of Jesus as supreme moral teacher. In this instance, he rested his case on the argument from prophecy and miracles, especially the great miracle of the Resurrection. Accept that as fact, Vaughan argued, and you could then accept all other miracles and dogmas, including the Ascension and Immaculate Conception, without difficulty.[9]

That was probably going too far for most of the Protestants who heard Vaughan, but they were prepared to overlook his more Catholic arguments for the sake of his general defence of Christianity. After his death in 1883, there was a surprising tribute to Vaughan as an apologist in the *Protestant Standard,* for the editor of the journal was Dr Zachary Barry, an Irish Protestant and inveterate opponent of Rome. Something of an apologist himself, Barry praised Vaughan's lectures to undergraduates at the University of Sydney and conceded that his recent Lenten lectures had been "for the most part thoroughly scriptural and evangelical". But the free-thinkers regarded Vaughan as thoroughly obscurantist. Charles Bright had remarked of him on one occasion that "the Evolutionists seem to be as terrible to him as the Copernicans were to his predecessors some three centuries ago."[10]

There were various responses to the challenge of the freethinkers among Protestants. Some seemed to regard the threat complacently. For Bishop Barker church extension was the principal means of resisting the spread of infidelity in society. But when he mentioned the matter to the Sydney synod in 1880, he also asked his clergy to deal with the difficulties the Scriptures presented to thoughtful, enquiring minds, recommending the publications of the British Christian Evidence Society.[11] Others saw evangelism as the best weapon against secularism and so encouraged special missions. Most of the visiting evangelists could be depended on to denounce free-thought and defend the Bible against its detractors, although they were obscurantist in their attitudes towards modern science and biblical criticism.

There were only a few churchmen early in the 1880s who thought that Christianity should be publicly defended against the calumnies of the freethinkers. One of these, the Reverend Hans Mack, unsuccessfully proposed in 1882 that the Wesleyan Conference should establish a lectureship to set forth "the claims of natural and revealed religion against the various forms of infidelity". The best way of counteracting "vaunting scepticism", according to another minister, was with "sermons full of old Methodist doctrine, full of the spirit of Christ, and imbued with the power of the Holy Ghost".[12] Similarly, the *Presbyterian* told ministers in 1884 to leave apologetics alone. The simplest, most effective method of dealing with sceptics, it advised, was to live and teach Christianity by the example of the Bible; but two years earlier it had argued that ministers should be sufficiently versed in apologetics to show that "Christianity is no bubble, and the Bible no fable". Even then it was reluctant to see Presbyterian ministers debating publicly on religion, and advised them not to reply to the assertions of James Greenwood, a former Baptist minister turned secularist. Greenwood had taunted that "not a clergyman in Sydney . . . implicitly believes in the dogmas . . . he teaches".[13]

Dr Zachary Barry was one of the first to take up a public defence of religion in Sydney. In August 1876 he delivered a series of sermons on "Christian Free-Thought" on Sunday afternoons in the Victoria Theatre. Barry dealt with many of the objections raised by freethinkers, particularly the apparent inconsistency between science and the Bible, but he did not give much more ground to science than Bishop Perry of Melbourne had done in his celebrated lecture on the subject in 1869. Both Perry and Barry dismissed the theory of evolution, as also did most colonial scientists at the time. The age of the earth did not trouble Barry, for clerical geologists had earlier harmonized the account of creation in Genesis with the findings of geology by interpreting the days of the first chapter of Genesis as periods of indeterminable length.[14] This was a superficial solution, for Genesis placed the appearance of the sun on the fourth day, after the creation of night and day and of vegetation, not to mention the two different stories of creation with their irreconcilable ordering of events.

But few noticed these problems in 1876 or 1880. The veteran Wesleyan minister, W.B. Boyce, adopted this harmonizing of Genesis and geology in his lectures on higher criticism of the Bible in 1878. Boyce also had less to say against the theory of evolution than against the sceptical theories of the inspiration and compilation of the biblical writings emanating from the University of Tübingen in Germany.[15] This harmonizing of Genesis and geology did more than resolve for Christians the apparent contradiction between religion and science. It also substantiated the divine inspiration of the Bible, as Canon Scott pointed out in a paper read to a clerical conference at Goulburn in October 1881. The Bible, he observed, told of stages of development without the aid of modern science.[16] It was the same with modern astronomy, although the study of it had led the popular lecturer on astronomy, R.A. Proctor, to abandon his vocation to enter the Anglican ministry. Proctor's visit to Sydney in September 1880 gave James Jefferis the opportunity to lecture on "The Highest Teachings of Astronomy". These teachings provided, he claimed, "stupendous proofs of design", thus reinforcing the argument of Archdeacon Paley's *Natural Theology,* that is, that nature in its intricate design and function testified to an intelligent Creator.[17] This became the standard defence for belief in the existence of God in nineteenth century Christian apologetics.

Almost every churchman in the early 1880s maintained that there was no conflict between religion and science, and Mr Justice Higinbotham said much the same in a controversial lecture on the topic in August 1883. But Higinbotham meant the simple but sublime religion of Jesus rather than the orthodox teaching of the churches.[18] Most churchmen had conceded very little to science, especially on the theory of evolution. The *Weekly Advocate* spoke for many when it declared in 1882, on the occasion of Darwin's death, that his theory was "essentially atheistic" and "a deadly foe to revealed religion". But informed laymen were beginning to take a different view, as articles in the *Sydney University Review* and the *Victorian Review* in 1882 indicated. Ultimately, ministers also came to see that they defended Christianity better by accepting the theory of evolution than by resisting it. In October that year the Chairman of the Congregational Union, the Reverend J.F. Cullen, pointed his denomination in this direction in his address to the annual assembly. "That evolution is the great law and method of creation", Cullen protected, "may surely be believed without violating the indispensable idea of a Creator." After all Darwin himself had admitted "a First Cause". At the same time, Cullen warned against hasty conclusions, for or against evolution.[19]

A more accommodating attitude towards modern science was also evident in some of the lectures given under the auspices of the YMCA in the early 1880s. Apologetic subjects were prominent in the winter lectures the association organized. They did not attract large audiences, although distinguished laymen as well as clergymen were among their lecturers. Some of them, such as Alexander Gordon, an evangelical Anglican, a lawyer and a Member of the Legislative Council, offered traditional defences of Christianity. In August 1880 Gordon lectured on "Freedom of Thought", but was more concerned to limit than to extend that freedom.[20] A more positive attitude was apparent in Dr (later Sir Arthur) Renwick's lecture on "The Realm of Knowledge and the Realm of Faith" in July 1882.

Dr Renwick was a physician, and in religion a Congregationalist. He was also a Member of Parliament and secretary for Mines and was prominent in the affairs of charitable institutions. Well acquainted with the discoveries and speculations of science in the nineteenth century, this layman did not repudiate scientific progress. But he pointed out that there was still much unknown to

Sir Arthur Renwick, physician, politi
and lay apologist. Presumably take
Sydney around 1900. (Photo courtes
Mitchell Library, Sydney.)

Josiah Mullens, Chairman of the Syd
Stock Exchange, amateur archaeolo
and lay theologian. Taken in Syd
probably around 1890, when he reti
(From *100 Years ago and now. Mu*
and Company 1860-1960 provided
Mr. F.H. Mullens.)

science. Its teachings had to "be made more perfect before its limits and full meaning [could] be truly realised". Thus, like Cullen, he cautioned those who would draw hasty conclusions about inconsistency between religion and science. As far as evolution was concerned, he observed that Darwin had allowed that unknown causes were at work. Ultimate and satisfying knowledge came not from reason or the discoveries of science, but from faith. Belief was "the primary condition of reason", he said — not Abelard's "know that you may believe" but Anselm's "believe that you may know". "Amid the unrest of intellectual inquiry, and the dimly comprehended conceptions of science", faith in Christ brought "the anxious soul. . . a peace which the world can neither give nor take away".[21]

Another layman who lectured for the YMCA was Josiah Mullens, chairman of the Sydney Stock Exchange (1874-89). Also a Congregationalist, Mullens was cultured and learned, especially in Egyptology, archaeology and the Bible.[22] In a lecture delivered in July 1884 he offered a modified view of the inspiration and authority of the Bible; it was not to be worshipped as a fetish. Scientific chronology was not to be found in the early chapters of Genesis, but the Bible had nothing to fear from science; Egyptologists and Assyriologists had confirmed the accuracy of biblical history. Cruder notions of God and morality did not trouble him, for he pointed to the "true evolution" in the understanding of God in the Old Testament. Mullens's more liberal interpretation probably went further than many would have liked in 1884. Similar views of his in 1881 provoked the *Presbyterian* to say that, as Mullens did not accept all the inferences that scientists drew, he should not mind if the journal did not accept his hypothesis of pre-Adamite man.[23] But few would have objected to his appeal to archaeology, for it was to become an important feature of the conservative defence of the Bible.

As well as these lectures by thoughtful and informed laymen, the YMCA and a committee of churchmen sponsored the visit to Sydney of Joseph Cook, an American apologist. A Boston Congregationalist descended from one of the Pilgrim Fathers, Cook had been educated at Yale, Harvard, Andover Theological Seminary and then at German universities. After touring Europe and Palestine he returned to Boston where he earned fame from his Monday lectures, in which he sought to reconcile science with revealed religion. Staunchly evangelical in his theology, he was, according to the *Presbyterian,* "a profound theologian and a thorough scientist". There was great exaggeration in both these epithets, but Cook impressed his audiences with his claim to knowledge in both fields, and he had the gift of assuring Christians that they had nothing to fear from modern science.[24]

Cook's fame had gone before him, and people stampeded for seats at his first lecture in the Protestant Hall in 11 July 1882. Leading churchmen and many politicians were there in the packed audience, with W.J. Foster, one of Sydney's leading evangelical laymen, presiding. The crowd cheered as Foster welcomed Cook — "a champion of revealed religion ... a staunch friend of science and philosophy ... and of freedom of thought" and, above all, "a pronounced indefatigable exposer and demolisher of infidelity". Cook stood to speak amid a storm of applause. At his first lecture he proceeded to demonstrate belief in immortality by appeals to conscience, physiology and revelation. He corrected a popular "misconception" about Darwin, by pointing out that "the great naturalist" had "always asserted that the first living matter was supernaturally created". Cook may have helped Christians to come to terms with modern science, yet his theology remained conservative, especially on those points on which freethinkers attacked Christianity. In subsequent lectures he defended the substitutionary theory of the Atonement and the doctrine of eternal punishment; in "The Failures of Unbelief" he claimed triumphantly that in America and Germany orthodox Christianity was gaining the victory over rationalism and infidelity. These lectures proved so popular that Cook was invited to give a second series the following week in Pitt Street Congregational Church, which could accommodate a larger audience. These later lectures were directed more specifically at spiritualists and freethinkers, although in his last public lecture, at which the colonial treasurer, James Watson, presided, Cook ventured into political economy, expounding the gospel of Free Trade. Incidentally, like most visiting evangelists, Cook also gave a lecture to men only in the Theatre Royal on Sunday 23 July, at which he prescribed "remedies for besetting sins".[25]

A small number of Protestant churchmen would have found Cook's theology too narrow for them. He moved on about the same intellectual plane as the more prominent freethought lecturers, such as Charles Bright and Thomas Walker. But he was not willing to debate with them publicly. He refused a challenge from Walker in Melbourne, ostensibly because freethinkers were connected with schemes for immorality (such as the promotion of birth control). The assumption that unbelief and immorality went together was common enough, but the New South Wales *Presbyterian* thought Cook was offensive to the moral freethinkers of Australia.[26] Few Protestant churchmen, however, were willing to face the freethinkers in open debate. One exception was E.C. Spicer, a young Anglican clergyman.

In 1883 Spicer published a lecture entitled "The Harmony between Geology and Genesis'', in reply to another lecturer's attack on the Bible.[27] This provoked Charles Bright to challenge Spicer to public debate on the question: ''Are the Statements of Science and Genesis Contradictory?'' The debate took place during 22-23 May 1883 under the chairmanship of the politician, George Reid. Bright dwelt mainly on the two accounts of creation in Genesis with their inconsistent ordering of events, but also raised other problems such as the Hebrew cosmology of Genesis, the longevity of Methuselah and the old chestnut of Cain's wife. Spicer began his defence with the usual interpretation of the days of Genesis as an age and asserted the harmony of the account with geological findings. He did not tackle the question of the two accounts, but Bright would not let it rest, insisting that the Bible should be taken literally and that days meant days of twenty-four hours. Spicer would not be bound to a literal reading of the King James Version (the Revised Version of the Old Testament had not then been published). He appealed to the Hebrew text and took the two stories to be different accounts, one a general account of the creation and the other of the covenant relationship between God (under the name Jehovah) and man. This was a neat evasion of the problem. But, while he sought to solve the problem of Cain's wife by reading ''Adam'' as the name of a clan or dynasty, he was no match for Bright. The audience was hostile to him and as the debate wore on he retreated into a somewhat obscurantist position, imputing immorality to the famous English secularist, Charles Bradlaugh. Affirming the infallibility of the Bible, he declared that scientists were not competent to pronounce on theology, which was itself another science. Nevertheless, he thought it worth quoting that 617 scientists had asserted that there was no contradiction between the Bible and science.[28]

No one thought Spicer had fared well. The *Protestant Standard* admired his zeal, but not his reasoning; the *Presbyterian* dismissed him as ''an intellectual stripling'' whose defence was of ''a hither and thither nature''; and the *Weekly Advocate* thought him no match for the polished and experienced Bright.[29] Bishop Pearson of Newcastle defended Spicer on one point only: his use of texts other than the Authorized Version of the Bible. Otherwise he thought Spicer's defence quite inappropriate, as he made clear in the ''Letters for Sunday'' series in the *Echo* in June 1883.

What had begun as a debate between a clergyman and a freethinker became a newspaper controversy between the conservative cleric and a liberal bishop. A Broad Churchman, Pearson's attitude was evident in a paper he read to the Melbourne Church Congress in 1882. On this occasion he had warned against regarding doubt as a product of immorality and exhorted Anglicans to recognize the difficulties in the way of belief, and not to increase them by multiplying "*credenda*". At the same time, he welcomed modern science's testimony to an ordered creation.[30] But he had no sympathy with forced attempts to harmonize the Genesis story with science. "The exposition of the word 'days' is no part of my creed", he wrote in his first letter. In the second letter Pearson claimed that if Christians adopted the attitude to the Bible which he advocated, "many of the arrows from 'Freethought's' quiver would fly quite harmlessly over our heads". He conceded that the writers of the Old and New Testaments might have cherished unscientific notions of nature and matter, and were also unaware of lands beyond their own circumscribed world, especially of the continent of Australia. On this point, Pearson imagined the freethinker protesting that it was folly to believe that there could be any inspiration in men so ignorant or mistaken, while some pious Christians would try with ingenuity to prove that the biblical writers were not so unscientific after all. He was content to leave these extremists to their own arguments, confident that whatever the salvation of his soul depended on, it did "not depend on David's acquaintance with the mysteries of the union of oxygen and hydrogen". In conclusion, he questioned whether men had the right to seek for any knowledge in the Bible "but that of a practical and spiritual character".[31]

In his third letter Pearson took issue with Spicer on the use of the "Word of God" as applied to the Bible. "That title of Divine honour" should more accurately be applied "to Christ himself, as being in speech and deed, in life and death and resurrection, the very utterance of the Father's mind and will to man". Scripture testified to this, but Pearson also pointed out that there was the historical "witness of the visible Church to her Lord . . . Every place of Christian worship [was] an evidence of Christianity". If Protestants could learn that, they would be able to counter many of the objections to the Bible without need of "recourse to a theory of its absolute infallibility on all subjects which are named in it".[32]

Not many churchmen took the same relaxed attitude to the controversy between science and the Scriptures as Bishop Pearson, although Bishop Moorhouse in Melbourne held just as liberal a view of the Bible.[33] Churchmen in Sydney appeared more nervous about the challenge to religion. After the Bright-Spicer debate the *Weekly Advocate* declared that the revolt against the Bible had reached such proportions in Sydney that the churches should bestir themselves to defend the truth.[34] An association for the defence of Christianity had already been formed.

Organizing to Defend the Faith

In January 1883 an enthusiastic lay apologist, H.G. Picton, took steps which led to the formation of the New South Wales Association for the Defence of Christianity on 9 April 1883. The founding members were mainly evangelical laymen, with some ministers of the various denominations but not their leaders. The doctrinal basis of the association was evangelical — "the divine inspiration and supreme authority of the Holy Scriptures" and "the divinity and all-sufficient atonement of the Lord Jesus Christ". It aimed to combat the antagonists of Christianity by lectures, discussions and the dissemination of anti-secularist literature.[35] The *Presbyterian* gave it no encouragement. The YMCA lectures, it observed, delivered by "the ablest minds", had attracted but small attendances and, in any case, it thought that ministers would be better employed attending to "their proper duties" than engaging publicly in apologetics. After all, it concluded, "sceptics are more at fault in their hearts than their heads." But it did concede that the dissemination of anti-secularist literature might do some good.[36]

The strongest support for the Christian Defence Association came from Zachary Barry and his weekly, the *Protestant Standard,* which rebuked the *Presbyterian* for its wet-blanket attitude to the new association. Its formation, the *Standard* declared, should have been hailed with "cheering applause".

> The battle now is not for this Church or that Church, but for Christianity; whether we shall have a Bible or no Bible; a Sabbath or no Sabbath; whether the confusion of teaching and wild theories shall supersede the old Book which has been the guide of multitudes to Eternal life; or whether there be such a thing as Eternal life at all, and whether man does not perish like the beast of the field.

To confront "infidelity and scepticism" in public places was imperative, it argued.[37]

The Defence Association began holding weekly lectures in June 1883. Its apologetics were, on the whole, traditional and conservative, and antagonistic rather than accommodating to modern science, apart from the harmonizing of Genesis and geology. In "A Chat about Evolution", for instance, one of the committee, Mr J. Pottie, dismissed Darwin's theory with the remark that its proponents were "all at sixes and sevens"; yet "this was the myth foolishly advanced by scientists to displace the Genesis and the Apocalypse of the Bible."[38] The defenders of the faith were soon to see this argument turned against themselves.

As the association was not getting the support it sought from the

Christian public, it held a meeting on 1 October 1883 to explain and promote its objects, which had come under some criticism. Alexander Gordon was the main speaker in defence of the association's aims. He saw in the word "defence" the implication of an attack, which made it necessary for those who professed Christianity to join forces in resisting it. This, he claimed, was essential for the preservation of their civilization, because Christianity gave to their society something which all the great civilizations of the past, and those contemporary civilizations of other religions, lacked. Other speakers sang a refrain to this hymn of self-praise, but the Quaker, Alfred Allen, who was on the platform with the other speakers, struck a discordant note. He protested that the constitution was too illiberal. He did not believe in the inspiration of the Scriptures, but of the writers of the Scriptures. Allen was not allowed to move an amendment, but Picton attempted to placate him by claiming that the association believed "exactly what Mr Allen believed", only that it was differently expressed.[39] This was to cover up rather than to remove the difference.

This latest exposition of the principles of the Christian Defence Association did not impress the *Weekly Advocate*. It had apparently changed its mind since its earlier call for the churches to defend religion. The association had adopted a "somewhat pretentious title", it sneered, and questioned whether anyone could "seriously think that the Ark of God [was] in danger".[40] The liberal *Evening News* was also critical, but for different reasons. Offended by the arrogance and presumption of most of the speeches made at the recent meeting, it thought that Christianity stood to lose more than it could gain by such an association.

> In spending their strength in defending the dogma of the infallibility of the Bible the churches are making a grave mistake; for nothing could be gained if the dogma were to be proved true, because there would still exist to confuse the enquirer a variety of interpretations, and Christianity does not require for its successful operation to be supported by any such dogma. Christianity can sustain no harm if it should be proved that the world was not made in six days, or that a fish did not swallow JONAH, or that the Psalms contain certain prayers that ought never to have been uttered by any religious man; but it will suffer if it can be proved that its great law of sacrifice is not adapted to human circumstances. . .

The *Evening News* clearly did not have much sympathy with orthodox religion; it admired Higinbotham's distinction between the creeds of the churches and Christianity, and claimed that "the life and principles of JESUS" were appealing increasingly to educated people. If these were explained simply from the Gospels, "without reading into them systems of metaphysics", it argued, there would be no need to organize to defend the faith, "or to complain that the churches have lost the influence over the people they once enjoyed".[41]

Some who did not support the Christian Defence Association nevertheless thought some kind of defence of religion was necessary. One of these was Dean Cowper, who set up a Committee on Christian Evidences in the diocese of Sydney in May 1883, during the interregnum between Bishop Barker and Bishop Barry. This committee organized lectures on apologetic topics, given by leading clergymen in St Andrew's Cathedral on Tuesday evenings; some of them were repeated in suburban parishes.[42]

Why Cowper set up this committee when a Defence Association had just been formed is an interesting question. The association's conservative basis probably did not worry him, although Bishop Pearson would not have liked it. Cowper might not have approved of a movement formed and led by laymen, and patronized by the independent Zachary Barry. Several of the leaders of the association were also prominent Orangemen, but this should not have been too objectionable to an Evangelical. Nor should its interdenominational character have worried him for he was a member of the non-sectarian Lord's Day Observance Society. The most plausible explanation is that Cowper found the Defence Association too aggressive in its attitude towards the freethinkers. He might have thought that such a group of narrow enthusiasts would bring colonial Christianity into disrepute. His main concern was to provide informed support for Anglicans in a time of testing, and he used both evangelical and liberal lecturers, including Bishop Pearson.

The Christian Defence Association was not discouraged by its critics. At its annual general meeting in April 1884, it reviewed its work with pride. It had given thirty-one lectures, some dealing with objections to the Bible and Christianity, and others attacking "infidel theories". The *Protestant Standard* claimed that the association enjoyed the patronage of many prominent Protestant ministers, adding: "Of course no priest of Rome has dared patronise it, for Rome dreads the Bible, which is freely used at these lectures."[43] The extent of support for the association was exaggerated, but before long the leading ministers of Sydney were to support a united movement to defend Christianity.

It was Bishop Alfred Barry who drew the Protestants together to form a Christian Evidence Society. A scholarly and experienced apologist, Barry had been the Boyle Lecturer in 1876-78 and subsequently was to be the Bampton Lecturer (1894).[44] Like his namesake, Zachary Barry, the bishop believed that the main issue of the day was not in the contending forms of churchmanship, but in the greater conflict between secularism and Christianity. But Alfred Barry was a man of broader spirit and outlook, and it must have grieved him on his arrival in New South Wales to find the apologetic movement divided between an association which did not command widespread support and a little known Anglican committee. Barry had been associated with the British Christian Evidence Society and at a meeting of the Committee on Christian Evidences in September 1884, he proposed the formation of a similar society in Sydney. He hoped not only for the cooperation of the main Protestant denominations but also of Roman Catholics.[45] With the backing of the Anglican committee, Barry set out to win this wider support, although some of his fellow Anglicans were probably sceptical as to the probability of Catholic cooperation. Certainly the Catholic press treated Barry with respect, but to expect Catholic cooperation at that time was rather sanguine.

Ministers of the principal Protestant denominations accepted Barry's proposal with enthusiasm.[46] Although most of them had cold-shouldered the Defence Association, they were concerned about the secularists' campaign against Christianity, and Barry gave the apologetic movement a leadership they could respect. The Christian Defence Association decided to merge with the Christian Evidence Society, probably realizing it would not command much support in competition with the society Barry was forming. Although the Christian Evidence Society adopted the same doctrinal basis as the association, its objects were stated less aggressively. It sought first, to promote the intelligent study and knowledge of the evidences of Christianity and, secondly, to meet the various forms of modern doubt and objections to Christianity. It hoped to achieve these aims through lectures, classes on Christian evidence with examinations and, of course, the circulation of literature. To this end it hoped to establish a library.[47] But the aims, and even the basis of the society, could be interpreted in several ways, as was clear from the beginning.

A large crowd thronged into the Protestant Hall for the inaugural meeting of the Christian Evidence Society on Tuesday 18 November 1884. All the leading Protestant clergy were there and a number of distinguished laymen. There was a message from the newly-arrived Catholic Archbishop, Dr P.F. Moran, pointing out that his clergy could not take part in the movement, and hoping somewhat cautiously that the society could do some good. The *Freeman's Journal* also wished it well, but did not expect too much of it because it believed the Protestants had abandoned the rock of truth for "the shifting sands of private judgment", which pre-empted any common ground for cooperation with Catholics. The *Weekly Advocate,* however, was not at all surprised that Moran declined Barry's invitation for Roman Catholicism, it asserted, could not welcome enquiry. There were also limits on the extent to which many Protestants would welcome enquiry into their beliefs, although they did believe that their faith would "stand up in the open light of day".[48]

Membership of the new society, Barry told the meeting, was open to all who confessed faith in Jesus Christ as Lord and Master, a statement perhaps open to broader interpretation than the stricter evangelical clauses of the doctrinal basis. Some of Barry's subsequent addresses showed that he held a modified view of that basis anyway, and his ideas of the society's tasks differed a little from some of its supporters. As he saw it, the greatest danger to Christianity was not from "avowed and distinct infidelity", but from ignorance and indifference. And he shrewdly observed that attendance at the freethought lectures would not be so large were it not for the musical and semi-dramatic entertainments which they featured. While they could not ignore the attacks from infidelity, the main task would be instruction in the outlines of Christianity, since too many practising Christians were hazy about the grounds of their faith. He also hoped that the society would help to correct the impression that Christianity was unnatural and other-worldly, indifferent to material progress and the issues of this life, or that it was opposed to learning, culture or modern science. So Barry clearly did not seek to defend old orthodoxy, but rather to reinterpret the Christian faith to modern man. He thought that the questioning of modern times had driven Christians to the central truths of their faith enabling them to distinguish between human tradition and essential Christianity. Thus it had aroused "a deeper spiritual and more thoughtful life in the Christian Church".[49]

Dr Robert Steel, one of the leading Presbyterian ministers, displayed a different spirit in his speech moving the adoption of the society's aims. He was more interested in confounding infidelity than in restating Christian belief. He took little account of "honest doubt", quoting the dictum that "faults of life breed errors in the brain", and alleged that some secularists wished to cover up immorality or breaches of the social order, or were simply hedonists. One of those so traduced, Thomas Walker, was present and Bishop Barry gave him leave to speak. Courteously, Walker welcomed the formation of the society and challenged its members to come out and debate openly with freethinkers; he was ready to meet anyone from Picton to Barry. The bishop thanked Walker for his suggestions — at which time some of the audience hissed — but told the secularist that the society was not devoted to propagating contro-

versy but rather to bringing out the truth.[50] Barry could have held
his own with Walker or any other freethought lecturer, but he was
more concerned to commend the Christian faith to the community
at large than to score points in a public debate, which to many would
have been little more than entertainment.

The society's first lecture series began on 15 May 1885, with a
large and eager audience. There was a devotional opening: a hymn, a
prayer and an anthem, "O taste and see how gracious the Lord is",
by the Evangelistic Choir. Bishop Barry explained that as Christian
men they had decided on such an opening; he invited those who
could not take part to be reverential witnesses or, alternatively, to
enter in the pause before the lecture.[51] Not too many outsiders, it
seems, came to these lectures anyway, but the public was kept better
informed of the Christian Evidence Society's lectures than it was of
the freethinkers' utterances, for the daily press gave generous cover
to the former and continued to ignore the latter.

Bishop Barry gave the first lecture, entitled "Christian Evidence
and Christian Faith". From the outset, he reaffirmed his view that
the society was as much for the instruction of believers as the conversion of unbelievers. As Pearson had done before him, Barry
claimed that Christ and Christianity were the two great evidences of
the Christian faith. His argument rested largely on the claim of
uniqueness both of Christ as a person and of Christianity as "a
Divine Philosophy". While he admitted that there was a difference
between ideal and actual Christianity, he claimed that, for all its
defects, historic Christianity had been an influence for good and
social progress; he quoted C. Loring Brace's *Gesta Christi,* a popular
book with Protestants, which attributed all moral and humane
progress to Christianity.[52] As to the divine nature of Christ, Barry
appealed to his unsurpassed goodness and his miraculous works,
above all his Resurrection. There was nothing particularly original
here, but Barry stated the case eloquently and persuasively enough
for a Christian audience. As for agnostics, the *Presbyterian* thought it
all too "scholastic and high class" for them to follow and pleaded
that future lectures be simpler.[53] It would probably have been hap-
pier to see a more direct attack on "infidelity".

The subsequent lecturers, however, mostly followed the pattern
set by Barry. Dr Steel dealt with "The Bible and Science". He presented the usual harmonizing of Genesis and geology, but also
argued that the Bible taught religious and moral truth rather than
science. Several lecturers argued for the superiority of Christianity
over other religions and systems of morality. In his lecture on
"Man's Need of Religion", Dr Kinross, principal of St Andrew's
College, asserted that Christianity produced the highest morality

and met the deepest needs of men. Dr Jefferis's case for Christianity in his lecture on "Christianity and Buddhism", which revealed more a knowledge than an understanding of Buddhism, consisted largely in the claim that Christianity was found among the "progressive" nations of the world. Alexander Gordon concluded the series with an exposure of "the deficiencies and incredibility of pre-Christian systems" compared with "the completeness and truth of Christianity and the Bible". Generally, the apologetics leant heavily on Paley and Butler and the *Gesta Christi* theory was implicit in several lectures.[54] They did not go far in meeting the problems that arose from modern science. One exception was the lecture on evolution by Canon Sharp, warden of St Paul's College, Sydney University.

In rather constrained tones, Canon Sharp pointed out that the theory of evolution was "powerless to deny the existence of a Creator" and could not "undermine the force of the argument from design". He conceded that Paley's argument might need to be rewritten in the light of Darwin's theory; even so, evolution seemed to strengthen the old argument by supplying an explanation of pain and waste in nature, a point which had commended the theory to some English churchmen. Sharp saw no problem for the biblical account of creation. Evolution was a question of the method and, in any case, the image of God in man was a spiritual, not a bodily image, so that, even if it were *proved* that man was part of the evolutionary process, the finding could not disturb the Christian faith.[55] Sharp might not have persuaded many to embrace the theory of evolution; he was careful to make clear that he was speaking hypothetically of evolution ayway, but he probably helped some Protestants take a less hostile attitude towards the Darwinian theory.

These lectures of the Christian Evidence Society were fairly restrained, as far as the antagonists of religion were concerned. But the society did not ignore them altogether. In November 1885 it appointed H.G. Picton, the founder of the former Christian Defence Association, as its public lecturer and agent, at a salary of £250 per annum. Picton had considerable experience in "contending for the faith", and for a few months in 1885 conducted a Christian evidence class in St Andrew's schoolroom. His work for the society included lectures in suburbs and towns and in "the large workshops of the colony". At Newcastle he was reputed to have "put to silence the blatant leaders of secularism". But his principal work was to reply to the freethought lecturers in Sydney. He did not engage them in public debate, but in February 1886 he began attending the Gaiety Theatre on Sunday nights to take notes from the freethought lecturer, W.W. Collins, editor of the *Freethinker*. Picton would reply the following Friday night before overflowing audiences in the YMCA Hall. These lectures were later published as penny pamphlets under such titles as ''Darwin or Moses''; ''Evolution v. Creation''; ''Alleged Gospel Discrepancies''; and ''Can a Man Know God?'' The latter, commended by the *Protestant Standard* as ''a great antidote to the secularist poison'', sold out quickly and ran to another edition. None of these pamphlets seems to have survived, but, according to the *Australian Christian World,* Picton exposed the ''fallacies'' in the Darwinian theory and showed that archaeology confirmed the biblical record.[56]

Picton lectured in Brisbane as well as in Sydney suburbs and towns in New South Wales until March 1887, when he left the colony to lecture in England. He later returned to Australia and lectured in Melbourne. At one of his last lectures in Sydney, an example of his success was the presence of T.W. Hawkins, a former vice-president of the Australia Secular Association, who had lectured in opposition to Picton. During a long illness he had been converted back to Christianity by Picton's arguments. About the same time another secularist, W.J. McCloskie, a former secretary of the Sydney Secular Association, became a Christian and a keen supporter of the Christian Evidence Society. He had been disillusioned with the cupidity of some secularist lecturers, their malice towards each other and the dissidence within the movement. A few years later the chairman of Collins's meetings also renounced secularism and joined the Salvation Army.[57] There were as well occasional death-bed conversions to secularists, and the evangelists W.G. Taylor and J.S. Austin claimed to have converted freethinkers in their campaigns.[58] It was the conservative Evangelicals, the group to which Picton belonged, who managed to win secularists back to the faith. This was not as strange as it may seem, for coming from an evangelical background themselves, the secularists were more susceptible, especially on their death-beds, to the old arguments and appeals than to the unfamilar reasoning of the more liberal apologists like Bishop Barry and Canon Sharp.

Picton was no great intellectual, but neither were many of his opponents. He carried on the style of apologetics initiated by the Christian Defence Association, relying on denigration and ridicule more often than reason. He frequently linked infidelity with immorality and highlighted disagreements among secularists in Australia and Britain. One of his last lectures — ''Secularism Unmasked; or, the Cat Let Out of the Bag'' — provoked a letter of protest in the *Protestant Standard* from Charles Bradlaugh in England, whom Picton had traduced, evidence at least that the secularists did not ignore him. Picton also focused on divisions of opinion among scientists in his last lecture in Sydney, "Our Noble Ancestors; or, Have We Come from Monkeys?" In this instance he was concerned not so much to deny the theory of evolution as to defend the necessity, indeed the priority, of an "intelligent creator", and thus to refute the secularist's claim that evolution proved the Bible untrue.[59]

While Picton took on the freethinkers, the Christian Evidence Society offered another series of lectures in 1886 on the Bible, seeking to correct misguided notions about what the Bible really was. Bishop Barry opened this series with a lecture awkwardly entitled "What is of Faith as to Inspiration?" He had chosen to deal with the structure and inspiration of the Bible for two reasons: he believed, like Bishop Pearson, that in nine out of ten cases the attacks on the Bible from freethought lectures came from "sheer ignorance" on their part of what the Bible actually was; and secondly, he wished to give some positive instruction rather than "mere polemical attack or defence". What he had to say was really addressed to Christians, with the hope of bringing them to a more intelligent view of the inspiration of the Bible and a more liberal interpretation of the doctrinal clause of the society. Barry thought that no perfect theory of inspiration could be framed, but he espoused the view of Bishop Westcott, adopted by others, including Bishop Camidge of Bathurst, that it was the human authors of Holy Scripture, rather than the Bible itself — "not the pen, but the penman" — who should be regarded as inspired. The Bible, as a whole, was a record of divine revelation, but the Spirit of God spoke, not through mere "mechanical instruments", but through "living, thinking men"; however, even inspired men might grasp and transmit the truth of revelation imperfectly. Thus there was, Barry argued, an evolution in revelation — "a progressive revelation of God" leading up from the "imperfect and preparatory" revelation of the law and the prophets "to the perfect law and teaching of the great Prophet of prophets, the revealer of God in Himself". He conceded that the very early chapters of Genesis might be a symbolical narrative but he affirmed the "Absolute historical truth" of the biblical record, including the miraculous elements, "from the Flood onward". He concluded that the Bible, taken as a whole, was "the most perfect revelation which human nature was capable of receiving": in this sense it was the eternal word of God.[60]

This was a cautious and a not altogether consistent statement, for it was not easy to reconcile the claim to absolute historical truth with the insistence on the imperfect human elements in the Bible, and even its "moral and spiritual truth", especially that contained in the Old Testament, had to be discerned by reference to the character of

Christ. But Barry had opened the door to a different and more liberal view by not attempting to defend the early Genesis stories as history, and also by the notion of progressive revelation, although he did not spell out the implications of this idea. The same idea was present in one of the last lectures in the series, "The Relationship of the Old to the New Testament", given by T.E. Hill, the controversial principal of Moore College, in August 1886. Hill argued the importance of the Old Testament in understanding "the sum and climax of all Divine revelations" in the New; and that it was necessary to know a little about the progressive nature of revelation to appreciate "the more elementary lessons" of the Old Testament. Protestant churchmen were beginning to embrace this notion of progressive revelation, so shocking when first stated by Benjamin Jowett in *Essays and Reviews* in 1860. A concept of progressive revelation, Jowett argued, would relieve Christians of the burden of defending stories and ideas such as the slaughter of the Amalekites and the imprecatory psalms. But few admitted as frankly as George Clarke, in a sermon he preached in Hobart in August 1885, that there was "defective truth and defective morality" in the Old Testament.[61]

The year 1886 was the most successful for the Christian Evidence Society; it campaigned on two fronts, with Picton attempting to confute the freethinkers and Barry and others trying to lead the Christian public to a more enlightened understanding of the Bible. It enjoyed vice-regal patronage and the support of several leading citizens; Sir Henry Parkes, Sir James Martin, chief justice, and the mayor of Sydney, Alderman Riley, were some of those who presided at its lectures and meetings. Sir Frederick Darley, successor of Sir James Martin, and two other judges, Sir William Manning and Sir George Innes were the society's vice-presidents in 1887. But from 1887 the society went into decline. At the annual meeting in April 1888 Bishop Barry admitted that support for the society was dwindling. A series of lectures that winter did not attract good attendances either. The society also distributed leaflets among the crowds that gathered on the Sydney Domain on Sunday afternoons. At the next annual meeting in April 1889 it was decided to suspend the lecture programme, although a small committee was appointed to watch over the cause of the defending Christianity, and ministers were exhorted to deal occasionally with "the branches of Christian evidence" from the pulpit.[62]

Bishop Barry's imminent departure from Australia was one reason why the Christian Evidence Society decided to discontinue its apologetic lectures. Barry, "so courageous a champion of the faith", had been the driving force behind the apologetic movement since he came to Sydney in 1884. But there were other important reasons for the decline in interest. In June 1887 Sir Henry Parkes closed the theatres against the freethought Sunday lecturers, because free-thinkers and republicans had broken up meetings in the Town Hall in connection with Queen Victoria's jubilee (see chapter 7). This peremptory action had virtually silenced the organized opposition to Christianity, although the secularists opened their own hall three years later. But they no longer attracted the crowds to their lectures. Once the freethinkers were driven from their accustomed platforms much of the urgency of the apologetic movement was lost. Changes in religious thought towards the end of the decade also made the intellectual defence of Christianity seem less necessary.

Religious Thought at the End of the Decade

Bishop Barry thought that the Christian Evidence Society had con-tributed to a liberalizing of thought among Christians. In line with its original aims, it had cleared up some of the difficulties about the Bible and had explained "the deep truths of Christianity", not to sceptics but to Christians, "who sometimes held their convictions with more of tenacity than of reason". The society had shown a cer-tain tolerance to modern science, so much so that it had sometimes been criticized for allowing lecturers such wide latitude in their ideas. In his final address to the society in April 1889, Barry viewed the relationship between belief and unbelief optimistically. He thought that there was more sympathy and respect between believers and non-believers than there had been. He predicted a revival of faith "which would assimilate all that was good and true" in modern thought, as Christians moved "closer and closer to the great truths of humanity as embodied in Christ". There was the same optimism in H.L. Jackson's paper on "The Church and Modern Thought", read to the Anglican Church Congress in Sydney in April 1889. Jackson argued that the churches had gone through a necessary destructive period that cleared away the rubbish of the past; now a "New Theology" was about to usher in another reformation.[63]

Churchmen in other denominations were also conscious of being liberated from the theological systems of the past. George Clarke reviewed the changes in religious thought at the Intercolonial Con-gregational Conference in Adelaide in September 1887. He com-mented on the increasing numbers of intelligent and devout believers who were regarding the Bible in a different light. They could see with more confidence that it was "a revelation of man as well as a revelation of God . . . not the divine word, pure and simple". A humanized theology had accompanied these changes. Congregationalists had forsaken the "slightly softened" Calvinism of their fathers, realizing that "a true theology must be a product of the heart as well as of the head". With this kind of thinking the doctrine of eternal punishment was itself damned. The same process was evident in colonial Presbyterianism. Members of the General Assembly applauded the Moderator, John Auld, in March 1888, when he declared the Westminster Confession inadequate and called for a new statement of faith. The debate between Calvinists and Arminians was a thing of the past, according to the Moderator in 1890, T.E. Clouston. The *Sydney Morning Herald,* then edited by a former Wesleyan minister, William Curnow, praised these signs that the churches were identifying with "the reforming movements of the time".[64] The decision of the Wesleyan General Conference in 1890 to relax the rule that members of Methodist churches should attend a weekly class meeting suggests that Methodism was changing too, even if not as fast as the Anglican, Presbyterian and Congregational Churches.

Conservative views were still aired and obscurantist attitudes still adopted by a few. One of the Christian Evidence Society lecturers in 1888, Dr Thomas Porter, attempted to refute the theory of evolution, and in March 1889 the Presbyterian Moderator, this time Dr Archibald Gilchrist, denounced evolution as atheistic and clearly irreconcilable with revelation.[65] But there was a growing acceptance of the Darwinian theory among Protestants in the 1880s. Dr Thomas Roseby had come to terms with evolution as early as 1876; and in his Livingstone Lectures, given under the auspices of Camden College in October 1888, he argued that evolution through natural selection was "simply a question of divine method". Evolutionary theory was completely consistent with a theistic view of creation: "Unless the whole scheme of nature had first existed in the thought of God, it would never have been *realised* in the facts of experience." Confident that the living God was behind all the processes of nature, Roseby viewed evolution optimistically. It was an irreversible ascent in which man's nature and destiny as a child of God were still unfolding.[66]

Other theologians with some experience in science, forerunners of Teilhard de Chardin, had also married science and religion. One of these was the Scotsman, Henry Drummond, who, influenced first by Moody, studied science. He produced a synthesis of evolutionary biology and evangelical doctrine in his book, *Natural Law and the Spiritual World* (1883). Bishop Barry quoted Drummond with approval and Dr Jefferis was credited with promoting Drummond's book in Sydney. But Roseby dismissed Drummond as "most unsatisfactory" on science and "most misleading" on religion. However Drummond helped many Protestants come to terms with evolution, especially students, who flocked to his meetings during his visit to Australia in 1890.[67] An English Methodist, Dr W.H. Dallinger, also helped to change Protestant attitudes in his Fernley Lectures in 1887. At least the *Weekly Advocate* in Sydney reversed its attitude: "Let it no longer be supposed that a Theistic theory of evolution is inconsistent with the fullest and most reverential faith in the Christian revelation." Similarly, the *Presbyterian* told its readers in 1890 that they need not trouble themselves as to how they came into existence, for "a Great First Cause is necessary to the evolutionary hypothesis".[68]

It was much the same with attitudes to the Bible. Archaeology buttressed the conservative view of the Bible as an infallible book for a while. At the annual meeting of the Christian Evidence Society in June 1887 Dr Steel declared that the spade was one of the "greatest arguments in favour of Christianity", and even asserted that archaeological evidence "entirely corroborated" Moses' story "of the creation, the fall, and the flood". Cardinal Moran also claimed in a lecture in 1885 that archaeology confirmed the authority of the "inspired books".[69] But archaeology was not always embraced so uncritically. In an address to Australian Congregationalists in 1892, William Roby Fletcher pointed out how much archaeology supported the biblical record, and advised caution as far as the theories of German higher criticism were concerned. Yet Fletcher went a long way to accepting some of the conclusions of modern biblical scholarship, which disposed of the old theory of verbal inspiration and allowed for the composite nature of the Pentateuch. Two years later the Reverend George MacInnes proclaimed the death of the theory of verbal inspiration from the moderatorial chair in the Presbyterian General Assembly; another minister, George Grimm, replied with a moderate defence of the "plenary inspiration" of the Bible, but MacInnes's view was that of a growing number in his denomination.[70]

The Christian Evidence Society could claim a little credit for these changes, but they were as much reflections of changes that were taking place in Britain and North America. Publication of the Revised Version of the Bible in the 1880s helped to modify attitudes, but more important was the acceptance of higher criticism by British biblical scholars. They had mostly preserved their theological orthodoxy while accepting new conclusions as to the date and the composite authorship of much of the Old Testament, thus accepting some of the conclusions of the formerly-damned German scholars.

The publication in 1889 of *Lux Mundi,* a collection of essays by younger high church scholars, showed that modified and critical views of Scripture were also consistent with Anglo-Catholic theology. Although the walls of resistance to evolution, higher criticism and a liberal theology still stood here and there, they were being eroded. By the turn of the century most Protestant ministers had modified their views on biblical inspiration and had come to terms with modern science.[71]

But whether the new thinking had percolated through to the pews cannot be answered confidently. Laymen who attended the lectures of the Christian Evidence Society or church congresses and conferences would have been exposed to the new thought, and the concerned among them probably welcomed it. The more liberal preachers expounded their beliefs from the pulpit, although others might have feared to disturb the faith of their congregations. But where a layman espoused the new thought himself he might become one of its promoters, even in the Sunday school. James Backhouse Walker, the son of a Quaker, brought up his Bible class in Davey Street Congregational Church, Hobart, on liberal biblical scholarship. He had earlier come under the influence of George Clarke; "his teaching was just what was necessary to lead me without too great a shock to wider views of God and religion." In 1887 Walker dealt with the early chapters of Genesis in his bible class of youths, attempting to provide a reasonable explanation of the early allegorical chapters. To this end he

> endeavoured to work out the spiritual side of the story, and show them that there are great spiritual truths for us which are taught there — that the truths are just as living today; and, to see this we only need look under the old picturesque and figurative language in which the Semitic races clothed all their ideas — giving a concrete form to subjective truths.

He saw a reasonable interpretation of the early biblical stories as vitally necessary, if Christianity was to maintain the allegiance of young people.[72]

It is unknown how many bible class teachers there were like Walker. Perhaps Josiah Mullens exercised the same influence over his bible class in Burwood Congregational Church. In any case, it is significant that Walker approved the "reasonable solutions" offered in a "Handbook of Biblical Difficulties", produced by a writer of the Sunday School Union. He also found that even "the ultra orthodox 'Notes on the Lessons' of the Sunday School Union actually interpret the story of the Fall as allegorical".[73] From this it can be assumed that, in so far as Sunday schools followed these lessons, and many did, they were encouraging a modified view of the nature of the Bible.

Thus from the late 1880s any person, young or old, who was troubled by aspects of the Bible and its relationship to modern science could find intelligent and sympathetic teachers prepared to help resolve the difficulties, unlike those casualties of the old evangelical theology who became freethinkers. But such troubled souls were always a minority within the churches. Ministers with a liberal theological outlook, like Jackson, tended to exaggerate the importance of intellectual difficulties, especially in reference to those outside the churches.[74] Admittedly, working-class men had gone to listen to the freethinkers, but not because they were disturbed by Darwin or perplexed about the Bible. What did they know about evolution or the Bible anyway? They enjoyed the irreverent attacks on churchmen whom they despised for reasons other than the alleged conflict between science and religion, as the layman, T.J. Hebblewhite, argued in a trenchant reply to Jackson's paper to the Anglican Church Congress.

Judging from 'The Ordeal of Faith", a poem he had published in the *Centennial Magazine* in 1889, Hebblewhite realized what a struggle it was "to keep the flickering spark [of faith in Jesus of Nazareth] alive".[75] But in an article on "Artisan-Scepticism and Empty Churches", he dismissed the intellectual difficulties of the working classes, of which Jackson, "the Rev. Onesimus Dryasdust", had made so much. "The greatest enemy" confronting the churches in the closing decades of the nineteenth century was

> not the aggressive and blatant atheism that hires a hall and, armed with a mutilated version of Darwin and a bundle of pamphlets by Bradlaugh, undertakes to hound God out of His own universe in something like a hour and forty minutes by the clock; but a cold, unreasoning, expressionless unbelief that chills the very springs of devotion and hems life in on every side with a frigid atmosphere of aimless, hopeless, devil-may-care materialism.

He also dismissed as "frivolous" the various suggestions that were offered to make church services more attractive to the working classes.

The problem was too deep-seated for such superficial remedies. It arose out of an unjust economic order, and the discontent this engendered was fraught with more danger for the churches than the challenges from science and philosophy. The churches, Hebblewhite charged, were partly responsible for this "monstrous growth" of injustice, because of their "tacit acceptance of principles which contravene the very axioms of morality", not to mention Christianity with its gospel of "love and brotherhood". But would the churches seriously take up "the question of a more equitable distribution of wealth", instead of tinkering with "little two penny attractions to draw the 'poor misguided masses' "? Hebblewhite had more hope of "the Ethiop changing his skin".[76]

This touched a weak point in contemporary Christianity — its relationship with the working classes, more particularly with the trade union movement. There had been papers on this question at the Sydney Church Congress earlier in 1889, under the unpromising title, "The Church in Relation to the Various Grades of Society". The four speakers under this theme all concerned themselves with the working classes. But Hebblewhite made no recognition of these speakers in his criticism of Jackson and churchmen generally. One of them, S.B. Holt, rector of Deniliquin, exhorted his fellow clergy to master economic questions and to put "more of the human and less of the doctrinal" into their sermons. A "sympathising humanity" pervaded the Sermon on the Mount, and a preacher could not expound the "Holy Book" adequately if he was not interested in social and economic concerns.[77] Others, also including Jackson, realized that it was not enough to prove Christianity to be reasonable; it had to be shown to be relevant, particularly to the question of social justice.

6

Applying the Gospel

It has been generally assumed that the church interest in social questions began in the 1890s, prompted by the Maritime Strike of 1890, the rise of the Labor Party, which secured parliamentary representation in New South Wales in 1891, and the social distress associated with the depression of the 1890s. It has been claimed in reference to the 1870s and 1880s that "Australian trade unionism grew virtually without religious acknowledgement", and that preaching "rarely ever touched on any question of public life or morals".[1] Historians have mostly found the 1890s more fascinating than the preceding decade, but a closer investigation of the 1880s shows that churchmen were more interested in social questions and had more to say about trade unions and the problems of capital/labour relationships than many have assumed.

In a lecture on "The Enfranchisement of Labour" in June 1878, James Jefferis attributed the alienation of workers from the churches in part to an "undue reticence in the pulpit about matters of the utmost importance to man's life". Too much time was spent "explaining the Gospel, which does not need much, instead of applying the Gospel, which is greatly needed". Since Christianity belonged to the whole of life, preachers were entitled to speak out on matters affecting society. But it was a general rather than a specific application of Christianity to social questions that Jefferis had in mind, for the pulpit was not to engage in party strife, nor to propose precise solutions to pressing problems, "but to lay down [those] principles and truths. . . of eternal obligation" which should guide parliaments, chambers of commerce, trade unions and "the conduct of the individual man . . . in every department of life".[2]

Jefferis's Sunday evening lectures were devoted to "applying the Gospel"; and he was not always as general in his discussion of social questions as he counselled. In his lecture on "The Chinese and the Seamen's Strike" in December 1878 he argued that the Chinese should be paid the same wages as Australians, that their living conditions should be improved and that they should have Chinese women living among them. Thus he offered more than pious exhortations to love and brotherhood. But one swallow does not make a summer; and much that Jefferis himself said might seem to confirm the view that, on the whole, the pulpit neglected social questions. So might a statement from the *Presbyterian* in 1888, observing that the prevailing opinion at the beginning of the 1880s was that the pulpit should preach "the simple gospel", dealing with the fall, redemption and regeneration.[3] But, in fact, while few churchmen sought to apply the gospel as consistently and self-consciously as Jefferis, there were many occasions on which the pulpit or the religious press commented on strikes, trade unions and capital/labour relations. Furthermore, there should be no misunderstanding about "the simple gospel"; implicit in it was a social teaching that informed the attitudes of pew and pulpit to the issues of the day.

Evangelical Protestantism inculcated the old Puritan virtues of industry, thrift and sobriety, which to a large extent coloured the attitude of Protestants to questions of poverty and social justice. In 1880, for example, William Taylor, a Baptist minister, wrote that Christianity was no friend to idleness. Every Christian was to have some occupation or calling and to carry on his business with diligence, which, "if associated with prudence seldom fails of its reward"; for according to the biblical precept, "he becometh poor that dealeth with a slack hand, but the hand of the diligent maketh rich." There was no doubt that these virtues did promote a degree of prosperity, as Carruthers boasted concerning Methodists; the position of the Protestant churchgoing community on the whole seemed to confirm it. By the same token, the Catholic hierarchy, concerned to see the position of Catholics in colonial society improve, exhorted the faithful to adopt the same virtues and discipline.[4]

This teaching was an implicit rebuke to working men. They had to learn that "competence, comfort and wealth are the appropriate rewards of industry, temperance and thrift", the *Australian Christian World* observed in a comment on riots of the unemployed in London in 1886. To teach men otherwise was to do them a grievous wrong and to promote indolence and public unrest. Similarly, the *Presbyterian* postulated in 1890, during the Maritime Strike, that men had "themselves to thank or to blame for their present position", for it averred there was "a fair field [open] to all who had the power and will to rise".[5] It had been, until 1890 anyway, an age of opportunity, in which enterprising tradesmen could establish small businesses which had a good chance of prospering. But still, the notion was simplistic and bespoke an unsympathetic attitude towards the poor.

At the same time, most Protestants recognized an "honest poverty" caused by misfortunes, such as the illness or death of the breadwinner, or by social factors beyond the individual's control. These were the "deserving poor" and they had a proper claim on the sympathy of the wealthy, whose duty it was to assist them. But the "undeserving" drunkard or ne'er-do-well might have a wife and children to share his poverty, and these too had to be helped. Even if he was alone in his poverty, hardly anyone thought that he should be left to perish from hunger or exposure. Protestant philanthropy supported a number of charitable institutions and societies, chiefly the Benevolent Society of New South Wales, the Sydney City Mission and the City Night Refuge and Soup Kitchen. As well as these agencies, there was the Ladies' Evangelistic Association which distributed charitable relief to poor families in Sydney. There were similar institutions in other Australian cities. These bodies were constituted on a non-sectarian basis but they were financed and staffed by Protestants. Alongside them were a number of Catholic institutions, including the Society of St Vincent de Paul, established in New South Wales in 1881. The charitable institutions enjoyed some state subsidies to carry on their work and the State exercised a limited role in direct relief of the needy. But the relief of poverty rested largely on Christian philanthropy.[6]

This was how Protestant churchmen believed it should be, or so James Jefferis argued in his lecture, "Australia Christianised", in Adelaide in June 1880. Some forms of state relief, he considered, only intensified the evils of poverty. Nevertheless, he allowed the State a certain role; it should intervene to remove the recognized causes of poverty, such as overcrowded conditions and uncontrolled immigration, and to curb gambling, intemperance and prostitution. It was also the State's duty to regulate and reform schemes of relief, so as to prevent rather than perpetuate poverty. Jefferis looked for schemes which would help the poor to help themselves. His wife, Marian, was one of the leading figures who sought the introduction of the boarding-out system, which placed destitute children in foster homes as an alternative to the larger barrack-type institutions of the Randwick and Benevolent Asylums. She also established "cottage homes" in the community to care for such children. But although the State might regulate, it should not supplant private charity, Jefferis maintained. Christian philanthropy was to be encouraged. It was the Christian's duty, as another Protestant churchman explained, to use the wealth God had given him to support both religion and works of charity and usefulness, in which he could not engage himself.[7]

The care of the poor was one thing; the causes of poverty quite another. While churchmen in the 1880s regarded inequalities of wealth in society and a degree of poverty as inevitable, they regarded much poverty as unnecessary — the result of idleness, improvidence and vice. The latter meant, in particular, gambling, prostitution and, above all, intemperance.

The Churches and Temperance

Intemperance was for most churchmen in the 1880s the principal cause of unnecessary poverty in society. During this decade the temperance movement, which earlier in the century did not enjoy the wholehearted support of the churches,[8] strengthened its hold on the Protestant denominations. Between 1874, when the Church of England Temperance Society was established in the diocese of Sydney, and 1889 the principal denominations in New South Wales set up their own temperance or total abstinence societies. Sunday schools promoted temperance, particularly through Bands of Hope, and annual temperance sermons became the custom in several denominations. The Woman's Christian Temperance Union was introduced to New South Wales in 1882 and Victoria in 1885,[9] and a number of Gospel Temperance missioners came to Australia during the decade (see Chapter 3). All in all, there was a sustained campaign within Protestantism from the 1880s onwards to persuade people in the congregations to adopt temperance principles, which came increasingly to mean teetotalism. It is some testimony to the success of the campaign that by 1890 many Protestant churches had substituted unfermented grape juice for wine in the communion service.

Australian Catholicism also had its temperance movement, dating from the early days of the colony of New South Wales. It was strengthened by Cardinal Moran, who came to Australia bearing the reputation of a temperance reformer. He founded the Catholic Total Abstinence Association in 1885. But Catholics in Australia were not prepared to cooperate with Protestants in the temperance cause, as Cardinal Manning did in England, and as Catholics had done in New South Wales in the 1830s and 1840s. Soon after Cardinal Moran's arrival in Australia, he declined the Local Option League's invitation to become one of its vice-presidents, on the grounds that he had to avoid political agitation! Pastoral considerations most probably led him to turn down this opportunity to promote a degree of unity between Catholic and Protestant. Such a public role would not have helped Catholic unity, for quite a number of Catholics were licensees of hotels; some were prominent in the Licensed Victuallers' Association and one, J.M. Toohey, was a leading brewer. Apart from this, Moran did not want Catholics mixing with Protestants in the temperance movement, and in 1885 the bishops at the Plenary Council instructed priests to establish parochial temperance societies to discourage Catholics from joining societies outside the pale of the Church.[10]

Nevertheless, Moran spoke against intemperance in terms similar to the Protestants, as one of the greatest social evils of the day; and the Australian hierarchy considered it a besetting weakness of the Irish, which kept them socially depressed and also corroded religious faith and devotion. Moran, himself, was not averse to legislation discouraging intemperance and he had taken parts in movements for legislative restriction of the liquor trade in Ireland. He endorsed the principle of local option and suggested to the Local Option League that it should press for Saturday afternoon closing of hotels, because it was "the most dangerous day for the working man". But the Catholic temperance movement mostly relied on moral suasion of the individual, partly from discretion of conviction, and partly because the public temperance movement was dominated by Protestants.[11]

At the beginning, the temperance movement generally was also based on moral suasion, but by 1880 its mood had changed. At the opening of the International Temperance Conference in Melbourne in 1880, the Victorian politician and prominent temperance advocate, James Munro, said that there had been a good deal of talk "about moral suasion and legal suasion" some twenty-five years earlier, but "throughout the whole world, those ideas had become united, and now the fixed principles adopted by all leading abstainers were total abstinence for the individual and prohibition for the State".[12] As far as Protestants were concerned, this was some departure from the evangelical principle of social reform through individual regeneration, and the liberal principle of minimal restriction of the freedom of the individual, and of free trade for that matter. But intemperance and its consequences were regarded as so serious as to require exceptional remedies.

A vast amount of disorder and distress was laid at the door of drink. A speaker at the Anglican Church Congress in Melbourne in 1882 attributed 90 per cent of crime, 75 per cent of divorce cases, 45 per cent of lunacy and 60 per cent of general disease to strong drink. Bishop Linton, of the Riverina, subscribed to this view in a paper to the Sydney Church Congress in 1889. Drink was also blamed for the greater amount of poverty that existed then. According to the Reverend F.B. Boyce, an Evangelical and one of the leading temperance reformers in New South Wales, drink was the cause of two-thirds of pauperism. Richard Sellors, a Wesleyan minister, told the Intoxicating Drink Inquiry Commission in New South Wales in 1886 that a large degree of poverty was preventable because it was due to intemperance.[13]

Thus to many temperance enthusiasts legislative restriction or prohibition of the liquor trade was the most imperative of all social reforms. A letter to the Melbourne Temperance Conference from the Reverend H.A. Thompson, president of Otterheim University, USA, proclaimed temperance reform as a panacea for all social and economic ills. In deploring the size of the "Drink Bill" he quoted another American authority:

> Because this capital is so misspent, our jails are filled with criminals, our poorhouses with paupers, our asylums, homes, and charities with dependents, and our industrious sober citizens burdened with taxes that would not be needed but for this work of liquor. What nation or people can long exist or prosper who spend or waste the value of so much labour for poisonous drink? Can we wonder that we have many panics, hard times, and stagnation of trade?[14]

A few questioned these exaggerated claims. Among the witnesses called before the Intoxicating Drink Inquiry in 1886 was the Reverend C.H. Rich, Anglican chaplain of Darlinghurst Gaol, who took the claim that 90 per cent of crime was due to drink "*cum grano salis*". The police report showed that drunkenness formed part of the charge in around 60 per cent of arrests between 1881 and 1885; its author, Inspector General Fosbery was disposed to condemning the menace. The president of the Intoxicating Drink Inquiry Commission, Alexander Oliver, pointed out that arrests for drunkenness in the period had actually fallen from 6 per cent to 5 per cent in the metropolitan area. But Fosbery did not think the figures indicated an improvement; the slight decrease was among the number of females arrested for drunkenness. Another witness, Dr Manning, inspector general of the insane, estimated that 5-6 per cent of cases of permanent insanity were attributable to drink, and in 1886 around 11 per cent of admissions to asylums were considered to be caused directly or indirectly by intemperance. This was lower than the figure of 13-14 per cent given for England and much lower than the 45 per cent or more estimated by temperance reformers, as the government statistician, T.A. Coghlan, could not forbear to point out.[15]

The relationship between poverty and intemperance was hardly questioned in the 1880s, although Bishop Barry suggested to the Drink Inquiry that the drinking habits of the working classes might be the result of poverty and bad living conditions, rather than the cause of it. In East London in 1887 Charles Booth found the proportion of poverty due directly to drink to be much lower than popular estimates. In the cases he investigated he concluded that drink was responsible for the misery of 13 per cent of the poor and 14 per cent of the very poor.[16]

In Australia, Sir Henry Parkes believed that intemperance was a serious cause of poverty and misery among the working classes; it was for this reason, he explained in 1884, that he was "a friend of temperance". But Bishop Barry did not think intemperance was any greater among the working classes in Australia than in England; in fact, he rightly suspected that it was less than in Britain, where nearly thirty gallons of beer per head of population was consumed annually compared with around twelve in New South Wales and twenty in Victoria. But few consulted the statistics and so there were varying opinions as to the prevalence of intemperance in Australia. Inspector General Fosbery and Sir Alfred Stephen thought that drinking habits had improved among "gentlemen", but Bishop Barry had found intemperance among the middle and upper classes of the colonies to be much more prevalent than in England. Fosbery and Stephen thought that intemperance was increasing among the young and women; but the arrests among women for drunkenness suggested the opposite and Dr Manning thought that the youth of the colony were "very sober". Dr Jefferis also did not think that youth were much given to drink and doubted whether there had been any increase in intemperance generally in proportion to the increase in the population. Beer had become the most popular drink by the 1880s, but its consumption per head of population, as well as that of wine and spirits, was actually decreasing in New South Wales in the 1880s; there was a noticeable decline in Victoria during the next decade. The amount of beer drunk in New South Wales fell from nearly fourteen gallons per head in 1885 to just under eleven gallons in 1889, and in Victoria from twenty gallons per head in 1888 to twelve in 1898.[17]

But temperance reformers were convinced that intemperance was increasing and ruining the country, as F.B. Boyce argued before the inquiry. The commissioners questioned his computation of the national "Drink Bill", but nothing could dissuade the reformers from their stand. The temperance reformers were really prohibitionists. One speaker at the Centennial Temperance Congress in Sydney in 1888 declared that to argue for a man's right to sell drink was like arguing over his right to sell rotten fish or bad cheese. If they could not have prohibition, local option was "the next best system", J.D. Langley, a future bishop of Bendigo, told the Intoxicating Drink Inquiry. Complete local option, which would allow voters to decide against licences in their electorate, was the aim of the temperance reformers in the late nineteenth century. Their campaign focused on the public house: 95 per cent of drunkenness could be traced to drinking in public houses, Sir Alfred Stephen reported, a man who drank wine for the good of his health. In vain might the brewer Toohey try to lay the blame on licensed grocers. The commissioners agreed that the best way to reduce intemperance was to reduce the number of public houses, which had grown like church buildings in the 1880s. The Licensed Victuallers' Association also thought that there were too many, and might have cooperated with Local Optionists in closing low class houses and improving standards all round.[18] But the temperance men would make no pact with the devil. They were at war with drink and the drink trade.

Churchmen and the Labour Movement

Temperance propaganda implied that poverty and hardship in society was due to the drinking habits of the working classes, who mostly drank in public houses. But espousal of temperance reform did not necessarily preclude sympathy with the labour movement in its struggle for better wages and working conditions. James Jefferis is a case in point. In his lecture, "The Enfranchisement of Labour", he reviewed the relations between capital and labour over the centuries and especially in the nineteenth century. He drew more on English than Australian experience. He had been in England when the Reform Bill of 1868 was passed, and since then he thought that there had been a new recognition of the rights of labour. Up to then the theory had been that capital had rights and labour had duties, but, he claimed, "the law now deals with the capitalist and the workman as upon the same level." Labourers could now vote, and their right to combination and to strike was recognized. He attributed this progress in part to the influence of the more liberal colonies on the mother country, but recognized that much of it was due to trade union action. He would not have anyone abuse the unions. "The combination of workers is essentially just and actually necessary", he affirmed. He believed neither that "the character of the British workman had deteriorated", nor that higher wages, shorter hours and greater independence would destroy Britain's commercial pre-eminence. He was convinced that "with better food and a better home, and more leisure and manliness" both the English and the Australian worker, would do more and better work.

In the same spirit, Jefferis also conceded that the progress of the worker had been achieved through battles "in which law, and learning, and even religion herself, have too often been found fighting for an evil cause". Yet he distinguished between religion, as represented in the Established Church and other leading denominations, and the spirit of Christianity. The latter had had most to do with the enfranchisement of labour, for the gospel was "the true Charter of liberty". He saw no complete victory until the country's labour had "become permeated with the Spirit of the Gospel". For this reason, the alienation of the working classes from the churches was a question of the greatest importance. But the elevation of the working classes also depended partly on working men learning thrift and temperance. While he looked to some degree of legislative reform, he did "not think that the mighty passions which defile and degrade human nature [would] be conquered by anything short of the still mightier passion of religion".[20]

There was ample recognition of trade unionism here in this lecture and a large degree of sympathy with the labour movement, even if it was patronizing at times. His frank recognition of the reactionary role of religion was refreshing. All in all, it was an unusual utterance for the time. Most Protestant churchmen were still a little chary of trade unionism around 1880; and strikes aroused in them a fear of a new tyranny, the tyranny of the worker, as the *Presbyterian* warned on the occasion of a miners' strike at Newcastle in 1880. It recognized the right of both employers and employees to combination, but it thought that there was more danger to society from the combination of workers, especially when they sought to prevent some from working during strikes. The "scabs" evoked its admiration and it exhorted all workers to exercise their liberty of choice, for it was better to work for low pay than to be idle and depend on charity. The *Independent* commented in 1882 that trade unionism was displaying a perverted idea of cooperation which amounted to tyranny, although it did not want to see a return to the old tyranny of capital over labour. It thought that class conflict could be avoided altogether by genuine cooperation between capital and labour to make the most of resources, "whether of money or human tissue".[21]

Comments could be less sympathetic. In 1886 the *Independent,* then under a new editor, distinguished between the hardworking, home-owning artisans and the disreputable workers, who only worked to get drink. These latter, it claimed, fomented disaffection and promoted strikes.[22] Harsh criticism also came from the newly established interdenominational religious weekly, the *Australian Christian World,* in 1886. Edited by J.D. Hennessey, a Congregationalist and formerly a Wesleyan minister, it was mistrustful of trade unionism. In a comment on the waterside strike in Melbourne in 1886, it blamed the workers for their "disinclination to do a fair day's work for a fair day's wage". The labour movement, it thought, was trying to reverse "the true order of things".

> The men who, by their wisdom and energy have accumulated sufficient wealth to employ others, are certainly better able to rule than those who, however worthy as citizens, have not had brains enough to raise themselves out of the ranks of manual workers.[23]

James Jefferis, Minister of Pitt Street Congregational Church (1877-89). Presumably taken in Sydney, around 1880. (Photo courtesy of Mitchell Library, Sydney.)

These comments indicate that churchmen did take some notice of trade unionism in the 1880s, even if their attitude was not too friendly or sympathetic. Generally, evangelical Protestants did not think that regulation of industry was the way to better industrial relations. They looked to a Christian spirit to prevail among workers and employers. During a bus drivers' strike in 1882 the *Weekly Advocate* observed that if masters and men took as their slogan, "not slothful in business, fervent in spirit, serving the Lord", it would transform industrial relations. At the same time, it expressed some sympathy with the drivers who worked fifteen hours a day with little time for a meal.[24]

The Pauline teaching from the New Testament on masters and servants was often invoked as the pattern of good industrial relationships. In essence, it was an appeal to employers to be just and considerate to their workers and to employees to work hard and honestly. It was the basis of Catholic as well as Protestant teaching. Father P.M. Ryan appealed to St Paul's advice in a sermon preached in St Mary's Cathedral in February 1884. He did not want to deal with politics or social economy, but he did condemn idleness. It bred "poverty, crime, and misery in the humbler walks of life, and pride, immorality and selfishness among the rich". Man was obliged by the fall to work, but Christ had dignified and elevated labour by his own toil as a carpenter. Some, however, would employ and others would be employed. As to the responsibilities and duties of the employer and the employee, "mutual respect and a desire to act towards each other fairly, and honorably" were essential. The servant should show "respect for the worthiness of the master and a proper regard for his interests", but without toadying. The master should show "a kindly interest in the moral and general welfare of all in his service", being respectful of feelings and religious convictions. Above all, relations were to be ruled by the principle of just pay for honest work. This well-meaning but paternalistic concept of industrial relations anticipated the teaching of the papal encyclical *Rerum Novarum* (1891).[25]

Some churchmen, however, were not prepared to leave the question of industrial justice wholly to benevolence and a sense of fair play. They recognized that it was sometimes necessary for the law to redress wrongs. Trade unions had won many rightful gains for skilled workers, who by 1880 mostly enjoyed an eight hour day. But it was a different story with the more "respectable" occupations, especially shop assistants. Partly due to their pride, they fared poorly compared with tradesmen. They might have had the support of the trade union movement in a campaign for shorter hours but, as was pointed out at the Trades and Labour Congress in 1889, the shop assistants disdained "to mix with the horny-handed", and were generally apathetic in their own cause.[26]

But leading churchmen supported the early closing movement. Bishop Barry, Dr Robert Steel, Dr Jefferis and Dr Renwick were among its prominent advocates in the 1880s. "Perish business," exclaimed Barry at an early closing meeting in December 1885, "if in its process it [has] to use up the bodies and minds and souls of men". The Congregational Union and the Wesleyan General Conference endorsed the early closing movement in 1888 and the *Australian Christian World* took up the cause. Support from churchmen increased in the 1890s, for shop assistants continued to work long hours in New South Wales until 1900, when 6 p.m. closing of shops was introduced, with one late shopping night (to 10 p.m.) and a weekly half-holiday.[27]

Legislative regulation might also be needed where unions were strong as well as where they were weak. A few churchmen were coming to this view in the 1880s, especially as industrial strife became more serious. Trouble on the Newcastle coalfields in 1888 led some to contemplate government intervention. A strike loomed near in August when the miners' union demanded a new agreement on more generous terms. The dispute threatened the community more than any previous trouble, both because it would disrupt industry and transport and because the miners sought wider support for their protest at the unequal distribution of wealth in society.[28] The threatening disaster provoked some comment from churchmen and reflection on the state of industrial relations and the morality of strikes.

Dr Jefferis viewed the gathering industrial storm with grave concern, anticipating the reaction of churchmen to the Maritime Strike two years later. From his pulpit on Sunday 19 August 1888 he warned that a strike was impending "upon a scale of the greatest magnitude ever witnessed in Australia". While he still recognized the right of workers to combine, he now saw a danger of tyranny from trade unions. Even so, strikes were "sometimes necessary . . . the millenium [sic] being yet very far off". But a strike was "a declaration of war" having direct consequences on the workers, their dependants, their industry and, in the case of this dispute, on society at large. So, like war, everything should be done to avoid it; and it should only be embarked on for an adequate cause. Jefferis did not want to pronounce on that from the pulpit, but he made his position clear enough when he stated that, while the men might have a righteous cause in demanding a 5 per cent pay increase, their cause became unrighteous if it deprived others of earning anything, thus creating poverty, misery and hunger. This, society could not sanction; legislation was needed to set limits to such industrial disputes and to provide machinery for an "authoritative settlement" of them.[29]

This was further than some were prepared to go, although the Catholic *Nation* thought that the public should support the coalminers as long as they conducted themselves with honour and prudence. But the *Weekly Advocate* condemned the strike as immoral for much the same reason as Jefferis abhorred it. It thought that the time had come for the churches to enunciate the general principles of justice between men and urge them to settle their disputes by "some civilised and Christian method". Piously, it relied on Christian influence rather than state intervention or regulation. The *Presbyterian* reflected ambiguously on the morality of strikes and relative rights that needed defining, but the *Independent* took a clear enough line when the strike began. It was persuaded that questions of wages and conditions of employment would have to be settled by law courts, for capital and labour could no longer be left to fight their own battles. "Either State regulation or Socialism in its absolute form must come", it predicted, for "Laissez faire is played out in the estimation of the multitude". Unless the government intervened it saw only anarchy generated by labour unions on the one hand and by unions of capitalists on the other.[30]

The *Independent*'s view arose partly from free trade liberalism's principle of international arbitration to avoid war among nations. This principle enjoyed widespread support among Congregationalists and other evangelical Protestants. Some of them were active in the Sydney Peace Society, founded in the 1880s. The need for arbitration in international affairs was easily extended to industrial disputes, which Jefferis had depicted as a form of warfare. The Employers' Federation formed in New South Wales in 1888 also supported the principle of industrial arbitration, largely as a means of curbing union demands in a time of prosperity. But the good years were almost over, and as the economy tightened the unions lost the advantage they had gained in the 1880s and they began to look to arbitration. The 1889 Trades and Labour Congress carried a motion in support of "the establishment of Boards of Conciliation and Arbitration for the settlement of all disputes between Capital and Labor [sic] and so prevent strikes and lock-outs".[31] But the primary motivation of churchmen in seeking a system of arbitration was the preservation of law and order through a civilized and Christian manner of settling disputes.

Such an attempt was made to avert the strike at Newcastle. A Citizens' Conciliation Committee was formed and Canon A.E. Selwyn, Vicar General of the diocese of Newcastle, emerged as its leader. Both parties accepted Selwyn as mediator and negotiations began optimistically. Selwyn tried to soften the attitude of the colliery proprietors towards the men, but in the end he was used by them in an attempt to bring the men to heel. On Tuesday 21 August they handed him a sealed envelope containing a proposed agreement which could only be opened once the miners had withdrawn all demands obnoxious to the employers. The Conciliation Committee naively agreed to this approach, but Selwyn found the miners' representatives unwilling to negotiate until the proprietors' proposals were opened and set before them. He failed over several meetings to win their consent to the employers' scheme and the strike began on 24 August. The miners won some gains through the strike, but it was settled on the proprietors' terms.[32] Despite Selwyn's ineptness which made him appear an emissary of the employers, he and his supporters were not devoid of sympathy for the unionists.

Australian churchmen found an opportunity to express their sympathy with the labouring classes more warmly on the occasion of the London Dock Strike in 1889, although it was easier to speak out against social injustice when it occurred in England. At the same time, the Australian working classes did not seem too badly off compared with the poorly paid dockers of London, whose plight aroused widespread sympathy. There was a public meeting and mass demonstration on the Sydney Domain to raise funds for the dockers and appeals of support were made from the pulpits in Sydney and Melbourne. In an impassioned plea from his Pitt Street pulpit, Dr Jefferis told people who had no paper to tear a page from their hymn-books and write their promised gift on it.[33]

The appeal for the London dockers provided an occasion for more general observations on poverty and capital/labour relations. The *Presbyterian* was more restrained in its sympathy. While it thought the dockers had justice on their side and that women and children should not be allowed to starve, it also observed unsympathetically that the greater number of the poor had only themselves to blame for their "dependent condition". They lacked "the essentials of citizenship, viz., righteousness, sobriety, purity, economy and industry". John Fordyce, liberal minister of the wealthy Woollahra Congregational Church, expressed the opposite view. He made the appeal an occasion to attack both laissez-faire capitalism and the cherished principle of freedom of contract, which had once meant the "freedom to brutalise and degrade helpless children". Many good but short-sighted men, he observed, still thought that the interests of all were best advanced "by each seeking his own interest". These men, he exclaimed, "pray on Sundays 'Thy Kingdom come' ", yet on other days they worked to advance their own selfish ends; "as if God's Kingdom could ever come by every man seeking his own things!"[34]

Christianity and Socialism

This attack on laissez-faire capitalism was not entirely new in Australia. Socialist theories prompted a few churchmen to rethink their position on social questions in the 1880s, although some reacted with hostility. In 1886 the *Australian Christian World* denounced socialist theories as "the vicious outbursts of idle penurious agitators" who were attempting to disturb the proper order of things; "some must be rich and some poor, some gain distinction and honour, while others live in obscurity." Communism, it allowed, "may be possible in the millenium [sic], but not now". Cardinal Moran hardly sounded any different in an address that same year, although he also condemned unbridled capitalism. But he depicted socialists as men who deemed it "idle to earn an honest livelihood by industry", preferring instead "to pull down the rich man from the pedestal of power, and appropriate the wealth that does not belong to them".[35]

More sympathetic responses to socialism came from theologically liberal Protestants in the 1880s. They sought to show that Christianity was not necessarily hostile to socialism. In a lecture in St James's Church in September 1886 Bishop Barry explained that Christianity recognized and sympathized with both individualism and socialism. By individualism he meant equality of opportunity for all men to develop their abilities and powers. But this freedom could not be completely unrestricted, for experience had shown that left to itself capitalism would probably use up more than its share of the fruits of labour. Socializing forces were needed to check the excesses of individualism and subordinate it to the public good, but not socialist government. Law was one socializing force, as also were cooperation and combination exhibited in the trade union movement; Christianity wished it well. But the great socializing force for which Christianity stood was not law or combination, but "a spiritual force" which inspired men with a spirit of self-sacrifice in the service of their fellow men and of God. Thus Christianity was "true socialism". It also sought to preserve the small units of society, such as the family, and to leave room for charity and philanthropy; the latter, Barry pointed out, were vital features of the Christian socialism of Frederick Denison Maurice and Charles Kingsley. But the greatest difference between Christianity and secular socialism, he argued, was a matter of means; for the law of Christianity was development, not revolution.[36]

James Jefferis made similar points in a lecture on "Socialism in Germany", delivered in June 1878, and in a series of lectures on "The Socialism of Christianity" late in 1886. The former lecture was prompted by a report of the funeral of the German socialist, Augustus Heinsch. Jefferis deplored the atheism of German socialism and its attacks on Christianity, but he was confident that faith would triumph over unbelief: "A nation of atheists there never has been, and there never can be." But one aim of socialism he did warmly support was to lift "the toiling struggling masses into a more comfortable and a more honourable life by changes in the existing structure of society". Jefferis saw evidence in the preceding fifty years that the lot of the worker was improving; it would continue to improve if Christians as well as political economists found practical answers to the problems of justice and human dignity in industrial society. The solution did not lie in destruction, but through regeneration in which "the spirit of Christ becomes the regulating . . . power". In the later lectures he emphasized more the common ground between Christianity and socialism. But Christian socialism looked for a slow but sure progress towards the Christian state: slow, because it worked through the individual; sure, because it took account of the depravity of human nature. The evangelical teaching was evident here, but nothing of laissez-faire. Legislation was necessary to check individualism without destroying it. Both Jefferis and Barry attributed to Christianity the humanitarian progress of the recent past, such as the abolition of slavery and Shaftesbury's factory legislation. Monstrous inequalities remained, Jefferis realized, but he was sure that they would be abolished gradually by piecemeal legislation, by the cooperation of capital and labour, and above all through the spirit of Christ, "the great Social Reformer" and "the Regenerator of Society".[37]

Both Barry and Jefferis displayed a certain complacency about social injustices; but it came not so much from indifference as from a great faith in the progress of humanity under the influence of Christianity. They recognized the existing evils and did not blame the poor for their plight, as some of the Evangelicals did; but the prophetic passion of Jeremiah or Amos did not burn in them. Although they distanced themselves from the Catholic and conservative Protestant attitude of unswerving hostility to socialism, their implicit criticism of the injustices of the existing social and economic order probably made little or no impression on thoughtful working men outside the churches.

More trenchant criticism of the social order and warmer expressions of sympathy for the working classes came from Dr Tho.nas Roseby, who was also theologically more liberal. Born in New South

Wales in 1844, Roseby returned to the colony in 1888 after a long
pastorate in Dunedin, New Zealand, and a short one in Ballarat, Victoria. Well read in political economy as well as in theological and
scientific literature, Roseby was a persistent critic of laissez-faire
capitalism and its dogmas of "the Divine principle of competition"
and "freedom of contract". There was "a principle of Divine righteousness higher than that of the political economist", he told the
Victorian Congregational Union in October 1886. In a paper read to
the Intercolonial Congregational Conference in Melbourne in 1888
he attacked "the iron law of wages" and, as Chairman of the
Congregational Union of New South Wales, in November 1890 he
rebuked Congregationalists for preferring the "Gospel of
Manchester to that of Galilee" and admonished them to "throw off
the incubus of this superstition about *Laissez faire*". Roseby was also
caustic about Carnegie's "Gospel of Wealth" and its patronizing
attitude to the poor. Charitable institutions served a purpose but
they only dealt with effects. In his Christmas sermon in 1889, "Purple and Rags", he declared that "not charity, but justice" was
necessary to adjust the great gulf between the very rich and the poor,
by whose labour they were enriched.[38]

The ethical prophecy of the Old Testament underlay Roseby's
social teaching; the fatherhood of God and the brotherhood of man
and the quest for "the Kingdom of God and His justice" were leading ideas of his liberal theology. He proposed more radical remedies
for social injustice than most churchmen of the time. He was not
afraid to speak of "the reconstruction of society", although he
admitted to the Royal Commission on Strikes in 1891 that the
phrase sounded "ominous". In "The Labour Problem", a paper
delivered in 1888, he argued that the conflict between capital and
labour would not be solved "by any sumptuary legislation, prescrib-
ing rates of wages, and endeavouring to regulate the minutiae of
industrial relations", but "by the abolition of the conflict of
interests entirely, so that labour itself shall become at once its own
employer and its own servant". Roseby promoted this principle of a
blending of interests through the Federal Co-operative Association,
founded in 1889, and sought practical application of it in the depression in the 1890s.[39]

But cooperation was not the sole answer, for Roseby added that
the solution to economic conflict also depended on "both capital
and labour being admitted into full partnership with land". In his
advocacy of a system of taxation on land he was close to Henry
George, who had disciples in New South Wales, especially among
the urban middle classes and small farmers. But Roseby denied that
he was "a single-taxer". He expounded his theory on the national-

Thomas Roseby, Congregational Minister, amateur scientist and Christian socialist. Taken in Dunedin around 1884. (From *Moray Place Congregational Church,
Dunedin, New Zealand* by Thos. Gilray [Dunedin: 1912].)

ization of land in his sermon, "Purple and Rags", which he was to
repeat a number of times as a lecture in 1890. He based his teaching
on the Mosaic law: "The land shall not be sold for ever: for the land
is mine" (Lev. 25:23). A "substantial tax upon the unearned incre-
ment of land", he argued, would increase both the profits of indus-

try and the wages of labour. It would also contribute to public works, especially to education, and lighten taxation generally.[40]

These changes were comprehended in Roseby's overall idea of the quest for the kingdom of God and "His justice". But his vision of a Christianized society was not radically egalitarian. The progress of brotherhood among men and nations would not abolish "the distinction between purple and fustian" by substituting "a neutral tint of common gray", although it would "brighten and elevate the universal lot" of men. In the end the Christianization of society was not so much a political programme as a question of evangelization. Like Jefferis and Barry, and the more conservative churchmen, Roseby proclaimed that the answer to the great social questions lay in Christ, in regeneration, and in following his teaching in the Sermon on the Mount.[41] This took some of the offence out of his utterances.

Another of the more liberal churchmen in Sydney, H.L. Jackson of St James's Church, was a Christian socialist. In an address to the Intercolonial Charity Conference in November 1890 he stated: "Society must be reorganised upon a nobler and sounder basis, such as [that] contained in the 'platform' of the English Christian socialists." The short-lived *Banner and Anglo-Catholic Review,* which began publication in Sydney in 1890, also promoted Christian socialism. One writer found radical and political significance in the liturgy as celebrated by High Churchmen: "The Mass is full of deep popular sympathy, of downright and fearless Socialism." Precisely what all this meant was not clear; the founder of the English Christian Social Union, Bishop Westcott, admitted that "Christian socialism" was "a most vague phrase". The Church's function was not "to propose any social programme but to enforce eternal principles".[42] But churchmen did not agree about what those principles were, as Jackson found in 1890 when he moved in synod that the economic welfare of society depended on the acceptance and application of every man's right to work and the redistribution of the produce of labour. The motion lapsed when the synod adjourned for want of a quorum — "a very happy despatch", observed the evangelical *Record.*[43]

Churchmen in the 1880s touched fairly frequently on social questions in the pulpit in lectures and in the religious press. Their comments displayed a variety of attitudes. Some showed little sympathy for the trade union movement, were contented with the existing social order and viewed socialism with hostility. Others conveyed a positive sympathy for trade unionism and the improvement of industrial conditions and the living condition of the working classes, but their view of socialism was still critical. A few went further and looked for the reconstruction of society under the name of Christian socialism. The spectrum was much broader than the recent assertion that up to 1890 all churchmen "had supported capitalism" and that "ministers of the major non-Catholic denominations continued to do so". Hebblewhite's accusation in 1889 that the churches were losing support because the clergy preached outworn doctrines instead of bringing the social and economic order under the scrutiny of Christian standards was also somewhat wide of mark, especially as it was aimed at H.L. Jackson.[44] Some of those most anxious to restate the faith to modern man also cared keenly to see it applied to modern society. But they were a distinguished minority; most ministers, when they touched on social questions, still proclaimed the old evangelical doctrine of individual regeneration as the only way to reform society, and to that extent Hebblewhite had a point.

The Churches and Social Questions in 1890

There was considerable discussion of the question of politics in the pulpit early in 1890, some of it almost certainly provoked by Hebblewhite's article, even though it was not mentioned. But churchmen themselves were calling for more attention to social questions from the pulpit, as for instance at the Anglican Church Congress in Sydney in 1889. When the *New South Wales Independent* took the question up in January 1890 it maintained the traditional argument that the church's task was primarily spiritual; preachers would do more good, it claimed, by keeping "resolutely to the Gospel themes", and thereby inspire and influence the men who had to solve social and industrial problems.[45] The *Australian Christian World,* now under the editorship of E.J. Rodd, a Wesleyan minister, moved away from the accepted evangelical position. In a comment on Henry George's visit to Sydney in March 1890 it observed cautiously that there ought to be room in the pulpit for the application of Christianity to present day problems. It thought that the alienation of the masses from Christianity was due in large part to want of sympathy and understanding from churchmen, much the same view that Hebblewhite had advanced. In a subsequent issue it affirmed that the interest in social questions was a move in the right direction, but warned the churches not to abandon their "moribund theology" simply to deal with the problems of the day, for if the pulpit omitted "God and His Spirit, Christ and His Salvation" and supernatural power from its message, "the survival will be scarcely worth calling by Christ's name". The point had to be made, at least for the sake of a few enthusiasts. One layman complained to the

Australian Christian World in April 1890 that Henry George had so turned the heads of some ministers that a respectable businessman who owned an allotment of land was now "in most ministers' eyes a bloated monopolist, a land grabber, and the oppressor of the poor working man".[46] Such a preacher would have been unusual in 1890, but it is significant that there were some.

The *Australian Christian World* supported the social application of Christianity more emphatically from April 1890, when there was another change of editorship; the new editor was T.S. Carey, a Baptist layman from South Australia. In a comment on the Salvation Army in July 1890, the journal praised the Army's new programme of social work, but claimed that this did not go far enough. The churches had to take the side of the people "frankly and openly" against all oppression. In an essentially practical age, it argued, the gospel must not only tell penitent sinners how to find peace with God, but also constrain Christians to love their neighbours as themselves, and "honestly and equitably [to] share with the toiler that wealth which is far more the outcome of his industry than society has ever yet acknowledged". The "great Christian work" of the time, it concluded, was "the reorganisation of society in accordance with the principles of the Gospel". That same month a writer reviewing Edward Bellamy's *Looking Backward* (1889) questioned the view that the world only needed the gospel and conversion to God "in the generally accepted sense of that term". Social reform, he implied, might have to come first "to make the conversion of men in any widespread way at all practicable".[47]

At the same time, the Wesleyan *Weekly Advocate,* edited by the conservative Paul Clipsham, was doing all it could to reinforce the traditional view. In May 1890 it announced that Methodism's task was to contribute to "the conservation and perfecting of human society", as it had been from the beginning; for "faithful preaching, not of politics, but of the Word of God . . . saved English society at the end of the last century from the throes of revolution". It was confident that in Australia also the Methodist Church would be "one of the strongest safeguards against the evils which now seem so inseparably connected with Socialism". A speech on "Social Regeneration" by the colonial treasurer, William McMillan, son of the Methodist manse, gave the *Advocate* an opportunity to reply to the *Australian Christian World.* McMillan's speech, in a nutshell, was that "society is not to be regenerated by Acts of Parliament but by the grace of God." This idea found favour with the *Advocate*; if the churches preached "the need of heart religion" and helped men to get it, society would "need no political cataclysms to sweep away its evils, nor sweet influences of legislation to bind up its wounds".[48]

The *Australian Christian World* and the *Weekly Advocate* represent the opposite ends in the spectrum of social attitudes expressed by churchmen in the first half of 1890, before the Maritime Strike. The evangelical principle of social reform through individual regeneration, while it still had powerful advocates, did not have the field to itself. It had long been modified by some leading churchmen, and a few had gone even further in espousing some form of Christian socialism. Thus the Great Strike of 1890 is not the watershed in the social thought of the churches that it has sometimes been thought to be.

The responses of churchmen to the Maritime Strike, which began on 16 August 1890 and soon proliferated into something like a general strike in eastern Australia,[49] arose predictably out of the debate of the previous decade. As in the case of the Newcastle Coalminers' Strike in 1888, churchmen were profoundly disturbed by the social disruption caused by the strike and commended the Christian principles of mutual sympathy and respect as the means to resolve the conflict. A Wesleyan minister, the Reverend Rainsford Bavin, suggested that the captains and crews of the ships should say the Lord's Prayer together and observe the golden rule. Preaching in the Parramatta Presbyterian Church, the Reverend J.W. Inglis turned to the Pauline teaching on masters and servants to find light on the dispute. "Christian feeling", he declared, was the only remedy "for such malignant disorders", of which the strike was symptomatic.[50] This well-meaning advice was repeated frequently throughout the strike by concerned churchmen who were out of touch with the harsh realities of the industrial situation. Their admonitions fell on deaf ears.

The religious press, generally, was not sympathetic to the unionists' opposition to non-union labour. The *Presbyterian* and the *Independent* defended freedom of contract — individual liberty for men and masters — against the closed shop, although the latter journal was not as hostile to the unionists as the former. The *Weekly Advocate* recognized the right of combination, but when men tried to prevent the employment of non-union labour (which was plentiful in 1890) they were "using tyranny as a means of securing for themselves rights they denied to others". The *Australian Christian World* was more sympathetic, although it did not consider the strike justified. However, it observed that it was too late to attack unionism in defence of something called "free labour". Even though there were occasional excesses in unionism, it could not but rejoice in the general elevation of the toiler", which he owed "almost entirely to . . . Trades Unionism".[51]

James Hill gave a bolder defence of unionism from his pulpit in

Bourke Street Congregational Church on 28 September 1890: properly used, it "could not but have the sanction of Christianity". He found the defence of freedom of contract specious, for it was "a pretty theory" which in practice "resulted chiefly in the rich man grinding the face of his poorer brother". It was sometimes necessary, he contended, to sacrifice individual liberty to secure "a larger and more widely-permeating liberty". He predicted that trade unionism would be instrumental in bringing about "a juster and more righteous state of affairs" in the future. These views upset at least one member of the congregation, who "put the case for the masters" somewhat excitedly outside the church. Dr Roseby held similar views to Hill on unionism; he told the Royal Commission on Strikes that free labour was the greatest threat to the elevation of the worker.[52]

Roseby also led a group of ministers formed on 10 September 1890 to act as conciliators in the strike. This initiative came from the Sydney Peace Society, of which Roseby was a member. The ministers were unsuccessful because the shipowners refused to receive their deputation, although they had informal conversations with the Labour Defence Committee. The next week Cardinal Moran offered his services as a conciliator, and likewise received a good reception from the unionists, but not from shipowners. Protestant ministers in Brisbane were rebuffed by the employers when they attempted to mediate in the dispute there. "Social questions are outside the province of the pulpit", they were told.[53] The employers were clearly bent on unconditional surrender by the unionists.

How much impact did the words, statements and actions of churchmen make on the unionists? The report of the Labour Defence Committee condemned pulpit along with press and government. The clergy, it said, left public opinion "to grope amid the gloom of *sacerdotal* clap-trap", a harsh judgment on the pious exhortations to goodwill and mutual sympathy. Exceptions were made of Cardinal Moran, Dr Roseby, the Reverends H.L. Jackson and George Walters, the Unitarian minister, "and a few other clergymen for their Christ-like sympathy with the struggling masses". The majority had, it asserted, largely lost their "opportunities of well-doing among the workers of Australia".[54] The clergy it praised were among those who held the most radical theological as well as social ideas, except for Cardinal Moran, who, despite his epithet of "the radical Cardinal", was relatively more conservative.[55]

Cardinal Moran differed from the conservative Protestants in his open sympathy for the maritime officers in their claim for better conditions, and in his criticism of the ruinous competition that

Patrick Francis Cardinal Moran, Third Catholic Archbishop of Sydney (1884-1911). Taken
Sydney around 1886. (Photo courtesy of St Mary's Cathedral Archives.)

forced wages down. But while he generally approved of trade unions, which were "only another form of the old Catholic guilds", he defended freedom of contract during the strike and warned that unions were in danger of falling into the same kind of tyranny that they denounced. This was not very different from the utterances of some of the conservative Protestants, and he was close to them in his attitude towards socialism. In an interview in October 1890 he said that the only hope for trade unionism was "to keep quite free from any Socialist movement . . . The end and purpose of Socialist agitation is to overthrow society . . . Socialists are the vowed enemies of all religion." Some of his other statements during the strike sounded similar to those of conservative Protestants, such as his address on Sunday 28 September.

> If the principles of Christianity were observed and followed there would be less clamouring for law and order, there would be fewer appeals to justice and equity in their sternest and coldest forms, and . . . more reliance on kindness and charity . . . these Christian methods [are] often efficacious where justice and equity as recognized by the world [fail] in the settlement of disputes and in the re-establishment of social relations which [have] been rudely disturbed by misunderstanding and quarrels.[56]

It was his practical sympathy rather than these platitudes that earned the Cardinal the plaudits of the labour movement.

Cardinal Moran's social teaching largely anticipated the message of the papal encyclical on "The Condition of Labour", *Rerum Novarum,* issued in May 1891. This statement took the inequalities of society for granted and spoke of the blessedness of poverty; it defended charity as dispensed by the Church against the State's systems of relief. Despite its view of the modern world through a medieval window, it did have some positive things to say about trade unions, although it preferred Catholics to belong to Catholic trade unions. While it sought to defend the Church against incursions from the State, it did insist that the State had the duty to regulate industrial affairs where public peace or good morals and religion were concerned. It spoke of reasonable hours and conditions of labour, and of a "just wage" as being "enough to support the wage-earner in reasonable and frugal comfort". Needless to say, the encyclical emphatically opposed socialism, and against it defended "the inviolability of private property". But, it has been observed that what was "mentioned most often in *Rerum Novarum* was the necessity of true religion as a foundation for any right relationship between capital and labour".[57] Aside from its Thomistic arguments and general Catholic orientation, many of the encyclical's ideas had been expressed by some Protestant churchmen in the 1880s, Bishop

Barry and Dr Jefferis in particular, although not with the same air of authority and finality.

In Australia Catholics welcomed *Rerum Novarum,* if sometimes for different reasons. The *Freeman's Journal* was pleased to note that it insisted on the rights of property and individual freedom, so long as the exercise of these rights was "limited by Christian charity". Cardinal Moran saw in it an endorsement of the labour movement.[58] The papal teaching underlay his lecture on "The Rights and Duties of Labour" delivered before a distinguished audience in the New Masonic Hall on 17 August 1891. Moran spoke warmly of the rights of labour and recognized the abuse of "freedom of contract": it had been made "an engine of tyranny" instead of the charter of the worker's liberty. But he became unctuous and condescending when he spoke of the duties of labour. Expounding on *Rerum Novarum's* teaching on charity and religion, he pointed the poor to the consolations of heaven. The Church preached the gospel to the worker "to cheer and comfort him in his toil, to alleviate his burden, to teach him the true dignity of labour". His "privations" would be "the seed of spiritual blessings". At the same time, the Church, he said, warned the capitalist "not to place his trust in the riches and power he possesses", but to use his wealth as "a faithful steward . . . in the service of his Divine Master". It was "the Gospel of Wealth" from Catholic lips. The Cardinal's audience received the lecture well, but a few days later the Trades and Labour Council decisively rejected the motion of Peter Brennan, one of the Catholic members of the recently-formed Labor party, to thank the Cardinal for his "able and instructive lecture".[59] Nevertheless, Moran enjoyed much greater rapport with the emerging labour movement than most Protestant churchmen.

The reason for this is partly that more Catholics than Protestants seem to have been Labor voters, and it was in the Catholic Church's interest to cultivate them. Protestant congregations were largely middle class and many of them were supporters of the Liberal party or its equivalent. Yet Dr. Roseby and Archdeacon Boyce and a few other Protestant churchmen were more active than any Catholic churchman in promoting village settlements and other schemes of relief during the depression in the 1890s. They also advocated social welfare measures such as old age pensions and supported the movements for early closing of shops and women's suffrage.[60] But, although a Christian socialist, Roseby never became a supporter of the Labor party. The reasons for this are not entirely clear, but in his address to Australian Congregationalists in 1904 on "Social Unrest—Labour" he argued that the churches had to keep out of party politics and do justice to the best men in all parties. The tone of this paper was more conservative than his earlier utterances; "political and social changes, to be safe," he pointed out, "must not be revolutionary, but evolutionary."[61] This was hardly any different from Bishop Barry's position in 1886. So the most radical of Protestant churchmen grew more cautious.

Christian socialists were a small minority anyway; the branch of the Christian Social Union founded among Anglicans in Sydney in the late 1890s did not last long.[62] The *Weekly Advocate* had no time for the Christian socialists in 1890 — "political and religious faddists" with their "loose preaching of brotherly love and a sort of Christian communism". Opposed as it was to mixing religion and politics, it made two significant exceptions to its rule; on Sunday observance and temperance it was prepared to resort to those "sweet influences of legislation". Similarly, at the Anglican General Synod in September 1891, Bishop Saumerez Smith warned that the Church should generally not interfere in politics; its task was essentially to prepare for the Second Coming of Christ, for it was to this event that Christians looked for a solution to the world's problems. But where "social morality" or "the religious rights of the community" were concerned, and were silence might be construed as apathy or cowardice, the Church should speak. Smith probably had in mind the divorce question, Sunday observance and issues such as gambling and temperance.[63]

Evangelicalism did tend to inhibit a positive response to questions of social justice among many Protestants,[64] but it did not prevent Boyce from campaigning for measures of social reform, such as old age pensions. It was rather the interest in temperance reform which prevented Protestants from taking questions of social justice more seriously than they did. It also inhibited their sympathy for the working classes. Here again Boyce, the leading temperance reformer, is an exception to the rule. And Dr. Roseby is another; he saw intemperance as much a consequence as a cause of other social evils, a reaction to long working hours and poor living conditions.[65] But temperance reformers and their supporters mostly told a different story.

The temperance evangelist, William Noble, told his Sydney audience in 1886 that he had heard men declaiming on the Domain about over-production and the redistribution of wealth; but the temperance reformer, he claimed, had solved all these problems long ago. The trouble was that the working man spent too much of his money on drink and tobacco and left his wife with little to keep the home. The same argument was used at the International Centennial Temperance Congress in Sydney in 1888. One speaker asserted: "We should hear very little of poverty or of the 'unemployed question' if a stop were put to the drinking habits of our land."[66] The effect of these and similar utterances was to persuade many Protestants that temperance reform was the alternative to other programmes of social reform, especially those proposing the reconstruction of society.

Commitment to temperance reform not only coloured the view churchmen took of social questions; it also further alienated the working classes from the churches. This is not to deny the support there was for temperance among some working men. But there was bound to be some conflict between the claims of the temperance reformers, as they were presented in the late nineteenth century, and the aims of the labour movement. Labour leaders argued that temperance reformers mistook the effect for the cause, and the objected strongly to the implication of middle-class Protestant propaganda that it was chiefly the working man who needed to be protected from the evils of intemperance.[67] But these protests had little impact. Temperance had become firmly entrenched in Protestantism in the 1880s, and was to shape the response of most churchmen to social questions for years to come.[68]

Part Three

Christianity and the State

7

Defending Christian Institutions

The Evangelicals' principle that the churches should keep out of politics did not apply when the preservation of the Christian Sunday or other "religious rights" of the community were at stake. Being energetic lobbyists in these matters, they acted from the premise that Church and State were still properly joined. Anglicans generally took the view, and, in this area of religious rights, so did the voluntaryists. They affirmed as emphatically as other Protestants that Australia was a Christian country, and that the State should therefore uphold religious values.

This opinion was not confined to churchmen — it was apparently shared by some political leaders. Sir Henry Parkes, father of the so-called Secular Education Act of 1880, hoped that Australia would become "a great, free, independent nation based upon the broad principles of our common Christian religion". So he said from the chair of the Christian Evidence Society in August 1885. Non-believers were free to express their views: but,

> as we are a British people — are pre-eminently a Christian people — as our laws, our whole system of jurisprudence, our Constitution . . . are based upon and interwoven with our Christian belief, and as we are immensely in the majority, we have a fair claim to be spoken of at all times with respect and deference.[1]

This was precisely what Protestant churchmen thought; and it implied that Christianity was entitled to some support and protection — moral and legal, if not financial, especially to uphold the Sabbath and Christian marriage, the "two greatest institutions" brought to the world by Christianity.[2]

By 1880 both these great institutions were under threat. There were repeated attempts in Parliament to liberalize the law dealing with divorce, and the Sabbath was not being kept as churchmen believed the commandment of God and the law of the land intended it to be kept. The Sabbath was protected chiefly by two old statutes — the Sunday Observance Acts of 1677 and 1780. The former, a statute of Charles II, principally prohibited self-interested labour and trading on "the Lord's Day", but by 1880 it was honoured more in the breach than in the observance. The government, by providing Sunday train services, appeared to be one of the greatest transgressors of this law.[3] However those prosecuted under the Act were generally poorer people — Chinese gardeners, paper boys, fruit barrowmen, and occasionally Seventh Day Adventists who worked on Sundays; and the fines for such offences were usually nominal. The other statute, enacted under George III, outlawed public performances on Sundays for which admission was charged either by cash of ticket and also made the advertisement of such performances illegal. Also known as Bishop Porteus's Act, it was framed to protect religion from having to compete with entertainments and especially to shield it from ridicule. Yet freethought lecturers were charging admission to their Sunday-night lectures in city theatres, in which they entertained their audiences with attacks on religion, and a little music as well.[4]

Apart from these breaches of the Sunday observance laws, people generally were using Sunday as a day of recreation as well as, if not always instead of, a day for religious duties. After all, there were more and better opportunities for recreation than there had been in earlier days. An extensive system of public transport including railways, tramways, horse-drawn omnibuses and harbour steamers made possible a variety of Sunday outings and picnics which were appealing in the climate. The trend for the middle classes to avail themselves of those opportunities troubled churchmen and probably contributed to the decline in attendance at evening church services. At the same time, there was a movement, inspired by the Sunday Freedom League in Britain (founded in 1875), to open museums, picture galleries and libraries on Sundays. The English league enjoyed the support of a number of Broad Churchmen, including Dean Stanley of Westminster. He had a few counterparts in Australia, especially in Melbourne,[5] but most colonial churchmen were opposed to any liberalization of Sunday. It was a Catholic MP, J.J. Hurley, who introduced a motion in the Legislative Assembly in March 1878 to open the Museum and Free Public Library on Sunday afternoons. Hurley quoted Dean Stanley in support of his motion, which was carried in a thin House. It took the churches by surprise, and on 1 April a large gathering of churchmen condemned this "violation of the law of God" and resolved to pressure the governor, Parliament and the trustees of the museum and library to have the Legislative Assembly's decision rescinded. Petitions from churches and public meetings throughout the colony poured into Parliament, but to no avail. The next year at Easter, concerned churchmen inaugurated a "Week of Prayer for the Entire Sanctification of the Sabbath Day". But certain events in 1880 were to con-

Before His Most Sacred Majesty.

A prosecution for Sabbath-breaking, under the Act of Charles II.

A prosecution under the Sunday Observance Act of Charles II. (From the *Bulletin*, **24** November 1883. Photo courtesy of La Trobe Library, State Library of Victoria.)

vince them of the need to do more than pray for the proper observance of the Lord's Day.

At a meeting of subscribers of the School of Arts Reading Room
in August 1880 the freethought lecturer, Charles Bright, proposed
the opening of the reading room on Sunday afternoons, appealing
also to the example of Dean Stanley. Bright claimed that Sunday
opening would be a great boon to working men, and the spiritualist
lecturer, John Tyerman, flippantly observed that the ringing of
church bells on Sunday was harder work than Sunday opening would
entail for the attendants of the reading room. But Bright's and Tyerman's advocacy did no service to the cause, for their campaign made
it plausible to assume that a crusade against Christianity lay behind
the movement. Such was the tone of the debate and Bright's resolution was soundly defeated.[7]

Churchmen enjoyed another victory a month later when Sir
Henry Parkes, then premier and colonial secretary, prevented the
agnostic astronomer, R.A. Proctor, from delivering a Sunday-night
lecture in the Theatre Royal. Apparently prompted by the proprietors of the *Protestant Standard*, Parkes forbade the theatre to open in
the terms advertised only two days before Sunday 5 September.
Proctor's agent appealed unsuccessfully against the prohibition and
the lecture was cancelled too late to inform the public. A crowd of
between two and three thousand gathered outside the theatre on the
Sunday night, attracted perhaps by the publicity beforehand as much
as the subject itself. When it was clear that the lecture would not be
held, the outraged audience moved to the Oxford Hotel, Darlinghurst, and called for Proctor. He was pleased with this demonstration of public sympathy, but asked the protesters to disperse
quietly. Before they left they gave three cheers for the hero-
astronomer as well as for the Queen, and three groans for Parkes;
some repeated this performance outside St James's Church.[8]

The *Sydney Morning Herald* sympathized with the demonstrators,
stating that Proctor's lecture should have been allowed, and
observed that if Christianity needed protection the colony should
return to a state church and a fixed creed. Few in the churches,
however, were willing to apply the voluntary principle to the question of Sunday observance. The Presbytery of Sydney congratulated
Parkes on his action and the *Church of England Record* remarked that
it was one more proof "that God's command and man's welfare
strictly coincide".[9]

But Parkes told the Sydney Presbytery that he had not acted from
any religious motives; he had not invoked any Sunday observance
laws, even though Proctor's intended performance seemed clearly
to contravene the Sunday Observance Act of 1780. Another possible

authority was the Public Exhibitions Act of 1850 (amended 1873), which empowered the colonial secretary to suspend a performance "for the preservation of good manners, decorum or the peace", as well as to prohibit performances for gain or reward on Sundays, Christmas Day and Good Friday. The *Herald* thought that Parkes had acted on the authority of this Act, although he never acknowledged it; perhaps this was because Attorney General Robert Wisdom did not consider Proctor's lecture in breach of the law, which was not revealed until several years later. Thus the public remained uncertain of the authority under which Parkes had acted, while realizing that he had also been inclined to curb the activity of freethought lecturers in the past.[10] His action against Proctor pleased churchmen. Their reasons were not unmixed either, for as well as the campaign to enforce stricter Sunday observance there was also the movement to combat freethought. Yet in pleasing churchmen for whatever reason Parkes did not seek to endorse their sabbatarian principles and so appear to be the parsons' pawn. As for Proctor, he probably did not mind too much in the end as he delivered the lecture twice to crowded audiences in the New Masonic Hall on the Thursday and Friday of the following week.

Defending the Sabbath

Pleased though churchmen were with the premier's action, some of them thought that the time had come to revive the Society for Promoting the Observance of the Lord's Day, founded in 1856, but defunct since the 1860s. Veterans of the old society planned a large public meeting and sent several thousand invitations to working men to join them in defending the day of rest. But only 300 people, mostly evangelical Protestants, met at the Protestant Hall on Monday 11 October 1880 to re-establish the society. Archdeacon Robert King, who had been secretary of the old society, railed against the increasing desecration of the Sabbath: Sunday trains and trams and harbour excursions on a large scale; public houses open legally for a few hours and some illegally at other hours; the museum and public library open on Sunday afternoons; and above all the Theatre Royal being used on Sunday nights for lectures "pointedly opposed to our common Christianity". King acknowledged the few feeble protests there had been but said that too many religious people, by fearing the label "sabbatarian", virtually sanctioned the desecration of the commandment given to men "amidst the thunders of Sinai" — to "remember the Sabbath day, to keep it holy".[11]

Speakers at the meeting expounded arguments on defence of the

Robert Steel, Minister of
Stephen's Presbyterian Churc
Phillip Street, Sydney (186
93). (From *Centenary Histo
of the Presbyterian Church
New South Wales* by J. Ca
eron [Sydney: Angus a
Robertson, 1905]. Pho
courtesy of La Trobe Unive
ity Library, Melbourne.)

William Macquarie Cowpe
Dean of Sydney (1858-1902
Taken in Sydney probabl
around 1890. (From *Th
Autobiography and Remini.
cences of William Macquar.
Cowper, Dean of Sydney* b
W.M. Cowper [Sydney: Angu
and Robertson, 1902]. Phot
courtesy of La Trobe Univer
ity Library, Melbourne.)

Sabbath. Most Protestants, particularly Evangelicals, regarded Sunday as the Sabbath of the Decalogue. They believed that the apostles had, under divine authority, transferred the Sabbath from the last to the first day of the week to commemorate the Resurrection of Jesus Christ. Some invested the fourth commandment with a special significance. Dr Robert Steel, of St Stephen's Presbyterian Church, went so far as to say at a subsequent meeting, that while most of the Decalogue coincided with the laws of nature the fourth was the one commandment direct from Almighty God, and Dean Cowper held that the Sabbath rule was the crucial commandment because it stood between the first three enjoining duty to God and the remaining six defining duty to one's neighbour. [12]

These churchmen held that as the colony was a Christian country its laws should protect Sabbath observance. Furthermore, they claimed that the Sabbath was a British as well as a Christian institution, and was responsible for British power and prosperity; it had even made Australia "a land of love, of liberty, of light". Sabbath keeping was thus a social necessity, on which national prosperity and social stability depended. The turmoils of Europe were attributed to the "Continental Sunday". Humanitarianism was also invoked. The Lord's Day, said Cowper, was "the inalienable right of man conferred on him by his Creator"; lunacy and heart disease were products of needless Sabbath work. While Sunday reformers argued that working men needed more recreational facilities, sabbatarians claimed that they were the true friends of the working man for they were defending his day of rest. Banish religion and freedom is banished, Cowper argued, but sanctify the day of rest and oppression is ended. George Woolnough, a Wesleyan, remarked that even if the Sabbath were not divine it was humane. [13]

Thus the Lord's Day Observance Society urged that Christians, patriots and humanitarians uphold the Sabbath. King was not sanguine about influencing the government, but he trusted that the society would place some check on Sabbath desecration and at least register some protest against the secularization of Sunday. The society pressed for no change in the law, and spoke of a day of rest for all people — "of holy rest if they themselves should be happily so inclined". [14] But if they sought no new legislation the sabbatarians certainly meant to have the old laws applied to the letter.

In the churches at large most Protestant clergymen were strict sabbatarians, while some laymen had less rigid views. But there were also some differences among the clergy, especially in the Church of England. Of three papers by Victorian churchmen on the question of Sunday observance read at the Anglican Church Congress in Melbourne in 1882, one defended the status of Sunday as "the Sabbath"; the second advocated a religious observance of the day, but pleaded that it should not be too burdensome; while the third was more liberal and argued that the Church had to steer a middle course between secularism and sabbatarianism.[15]Broad and High Churchmen held more liberal views on Sunday observance, especially where recreational activities were concerned. Bishop Barry, for instance, did not subscribe to the sabbatarian view of Sunday and dismissed the claim that the apostles had transferred the Sabbath to Sunday as "a baseless figment". Jackson of St James's Church also dismissed the sabbatarian argument in a lecture in August 1885. He exposed the hypocrisy and harshness of strict sabbatarianism, past and present, and appealed for more liberal Sunday observance. The *Weekly Advocate* found his views "decidedly lax" and the *Presbyterian* dismissed his lecture as "more Papistical than Protestant". But Jackson had imposed limits, such as doing nothing that would entail work for others, and he certainly did not want to see Sunday secularized. Bishop Barry was also concerned to check what, euphemistically, he called "Sunday trading".[16] These men took a more liberal stand on the use of trains on Sundays and the opening of museums and libraries, but they did share some ground with the stricter sabbatarians. This made possible a common Protestant front on Sunday observance, although not under the name of the Lord's Day Observance Society.

Catholics mostly held a freer view on the issue, although one Catholic politician took a sabbatarian stand in Parliament in 1882 in opposition to the Sunday opening of the National Gallery. Some Catholics delighted in denouncing "the black-coated Puritans" and their miserable Sabbath; one denied that Sunday was the Sabbath or even that Adam had received any command to keep the seventh day holy. This was not the official view, for the Pastoral Letter of the First Plenary Council in 1885 declared that the fourth commandment retained its original authority "quite as fully as the others", and the encyclical *Rerum Novarum* (1891) defined Sunday as a day for rest and religious observances "sanctioned by God's great law". Cardinal Moran, observing that Sunday in many countries was devoted "to dissipation and distracting secular pursuits", even suggested that the matter of Sunday observance might be an area for Catholic-Protestant cooperation, if such were possible. This did not imply a sabbatarian view for the Catholic position was closer to that of the Broad and High Anglicans; but Catholics were no more favourably disposed to the use of the theatres on Sunday by freethought lecturers than any Protestant.[17]

After its revival the Lord's Day Observance Society embarked on a futile campaign for the abolition or reduction of Sunday trains. The strict sabbatarians found little support in the community or sympathy among politicians for this part of their programme. Sir Henry Parkes defended government enterprise on Sundays as a matter of necessity and mercy. Indeed, the trains served in emergencies such as illness and bereavement, but the necessity consisted more in the revenue that Sunday traffic provided. In 1882 John Lackey, secretary for Public Works, told a deputation of devout ladies that the government did try to keep Sunday traffic to a minimum, but some traffic was inevitable. He reminded them that the locomotives which drew livestock to the Monday markets also brought many of the faithful to Sunday services. Thus, while Sunday outings by train might provide an alternative to church services, they also made it easier for some people to attend them, and churchgoers patronized the Sunday morning trains despite objections from the pulpit. Ministers of the central city churches, of course, did not object to people coming to church by train. One train-travelling churchgoer went so far as to suggest that the "church-trains", at least, should be protected from larrikins, who, by playing secular tunes offended churchgoers as they journeyed home "just after worshipping the Almighty".[18] A few notable churchmen, such as Bishop Barry, upset the sabbatarians by travelling on the Lord's Day. Dr Roseby held that train travel to religious services came under works of charity and mercy. But J.S. Austin, a strict Wesleyan, rejoiced at the end of his life that he had never found it necessary to use public transport on Sundays, except to conduct funerals. Undeterred by its want of success in this matter, the Lord's Day Observance Society continued to carp about Sunday trains, especially their use by churchgoers and ministers of the Gospel.[19]

The Society also sought to end the Sunday opening of the museum and library and to prevent any extension of this to other cultural institutions. In March 1881 it rallied to the support of Ninian Melville MP, an undertaker, Primitive Methodist and ardent sabbatarian and temperance advocate, who moved a motion in Parliament to terminate the opening of the museum and library on Sunday afternoons. The opening of cultural institutions on Sundays, he asserted, was the work of freethinkers and amounted to "State aid to infidels". Despite a large public meeting in support of the motion the night before it was introduced, and Parkes's outspoken disapproval of Sunday opening, the House voted against Melville. Sabbatarians had more success in Melbourne in 1882. The trustees of the public library decided to open it on Sunday afternoons, but after six weeks Parliament voted to close it.[20]

In September 1881 Henry Copeland proposed in Parliament that the new art gallery in Sydney should also open on Sunday afternoons. Nominally an Anglican but strongly anti-clerical, Copeland held that the churches ought to have jurisdiction only over those who professed to belong to them, but nominal adherents made up most of the population. His proposal nevertheless stirred the Lord's Day Observance Society to action and the Legislative Assembly narrowly rejected Copeland's motion. He tried again a year later, and this time provoked a long debate. He argued that there was nothing in his proposal to hurt the churches and much to benefit the working classes. He did not think attendants in the cultural institutions objected to Sunday work "because they found they could get through all their prayers and religious duties, and still have 10 s[hillings] to the good".[21] But this did not allay the fears of those who perceived the threat of secularism in Copeland's proposal.

"We are either a Christian country or we are not", Parkes postulated and Sunday opening was a form of state aid to competitors of the churches. He also argued that the churches deserved protection because they helped the progress of civilization and promoted sound morality, while the movement for Sunday opening was comprised of enemies of Christianity and good government. New South Wales should follow Britian rather than the Continent. Parkes also pointed out that not a single voice of the working classes, for whose benefit the reformers claimed to be working, had been raised for Sunday opening although there were 10,000 petitioners against it. The debate was adjourned and in the interim Copeland collected 24,000 signatures in support of his motion; the society and the churches were busy on the other side, but they secured only 22,000 signatures. In September 1882 the decision of the year before was reversed by a majority of almost two to one, and the art gallery became another Sunday attraction in Sydney.[22]

This decision helped to make Sydney a slightly brighter place on Sundays than other Australian cities, but it filled churchmen with gloom. It is doubtful whether the working classes took much advantage of the new opportunities for enjoyment. Indeed, Daniel O'Connor, a Catholic politician who supported the motion, submitted that these cultural institutions would not attract iconoclasts or the irreverent, but only those of cultivated tastes from the higher walks of life.[23] This was precisely what worried some churchmen: churchgoers might not attend the evening service after an afternoon at the art gallery.

The outlook for the Christian Sunday seemed worse in 1883 when Sunday afternoon concerts began in the Sir Joseph Banks Pavillion at Botany. These concerts were more or less secular versions of the Pleasant Sunday Afternoon introduced in England. As well as classical music they featured lectures of general interest such as ''The

Life of Captain Cook". But, unlike the Pleasant Sunday Afternoon, the concerts did not seek to attract the working classes. An advertisement stated that audiences were required to be highly respectable.[24]

These Sunday afternoon concerts did not escape the notice of the Lord's Day Observance Society which sought their suppression along with the Sunday evening lectures in the city theatres. But Protestant churchmen could not count on much sympathy from the government, which had defeated the Parkes administration in December 1882. Premier Alexander Stuart, was a High Churchman with several Catholics in his cabinet. The Lord's Day Observance Society could only try to have the laws on Sunday observance enforced. A deputation approached Stuart in July 1884 to draw his attention to Sunday entertainments in theatres and elsewhere held for gain and openly advertised. These were not only contrary to law, Dean Cowper told the premier, but also injurious to the moral and religious welfare of the community. The apologist H.G. Picton, who was also in the deputation, claimed that they had no wish to suppress the lectures but only the entertainment associated with them. Subsequent discussion showed that claim to be hollow.

Stuart could not be persuaded that there was any breach of the law, which he read very literally. He pointed out that the Public Exhibitions Act did not mention music and singing among the forms of entertainment forbidden in the theatres on Sundays. When reminded by a solicitor among the deputationists, W. Russell, that this Act had presumably been used to close Proctor's "not objectionable" lecture, Stuart observed lamely that the lantern illustrations used by Proctor were "clearly more akin to a theatrical entertainment" than singing. At the same time, he warned the churchmen against making martyrs of protagonists on the other side by overstepping the bounds of the law; better to work to change public opinion in the matter. But the society obviously thought it safer to try to suppress the lectures themselves, as well as the entertainments, which they rightly thought made them more attractive. Submitting a shorthand report of a lecture by the secularist Dr Hughes, Picton described it as "one tissue of blasphemy from beginning to end". There were also laws against blasphemy, he pointed out to the premier. Stuart admitted this was a new objection and promised to look into it. The *Sydney Morning Herald* thought there was some point to it. While everyone had a right to express his views decently on religious subjects, it thought that there was "no very urgent reason" for tolerating or legalizing indecent attacks on religion.[25] But nothing seems to have come of Stuart's enquiry into the blasphemy laws and he gave the Lord's Day Observance Society little satisfaction. As far as it was concerned, the change that was needed was not in the law, but in its administration.

Theatre proprietors clearly had little to fear from the government over Sunday entertainments and disregarded the Sunday laws more blatantly in 1885. In November, the Opera House, formerly used by the YMCA on Sunday nights for its evangelistic services, introduced a series of "Sacred and Classical Concerts" on Sunday evenings. Not to be out-done, the Sunday Platform Association, which had always included some music in its programmes, promptly advertised its meeting as a "Concert and Freethought Lecture". The next year other theatres in the city and in some suburbs offered sacred and classical concerts under such names as "Grand Concert Spirituel". Sunday concerts had also begun in Melbourne about this time. The Sunday evening concerts in Sydney were potentially more serious competitors with church services than the freethought lectures. Since they were claimed to have a sacred content, they might have seemed an acceptable alternative to "going to church". Indeed, it was argued that the Sunday concerts did not keep people off the streets, as some defenders claimed, but attracted those who might otherwise have been attending church services.[26]

Other bodies now joined the battle. The Sydney Women's Prayer Union, formed during Margaret Hampton's mission in 1883, also campaigned for stricter Sunday observance. In July 1886 it presented Parliament with a petition 356 feet long, seeking closure of the theatres on Sundays and an absolute prohibition of Sunday entertainments. Blasphemous lectures, the petitioners claimed, were demoralizing the youth of Sydney; it was "inconsistent in a Christian country", they argued, to permit Sabbath-breakers to offend "tens of thousands of Christians.[27] Certainly concern for the Christian Sunday was spreading. That same year Protestant ministers formed the Sydney Ministers' Union. It enjoyed a broader basis of support among Protestant ministers than the Lord's Day Observance Society, and soon supplanted it as the main pressure group on the Sunday question.

From May to November 1886 the Ministers' Union sought unsuccessfully to discuss the suppression of the Sunday theatres with the colonial secretary, G.R. Dibbs, who gave the excuse that he had referred the question to crown lawyers. But the union grew impatient and on 3 November published its correspondence with Dibbs, including the opinion of Frederick Darley, soon to become chief justice. Darley had assured the union that the Sunday entertainments were illegal. While continuing to ignore the union, Dibbs did receive a deputation from the Pitt Street Congregational Church in December 1886, led by its minister, Dr Jefferis. He complained about the Sunday evening concerts in the Gaiety Theatre, immediately behind the church, pointing out that services were not only disturbed in the evenings but also by the rehearsals held on Sunday mornings. There would have been a case for action here under the existing laws, for in 1884 the Supreme Court had upheld the protection of religious services from disturbance. But rather than attract bad publicity through legal proceedings against the theatre, Jefferis hoped to persuade the government to enforce the law. However Dibbs told the deputation that he would submit to Darley's opinion that the concerts were illegal only if he gave it from the bench; until then he could do nothing.[28]

The Ministers' Union hoped for a better hearing from Parkes, who was returned to government in 1887. In February 1887 the union convened a meeting of the heads of Protestant churches which resolved to address a memorial to the premier through Bishop Barry, reminding him of the prohibition against Sunday entertainments for gain. Barry went overseas for some months, and as he had received no reply from Parkes, the anxious ministers decided to act without him.[29]

A deputation of ministers led by T.S. Forsaith, a Congregationalist, approached Parkes on Friday 10 June 1887. Forsaith told the premier that it was the duty of a Christian government not to tolerate any breach of the law for it was the guarantee to society of security and progress. The spokesmen for the deputation attributed growing immorality, especially among the young, to these implicitly sanctioned evasions of the law. In particular, they mentioned the lectures which ridiculed Christianity, although they were equally concerned about the sacred concerts. If there were any doubts about the existing laws they asked that these should be amended, but they also informed Parkes of Chief Justice Darley's opinion that the existing laws were sufficient to suppress the Sunday performances. The ministers wanted the premier to use the power he already possessed.

Parkes, newly in power after several years in opposition, did not intend to risk his government on the Sunday question. As subsequent events made it clear, Parkes considered the freethought lectures objectionable and the concerts harmless. This distinction was a change from the position he had taken in 1881-82, on the Sunday opening of the art gallery, but public opinion seemed to support it. Parkes's concern was how to suppress the secularist lectures without closing Sunday concerts as well. On the morning of the deputation there seemed to be no way out, so he showed little sympathy with the ministers on either account. He argued at first for the toleration of differing opinions and taunted them a little, asking why the concerts attracted so many and the churches so few, although in fact there probably were less people in the theatres in Sunday nights than in all the churches. The ministers were not abashed, and towards the end of the interview he promised politely to study the law and consult his colleagues.[30] It is doubtful whether he intended to do anything serious about the matter immediately, but by the end of that day, after a fiasco in the Town Hall, Parkes had changed his mind, at least about the toleration of freethought lectures.

At this time the colony was planning its celebration of Queen Victoria's Jubilee and democrats, republicans and secularists had successfully disrupted a public meeting at the Town Hall on Friday 3 June 1887. The following Friday evening, the day of the minister's deputation, the radicals wrecked a second meeting more spectacularly. After the police had cleared the hall the shocked civic leaders retired to the mayor's reception room to take counsel. Among them were representatives of the Protestant, Catholic and Jewish communities and all agreed that these irreligious men were the enemies of society, the throne and of God. They concurred with the chief justice that action was necessary to curb such "abuse of laws both human and Divine" that resulted in the desecration of theatres and public parks. Together they drew up a solemn declaration condemning the "riotous conduct of a disloyal minority" and pledged themselves to vindicate the loyalty of the people "to the laws, institutions, and Throne of the British Empire".[31]

The next day at noon Parkes closed the theatres against the "disloyal" and "blasphemous" freethought lecturers. The following Sunday evening a crowd of about six thousand gathered at the pedestal in Hyde Park — "within sight of the signposts of despotism, the Prince Consort's statue, the empty pedestal of the Queen's statue, and St James's Church on the other side". They shouted derisively when the police asked them not to disturb the service in the church. Thomas Walker, the prominent freethought lecturer, now a Member of Parliament, mounted the pedestal to address the crowd. He charged Parkes with acting under the effete law of George III and likened the chief justice the infamous Judge Jeffreys of "The Bloody Assizes", in his campaign to crush the freethinkers and secularists. The vast assembly resolved to send a deputation to Parkes to "beard the lion in his den". At the close Walker jeeringly called for three cheers for Parkes and the Queen and three groans for each resounded across the park![32]

The free Sunday advocates met Parkes the following Monday. He claimed falsely that he had not noticed the lectures until the ministers' deputation brought them to his notice the previous Friday. He conceded that he might have been too precipitate, but would not admit that the disturbance in the Town Hall had provoked his action. He took his stand on the Public Exhibitions Act, not the Sunday Observance Act of 1780. Theatre licences, he pointed out, did not authorize performance on Sundays, Good Friday or Christmas Day, adding that the lectures were offensive to the Christian majority of the population. The dissatisfied deputation returned to the pedestal to demonstrate against the premier and later appealed to the governor to protest to the Queen at this infringement of their liberty. A courteous refusal met the appeal, and the secularists and their 1,500 supporters could do no more than denounce Parkes again in another protest meeting at the pedestal in Hyde Park.[33]

Even if there was not a great deal of sympathy for the secularists, there was still some strong criticism of Parkes. The *Bulletin* depicted him as the pawn of the parsons, and the *Sydney Morning Herald*, which also stated that he had acted on behalf of the Ministers' Union, thought he was making martyrs of the secularists. Bishop Barry said later that Parkes had done exactly the opposite of what the churches asked. They did not want the freethought lectures put down by "real or fancied persecution", but to have the law applied strictly to all forms of "injurious . . . Sunday trading", which meant, in particular, Sunday lectures, concerts and newspapers.[34] Parkes had made no reference to Sunday observance laws; and he applied the law respecting the use of theatres most partially.

Parkes survived all criticism both inside and outside Parliament. Walker and the secularists had shocked public opinion more. Even though Parkes had to admit that he had acted without consulting the attorney general, and knew of no precedent for his recent action, an indignant majority upheld him, including a few who usually took an anti-sabbatarian stand. The Evangelical, W.J. Foster, said in justification of the government move that "gross blasphemy" should still be punished, not simply in deference to the Christian religion, but because it was so offensive to a large majority of the population. Certainly many were offended. Some 36,200 people signed a petition to support the closing of the theatres; it upheld that Sunday opening was both an infringement of statute law and "subversive of good government and morality". James Balfour wrote on behalf of the Lord's Day Observance Society of Victoria to congratulate Parkes for what he thought was the enforcement of Sunday observance laws.[35]

But Parkes thought that as colonial secretary he could allow an infringement of the law where he saw no danger of subversion. Accordingly, on 25 June he issued new regulations governing the use of theatres giving the colonial secretary sole discretion as to their occupation on Sundays. He told Parliament that he would allow the

A comment on Sir Henry Parkes's closure of the theatres. (From *Bulletin*, 18 June 1887.)
Photo courtesy of La Trobe Library, State Library of Victoria.)

use of theatres on Sundays for religious services, sacred concerts, and other concerts "not objectionable on moral grounds", but the government would not authorize lectures against Christianity or the monarchy.[36]So the Sunday concerts could go on, but the freethinkers were driven from their accustomed platforms.

Parkes's new regulations were high-handed and illegal, but in line with public opinion. Churchmen were displeased of course and a Supreme Court decision on Sunday newspapers in March 1888 added to their disquiet. The publication of Sunday newspapers began in 1886 and church congregations were disturbed to hear newsboys crying them in the streets outside. They were suppressed in Victoria, but the New South Wales court held that selling newspapers on Sundays was "perhaps the most innocent and least pernicious form of trading".[37]Such an opinion seemed to indicate to churchmen an urgent need to educate the public on the sanctity of Sunday.

The Wesleyan and Presybterian Churches appointed special Sundays for sermons about the Sabbath and in 1889 the Presbyterian General Assembly recommended a textbook on the Sabbath for Sunday school examinations. The desecration of the day of rest dominated the Reverend T. Owens Mell's address from the chair of the Congregational Union in 1888 and also Bishop Barry's pastoral address to his diocese in April 1888. Barry eschewed the term Sabbath, which he held was not applicable to Sunday, but his address had much of the earnestness of the serious sabbatarian as he called on all to rouse to the protection of the Lord's Day — that "priceless treasure" which had done so much to mould the British character. The spiritual element of Sunday observance should be left to spiritual influences alone, but the bishop expected the law to guard the day of rest so that those who did not want to observe the day religiously would have little else to do.[38]These views notwithstanding, the Evangelicals found Barry too lax because he condoned rail travel on Sundays.

All these protests weighed little with politicians, but Sydney was becoming a byword for the secular Sunday. The evangelist John MacNeil complained in 1888 that the city was well on the way to the "Continental Sunday" and in 1889 Henry Varley thundered about the desecration of Sunday in Sydney. The *Australian Christian World*, which thought Varley too severe, nevertheless acknowledged that Sydney held "bad pre-eminence" among Australian cities as far as Sunday observance was concerned. There was a demand for a freer Sunday in Melbourne, but the sabbatarian lobby, led by the Presbyterians, had largely managed to prevent it. If Sunday in Sydney was freer than in Melbourne, the *Sydney Morning Herald* was pleased. The older city had shown that cultural institutions could be thrown open on Sundays without jeopardizing the morals of the people. But a correspondent replied that these institutions were only opened for a coterie of secularists; had the churches organized their forces, he thought that it would have been a different story.[39] At this time a new and perhaps more effective campaign to save the Sabbath was taking shape.

The Presbyterian General Assembly initiated a move in March 1889 which led to the formation in June of a Council of Churches, composed of representatives of the six principal Protestant denominations (Anglican, Presbyterian, Wesleyan, Primitive Methodist, Congregationalist and Baptist). Similar councils were formed in other colonies in the next decade, although Anglicans did not always join them. The New South Wales council was formed chiefly to resist all further attempts to secularize Sunday and, if possible, to have existing infringements of the Sunday laws supressed.[40] The Christian Sunday had lately become essential to the preservation of Christianity itself; Dean Cowper told the Anglican Synod in 1889 that "the right observance of the Christian Sabbath is the bulwark of religion in the land." Similarly, at the Anglican Church Congress in Sydney, Archdeacon King made the dire prediction that if the Lord's Day fell it would not fall alone. It would "drag with it all other ordinances — the Bible — Public and Private Prayer — the Ministry — the Sacraments — and at the last Christianity itself".[41]

Education of the congregation was one of the tasks the council set itself, for some regular churchgoers were becoming lax about Sunday, perhaps taking Sunday afternoon excursions or visiting the gallery and museum. The council wanted the support of the Christian public in its crusade. In February 1890 it organized a preaching campaign of "The Claims and Value of the Sabbath" and on the last Sunday more than 150 ministers throughout Sydney preached on the Sunday question. The kind of arguments used at the formation of the Lord's day Observance Society in 1880 were repeated in many pulpits, but other voices and different arguments were now raised in defence of the Christian Sunday. The high church canon, Thomas Kemmis of St Mark's, Darling Point, asserted from his pulpit that those who promoted Sunday lectures, concerts and picnics were the disciples of Voltaire. The liberal Dr. Roseby declared that "the greed of avarice" was the only argument in favour of the secularization of Sunday. He presented a more sophisticated defence of the formal ceremonial aspect of Sunday observance. Wise routine was as necessary to life as the laws of gravitaton to the planetary system and even the most spiritual religion, such as Christianity, had to rely on some form of corporate expression. It depended for its existence on the congregation, with its "hymns of praise, this open Bible, this fellowship in acts of devotion"; one day in the week had to be set apart to preserve this routine. But this religious argument did not justify the legal protection of the Christian Sunday, so Roseby appealed as well to humanitarian considerations. The Sabbath law, he claimed, was "one of those many splendid Biblical protests on behalf of 'equality and fraternity'". Anything that tended to secularize the day of rest, including the " 'sacred and classical concert' ", meant work for the working man, in whose interests a freer Sunday was usually advocated.[42] Roseby, like Bishop Barry, thought that the use of railways to travel to religious duties was justified, despite the labour it involved for train crews. Apart from this, his views on the question hardly differed from those of the more conservative Protestant.

Thus most Protestant churchmen saw the Sunday observance laws as right and necessary in a Christian country; their concern was that they were being so flagrantly breached. If the government could not be persuaded to administer the law impartially, the Council of Churches determined to put the law to the test. Soon after the council's foundation, its secretary, John Walker, a Presbyterian minister, sued John Solomon, proprietor of the Criterion Theatre, under the provisions of the Sunday Observance Act of 1780. Walker had chosen his mark well, for the Criterion was the leading theatre providing sacred and classical concerts in 1889 and it was apparently attracting large houses. It was clearly an infringement of the law, but Walker also thought it necessary to disparage the content of the programmes which he claimed to have studied from past advertisements, finding nothing more sacred in them than ditties like "Rock-a-bye-Baby". This was quite untrue of the concerts advertised at the time Walker filed his suit. Programmes in October 1889 included the recitation of Leigh Hunt's *Abou Ben Adhem*, a variety of sacred musical items; some scenic displays, one of "Rock of Ages" accompanied by the hymn, another of episodes of the life of Jesus from the Nativity to the Resurrection, and a reproduction of Holman Hunt's popular painting, "The Light of the World".[43] The religious content was not so strong in later programes, but there were always some sacred items and none of the offensiveness that freethought lectures had contained. Parkes has suggested in 1887 that it was fear of competition that prompted the parsons to press for the closure of apparently wholesome Sunday entertainments. But the fear went deeper than that: Christianity could not be nourished for long on religious sentiment in the theatre. As Roseby argued, it needed fellowship and worship to sustain it. Besides, for most churchmen the Christian status of the colony was bound up with the defence of the Christian Sunday.

The Supreme Court delivered its judgment on *Walker* v. *Solomon* on 22 May 1890; it awarded Walker costs and the £200 recoverable under the Act. The verdict proved how arbitrarily Parkes had acted. He had authorized Solomon's Sunday concerts under the new regulations he issued in 1887 and the court ruled that he did not have this power; it dismissed the defence's argument that the Sunday Observance law of 1780 could not apply in New South Wales because there was no established church in the colony. The Australian Courts Act of 1828 had removed any doubt as to the applicability of the Georgian statute in Australia and the judgment in *McHugh* v. *Robertson* in Melbourne in 1885 provided a recent precedent.[44] But Chief Justice Darley and Mr. Justice Windeyer, both Anglicans, agreed that there was a need for up-to-date legislation to bring the law "more into harmony with rational modern ideas on the Sunday question". Windeyer commented that it was a grotesque law which allowed the performance of the *Messiah* by paid choristers before paying seatholders in a church, but put a theatre in which the same performance took place before a paying audience on the same level as a brothel. Mr Justice Foster disagreed with his colleagues' recommendation for a change in the law: he did not believe the day had come when either public opinion or the legislature would sanction any change.[45] Future events were to demonstrate the accuracy of Foster's opinion.

The judgment against Solomon pleased churchmen, although some who welcomed the verdict tried to appear reasonable and liberal in their attitude towards Sunday observance. Soon after the case James Hill said in Bourke Street Congregational Church that he was opposed to laws preventing people from amusing themselves on Sundays; he saw no reason why they should not hear high class music, but he objected to people making money out of it. The law that applied to butchers, bakers and other businessmen, he argued, also should apply to the entertainment business. The *Presbyterian* agreed that the "Continental Sunday" had to be resisted. It is doubtful whether many would have looked any more favourably on Sunday concerts if they were free and in any case they were unlikely to occur unless someone paid the musicians. The *Church of England Guardian* did venture to plead for a more tolerant attitude towards Sunday observance, especially for the sake of the young for whom Sunday could be such a dreary day. Probably written by Jackson, this article allowed a wider range of activity than many churchmen would countenance, but still objected to organized tennis parties — they might tempt or offend other people; and like Dr Roseby, the writer argued for Sunday observance as a social as well as a religious necessity. For all that, it provoked a sharp rebuke from Archdeacon

King, who pointed out that no competent authority had yet removed the fourth commandment from the Decalogue. [46]

When the court's judgment was published, the *Sydney Morning Herald* also demanded some amendment to the law and defended Sunday concerts. "No time should be lost", it declared "in putting an end to a situation that is intolerable". A few days after the verdict Colonial Treasurer William McMillan also told Parliament that new legislation was essential if people were going to take advantage of old statutes against the present-day "practical intention" of Parliament. But the government took no action on the matter until an enterprising individual began proceedings under the 1780 Act to recover about £40,000 from the *Sydney Morning Herald*, the *Daily Telegraph* and the *Evening News* for advertising the Sunday concerts. The bill introduced in July 1890 did not seek to repeal or amend the old law; instead it proposed to allow the government to waive the penalties provided by the Act. In passing the bill the colonial government was following the precedent of the British Parliament's Remission of Penalites Act of 1875 following the prosecution of Brighton Aquarium. There were some who wanted to repeal the old Act altogether, but the government refused to go that far, for the Sunday question was too vexed. The Remission of Penalties Act met the more limited objectives of the government.[47]The power remained to close objectionable Sunday entertainments such as the former freethought lectures, but the new Act gave the government the power to suspend the operation of the 1780 Act where it chose. Thus Sunday concerts could be immune from prosecution under the Act of 1780, but there was still the Public Exhibitions Act to get around. The Criterion and other city theatres gave up Sunday concerts after the Supreme Court's decision, but at Bondi Aquarium Sunday afternoon concerts continued to be held in defiance of the law, and in 1891, the SS *Invincible* staged a classical concert, entitled "Sunday Night on the Water". [48]

The government's half-way measure did not satisfy a member of the opposition, J.H. Want, a lawyer who had been attorney general in the Dibbs and Jennings governments in 1885 and 1886-87. Want thought that certain forms of Sunday trading and entertainment should be unequivocally recognized as legal, and in August he introduced a Sunday laws amendment bill to allow fruiterers, tobacconists and places of light refreshment to open for business on Sundays and to exempt Sunday newspapers and entertainments from the old Sunday laws. He claimed that he also was opposed to the "Continental Sunday", but argued that as Bishop Porteus's Act of 1780 was designed to prevent the ridicule of religion it ought not to apply to harmless entertainments and trading. But churchmen were

not at all persuaded. To some any liberalization of Sunday observance was virtually a ridicule of religion, and the *Protestant Standard*
criticized the double standards of a government that allowed the
prima donna to make money on Sunday but not the grocer; the Sunday laws should be observed and enforced absolutely or the day of
rest as recognized by the State abolished altogether. But Christians,
it added, would "in conscience sanctify it, whatever the world did".
That was not the usual line. The majority of churchmen acted as if
the future of religion depended on keeping all the legal sanctions for
Sunday observance and the *Presbyterian* had observed in June 1890
that the Sunday question would prove one of the most debated
social or political questions.[49] It was certainly the major question for
the Council of Churches which, despite the distractions of the
Maritime Strike, organized a massive campaign against Want's bill.
An army of volunteers was enlisted to canvass the colony for signatures to petitions. A record number of petitions and a total of
63,200 signatures, almost double the number which supported the
closure of the theatres against freethought lectures in 1887, poured
into Parliament from all over the colony. On 13 October, the night
before the date set for the second reading of the bill, there were
many protest meetings.[50] But the bill was never to reach the second
reading: it lapsed through the prorogation of Parliament in December. Nevertheless, meetings of protest still continued during that
month.

Want seems to have let the matter drop; at least he had tested
public opinion. Churchmen congratulated themselves that this
attempt to secularize Sunday had been averted. John Walker exulted
at the Presbyterian General Assembly in March 1891 that Want's
Bill was as good as dead, and crowed that the Supreme Court decision in his favour had resulted in the closure of Sunday entertainments. He was presumably unaware that some were still being held,
but it was no longer worth money to sue them. For all the efforts of
the churchmen, Sydney's Sunday remained freer than other Australian cities, with its library, museum and art gallery open to the public. It shocked Charles Alexander, the evangelistic song leader who
accompanied Reuben Torrey to Sydney in 1902 and Dr. Chapman in
1909. Alexander found Sabbath desecration in Sydney worse than in
Chicago, which was "the worst city in the world". It might have
been even "worse" than it was in Sydney had Protestant churchmen
been less persistent in their defences. If attempts to liberalize Sunday observance in the late 1890s failed, counter-attempts to
strengthen Sunday observance laws also failed. There was some
liberalization of Sunday trading in Sydney under the Labor government from 1910, when refreshment rooms were allowed to open.

But Bishop Porteus's Act remained in force in New South Wales until 1966, not without some effects.[51]

Contesting Divorce Law Reform[52]

The churches' campaign against the extension of the facilities for divorce in New South Wales was brief but intense compared with the battle against the secularization of Sunday. The institution of marriage virtually had been secularized by the Marriage Act of 1855 which, partly in the interests of religious equality, established that marriage was primarily a civil contract. While the Act provided for a civil marriage ceremony it presupposed that most marriages would by solemnized in religious ceremonies by ministers duly authorized by the State. Thus marriage remained intimately associated with the Christian churches and under colonial law, as in Britain, it was apparently indissoluble. In 1857, however, the British Parliament passed legislation which granted a man the right to divorce his wife for adultery. But simple adultery was not sufficient ground for a woman to divorce her husband. She had also to prove desertion for upwards of two years, cruelty or some unnatural offence. This legislation was adopted in the Australian colonies, last of all in New South Wales in 1873, and in 1881 the New South Wales legislation was amended to allow a woman to divorce her husband for simple adultery.[53]

Although this amendment was strongly contested both within Parliament and between the colony and Britain, there was not much opposition from the churches, apart from the Roman Catholic Church, which did not recognize the State's right to dissolve marriage on any ground. Protestants generally held that adultery was the one ground which Christ had allowed for divorce, and the law had gone no further than that.[54]But in the 1880s there were some who did want to go further, like some groups in Europe and North America where the divorce question was also under review. A new law adopted in France in 1884 allowed divorce on certain grounds including adultery, cruelty, habitual drunkenness and three years' separation.[55] That year three abortive bills were introduced in the New South Wales Parliament to extend the provisions for divorce. Of the two introduced in the Legislative Council, one sponsored by W.H. Suttor, proposed to allow drunkenness and venereal disease as grounds for divorce and the other, by W.B. Dalley, five years' desertion. A bill introduced in the Legislative Assembly by David Buchanan, a persistent campaigner for divorce extension, proposed to allow divorce after two years' desertion, a ground regarded by Scotsmen as "founded on the Scriptures".[56] Although these proposals failed, a more formidable advocate of divorce law reform now emerged in Sir Alfred Stephen.

Sir Alfred Stephen had opposed earlier measures to grant women the right to divorce their husband for simple adultery. Like the opponents of such a provision in Britain in 1857, he had argued in 1879 that a man's adultery did not have the same disastrous effect on a marriage as the infidelity of a woman, who was usually alienated thereby from husband and children. The erring husband, he maintained, often treated his wife with affection and continued to reside at home and to love the children. Besides, such a measure would put the laws of the colony at variance with the laws of Britain and the empire, an argument soon to be advanced against his own proposals for reform. In 1884 Stephen criticized Suttor's bill for not going far enough.[57] He had apparently resolved to go further.

Now in his eighties, Stephen had been chief justice of the colony from 1844 to 1873. He remained a person of immense influence and public stature in the Legislative Council, in various philanthropic movements and in the Church of England. His espousal of divorce law reform might seem something of a volte-face, but his position from 1884 onwards was not necessarily inconsistent with his opposition to a woman's right to file for divorce on the grounds of simple adultery; it was a different matter when women were deserted or suffered misery at the hands of drunken or brutal husbands. A supporter of the temperance movement, Stephen attributed a large percentage of crime and immorality to drink and his zeal for temperance and for divorce law reform stemmed largely from the same source. So much was this so that the leading clerical temperance campaigner, F.B. Boyce, noting that nearly all the grounds Stephen proposed for divorce were connected with drink, advised him to drop the bill he proposed and simply continue the fight against the root cause — liquor traffic. But Stephen could not ignore the effects; a long time on the bench had made him acutely aware of the misery some women suffered from the drunkenness and cruelty of their husbands and the consequent degradation of family life. It was for the sake of these unfortunate victims that he took up the cause of divorce law reform. In February 1886 he introduced a bill to allow desertion, drunkenness, repeated assault and long term imprisonment as grounds for divorce. This measure, he maintained, was in the best interests of morality, for deserted or battered wives were often induced to commit adultery or to turn to drink and prostitution.[58]

The *Sydney Morning Herald* cautiously supported Stephen's bill as a measure to check "the spread of pauperism and crime". The families of deserted wives and prisoners and drunken husbands

Sir Alfred Stephen, Chief Justice of New South Wales (1844-77) and champion of divorce law reform. (Photo courtesy of Mitchell Library, Sydney.)

themselves, it argued, usually became burdens on the State. Divorce would not necessarily solve this problem, but it did make remarriage possible.[59]The bill had many other supporters, mostly of those moved by compassion for suffering victims and the preservation of morality. Yet these reasons carried little weight with many churchmen, predominantly clergy, who flew to the defence of the Christian law.

Bishop Barry led the opposition to Stephen's bill. After its second reading Barry published his protest in a letter to the *Sydney Morning Herald*. Phrasing his comments with due respect for Sir Alfred, he nevertheless argued that Stephen had been carried away by exceptional cases of hardship and misery. Any relaxation of the law, could cause the breakdown of more marriages and, that aside, the proposed extensions were contrary to the command of Christ. They not only imperilled the sacredness of marriage, but the Christian faith itself. He called for a united stand of all Christians to oppose the bill.[60]

Barry hoped for Catholic as well as Protestant support and proposed through an intermediary, T.M. Slattery, that Cardinal Moran might join him in petitioning Parliament.[61]Despite its adamant opposition to divorce the Roman Catholic Church declined to cooperate with the bill's religious opponents. A week or so after Barry's initiative, Cardinal Moran explained his reasons in a Pastoral Letter. He conceded that the Anglicans deserved some praise for their opposition to the proposals for divorce extension, but stated that they were in a false position, having already recognized the State's right to dissolve the sacred bond of marriage in the case of adultery. The Catholic Church, on the other hand, did "not recognise any authority on the part of the Civil State to trench upon the Christian Sacrament or dissolve the marriage bond". Catholics, therefore, could only regard the bill as "another instance of the downward course invariably pursued by Civil Governments when they arrogate to themselves an authority in spiritual matters which Christ did not confer upon them". It is possible that Moran thought it inexpedient to cooperate with Protestants, but he also displayed more confidence in the obedience of Catholics to the teaching of their Church than Protestant churchmen seemed to expect from their flocks. All the same, Moran did not miss any opportunity to condemn divorce law reform in his public statements, and on one occasion described divorce as "a fashionable and social name for polygamy". The *Freeman's Journal* also attacked the bill as an anti-Christian measure which would legalize adultery and largely "undo the great good that Christianity had done for mankind".[62]Catholic politicians likewise opposed the bill in Parliament, and outside it some of them cooperated with Protestant churchmen in collecting signatures for petitions.

Bishop Barry could count on the support of almost all the Anglican clergy of the colony, with a few exceptions, such as his namesake, Zachary Barry, who took quite the opposite view. He thought the suffering, scandal and wrong caused by the lack of divorce facilities were "simply disgraceful to a Christian country". Like Cardinal Moran, one Anglo-Catholic held that "the laws of God and of His Church are unchanged and unchangeable" and that no State law could touch them,[63] But by and large the Anglican clergy believed it was essential for the State to uphold divine law. Dean Cowper, while removed from Bishop Barry on a number of points, was just as adamantly opposed to the extension of divorce facilities, and after Barry left the colony in 1889 it fell to him to lead the campaign against the proposed legislation. Bishop Pearson, more liberal than many on a number of questions, was also firmly opposed to a measure which, he argued, was not only contrary to divine law but also socially inexpedient. Easier divorce, he believed, would set brutal and drunken men free to find new victims. Majorities at diocesan and provincial synods and also the General Synod of Australia and Tasmania, were clearly opposed to divorce law reform. Although, officially, the Church of England was opposed to the reforms Stephen's bill would introduce, quite a number of Anglican laymen took the same line as Sir Alfred Stephen and the dissident cleric, Zachary Barry. One of them, G.H. Cox, who had also advocated repeal of the Sunday observance laws, told his fellow Anglicans that their Church would have to go with with the spirit of the age or be left high and dry.[64]

The response from the other Protestant denominations to Barry's invitation was generally less than he had hoped for. But some representatives of the Presbyterian and Wesleyan Churches, and also a few Catholic laymen, did meet with Anglicans at the Church Society House on Friday 16 April 1886 to protest against the divorce extension bill. The previous Sunday Barry had expounded the Christian teaching on marriage from the cathedral pulpit, taking as his text St. Matthew 19:3-9. On the basis of this passage he defended divorce for adultery, the only ground it seemed Christ had allowed. To go further than this was to set aside the Christian law. The bishop deplored the tendency to separate social and political questions from Christian faith and obedience. Christianity should influence all thought and action; and he claimed that in both England and the colonies "as yet the law had refused to give up the old Christian basis". For temporal law to break loose from the Christian law, "reverenced as it must be in the consciences of the great mass of their people who call themselves Christians", would be, he argued, to "inflict a deep wound on the moral well-being of society". At the protest meeting the following Friday Barry claimed that divorce was a Christian question, a non-sectarian issue. New South Wales was a Christian nation, despite the apparent separation of Church and State; the churches were therefore duty-bound to protest at any change at variance with Christian law. The argument that it was impossible to enforce the whole Christian law, which rested more on faith and willing obedience than on coercion, upon all society weighed nothing with him. He regarded the teaching of Christ as an inimitable law, and binding on all men and women.[65]

This was too restrictive for Barry's Presbyterian supporters, as Principal Kinross made clear to the protest meeting. He too took his stand upon the Scriptures, but Scottish divines regarded desertion as a scriptural ground for divorce, basing this on the teaching of the Apostle Paul. Kinross opposed Stephen's bill because it included additional grounds to those found in the New Testament. Most other Presbyterians took a more liberal view and did not share the Anglican opposition to remarriage. Thus the opposition to the bill was not as wholehearted as Barry hoped; nevertheless, the meeting agreed to petition Parliament not to pass the bill, and Barry submitted his own petition which became a model for several of the other petitions forwarded. The bishop's petition objected to the proposed amendment on three grounds: it was contrary to the law of Christ; it would harm the community's domestic and social life by impairing the sacredness of marriage; and it would put the law at variance with that of Britain and the other colonies.[66] Most other petitions against omitted the last point, but the first was what mattered most.

In vain might the *Sydney Morning Herald* rebuke the churches for shifting the debate from the question of social expediency to theological grounds. Apart from the minority of secularists and free-thinkers, there were few who were willing to treat the matter as a purely secular question. One opponent asserted that Parliament should deal with railways and other such matters, leaving alone laws the majority regarded as indissoluble.[54] There were some wildly extravagant claims as well. The sabbatarian Ninian Melville attempted to show Parliament that Stephen's bill was a secularist plot. He found himself in company with the Catholic, Daniel O'Connor, who asserted that the hardest-working supporters of the bill were the freethinkers who aimed "to wipe out all the great emblems of Christianity". The Anglican champion Edward Knox argued that the bill would be welcomed by those who sought to weaken the cause of religion, and the Catholic E.W. O'Sullivan condemned it as "antagonistic to the spirit of Christianity".[68]

But the character of Stephen himself, champion of the bill, made such charges ludicrous, and it was evident from the beginning that many respectable Christian citizens supported the measure. Bishop Barry knew better than to attribute the bill to secularism in any ideological sense. If it were carried, he recognized that it would be "mainly by Christian hands and on motives of compassion and philanthropy". Both within and outside Parliament Stephen defended his measure as "in full accordance with the will of Him who looks down with compassion on wretchedness", who "came to heal the broken-hearted, to preach deliverance to the captives and set at liberty them that are bound". It was this aspect of Christ's mission that Stephen's supporter, Chief Justice Darley, thought the ecclesiastics over-looked.[69]The proponents of divorce law reform were as confident that their proposal was Christian as their opponents were that it was not.

There was plenty of debate in Parliament and in the press over scriptural and historic precedents. The main advocate of the bill in the Legislative Assembly, John Cash Neild, although he wished to treat it as a civil and not a religious question, claimed that Wycliffe, the Protestant Reformers and Milton all approved of divorce, as well as the great Protestant apologist, Archdeacon Paley. Likewise, Sir Henry Parkes stated that, as a Protestant Christian, it was enough for him "to go to the great guides of the Reformation", Luther and Melanchthon. He was on safe enough ground, but Parkes seemed diffident when challenged by O'Connor to quote Melanchthon; he replied that he would rather set aside the religious argument altogether, since marriage in the colony had been secularized through a measure introduced thirty years before by a Catholic, J.H. Plunkett, and apparently supported by the Anglican and Catholic Churches. Still, to free the measure from any taint of secularism he pointed out that the petitioners for the bill represented "the solid Christian laity of the great churches of the country".[70]

In his debate with the Anglican Church in 1887 Stephen appealed to the *Reformatio Legum Ecclesiasticarum*, a draft reform of ecclesiastical law drawn up by a commission of divines under Edward VI. The proposed code included provision for divorce in the case of adultery, or desertion after three years or cruel and deadly hostility. Stephen claimed on the basis of the *Reformatio* that his proposals were "supported by Church authority", especially as the *Reformatio* would most probably have been adopted had Edward not died prematurely.[71]The Tudor draft might carry the authority of Cranmer and other divines, but Stephen's opponents pointed out that the *Reformatio* was not adopted under Elizabeth. Archdeacon King even speculated that its divorce provisions might have been

Churchmen, Sir Alfred and the wife-beater. (From *Bulletin*, 8 May 1896. Photo courtesy of La Trobe Library, State Library of

the very reason for its rejection. All it proved was that some Tudor churchmen held views on divorce "not consistent with the teaching of our Lord Jesus Christ", although their views were stricter than sixteenth century practice generally seems to have been.[72]

Christian opinion, either past or present was not unanimous in opposing divorce. In a defence of his reform in 1888 Stephen appealed to the early church fathers, the first Christian emperors, the Westminster Confession, the Protestant states of Germany, the Netherlands and the United States of America. By a very Protestant view of western history he depicted the ban on divorce as a device of the papacy. An anonymous supporter also pointed out that the High Churchman, Bishop Christopher Wordsworth, believed divorce for desertion was authorized in Scripture.[73] But none of this could change the opinion of his opponents.

Protestant churchmen agreed with Bishop Barry that the State should uphold the Christian law, but in the case of divorce, agreement on the law was difficult. Scottish law and the Westminster Confession led Presbyterians to conclusions different from Bishop Barry's. The Presbytery of Sydney debated the matter in June 1886 and finally resolved to support Stephen's bill in that it allowed divorce for "deliberate desertion". Some had reservations about some of the other proposed grounds, especially aggravated assault, although prominent Presbyterians were in favour of them all. Dr Steel supported Stephen wholeheartedly and in 1887 collaborated with him in publicizing the liberal divorce provisions of the *Reformatio*. Officially, Presbyterians appeared to be in favour of the bill, particularly in March 1887, when the General Assembly supported Steel's motion to petition Parliament in favour of divorce for desertion, as it was allowed under Scottish law.[74] Barry's arguments against divorce went too far for Presbyterians, who could not regard Scotland as less Christian than England.

The Wesleyans looked more united in opposition to divorce in 1886 when the "Committee for Guarding our Privileges" authorized the President and secretary of conference to petition against the bill; and the *Weekly Advocate* also opposed it. But the Annual Conference passed no resolutions on the subject, and in time it became clear that the Wesleyans were quite divided on the issue. In 1890, when Hans Mack, a consistent opponent of divorce extension, attempted to introduce a resolution at the Annual Conference it was pointed out that the Privileges Committee had considered the question and encountered such division of opinion that it decided to take no action. The General Conference did pass a resolution against divorce extension in 1890, but that only applied to Victoria. Dr Richard Sellors objected to any reference to New South

Wales, because of the dissension the question had aroused at the latest Annual Conference.[75]

The Congregational Union expressed no opinion on the matter and declined to take any definite action when Dean Cowper sought its cooperation in 1888. Some Congregational ministers signed petitions against the bill and Dr. Jefferis publicly condemned divorce as desecration. However the *Independent* was not outrightly opposed to the bill, as it held that the law had more "to do with men as citizens, not as Christians"; and G.A. Lloyd, one of Jefferis's deacons, stated in Parliament that Congregationalists were in favour of the bill. He was probably correct as far as laymen were concerned.[76]

The Baptists supported divorce extension. In April 1886, the Reverend Charles Bright, Chairman of the Union later that year, wrote an article for the *Echo* supporting divorce law reform and in May the union's executive committee unanimously approved Stephen's bill. Bright insisted that the teaching of Christ had to be taken very seriously, but so also did the fact that deserters, drunkards and brutal husbands had in effect broken the marriage contract, and thus the divorce had "practically taken place". The burden of sorrow upon the "unoffending and innocent person" was made "more poignant" because the law maintained "the miserable fiction" that marriage was an indissoluble institution for any cause other than adultery. The words of Christ, he argued, were addressed to individuals, and although Christianity was the perfect ethic, it was not to be applied inflexibly. (Similarly, Dr Andrew Garran, sometime editor the the *Sydney Morning Herald* and a Congregationalist, interpreted Christ's words as expressing an ideal of marriage not to be literally binding and legally enforced.) Once men had set the teaching of Christ aside, Bright continued, the State could no more restore what was lost than it could "raise the dead". Confronted by the breakdown of marriage it had to decide between two courses: "Either it must maintain a figment, and thus in many cases give license to evil, or recognise facts and relieve the innocent." He warned the churches not to be complacent in face of glaring evils, as if they had no remedy but the mouthing of medieval theology based on a hollow interpretation of one text of Scripture. The Christian response was to be determined by "the whole tenor of the teaching of the Divine Master"; like the Good Samaritan the Church had to show mercy and compassion.[77]

Sir Alfred Stephen must have welcomed such a defence, but it would seem that not all Baptists approved their leader's stand. A few years later a layman, Joseph Palmer, publicly regretted his denomination's endorsement of the bill and claimed that the majority of Baptists would be opposed to divorce if women were counted.[78]He may have been right, although women's groups, vocal as they were on Sunday observance and the liquor traffic, do not seem to have spoken out on the divorce question, apart from a few victims of broken marriages who supported the reform. On the whole, lay opponents were a dedicated minority. The opposition was largely clerical and predominantly Anglican.

These outspoken opponents of divorce did not elicit much response from the community at large, contrary to the expectation of the *Australian Christian World*. In 1886 the organizers only managed to collect 6,902 signatures, well below the number of those who signed petitions supporting the protection of Sunday. On the other hand, neither did the advocates of the measure win much public support. There were fewer signatures for the bill than against, but J.C. Neild asserted in Parliament that those for the bill were adult petitioners, while many who signed petitions against it were children[79]Such a claim might well have been true, but either way the public appears to have been indifferent.

The question did not seem to rate highly in the priorities of parliamentarians either, despite the intensity of the arguments from the few who cared strongly for or against. Stephen's bill lapsed in the Legislative Assembly in 1886 for want of a quorum. A second bill was passed at the next session of Parliament, notwithstanding Edward Knox's delaying tactics in the Legislative Council. Only half of the lower House voted on the bill and the majority of three to one constituted but a third of the house.[80] When on 13 July 1887 the governor reserved the bill for the royal assent he shifted the battleground from the colony to Westminster, and Anglican bishops, especially Bishop Barry in England at that time, did their best to have the measure quashed there.

Barry used every argument he could marshal in a letter to the secretary of state for colonies, Sir Henry Holland (later Lord Knutsford). He claimed with some exaggeration that there was strong opposition from large classes of people in the colony. The minority vote in the lower House strengthened his hand. He claimed that the bill got through largely because of the respect for its sponsor, Sir Alfred Stephen, and he argued that royal assent should be withheld until opinion in the colony could be judged more clearly and the question considered in other colonial legislatures. Alexander Gordon, who had returned to England, also wrote to the Colonial Office in London to support Barry's case, while Sir Alfred put the case for the bill through the governor, Lord Carrington. But the Colonial Office seems to have taken more notice of Barry and Gordon than Sir Alfred, and Holland suggested that Parliament should establish the feeling of the colony more fully before passing such a measure. This angered both Houses of the colonial legislature and many would have agreed with Dr Garran's assertion that the real reason for Westminster's decision was "the hostility of the ecclesiastical influence".[81]

Sir Alfred Stephen and Neild were nevertheless determined to get divorce law reform on to the statute books, despite the formidable ecclesiastical opposition. Between 1888 and 1890 five separate bills for divorce extension went before Parliament and all were lost through adjournment or prorogation of Parliament, assisted by the delaying tactics of a dedicated minority, foremost among whom was Knox. The debate became more intense in 1890 when the press received a record number of letters for and against divorce extension. Prophecies of revolt against religion and national apostasy were uttered anew. Canon Selwyn expostulated that Parliament would be overthrowing Moses and Jesus if it passed what he called the "Divorce and Adultery Extension Bill". But correspondents in the *Sydney Morning Herald* in favour of reform slightly outnumbered the opponents. The majority of petitions, however, were against divorce extension. Most of them came from Anglican clergy, who expressed opposition both to divorce and remarriage. But this intense campaign virtually marked the end of serious opposition from the Anglican Church.[82]

It must have become clear from events in Victoria in 1890 that churchmen could not stem the tide. A campaign for divorce law reform had begun in the younger colony after the movement in New South Wales was initiated, and there it also met with strong opposition from Anglicans in particular, on much the same grounds as those advanced in New South Wales. Indeed, opponents in the older colony supplied them with literature, but advocates of the measure in Victoria had also learned from the experience of New South Wales. William Shiels, the main proponent of the Victorian bill, conferred with Stephen on his way to London to put the case to the Colonial Office, and went armed with letters of introduction from Sir Henry Parkes and the Victorian premier. The governors of both colonies also recommended assent to the Victorian bill and there was support from South Australia and Queensland as well. The ecclesiastical opposition received short shrift from London on this occasion and on 13 May 1890 the Queen gave her assent to the Victorian bill for divorce extension.[83]

The Church of England had now to come to terms with wider provisions for divorce in Australia. No longer able to rely on legislative sanctions, it had to look to its own discipline. Thus Bishop Goe of Melbourne decreed that no clergyman within his diocese should remarry divorced persons or permit such marriages in his church.

There were to be regarded as "not joined by God". Such decrees were easier to issue than to enforce, as Zachary Barry made clear in an attack on Goe. He, for one, would not obey such a ruling as it was beyond a bishop's jurisdiction. The clergyman, after all, received his authority to marry from the State and not the bishop. The matter came up again at the General Synod in Sydney in September 1891, when the divorce law extension bill was before the New South Wales Parliament for the seventh time. After some debate this synod agreed that any measure such as the Victorian Act was "inconsistent with divine Law". It was not a unanimous decision; many laymen present dissented, and an attempt to include a ban on remarriage of divorced persons by Anglican clergymen failed.[84] Nevertheless, the attitude of the majority of clergymen was clear enough: they could be depended on not to countenance the remarriage of divorced persons. Decrees or synodical decisions would have made little difference to any who shared Zachary Barry's view.

The passing of the Victorian legislation apparently did not facilitate matters in New South Wales. The sixth bill lapsed for want of quorum in December 1890 and the fate of the measure seemed uncertain in 1891. Divorce law reform could not claim much attention in the political climate of 1891, and with Neild out of Parliament the measure lacked a committed advocate. Public interest was weak, although the *Sydney Morning Herald* kept the issue alive and campaigned for the introduction of another bill.[85] Neild, re-elected in June 1891, took the matter up and introduced the seventh bill on 12 August 1891. By March 1892 it had passed both houses and on 24 March it was reserved for royal assent. The Divorce Amendment and Extension Act was finally proclaimed on 6 August 1892. A minority in Parliament had continued to oppose it on religious grounds, but the churches did not put up much opposition at the end. Parliament received no petitions against this last bill, nor any supporting it.

The question churchmen raised by their campaigns to prevent both the liberalization of Sunday observance and of the divorce laws was whether or not the colony was a Christian country. If it was, as they believed emphatically that it should be, then its statute books should uphold Christian teaching on the sanctity of Sunday and of marriage. There were some in Parliament and the press who argued to the contrary that Parliament had to legislate not only for Christians but for the people as a whole.[86] But while most Parliamentarians agreed that the colony was Christian, some argued that the reforms were not anti-Christian. In the case of divorce it was easy to point to disagreement among the denominations, clergy and laymen, as evidence that churchmen were far from unanimous as to what the Christian teaching meant. The clerical advocate of divorce law reform, Zachary Barry, agreed with his adversaries that it was a religious question; but for him this meant that it was a matter of conscience. If the bill was passed, he argued, the State would "leave every conscience unfettered on the religious point". Some clergy, however, had inherited "a peculiar gloss on our Lord's words" and they wanted "the state by law to enforce that gloss and its consequences upon those who differ from them".[87] It was a pertinent comment.

A similar point had been made by a Victorian clergyman, Canon Robert Potter, a decade earlier in reference to the campaign against the liberalization of Sunday. According to Potter, the clergymen who sought stricter enforcement of Sunday observance laws were really troubled by "the inconsistent conduct of members of their own churches who disregard in fact what they profess to reverence".[88] Unable to persuade all their adherents to keep the Sabbath as they thought it should be kept, and fearful that divorce law reform would lead them to disregard Christ's teaching on marriage, many churchmen looked to the law of the land to buttress their diminishing authority. There was nothing novel here as far as Anglicans were concerned, but it represented a qualification of the voluntary principle among other Protestants, who, if divided on divorce, were almost unanimous on the Sunday question. The State might not fund the churches, but by its laws it was expected to support Christianity, and a rather Protestant understanding of it at that.

Divorce law reform was, to a degree, a step in the secularization of Australian society, but it should not be viewed simply though the eyes of its clerical opponents. The legislators did not think they had made the country less Christian by it. Against it must be set the measure of success churchmen enjoyed in preserving the Sunday observance laws. Admittedly, there were still differences of opinion on the Sunday question between the clergyman and his lay stalwarts on one hand and the ordinary layman on the other, who took the pulpit less seriously, especially if he was a Member of Parliament. So when churchmen used the law to close Sunday concerts, legislators provided for the remission of penalties. But the old laws for the protection of religion remained to restrict the scope of Sunday recreation. While those laws stayed on the statute books they suggested a Christian state, even if from some angles it looked secular. It was not the theocracy some churchmen seemed to want it to be, but neither was it a purely secular state. Church and State in New South Wales were tied, not by one cord, but by several slender threads; although one might be cut or weakened others remained.

8

Reinforcing Religion in the Schools

Public or state school education was one area in which the threads
tying Church and State were not all severed, and in the 1880s the
Protestant churches strove strenuously to preserve and strengthen
these remaining threads. This may seem surprising for the time
since the Public Instruction Act of 1880 has been treated in history
as a thoroughly secular measure, especially by some Catholic
historians.[1] Admittedly this legislation did something to weaken the
ties between Church and State in its withdrawal of state aid to
denominational schools, a measure which hit the Catholic Church
the hardest. The Act provided that from 1883 all church schools
which did not opt to come under the government had to suport
themselves financially, and thenceforth all public education was to
be under the authority of a minister of the Crown. This centralizing
policy in New South Wales was shared by other colonies. It was the
answer Australian colonial governments found to the problem of
providing universal schooling. The breaking of the Anglican
monopoly of state-supported schools led to no success in devising a
general system of public schooling acceptable to all, and in 1848
New South Wales adopted as a compromise a dual system of
denominational and national schools. At first the national schools
were the poor relations, but the Public Schools Act of 1866, which
placed both school systems under the Council of Education, altered
the situation, and the public schools (as the state schools were
known by then) increased while the denominational schools
decreased. The latter were mostly in the large centres of population,
while it was left to the government to provide schools in the more
sparsely settled country areas. A general system of education clearly
depended on the State rather than the churches, but denominational
anxiety about that education system still caused the government
problems. Smaller denominations resented the financial advantages
enjoyed by the larger denominations, and many Protestants objected
to concessions to Catholics. In 1874 the voluntaryists formed a Public Schools League to campaign for "free, compulsory, secular
education".[2] Their object was achieved in the passing of the Public
Instruction Act of 1880, although, ironically, education under the

new Act was not entirely free, not effectively compulsory and not exclusively secular.

New South Wales, in contrast to Victoria, did not attempt to resolve the religious difficulty by opting for a wholly secular system of public education. More conservative even in its liberalism than the daughter colony, New South Wales thought it not inconsistent with religious liberty and equality that some religious teaching in public education be provided. The religious provisions of Lord Stanley's Irish National System, which had operated in the colony's national schools until 1866, were enshrined in essence in the Public Schools Act of that year, largely at the insistence of the Anglican Church; and again in 1880 they were incorporated in the Public Instruction Act with little change. The religious content was a combination of general religious instruction and specific denominational teaching. Four hours a day were to be devoted to secular instruction, which under the Act's definition included "general religious teaching as distinguished from dogmatical or polemical theology". The seventeenth clause of the 1880 Act provided that an additional hour a day might be set aside for denominational instruction by visiting clergymen, including representatives of the Jewish faith. To facilitate this, special class rooms were to be provided for their use.[3]

The general religious teaching was to be given by the ordinary class teacher. For this he or she used the *Scripture Lessons* prepared for the Irish National Schools by the Protestant Archbishop of Dublin, Dr Richard Whately, with the concurrence of the heads of the Catholic and Presbyterian Churches in Ireland. These lessons were a selection of readings from the Bible in an independent translation. They ranged from the creation story through the sagas of the Old Testament to the gospel stories, with selections from the Acts of the Apostles, the Epistles and the Book of Revelation. Obscurities or archaisms were explained in footnotes and attempts were made to resolve the occasional conflict between Catholic and Protestant translations. An example was whether *metanoia* should be rendered as repentance or penance. The note explained that although for Roman Catholics penance implied essentially sorrow for sin, the word suggested a Catholic rite to Protestants. "While Roman Catholics are in no danger of being misled by the use of the words *repentance* or *penitence*, Protestants would be in danger of being misled by the use of the words *penance* or *do penance*". Some notes were interpretative, such as a comment on the first chapter of Genesis: "This image of God in man, is not in the body, but in the soul." Others were admonitory: "The love of this life, and its enjoyments, is a great temptation to deny Christ, and to renounce His religion, and whoever would wish to save his life in this world on such terms, will fail of eternal life in the next." In addition to these notes, difficult words and ideas were listed to be explained by the teacher and sets of questions were provided to test the child's grasp of each passage. These *Scripture Lessons* were not used for infants; they had "moral lessons", which included "the story of Creation, the Fall of Man, the Flood, and the lives of the Patriarchs, of Moses, Samuel, John the Baptist, and Christ".[4] Some diet! But much must have depended on how it was presented.

One teacher claimed in 1889 that many teachers resented the requirement that they impart this general religious teaching, some for conscientious reasons; and freethinkers, he asserted, used the lessons as a chance to ridicule religion. Most teachers, however, came from the religious middle classes, with Presbyterians and Wesleyans significantly above average in the profession. A good number of them were Sunday school teachers and some were frustrated by the regulation which forbade them to engage in lay preaching. Such teachers probably imparted the lessons conscientiously, and with what fervour we might gather from the claim of a retired teacher in 1894. Protesting against the complaint that state schools would become secular unless ministers of religion visited them, he did not see how the school system could become "purely secular" while it retained "its Scripture and moral lessons — setting forth God, as revealed by and in His son Jesus Christ the Lord in all His purity, unselfishness and holiness, crucified for the sins of the world".[5]

Teachers were not entitled to claim conscientious objection to providing the general religious teaching, but parents could withdraw their children from these lessons. Even these children were exposed to some degree of religious material for the public schools used the reading books of the Irish National System. Although they were seen to be stodgy and dated, the books were nevertheless well laden with extracts of religious and moral prose and poetry, strongly Christian in flavour; this was the case with most school readers of the age, unless, as in Victoria, they had been expurgated on doctrinaire secularist grounds.[6]

The religious provisions of the Public Instruction Act of 1880 were there by design and not by accident. The Public Schools League, dubbed the Secularist League by some, did not mean to exclude the religious provisions from state schools. Its *Manifesto . . . for Making Primary Education National, Secular, Compulsory and Free* acknowledged religious instruction as "supremely important" and stated that it had no objection to the *Scripture Lessons*, or to denominational instruction in schools provided that the latter was given at no cost to the State. That was as far as their secularism went.

Congregationalists, foremost among the voluntaryists, supported the public instruction bill at their Union assembly in 1879 and some of them expressed a preference for the word *unsectarian* rather than *secular* to deny the notion that they wished to exclude the Bible from the schools. The Presbyterian General Assembly also expected the *Scripture Lessons* to remain in the curriculum when it resolved to support Parkes's bill and the Wesleyan Conference emphasized the religious clauses in its petition in favour of the bill.[7] The Anglicans, at least the bishops, most clergy and a few laymen, opposed the bill, but this was mainly because it would withdraw state aid to church schools. They were hardly likely to oppose those religious provisions in state schools which they had fought to preserve in 1866.

The Catholic Church was the most vehement opponent of Parkes's public instruction bill in all its provisions. But the intemperate language of the famous "Joint Pastoral" of the Catholic bishops mostly was directed wide of the mark. It asserted the necessity for religion and education to go hand in hand, but denounced the public schools as "seed plots of future immorality, infidelity, and lawlessness". In "Hidden Springs", a series of lectures delivered in 1876, Archbishop Vaughan spoke of the movement towards free, compulsory, secular education in Australia as part of the sinister worldwide conspiracy against all forms of religion. His attitude remained unchanged in the 1879-80 controversy. Perhaps the apparent secularism of the earlier Victorian Education Act (1872) lent support to this view, but, whatever might be said against Parkes's measure, it could not fairly be called secular and godless. In a later speech Vaughan made a grudging acknowledgment of the religious provisions, but justified the Catholic view that the public schools were "strictly secular" with the assertion that before long the secularist current would "carry out of our public schools that miserable pretence at religion which has been introduced to save appearances".[8] This kind of attack was hardly calculated to win sympathy for the hierarchy's plea for fair play for Catholic children, but the authors of the "Joint Pastoral" had another end in view: to frighten the Catholics out of the state schools and to galvanize their support for a separate school system. Thus, paradoxically, a religious content in public education did not please the Catholic Church. Catholic MPs opposed the religious clauses, so much so that Captain Arthur Onslow, a supporter of state aid to church schools as well as the religious provisions in public schools, was amazed at "the most singular union between the secularists and the Roman Catholics".[9]

Avowed secularists in Parliament were few. David Buchanan opposed the religious clauses of the bill on the grounds that religious teaching should be left to churches and Sunday schools; but even he still wanted children to have the Bible as a reading book. It peeved one Catholic MP, John Dillon, that the advocates of the bill were "not secularists in the proper sense of the word"; he objected that the provision for special religious instruction would give the public schools a strong tinge of denominationalism. The Jewish MP, Henry Cohen, who supported a comprehensive system of secular schooling, quoted some of the religious material which ascribed Messianic status and divinity to Jesus, to show how offensive it was to Jews and Unitarians.[10]

None of these objections carried any weight with Parkes. When introducing the bill in 1879, the premier pointed out the New South Wales, in contrast to other Australian colonies, had sought "to carry religious teaching hand in hand with the secular instruction of the State". During the debate he declared that he would never drop the religious provision of the seventh clause; he did not believe that any nation could become great "without a profound faith". At the same time he thought his bill was "sufficiently secular for practical operation".[11]

Compared with Victoria, New South Wales had not adopted a very liberal solution to the educational dilemma. Jewish and other minorities had the right to opt out of the general religious teaching, but there was a general pervasiveness of Christianity in the schools. The scheme was supposed to be acceptable to Catholics, since it was based on the Irish National System to which the Catholic Church in Ireland had once been party. But no one in 1880 could have imagined that it would be acceptable to the Catholic hierarchy, although some, including Parkes, seemed to hope that the Catholic laity would accept the state school system, especially when faced with the costly alternative of providing their own schools. The threat to Catholic schools which the bill posed, however, helped to consolidate the Catholic community, as Vaughan appreciated. But to the Protestant majority the system was acceptable. Churchmen in Victoria cast envious eyes across the Murray; the Anglican Bishop of Ballarat, for example, congratulated Parkes on the passing of the Act and hoped Victoria would adopt its religious provisions, as Parkes confidently predicted would happen. Victorian churchmen campaigned for something akin to the New South Wales system, a fact which Vaughan and some other Catholic spokesmen failed to recognize when they quoted the opinions of men such as Bishop Moorhouse against state education.[12]

The Public Instruction Act had hardly been passed when a few began to fear that its religious content was being whittled away. The introduction of a new series of school reading books — the Collins Australian School Series — caused this anxiety. In September 1879, before the public instruction bill had been introduced, the secretary of the Council of Education, W. Wilkins, directed that the outdated second Irish reading book of the series be replaced by its counterpart in the Australian series. No instructions were given to replace the other books of the Irish series, but apparently the Collins series was being used in many schools. Inspectors' reports in 1880 indicated that the first and second Irish books were virtually phased out and it was left up to teachers to decide which books to use at other levels; they naturally favoured the modern Australian series. [13] Thus before the Public Instruction Act came into operation a feature of the old system had been slightly altered.

Such a change might be thought to have been a matter of small concern to churchmen, but the content of school reading books was a controversial issue in 1880. Victoria had only recently replaced the Irish reading books with Nelson's Royal Readers, "heavily expurgated to exclude references to particular religious faiths". In September 1880 the *Freeman's Journal* asserted that the same process was in operation in New South Wales, with the gradual replacement of the Irish books by a new series which it said only mentioned the name of God once and of Christ not at all. Exultingly, it declared that "schools from whose books the names of God and His Son are banished cannot be Christian", [14] as if this confirmed the wisdom of the Catholic denunciations of public schools. Even if its description of the Collins series had been accurate, it blithely overlooked the specific religious provisions of the public schools before and after 1880. Educational administrators clearly did not regard the reading books as part of those provisions, but it appeared that there were Protestant churchmen who thought that the reading books should also be vehicles of religious instruction.

One of these was Dr. W. Moore White, an Ulsterman and minister of St Andrew's Presbyterian Church, Sydney. White, who supported the Act of 1880 "*in its integrity*", took the matter up with the Minister for Public Instruction, Sir John Robertson, in November 1880. He complained that directives had been issued to teachers to apply for the Collins series, and that in many schools the Irish reading books had already been superseded by the Australian series of books "so secular in their character that the name of God is scarcely to be found in them". He argued that the Act's definition of "secular" implied the use of reading books with a religious content like the Irish series, quoting such selections as "The Christian Salvation" and "The Saviour Christ's Second Coming" from the fourth book and other specifically Christian excerpts, which Cohen had quoted for the opposite reasons. [15]

White's letter was distributed to district inspectors for report and comment. They denied that directives to buy the Collins series had been issued and stated that although the first and second Irish books were superseded the third and fourth were still in use. But some of the inspectors questioned the propriety of using the Irish books. One reported that the religious content was an embarrassment in classes where some children had different beliefs, and that secular reading books would avoid this problem. Another argued that the Irish books were not strictly non-sectarian, as the Act required; he thought quite reasonably that the framers of the Act expected the *Scripture Lessons* to be used for general religious teaching. As for teaching children to read, several inspectors defended the superiority of the Collins series as being more suited to the southern hemisphere and the time. Most took issue with White's assertion that the Australian reading books were "purely secular in the strictest sense of the term". The inspector of the Wagga Wagga district, D.S. Hicks, went to some length to show that "religious and moral instruction is interspersed in an attractive form through them." He found it incredible that a clergyman perusing the Australian reading books could fail to recognize this. As an example he quoted, from the second book, the words of the weeping parents of a deformed child:

"Poor little thing, to make thee well, we'd freely give our all: But God knows best!"

With this and many similar examples he concluded that White's charges could not be sustained.[16]

But this was not the kind of religious teaching White was looking for. Hicks's examples were theistic rather than Christian. Clearly, the definition of secular was the heart of the problem: the Collins series appeared secular compared with the old Irish series. What religious views it did contain were indirect, and White wanted the direct and didactic approach of the Irish books. His lobbying was not in vain for Robertson issued an instruction that the Irish books were to be supplied and used in the schools, and Parkes assured W.J. Foster in Parliament that there was no intention to dispense with them.[17]Thus educational standards were compromised by the requirements of religion.

White was sceptical of these pronouncements, and he would have agreed with another Presbyterian minister, J.M. Ross, who declared at a public meeting at Nowra in 1883 that New South Wales was rushing headfirst into secularism. A new standard of proficiency issued under George Reid, Minister for Public Instruction in 1883/ 84, seemed to give substance to this charge. The standard apparently made no mention of the Irish reading books, only the Collins series. White suspected that Reid intended to do away with the Irish books altogether, and in March 1884 he raised the matter in the Presbyterian General Assembly, arguing that Presbyterians had supported the Public Instruction Act of 1880 on the understanding that the reading books and the *Scripture Lessons* of the Irish National System would be used. The reading books, which contained lessons on the nature of sin, humility, benevolence and duty to parents, he maintained should not be withdrawn without public approval at a time when immorality and crime were increasing. The assembly judiciously declined to censure the Education Department, but it appointed White convenor of a committee to watch over the course of instruction in public schools.[18]

The *Weekly Advocate* also regarded Reid's instructions as evidence of an advancing tide of secularism, and the matter was raised in Parliament at the same time by Francis Abigail, a Congregationalist and a prominent Orangeman. Somewhat misinformed on the issue, Abigail asserted that the Irish reading books were being supplanted by books which contained no reference to the Creator. This in turn provoked an attack from secularists on the religious provisions of the Act, although most Parliamentarians were clearly in favour of general religious teaching in the schools. Even one Catholic MP, J. McElhone, supported it. It was pointed out that the Collins series was not to replace the Irish books, but to provide an alternative to them. The *Protestant Standard* was relieved that Reid's successors had retained the Irish books; had Reid had his way, it exaggerated, the Catholic charge of godless schools regrettably would have been true.[19]Like the *Freeman's Journal* earlier, it overlooked the specific provisions for religious teaching in public schools — and so had many clergymen.

Special Religious Instruction in Practice before 1884

Up to 1880 special religious instruction in public schools had been rather neglected by the churches. Anglican and Catholic clergy devoted their efforts mainly to certified denominational schools. Many of these schools received weekly visits, but during 1880 thirteen of fifty-seven Anglican and twenty of seventy-seven Catholic certified denominational schools received no visits at all from clergymen. Nearly two-thirds of the 872 public schools were not visited by a clergyman of any denomination in 1880. Of the remainder only about 75 received weekly visits more or less regularly and 82 per cent of these visits were made by Anglican clergymen.[20]

The legislators were not unaware of this neglect and it may be wondered that this facility was retained in the Public Instruction Act of 1880. While the bill was before the House, a report on the attendance of clergy at 105 public schools for the three years up to December 1879 was tabled. Of the 6,000 visits made over the period, two-thirds took place in 1879 and 88 per cent of the total were made by Anglican clergy. Most other denominations visited the schools infrequently, and the Baptists did not visit any of them in that time.[21] Ironically, in view of the poor showing of the Catholic Church, it was Michael Fitzpatrick, a Catholic MP, who defended the inclusion of the facilities for special religious instruction. He argued that, although the religious bodies had shown little disposition to use these facilities, they should be retained "because in future years they might determine a different course". Critical of his own Church's education policy, which earned him denial of a Catholic burial in 1881, he perhaps hoped that the Catholic Church might change its attitude towards public schools. At any rate, he pointed out that the Church of England had recently determined to make more use of its opportunities.[22]

The increase of visits by clergymen to public schools in 1879 was evidence of a new interest among Anglicans in providing religious instruction. Although it was largely at the insistence of the Church of England that the religious provisions of the Irish system were preserved in the Public Schools Act of 1866, Anglican clergymen generally paid little attention to them up to 1875, being content with providing religious education in denominational schools. The most ardent champions of church schools affected to despite the public school as godless, but at his synod in 1875 Bishop William Tyrrell of Newcastle, a High Churchman, refuted this "untruthful disparagement". Public schools were not averse to religious teaching, he explained, but they assigned part of the responsibility to pastors and parents. However, strong opposition met Zachary Barry, a prominent supporter of the Public Schools League, when he called on the Sydney diocesan synod in April 1875 to provide the measure of religious instruction allowed by the law in public schools. The majority of the synod, including Bishop Barker, saw Barry's proposal as an attempt to compromise the Anglican stand in defence of denominational schools, and much was said against the public schools and the difficulties of giving instruction in them. Nevertheless, later that year the Provincial Synod of New South Wales endorsed a recommendation of the bishops that Anglicans should attempt to carry out systematic religious instruction in both public and denominational schools with the use of paid and unpaid teachers to assist the clergy.[23]

This decision helped to change the mood in the diocese of Sydney and in December 1875 the synod set up a committee to work out a scheme for systematic religious instruction in the diocese. The following June the synod accepted most of the committee's proposals, including recommendations for the use of voluntary and paid helpers and a Scripture prize to encourage diligence in the pupils. In 1880 the committee presented a syllabus which essentially consisted of lessons from the Bible, the Apostles' Creed and the Catechism. It also reported that most metropolitan schools were receiving weekly visits, twice-weekly in some cases, which the committee thought should be the minimum. Country schools, however, were not visited as regularly and some not at all.[24]

With the passing of the Public Instruction Act in 1880 there was even greater emphasis on the need for the Church to undertake religious instruction in public schools. Bishop Barker and Bishop Pearson both charged their clergy with the duty to avert any further secularization of the system. At a public meeting in August 1880 to enlist support for the Anglican programme of religious instruction in public schools, Barker admitted his preference for denominational schools; but he foresaw that by the end of 1882 many of these schools in the suburbs and country would cease to exist. Anglicans had to make the most of the opportunities open to them in public schools, where almost all of their children would soon be taught. Barker dismissed the contention that he was jeopardizing the future of church schools, and emphatically denied that action by the churches after so long a time might provoke the repeal of the religious provisions.[25]

Other supporters of denominational schools likewise commended the programme in public schools, but some members of the Church of England Defence Association, usually High Churchmen, disapproved of the attempt to organize religious instruction in public schools. Committed to seeking a change in the law that would restore state aid to denominational schools, they deplored any softening of the Anglican position; one of them likened Barker and his supporters to rats deserting the sinking ship. The banker, Shepherd Smith, who was actually on the platform with the bishop at the meeting, wrote later to say that he disapproved of the programme and thought "a purely secular State-paid system" would be better for the time being. Smith was sympathetic to the Roman Catholic position and another critic wished the Church of England would be as "outspoken and logically consistent as the Church of Rome". On the other hand, the *Sydney Morning Herald*, while critical of some things said at the Anglican meeting, welcomed Barker's programme as evidence of "healthy co-operation between that Church and the State". The Church was facing the facts of the situation and dealing with them "in a practical manner". This opinion was reasonable. After all, of the alternatives, were any practical? Anglican church schools had been diminishing ever since the passing of the Public Schools Act in 1866; the number of certified Anglican schools in the colony had almost halved from 115 to 1870 to 63 in 1880.[26] For a long time the majority of Anglican children had been attending public schools. The Act of 1880 was to make Anglicans take their responsibility to those children seriously.

The systematic visitation of public schools was a formidable undertaking made more difficult by high church opposition in the one hand, and the distaste of some persons for the task on the other. A few argued that it was not the clergyman's role and others that clergymen were unsuited to the work. The latter may have been true, but Bishop Pearson had little patience with such an excuse. "A clergyman", he exclaimed, "might as reasonably say that he cannot read prayers, or that he cannot preach, as that he cannot instruct the young of his flock in the elements of Christian faith and duty."[27] But the prospects of giving religious instruction to children in a small country school were not very encouraging, compared with a large town or city school where a visiting clergyman might have the use of a separate room, although not always for the classes of smaller denominations. A Baptist minister who attended Cleveland Street Public School for a time in 1875 complained that he had to give religious instruction in a hall in which there were constant comings and goings. But there were more complaints about difficulties in country schools, where the clergyman was usually obliged to teach the children of his denomination in outbuildings or under the shade of trees. So the parson would probably not visit the small school in hot, cold or very wet weather. The teacher might also frustrate his task, as in one case where a teacher allegedly prevented religious instruction classes by persuading parents that it was undesirable to take the children outside in inclement weather. It is of little wonder that Bishop Thomas of the diocese of Goulburn should remark that the privilege of visiting schools would be more appreciated by the clergy if suitable accommodation was provided.[28]

There were other difficulties that made visits to country schools infrequent. Often, within one rural charge, there would be a number of small schools usually some distance apart. Bishop Pearson, defending his clergy in 1882, gave an example of one parish with seventeen schools; the clergyman and his wife visited one school three times a week and a catechist visited another four schools weekly, but twelve were not visited at all. The clergy, he protested, could not do the impossible.[29] It was generally recognized that catechists and other lay helpers were needed if the Anglican Church was to reach most of its children in the schools.

If the task was so difficult for the Anglican Church with all its resources, it was much more so for the other Protestant denominations. Yet the Presbyterians and the Wesleyans were stirred to some realization of their opportunities, by the Anglican initiatives in large part. Bishop Barker had suggested to his synod in 1880 that other Protestant children might attend Anglican instruction if their own pastors did not visit the schools, and he told the public meeting in August 1880 that children of other denominations were attending Anglican classes despite a protest in one instance, presumably from a Presbyterian. The Anglican clergyman concerned obtained the written consent of the parents and the children continued to attend his instruction. The low church bishop did not seem to regard this as proselytism, for the children were to receive nothing more than Scripture and the Apostles' Creed. [30]

To have children of different creeds in one religious instruction class was not unusual. There were complaints that children went indiscriminately to any minister and that teachers had sometimes to prevent Jewish children from attending Christian classes. Ministers who visited schools probably did not worry about the composition of their classes, but it was a different matter when a bishop advertised for the attendance of children of other denominations at Anglican classes. The *Weekly Advocate* warned Methodists that special religious instruction would become a proselytizing agency if they left their children to be shepherded by other churchmen in the schools. The next Annual Conference enjoined Wesleyan ministers to take advantage of the Act's provision for special religious instruction. Some ministers did so gladly, but there were those who complained of difficulties and disappointing results. [31]

It was much the same with the Presbyterians. In December 1880 the *Presbyterian* also reported the Anglican efforts and reminded its readers that the Act gave Presbyterian ministers an opportunity to teach children they would not meet on Sundays. In a subsequent issue it advocated a combined Protestant programme, perhaps as a way around the problem of proselytism. But special religious instruction was generally seen as denominational, and in March 1881 the Presbyterian General Assembly expressed its gratitude for the facilities and recognized the obligation that lay upon that Church to use them. Presbyterians, however, were divided on the matter; the Moderator's casting vote was required in the Presbytery of Sydney in February 1882 to carry a resolution to take advantage of the provision. This prompted a critical layman to remind the reluctant parsons that the youth of the colony were the hope of the Church, adding tartly that if they would have full coffers and churches they would have to do more than baptize and bury.[32]

The Baptist and Congregational denominations were apparently not much troubled by the possibility that Anglican clergymen might instruct their children in the public schools; or at least they did not discuss that matter in their assemblies early in the 1880s. In the case of the Baptists there was a lingering suspicion of any kind of connection between religion and the State, but this did not apply so much to the Congregationalists. They had expressed their approval of the Bible in the schools, and a few Congregational ministers visited the schools in 1879 and 1880, usually where Anglicans were attending more or less regularly. But it would have been almost impossible for Congregationalists to provide religious instruction for their few, scattered adherents in most schools. They were hardly encouraged to embark on the task, and, if they thought about it, it must have occurred to some that a widescale effort on the part of the various churches to exploit the seventeenth clause of the Act would mostly find their children at the feet of another pastor, probably Presbyterian or Wesleyan rather than Anglican. Furthermore, the success of their Sunday schools gave them less incentive to look to the schools for pastoral opportunities. This was true also of the Wesleyans, whose share of Sunday school attendances was well above their percentage in the population.[33]

The interests of the Protestant denominations, apart from Anglicans, really lay in a cooperative programme of instruction in the schools. Questions of ecclesiastical polity aside, there were no doctrinal hindrances to an interdenominational scheme of evangelical instruction. Some even envisaged a scheme embracing Anglicans. The *Presbyterian* seemed to have this in mind in 1880 when it advocated that Protestants should combine their resources. It argued that they could hardly condemn Catholics for not cooperating with the Act if they themselves could not work together. Such an arrangement would obviate the problem of proselytism threatened by the Anglican initiatives. But few took the suggestion very seriously in 1880, although when it was raised again in 1882 Protestant ministers in Newtown agreed to give daily religious instruction based on the International Sunday School Union lessons. They laid their scheme before the Minister for Public Instruction, F.B. Suttor, in August 1882. He did not oppose the scheme, but told the ministers it was a matter between them and the parents of the children concerned. If the parents agreed he assured them of cooperation from the teachers.[34]

The following February the group put its proposal, now reduced from daily instruction to three lessons a week, to the district school board, seeking approval to approach the parents. They also requested the use of two large school rooms and the assistance of teachers to keep order. The board questioned the legality of combined religious instruction; even if it were permissible, it rejected the proposed programme as too disruptive to the school, despite the Act's provision for one hour of religious instruction daily, and as unwarrantably burdensome on the teachers. The *Sydney Morning Herald* supported the board. It maintained correctly that the Act clearly intended dogmatic or denominational instruction to be given under the seventeenth clause, and in any case it doubted whether the scheme would work.[35] Thus the prospects for combined teaching were not very encouraging. The seventeenth clause had been an attempt to come to terms with denominational differences and with some point when it sought to cater for Catholic and Protestant. But there was little peculiarly denominational teaching in the Anglican syllabus of instruction, a point Bishop Barker used to justify the presence of Presbyterian children in Anglican classes. At any rate, the Act was to be interpreted more liberally the following year when the Protestant churches sought to put some life into the religious provisions of the Act.

The Religious Instruction Movement, 1884

It was largely due to Bishop Barry that religious instruction in schools became a public issue in 1884. Barry came to New South Wales in that year with every intention of taking up the matter, drawing on the experience he had gained in England. He had helped frame the religious provisions of the London School Board under the Forster Education Act of 1870 and before coming to Australia he had discussed the provisions of the Public Instruction Act with Parkes in London, who had explained its religious provisions to him.[36]

Barry declared his policy on religious education at an Anglican meeting on 1 May 1884. He urged Anglicans to preserve such of their own schools that had survived the withdrawal of state aid in 1883. (The diocese of Sydney had ten former certified denominational schools in 1884, all in the metropolitan area.) In the public schools he thought it the duty of Anglicans to see that the best use was made of the *Scripture Lessons* and the opportunities for special religious instruction. Barry recognized that the cooperation of other denominations would be necessary to make the religious provisions of the Act work most effectively, and he thought that Anglicans could work "in concert" if not "in combination" with them. The question of the day, he maintained, was not whether children would grow up Anglican or Presbyterian, but whether they would grow up Christian or not — whether Christianity rather than secularism would remain the unifying faith of society. Barry hoped that all denominations might show that they wanted "to work for Christianity and not merely for churchmanship".[37]

Bishop Barry's overture evoked a warm response from one of Sydney's leading Protestant ministers, James Jefferis, who delivered three Sunday evening lectures of religious education in the Pitt Street Congregational Church soon afterwards. It was not only the invitation to cooperate that struck a sympathetic chord among other Protestants including voluntaryists, but also the issue of the day as Barry compellingly defined it — Christianity or secularism. Jefferis recognized the far-reaching implications for society that would come to pass if the problem of religious instruction in schools was not adequately resolved in favour of Christianity. The one mighty hope was for the words of "the Great Teacher" to calm the "tempest of human passion which threatens to submerge the existing order, and destroy the very fabric of society. Our children must hear them, must learn to reverence them, must be trained to obey them."[38]

Jefferis's first lecture dealt with the instruction of children within the church, principally through the Sunday school. Voluntaryists had held that church and home were the only appropriate places for religious instruction, but the challenge to Christian belief and the threat to Christian institutions, which Jefferis portrayed so luridly, helped to change their minds on the relationship of the State to religion. As a voluntaryist and aware of possible accusations of inconsistency, Jefferis began his second lecture, "Religious Teaching in Public Schools", by refuting the charge that those who believed in "a free church in a free state" were secularists in national life; the antithesis of secularism, he asserted, was religion, not the church. Every state "must rely on a religious basis", and so, he maintained, Congregationalists believed "intensely in a vital union between religion and the State", as distinct from the union "between a church and the State".

Jefferis was virtually saying that common Christianity was the established religion of the land, and by implication ought to be taught to the children of the land. In a statement wrongly understood by his Catholic critics to indicate a very recent change of heart, he confessed that once, in his zeal for religious liberty, he had advocated the exclusion of religious teaching from the schools; but as he subsequently made clear, on coming to New South Wales in 1877 he happily joined the ranks of the Public Schools League and altered his motto to free, compulsory and *unsectarian*.[39] Now he would rather have officers of the State teaching religion than allow children to pass through the schools without learning about "the living God".

He saw the Irish National System as the best vehicle for religious education in a colony like New South Wales. It was "as fair and free" as any in the world, and the *Scripture Lessons* compiled by the admirable Dr Whately contained nothing offensive to Protestant or Catholic. As an example of their impartiality Jefferis quoted the note on the translation of *metanoia* as penitence rather then penance. But he felt too much fuss had been made of the content of the reading books. Although he thought it desirable to include some Christian history and biography in school readers, children should learn from books of literary excellence. While the *Scripture Lessons* were used it mattered little if the reading books were "secular". But he was strongly critical of the proportion of marks allocated to teaching the *Scripture Lessons*. He calculated that they represented only one twenty-seventh of the marks awarded to teachers, which, he argued, showed little esteem for this part of the curriculum and was contrary to the intentions of people and Parliament that state education should be religious. He also called for the exclusion from the state teaching service of those unwilling or incompetent to teach the *Scripture Lessons*.[40]

This provocative utterance, amply reported, might have prompted the recently appointed Minister for Public Instruction, W.J. Trickett, to visit Paddington Primary School on Monday 19 May where he found the *Scripture Lessons* used and religious instruction being given by Anglican catechists.[41] In any case, Trickett went to hear Jefferis the next Sunday evening when he spoke on the special religious instruction permitted under the seventeenth clause. Without giving much credit to Anglican efforts, Jefferis admitted that the clergy "as a whole declined to accept the trust, declined to discharge the duty". The main reason for this, he confessed rather abjectly was not the lack of will, but the lack of competence. Jefferis wanted to see the work left to those ministers with "a special aptitude", assisted by paid teachers who would devote themselves entirely to this work in schools. Such a scheme required cooperation among the denominations and ample funds. Lack of cooperation, Jefferis thought, was largely the fault of the Church of England, partly because it had plumped for an alternative system of educaton and was only of late coming to terms with "the national system", and also because of the disdain of some Anglicans for ministers of other denominations. But he spoke warmly of Bishop Barry and pledged the cooperation of Congregationalists in what he hoped would mark a new turning in religious endeavours.[42]

Yet Jefferis did not propose to cooperate in a scheme of

denominational instruction. The inculcation of "special creeds and dogmas", if it had to be done, was the work of the denominational Sunday schools. In the public schools children should be taught the truths that all creeds shared. But was this what the Act envisaged? Jefferis knew perfectly well what the law laid down: "the religious instruction to be given shall in every case be the religious instruction authorised by the Church to which the clergyman or other religious teacher may belong." Still, he argued that they were bound "by the spirit of the law even more than by its letter". Whether he interpreted the spirit of the law correctly was another matter. The Act already provided for general religious teaching of a kind supposedly acceptable to Protestant and Catholic, and its intentions beyond that were to allow each denomination access to its own adherents. Jefferis seemed to want something in between the provisions for general and denominational instruction. He advocated that the "Evangelical churches", by which he meant the Anglican as well as other principal Protestant denominations, should combine to authorize approved instructors to carry out special religious instruction in the schools on behalf of them all. The differences between them, he maintained, were small compared to the great body of truth they all received. The course of instruction he envisaged included both Scripture and the principles of natural religion. "Living religion grows not by the doctrines, but by the narratives of the Bible", he quoted from Jean Paul Richter, a German writer who "championed a cheerful Christianity, free of dogmas". As well as the course of instruction he thought that the hour of special religious instruction might include a form of prayer to open the school day and a hymn, although he did not want to see the hour become a religious service. The programme he envisaged was essentially Protestant in its non-dogmatic concept and scriptural basis, but it did not trouble Jefferis that Catholics would not cooperate. The schools offered them the same facilities and if they did not avail themselves of them, he declared, "the sorrow is ours. The blame and the loss are theirs".[43]

Jefferis had proposed some meaty matters for consideration at the meeting Bishop Barry convened on Tuesday 27 May 1884, when Anglicans sat down with Presbyterians, Wesleyans and Congregationalists. Barry had invited the Catholics to cooperate, but they declined, and the Baptists also stood off. The proceedings of this meeting were private, but it appointed a committee of four to draw up proposals for more effective religious teaching in public schools. Four weeks later the church leaders met to consider the committee's report which showed the influence of Jefferis, but the hand of Dr Moore White, the campaigner for Christian reading books, was also discernible. Above all, it embraced Bishop Barry's proposal for concerted action in special religious instruction. Recommendations included that the general religious teaching under clause seven of the Act be given regularly throughout the schools; that the reading books have some religious and moral content; that greater weight be given to marks awarded for Scripture; that the Department of Public Instruction consider the capability of teachers to give general religious teaching as part of the qualifications for teachers and that they be given some training in teaching *Scripture Lessons*, and that schools open with a brief act of worship. The committee also submitted that all these proposals should be extended to the few high schools as well as to primary schools. As for special religious instruction, it recommended a joint board consisting of two representatives from each participating denomination to watch over the course of general religious teaching as well as to coordinate the work of the churches in giving religious instruction, hoping both to promote harmony among the churches and to prevent undue interference with the work of the school. The committee opted for denominational religious instruction within the terms of the Act. The board's function was to see that, as far as possible, all children (whose parents did not object) received special religious instruction. Where a denomination supplied no teachers it was proposed that the board would appoint teachers accredited by all the denominations to teach its children; such teachers would pledge not to proselytize. This provision was a tacit admission that even under the proposed new scheme it would be almost impossible to provide denominational instruction for all children. At Barry's request, the scheme was provisionally to be confined within the boundaries of the diocese of Sydney, although he intended to recommend it to the bishops of his province;[44] as yet it lacked the formal sanction of all the denominations involved.

The scheme was to be laid before the Minister for Public Instruction on Friday 27 June, but lack of unanimity among the churchmen who devised it became evident the day before, when the *Sydney Morning Herald* published the objections Jefferis had made in committee to Barry's proposal to organize denominational religious instruction by all the churches. Jefferis argued that the proposed scheme would foster the sectarian spirit and present children with "the sad spectacle of a divided Christendom in a more open and visible way than before". Such a "parcelling out" of children he claimed to be contrary to the "general feeling" of parents, although parents were more probably indifferent. More to the point were the educational disadvantages Jefferis indicated. The denominational scheme would prevent a rational division of children into ages and ability, particularly for the small denominations, who, in many cases, would have to take all their children in one class. Thus there were obvious disadvantages to the small denominations in Barry s scheme as well as some to the schools, such as having to organize a number of denominational classes of varying sizes. So once more Jefferis advocated his syllabus of scriptural instruction to combined classes.[45]

On the morning of the deputation the *Herald* published Bishop Barry's reasons for not accepting Jefferis's sceme of combined religious instruction. The committee sought to implement the law which provided for a "dual system" of general and denominational religious teaching. This was the creation of Parliament, not of churchmen, Barry pleaded. But Jefferis replied ironically that the legislators, like Moses allowing divorce, had given the denominational provision " 'because of the hardness' of the sectarian heart". Furthermore, Barry's committee was prepared to go beyond the law in some cases. The bishop thought the Act might be interpreted to allow combined religious instruction in those small schools where denominational instruction was impracticable.[46]

This was some concession to Jefferis's argument, but Barry had such a strong preference for denominational instruction that he was determined to have it wherever it was practicable. His call to work for Christianity and not one form of churchmanship or another became more limited in practice. Jefferis had espoused the bishop's professed idealism more fully than he did himself, but admittedly it was easier for him as a member of a small denomination to stand by "the spirit of the law".

There were a few in the larger denominations who shared Jefferis's viewpoint. In a sermon in St Stephen's Presbyterian Church on 8 June Dr Robert Steel advocated combined classes for Protestant children, chiefly on the ground that denominational classes would be impossible in some places. Zachary Barry also supported unsectarian biblical instruction and predicted that if the bishop did not concede this his scheme would end in ruins. The Wesleyan J.H. Fletcher, on the other hand, thought Jefferis's proposal good, but, with its use of paid teachers, too difficult and costly to implement. Meanwhile, he argued that Methodists could no longer neglect their children in the schools.[47] Others might have sympathized with Jefferis but did not want to appear unwilling to cooperate with the bishop, who had shown such unprecedented goodwill.

While churchmen argued over these details the *Sydney Morning Herald*, a staunch defender of the Public Instruction Act and chary of stirring up sectarian strife, was generally critical of the scheme

"The New-Chum and the Wasps' Nest". (From *Bulletin*, 12 July 1884. Photo courtesy of Trobe Library, State Library of Victoria.)

Barry's committee had devised. It thought that the clergy were quite out of bounds in assuming to watch over the course of general religious instruction in schools. It considered the proposal to test and train teachers for teaching the *Scripture Lessons* quite improper; the department needed good teachers rather than good Christians, it averred. This was reasonable enough, but good teachers had to know their subject. Was it so unreasonable to ask that only the fit and willing should teach the *Scripture Lessons?* As there was a conscience clause to excuse children from the *Scripture Lessons*, perhaps teachers could be similarly exempted. But what the churchmen were proposing was more radical: they wanted to make competence in Scripture a principle of selection for the teaching service. The *Bulletin* did not miss the irony: the "Dissenters" were proposing a "new Test Act".[48]

As to opening worship, the *Herald* thought that it would be harmless enough in itself, but undoubtedly offensive to Catholics. The Protestant churchmen argued that "some kind of worship of the Almighty" was essential to an effective system of religious teaching, and thought that a rite acceptable to all could be devised. After all the Lord's Prayer was universal to all Christians and "of all forms of religion in the world hymnody was the most catholic", Barry pointed out. Jefferis did not think that Catholics could object to the Lord's Prayer and a simple hymn in an unconsecrated building. However the *Freeman's Journal* had already accused the Protestant churchmen of trying to turn the state schools into "Protestant Denominational Schools" and the *Herald* concluded that it was largely "a Denominational system" which Barry's committee was looking for; as such it thought it had little chance of public support.[49]

In face of the counter-arguments hot off the press, the churchmen began to justify themselves when they met the Minister for Public Instruction that Friday morning. Bishop Barry reminded Trickett that the deputationists represented 75 per cent of the children in schools, and they did not think that minorities should interfere with a programme which "the great majority of the community emphatically endorsed". Minorities had the right to abstain or withdraw, not to overrule the majority. If religious truth were absent from the schools, he added, some other principle would be sure to take its place. Josiah Mullens was confident that children could be taught that there was a great law above them which had divine sanction, "without trenching on the idiosyncrasies of any persons whatsoever". While they would have liked to see the whole Bible in the hands of school children, the churchmen told Trickett that they were content with the Irish *Scripture Lessons*, because the text had originally been agreed to by Protestant and Catholic.[50]

The deputationists assured the minister that they did not wish to go beyond the law; only to see it carried out in letter and in spirit. But they found that Trickett interpreted the Act in a stricter and more secular light. While he affirmed his own belief in the importance of religious instruction he argued that "the State could not undertake to be a religious instructor of the people" in such a community of mixed religious faiths. This was hardly consistent with the specific provisions for religious teaching in the Act, especially as Trickett went on to defend his department's administration of the Act, including the teaching of the *Scripture Lessons*, which he said were given daily. But he could not allow teachers to comment on the lessons, and so introduce sectarian interpretations. Nor could he see how teachers could be tested for their fitness to give the lessons since the department was forbidden to enquire into teachers' religious beliefs, to which Jefferis and Mullens replied that they only wanted teachers tested on the actual books in use. Nevertheless, Trickett conceded a point to the churchmen by increasing the marks allocated for Scripture from forty to sixty; he could go no higher, he explained, since children received much of their religious knowledge at home and at church as well as school, a point which had been made in the press by the chief inspector of schools earlier that month.[51]

As to the reading books, Trickett replied that the Collins series were supplementary to the Irish books, but he added that the department could not be bound to use only books with religious and moral content. Some of the deputation murmured their assent to this reasonable stand, but they were less pleased with Trickett's response to the proposal for opening prayers in the schools. That, he said, would be "an absolute religious ceremony" which some would find very objectionable. Less convincing was his opinion that religious instruction could not be given in the high schools. The government took the same stand in 1891 when Dean Marriott, of the diocese of Bathurst, raised the question again: he asked indignantly if the public school system was "to be [part] religious and part irreligious".[52]

So the deputation took leave of Trickett somewhat disappointed. Being a member of a government which included several Catholics, Trickett was no doubt aware of the Catholic reaction to the movement Bishop Barry had initiated. A month earlier Sir Patrick Jennings, a member of the Cabinet, had condemned what he considered an attempt to turn the public schools into Protestant schools, and thus increase the injustice to Catholics. So the safest course for Trickett was to stay strictly within the law, and to softpedal, although not to disavow, the religious aspects of the education system. Yet he was prepared to interpret the law liberally at one point, the question of combined teaching under clause seventeen; he assured Jefferis there was no legal hindrance to such a programme.

In this respect the *Sydney Morning Herald* took a similar line. It thought that the churchmen should have set their own house in order before going to the minister to complain about the way teachers carried out the general religious teaching under the seventh clause. There was no sense in trying to make the clause more Protestant. Religion should be taught by religious men; and to that extent it agreed with the deputationists. But it drew a different conclusion. The churchmen should forget the seventh clause and throw all their zeal into animating the seventeenth clause. Previously the *Herald* had supported the view that this clause allowed only denominational religious teaching; now it supported the principle of combined Protestant teaching in the schools, pointing out to Bishop Barry that if the Protestant churches could not work together in the schools it would not be because of any law restraining them.[53]

Much as the Protestants might differ with one another, they could not accept these views. They interpreted the Act in the light of what they believed were the legislators' intentions; Parkes, after all, had stated expressly that New South Wales intended religion and education to go hand in hand. In a letter a few days after the deputation Barry recalled his conversation with Parkes in England, through which he had gained the impression that the seventh clause was a recognition of a national faith, quoting also Parkes's speech in Parliament about the need for "a profound faith". This faith, Barry maintained, was the belief all Christians held in common — a faith based upon the Apostles' Creed, the Lord's Prayer, the Ten Commandments and the like. The *Scripture Lessons* used to impart that faith, he could not resist saying, had been accepted by Catholics "of less Ultramontane age". A few days later Jefferis also asserted from his pulpit that the State had to deal with the people as a Christian nation, yet recognize the diversity of Christian thought. It was the principle of the Act, he thought, to exclude sectarian dogmas and include the doctrines characteristic of Christianity.[54] He was not on safe ground in attempting to exclude denominational teaching, but he spoke of unsectarian religious instruction more confidently than before, now that Trickett had removed doubt as to its legality and the *Herald* had supported the principle.

The Catholic Reaction

Barry's movement inevitably opened up Catholic wounds inflicted by the Public Instruction Act. Barry had, of course, cherished hopes of Catholic cooperation, and some Catholics understood him to share their views on the need for religion in schools. But they did not understand that Barry regarded the provisions of the Act of 1880, with some gingering up, as the best means to hand of meeting that need. It amazed Catholics to see Barry accept "the Dissenters" as allies, men who "but a few years ago combined to blot Christianity out of the schools, and to place Secularism in its stead". Barry would have found the Catholics more faithful allies had he decided to work for the overturn of the Act of 1880 and the restoration of state aid to denominational schools, chided "Presbuteros", a columnist in the *Freeman's Journal.*[55]

Not only did Catholics misunderstand Barry, but they misrepresented the character of the Act of 1880 and the attitude of other Protestants towards it. The publication of Jefferis's sermons in May caused the *Freeman's Journal* to marvel at the "religious recantation" of this champion opponent of religious instruction in public schools. His sermons, it thought, by implying that there was some deficiency of religious instruction in the public schools, confirmed all Vaughan had said of those schools in 1879. Now, it argued, the colony was entering the second stage of the education controversy, the move to turn the state schools into Protestant schools. The supporters of the Public Schools League, it proclaimed, were not sincere when they advocated "secular" education, but it claimed that that was as much as public opinion would stand at the time. At last their true Protestant intentions were revealed, the journal gloated.[56] Thus there was no hope of Catholic cooperation in strengthening the religious provisions in public schools.

Catholics, however, knew well enough what the religious provisions of the Act were and the opportunities open to them under it. As the Protestant campaign got under way the *Freeman's Journal* asserted that the seventh clause was meant to be meaningless, and in July "Presbyteros" prophesied that the religious clauses which, like Vaughan, he thought had been retained for appearance sake, would remain only until the clergy took them seriously; then they would surely be repealed, leaving state education quite secular. This, in fact, was just what the Catholic Church wanted. Officially, it regarded the religious provisions with disdain; archdiocesan authorities advised Barry in June that they were not prepared to take any steps on behalf of the large number of Catholic children attending public schools.[57] To the Protestant contention that Catholics of a less ultramontane age had consented to the religious basis of the state schools, Catholics replied with the charge that Dr Whately, "the great liberal archbishop", had himself described the *Scripture Lessons* he compiled as "the great instrument of conversion".

Whately's words were recorded by his "Boswell", Nassau William Senior, and published by his daughter. Catholics took this as proof positive that the Protestant archbishop, while professing to be work-ing for the best interests of Catholics in Ireland had, in fact, been carrying out a proselytizing tactic. But Whately's statement was uttered impulsively on hearing of the Catholic charge that some conversions to Protestantism had been won by bribing poor Catho-lics with food and blankets. Afterwards, he attributed the success of the Protestant missionaries to their having learned Gaelic. Here was no proof of the sinister intent of the *Scripture Lessons*, but the words were reported and handed down uncritically from one generation of Catholics to another.[58]

Nevertheless, there were some Catholics who disagreed with the Church's line on the education question. In 1884 the *Church of Eng-land Record*, admittedly not the most reliable witness in this case, rumoured that "enlightened Catholics" were advocating that Catho-lic children should attend public schools, and that some priests were prepared to give religious instruction in them. As it was, 17 per cent (22,606) of the children in state schools in 1884 were Catholic.[59] The denunciation from the pulpit of "bad Catholics" who sent their children to those schools suggests that some decided against the teaching of the Church; not surprisingly, either, if they happened to contrast the facts about the public schools with what their preachers said of them. Of course some Catholic children had no practical alternative but to attend a state school. Was it right that they should be deprived of all religious instruction in day school? Were not "some fragments" of Christian teaching better than "absolute secularism", as Bishop Lanigan conceded in an unguarded moment? This line of thought prompted an anonymous correspon-dent in the *Freeman's Journal* to say that it was difficult to see how "a little religious teaching" in public schools could increase the Catholic grievance, upon which the editor commented that they objected to paying for Protestant education.[60]

It was not only the general religious teaching that Catholics regarded as Protestant, but also the teaching of English and Austra-lian history in schools. The curriculum covered the controversial areas of the English Reformation as well as other areas involving Protestant-Catholic conflict and England's relations with Ireland. Although teaching was to be non-sectarian, there was the tendency to present "the facts" of history from the Protestant Whig bias. Not surprisingly then, Catholics objected to history in public schools.[61] Religion and history both should be taught from books and by teachers approved by the Catholic Church, and only in Church-run schools. Otherwise neither of these "sectarian" subjects should be taught at all. Thoroughly secular education in mixed religion schools was "safer" than something like the Irish National System, Father Collingridge explained to those "enlightened Catholics" and puzzled Protestants alike who failed to understand the official Catholic position.[62] Thus, while Catholics warned of the dangers to society from godless education, Protestants, who generally agreed with that sentiment, could not count on Catholic cooperation in seeking to ensure that public education in New South Wales did not become just that. Motivated largely by fears of proselytism, Catholic authorities insisted on the one hand that public schools should be absolutely secular, and on the other that they should be denounced as godless.

So it was that in welcoming the new Archbishop of Sydney, Dr P.F. Moran, in September 1884, Dr Sheridan, the administrator of the archdiocese, could misinform him that, "here, as elsewhere, the great struggle of the day is against infidelity and secularism in education." The education question featured prominently in the archbishop's early addresses. He denied that the State should be schoolmaster; whenever it undertook to educate children it began "a crusade against all religion". But the State should distribute its funds to all who taught the arts and sciences irrespective of whether or not they taught religion. This attitude displayed the same indifference to the problem of providing schools in remote places which the denominationalists had always shown. Catholics looked to Anglicans as potential allies in their campaign to restore state aid to denominational schools, but prospects for such a combination were remote in 1884. Most Anglicans had accepted the "secular" settlement and were determined to make the best use of its religious provisions. Moran chided Bishop Barry for abandoning his principles as a denominationalist to become the champion of state education. When Barry arrived in the colony, Moran romanced, the bishop found the state system "a sort of godless monster that was spitting fire at every religion"; but he had discovered that by feeding and fostering it he might turn it "into a very pious Protestant". Catholics would not be fickle enough to abandon their principles for some compromise under the State. Barry granted them the rights of a minority — justice was that right. Catholics would wait until justice prevailed in "payment by results".[63]

Thus the new prelate confirmed the Catholic policy to shun the public schools and the Catholic children in them. He also supported the Irish-Catholic suspicion that Protestants used public schools for proselytism. This charge brought a letter from Trickett asking the archbishop to provide particular instances, to which Moran lamely replied that he was not speaking of New South Wales, but from past experience. The *Sydney Morning Herald*, ever ready to defend the education settlement, also took exception to Moran's statements. There was nothing in the public schools to which Catholics could object, it maintained, reminding the archbishop of the large number of Catholic children attending them. The Catholic clergy, it observed, preferred to leave them "without any religious instruction whatever" rather than teach them in a public school. That might be "a consistent course", it conceded, but it failed to see that it was "remarkably Christian". It found Bishop Barry's policy "far worthier of [the] Christian teacher" that he was.[64]

The Secularists' Protest

Throughout the debate the *Sydney Morning Herald* defended the comprehensive — and the Christian — character of the state school system. It made the latter point most clearly in reaction to the secularists' attempt to get into the wrangle. They might have been expected to press for the repeal of the religious clauses of the Education Act, but, surprisingly, the Australian Secular Association sent a deputation to Trickett a few days after Barry's party to seek permission to teach their secularist views under the seventeenth clause. They probably did not expect their request to be granted, but it was a way of protesting against the religious provisions in the Act. They claimed that if others were allowed to teach their dogmas in the schools secularists should be allowed to give their teaching, presumably to those of their own profession. Uncertain of how to treat this novel request, Trickett expressed a doubt that the secularists were a religious body and asked them to submit their views to him in writing. The *Herald* thought Trickett could have answered them straight off, for, as far as it was concerned, the meaning of the Act was plain enough: its formulas recognized implicitly that Christianity was the religion of "ninety-nine hundredths" of the population and no exceptions were made for the minority of secularists any more than for Mohammedans. The newspaper was adamant that it was for Christianity, and Christianity only that the Act made its religious provisions.[65] This emphatic stand must have pleased Protestant churchmen.

It was "morals without theology" that the secularists claimed they wished to teach in schools. Reluctant to answer them in the uncompromising terms that the *Herald* had used, Trickett pointed out that, even if such instruction were permissible within the provisions for religious instruction, he could see no need for such teaching since the teachers were already instructed to impart "the principles of morality, truth, justice and patriotism". The *Herald* approved of Trickett's stand, affirming that the seventeenth clause presupposed religious teaching in which there was some "recognition of the supernatural". In New South Wales this meant Christianity. Indeed, it asserted that the doctrine which underlay much of colonial legislation, including the Education Act, was that "Christianity ... supplies an element which the law of the land ought not to be without." The secularists could try, if they would, to change the law which recognized the religion of the great majority.[66]

Only the *Bulletin* defended the secularists as the genuine dissenters in the community, willingly counting them among "other religious bodies". But not all secularists wished to be regarded as religious. At a rowdy meeting later in July, some objected to a resolution supported by some of the leading freethinkers, that the State was not competent to say what was and was not a religion, and thus to exclude some from the schools. Nevertheless, the motion was carried as was another one in which the secularists, acting more consistently, pledged themselves to fight for the removal of the religious clauses from the Education Act "to make it entirely secular".[67] But they had even less hope than the Catholics of upsetting the education settlement.

The Results of the Religious Instruction Movement

Many of the immediate objectives of Bishop Barry's movement did not get far with the government in 1884. It remains to be seen how much success it had with the churches on whose cooperation Barry's scheme depended. The Anglican synod of Sydney considered the plan in July 1884 where it was opposed by a minority of High Churchmen. These opponents maintained that it was the Church of England's business to teach Anglican children in Anglican schools, and so they renewed the call for state aid. It was not a realistic stand, marked as it was by strong antagonism to the public schools where for long most Anglican school-children were to be found. Like the Catholics, Shepherd Smith condemned the bishop's scheme as a "Protestantising, proselytising proposal". Barry reminded him sharply that it was Catholics, not Protestants, who refused to cooperate in religious instruction in schools. The overwhelming majority in the synod supported Barry's idea of establishing a joint board to regulate the churches' activity in the schools. In October the bishops of New South Wales issued a joint declaration on religious teaching in public schools indicating their general support of Barry's policy to make the best use of the Public Instruction Act. The bishops exhorted their clergy to avail themselves of the opportunity given them "at a very critical time", but did not mention cooperation with other denominations.[68] Not every bishop was as ready as Barry to work with other Protestants.

Prospects for cooperation within the area of Barry's diocese looked fairly hopeful. Presbyterians, Wesleyans and Primitive Methodists each appointed two representatives to the board. But the Congregationalists declined to join a board which would "strengthen and regulate the separate denominational agencies". This was something of a blow, although not unexpected. Jefferis, who had done much to promote the movement in its early stages, and his fellow Congregationalists now seemed to be sabotaging Barry's scheme. Many were loath to disagree with the bishop they respected, especially when they were being treated generously in the matter of representation. Most, however, thought they had to stand alone for "the perfect liberty of unsectarian Christianity". Some also feared that the separation of children into denominations would provoke ridicule from the critics of Christianity and religious jealousy and bitterness among the children, or that in a segregated system the children of minorities might end up with the larger denominational groups. By declining to join the board, the union assembly confirmed Jefferis's stand that "a system of combined, voluntary and unsectarian religious instruction" was desirable for all public schools in the colony. The Baptists, who had shown practically no interest at all in the facilities for religious instruction in schools, also declined to join the board.[69]

The *Presbyterian*, which had advocated a scheme similar to the Congregationalists' in 1880, now condemned the union for keeping the denominational barriers at full height. The *Sydney Morning Herald* also took issue with Jefferis, reversing the stand it had taken in July in favour of combined instruction. It accused the Congregational Union of cutting itself off from "that united Christianity which it so highly esteems". Congregationalists, it argued, were asking too much in expecting the denominations to sink their differences far enough to mount a scheme of unsectarian special religious instruction. Furthermore, it now questioned Trickett's interpretation of the law as allowing combined teaching. Trickett's opinion was not the law, it pointed out — the next incumbent might well interpret it differently.[70]

For all this, there was an underlying consistency in the *Herald's* position. It opposed any change to the education settlement in the provision it made for religious instruction. Because it regarded religion as essential to morality and social stability, it was keen to see

the provision for special religious instruction in schools imple-
mented systematically, regardless of how this might best be done; it
now gave its full backing to Barry's plan, apparently persuaded that it
would work. Its rival, the *Daily Telegraph*, although more sympathetic with Jefferis's position, thought it impractical at the time,
and argued that Barry's plan for systematic denominational instruction had to be supported as the next best choice.[71] It hardly seemed
wise to support an alternative when the Presbyterians and the
Wesleyans had thrown in their lot with the Bishop.

But the support of these two denominations for Barry's scheme
was not unqualified. In May 1884, just as Barry's movement was
getting under way, the *Presbyterian* had argued for religious instruction to be given by the teacher and not a visiting clergyman. This
presumably meant general teaching only rather than denominational
teaching. In March 1885 the incoming Moderator, Roger McKin-
non, told the General Assembly that he had little sympathy with
denominational instruction. He advocated that the common principles of the faith be taught to combined classes, and that the rest be
left to parents and Sunday school teachers. This was essentially what
the *Presbyterian* had recommended in 1880, and such a scheme
came into operation in Newcastle in 1884 without the Anglicans,
whom the *Presbyterian* rebuked for aloofness (in the same issue that
condemned the Congregationalists for insisting on combination). In
Newcastle the Protestant ministers were giving instruction to large
classes in ten schools, one of the participants reported enthusiastically to the Wesleyan Conference in February 1885.[72]

In Sydney some Wesleyans were not convinced of the necessity of
special religious instruction at all. Although J.H. Fletcher had
supported Barry rather than Jefferis in 1884, he was facscinated by
the *Scripture Lessons*, which apparently he had not read before the
controversy arose. In his retiring address as President of the
Wesleyan Conference in January 1885 Fletcher acknowledged that
the law provided "a rich and varied feast" under what it called non-
dogmatic and non-polemical religious teaching, with lessons ranging
from the Creation to Final Judgment. If such topics were "non-dog-
matical and non-sectarian", he concluded, so long as children were
taught them, "we do not care much if they never hear anything all
their lives about what is dogmatical and sectarian." This
"exposure", as one newspaper columnist saw it, of the amount of
religion being taught in "secular" education goes a long way to explain the lack of enthusiasm for special religious instruction among
Methodists. But the fear of proselytism also lingered on. In September 1885 the *Weekly Advocate* was disturbed that some Methodist
children were still receiving instruction from Anglican clergymen

and suggested that "the true policy of the minor Churches" might be to seek the repeal of the seventeenth clause, but to support the retention of the *Scripture Lessons*. At the same time it thought that they should strengthen the work of their Sunday schools.[73] There was no serious move to have the seventeenth clause repealed, but Wesleyan priorities were clear.

Thus the prospects for Bishop Barry's scheme of cooperation were not promising. The joint board was formed, but it had a short life. It met four times up to July 1885 and achieved little in that time. According to Barry the board had difficulty in obtaining accurate information on the amount of religious instruction actually being given by the Protestant denominations,[74] which is not surprising in view of the lack of enthusiasm among many churchmen. Barry spoke no more of it after July 1885, so it seems to have lapsed around this time. However Anglicans continued to promote the work in schools much as before, without reference to the other denominations.

So the cooperative scheme failed. And what difference Barry's movement made to the amount of special religious instruction actually being given in the schools by the various denominations is difficult to gauge. The government statistician, T.A. Coghlan, did not seem to think it made much difference. He wrote in 1887 that the clergy of the various denominations had taken advantage of their oportunities under the seventeenth clause "to some slight extent". This was not quite fair to the Anglicans who were making an earnest effort to reach their children in the schools, and doing it with lay support, by way of a few voluntary and some paid instructors; there were fourteen of the latter at work in schools within the Sydney doicese in 1885. Barry pleaded continually for more manpower and money, but by 1889, almost at the end of his episcopate, he could claim that Anglicans were reaching only about 75 per cent of their children in the schools. They never reached more than 80 per cent over the next twenty-odd years. Perhaps that was impressive enough in view of the number of country schools. The most regular visiting, of course, was done in the metropolitan schools and in the larger towns, and for some years small country schools received infrequent visits or none at all.[75]

Despite the misgivings some Presbyterians and Wesleyans expressed about special religious instruction, there was an improvement in the attendance of ministers of these two churches in the mid 1880s, a fact which the *Sydney Morning Herald* attributed to Bishop Barry's movement. However it was due as much, if not more, to the increased Anglican efforts before Barry's arrival in the colony. Returns for attendance at metropolitan schools in 1883 and the first half of 1884 published in the *Herald* showed Anglicans contributing about 70 per cent of all the visits compared with around 90 per cent in 1880. (The Anglican proportion would probably have been higher if country schools were included.)[76]

In February 1885 the Wesleyan Conference affirmed the "paramount importance" of religious instruction in schools and appointed a committee to organize the Wesleyan effort. But in 1887 the conference rejected a proposal to use paid agents, although voluntary helpers were acceptable; and a debate in 1889 revealed that there were ministers who were still not convinced that the work was theirs to do, or that special denominational instruction ought to be given in the schools anyway. In vain did the head of the religious instruction committee, the supernumerary Joseph Oram, hold the spectres of Hume, Paine and Voltaire before his brethren. The conference reappointed its religious instruction committee, but halfheartedly, and Oram reflected gloomily: "As the matter now stands, I suppose every man will do as he likes".[77] The next year the committee was not reappointed, and Oram's speculation became fact.

The story is rather similar for the Presbyterians. In spite of the Moderator's lack of sympathy with the cause in 1885, the General Assembly gave its Sabbath Schools Committee the responsibility for promoting religious instruction in public schools. Although the committee remained preoccupied with the Sunday school, the report for 1892 indicated that some Presbyterian ministers were attending the public schools; they made 2000 visits that year, but only to 231 schools. The convenor pleaded that there were only about 120 "settled ministers" and a few years later the Presbyterian statistician thought their effort was "considerable". But it did not match the effort of the Anglicans, and the government statistician's comment in 1905 that apart from the Church of England the churches did not take advantage of the seventeenth clause "to any great extent" was not unfair.[78]

The Anglicans, of course, had greater incentive to visit the schools, for with the largest number of adherents and many of them not in close touch with the Church, the schools presented them with a valuable pastoral opportunity. This was less so with other Protestants, whose denominations were too small in any case to maintain systematic programmes of instruction. It was in their interests to combine in the kind of programme that Jefferis and others advocated, but some wondered how necessary that was in view of the general religious teaching that was already in the curriculum. Many were content to leave the rest to home and Sunday school, or to a lesser extent to the church colleges such as Newington College, Scots College for boys, and Presbyterian Ladies' College and

Wesleyan Ladies' College. These church schools aimed to give "a high-class Christian education", but to a limited number of children.[79]

There were opportunities for the Catholic Church among its Catholic children in public schools (17 per cent of the total enrolment in 1884, 14 per cent in 1890), and Dr Sheridan, former Vicar General of the archdiocese, seemed to recognize this when he enquired in 1888 if a priest might use the hour allowed under clause seventeen to hear children's confessions in his home.[80] The reply from the department does not seem to have survived, but it was probably unfavourable. In any case the official policy of the Catholic Church was opposed to making use of the facilities in any way at all, even though a few Catholic priests did visit schools from time to time, most probably to arrange to meet Catholic children outside school hours. Not only was sending children to state schools discouraged, but Cardinal Moran threatened those Catholic parents who persisted in sending their children to them when a Catholic school was available, with exclusion from the sacraments. Catholic Sunday schools were expected to cater for those children who attended state schools when no Catholic school was at hand. This policy did not win the Catholic Church any sympathy from the Protestant community. The *Sydney Morning Herald* in 1888 bluntly accused the Roman Catholics of hypocrisy for refusing to provide religious instruction in public schools and at the same time denouncing them as godless.

> What other term can we use when we find men who in words proclaim their convicton that religious instruction is the one thing necessary to save the country from ruin, declaring by their action that if they cannot give religious instruction exactly in their own way, it may go to the winds — and the poor uninstructed children after it — for anything they care?[81]

But it was not in fact the "godlessness" of New South Wales public schools to which Catholics actually objected, but the religiousness expressed in the general religious teaching and to a lesser extent in history teaching. Cardinal Moran made this objection clear in speeches later in the decade when he asserted that the public schools taught "a special form of Protestantism". In fact he avowed that this undenominational religious teaching was "not Christian religion at all".[82] This was precisely the religious character of the public schools which Protestant churchmen and the Protestant press defended as the basis for a comprehensive school system.

Education in New South Wales, then, was not a classic example of the separation of Church and State so much as a working model of a modified relationship between the two. Despite the withdrawal of state aid to denominational schools, the Education Act preserved "friendly relations between great religious and State institutions", in the words of the *Herald*. The newspaper defended the Church of England for working with the State "as fellow-labourer". To its credit, that Church had "recognized in such a practical and efficient way the duty of looking after the religious interests of the young, instead of seeking shelter for its own remissness under a supposed dereliction of duty on the part of the State".[83]

Although the other Protestant denominations did not make the same effort to give special religious instruction, they did recognize the religious character of public schooling and it was to defend that character that they supported Barry's initiative in 1884. The "New South Wales System" became the model that churchmen, particularly Anglicans, sought to see introduced in Victoria and South Australia in the late ninteenth century. Dr Jefferis, who returned to Adelaide in 1894, commended it to South Australians as the solution to the problem of religion in education, although he wanted only the general religious teaching given by teachers. Anglicans valued more the right to enter the schools to give denominational teaching.[84]

It was the middle of this century before Victoria and South Australia overcame "the religious difficulty". Their solutions fell short of the New South Wales model, but at least they had secured Catholic cooperation.[85] Protestant churchmen and statesmen in New South Wales were confident that they had solved the problem in 1880, even though some churchmen wanted more religion in schools than the Act allowed. Parkes proudly predicted in 1889 that "our system will always rest on the cardinal principles of our common Christian religion". As far as Catholics were concerned, he might have said "our common Protestant religion", but, with that qualification, his prophecy held good for nearly eighty years. In 1964, when the Renshaw Labor government attempted to broaden "general religious teaching" to include all the great religious and ethical systems of the world, thus depriving Christianity of its unique place in the syllabus, Protestant churchmen once more rallied round the Anglican primate, Archbishop Gough. Their loud protests forced a compromise through which Christianity and the Bible, though no longer exclusively taught, retained a special place in state education.[86] Thus in this area Church and State remained tenuously tied for a little longer.

9

Public Recognition for God

The tenuous ties that bound Church and State in the 1880s were not reassuring enough for Australian churchmen. The attack on Christian institutions and on Christianity itself nurtured their fear that secularism would subvert the Christian character of the country. So they looked for ways of reinforcing religion in society and restoring what some of them thought they had lost in the battles against state aid to religion and church schools since the 1860s. The distinguished British Nonconformist divine, Dr R.W. Dale, during his visit to Australia in 1887, noted that many he met were "uneasy on account of what they describe as the secular character of the Australian State". While they would "strongly resist any attempt to establish or endow a Church", he observed, "they have a vague craving for what they describe as a formal and public recognition by the State of the authority of God."[1] At the Intercolonial Congregational Conference, held in Adelaide to celebrate the golden jubilee of Congregationalism in South Australia, Dale heard the Victorian Congregationalist Alexander Gosman tell the assembly that the time had come for Congregationalists to rethink their attitude "with regard to the relation of the State to religion and to the Churches". He argued that although the State had "disestablished that portion of the Church formerly endowed and exclusively recognized by it" there was no need for it to cease being religious. Were they as churches, he asked, to withdraw from all political affairs, and let secularism "come in upon us like a flood, and sap the foundations of a civilization that has taken centuries to build up"? It would be "perilous to claim that "the State has nothing to do with religion", for if the State ceased to be religious, it became "not *non*-religious" but "*ir*-religious".[2] If the champions of voluntaryism could speak like this, how much more must Anglicans and Presbyterians, and even Catholics, have craved for the public recognition of religion.

The Churches and the Sudan Contingent, 1885

This desire of the churches to be recognized by the State was made very obvious in February 1885 when the New South Wales government decided to send a contingent of soldiers to assist Britain in the Sudan, after the murder of General Charles Gordon in Khartoum. The government's action was unconstitutional and the worth of the cause debatable, but this gesture made by the acting-premier, W.B. Dalley, an imperial federationist, fired the imagination and patriotism of most Australians; and the other colonies envied Dalley his coup. Among the few public opponents of the government's action were Sir Henry Parkes, out of Parliament at the time, and Dr Jefferis, but he waited until the soldiers were on the high seas before voicing his dissent. These two did not find themselves in congenial company, for the secularists were among the most outspoken critics of the expedition.[3]

The churches were swept along in the swelling tide of patriotism that engulfed the country. Even those churchmen who could not suppress their doubts found reasons for supporting the expedition. The *Protestant Standard* could not defend Dalley, but it dissociated itself from his secularist critics by indicating its confidence that the colony would profit from the experience. Similarly, the *Presbyterian* was "not fully convinced of the propriety of the step"; but it pointed out that there could be no going back once the offer was made for the honour of the colony was at stake. In any case, it considered, "the moral effect" on Britain and the other colonies of the New South Wales contingent would be "the chief asset in the undertaking".[4]

The great concern of the churches was that the religious needs of the soldiers should be recognized. The various denominations supplied their men with prayer books or hymnals and other religious literature and the local auxiliary of the British and Foreign Bible Society provided the contingent with copies of the New Testament. But they wanted to do more than this. Several colonial clergymen offered to go with the contingent as chaplains, but the government, perhaps afraid of sectarian squabbles, decided to entrust the care of its troops to British army chaplains. The government also turned down the offer of the Catholic Sisters of Charity to accompany the contingent as nurses. The contingent, the *Presbyterian* lamented, would "go forth panoplied with every requisite save that which has to do very specially with the spiritual life".[5]

But Bishop Barry was not prepared to see the matter rest there. More than the spiritual welfare of the men, the status of the churches in colonial society was also at stake. So Barry decided to enlist Archbishop Moran's aid to press the government on the matter. In a rare cooperative bid, the two prelates persuaded the government to change its mind, and the day before the farewell church parades they received the gratifying news that the Reverend H.J.

Rose, Anglican, and Father C.P.F. Collingridge would go as chaplains to the contingent. The *Presbyterian* gloated that the appointment of chaplains with government salaries must have been particularly galling to the secularists, and no doubt it was.[6]

So there was nothing to mar the joy of the churchmen on Sunday 1 March 1885 when they preached to the departing troops, apart from rowdy and irreverent behaviour. Yet Bishop Barry betrayed some uneasiness of conscience over the expedition itself. He prefaced his sermon with the explanation that it was not the preacher's office to discuss the policy or justice of the Egyptian war, or the way and spirit in which the colony had offered its contingent. Although as a citizen he had a right to an opinion, and even the duty of expressing it, it had no place in a service offering prayers of intercession for the men going forth "to embody . . . the spirit of loyalty in this colony to the old mother country". With some reflections on just and unjust wars and a denunciation of "military spirit", he felt his congregation to draw its own conclusions, and went on to unfold the "meanings" behind the event — the expression of loyalty to the mother country and above all "the glory of voluntary devotion and self sacrifice" for one's own country.[7]

There was nothing of this uneasy compromise with popular patriotism in the Catholic archbishop's sermon to the Catholic troops. Apparently pleased by his co-religionists's coup in offering the contingent, Moran told his congregation that war was within the providence of God, who was the Lord of the Battles as well as the God of Peace. But the archbishop did not share Dalley's imperial sentiments; he said nothing about Britain and the empire, but focused instead on the meaning of the event for Australia. The "blue flag . . . gemmed with the Southern Cross" was taking its place on the battle fields of the world for the first time; and it was being unfurled in "the best interests of civilisation and peace", for the cause could bring no "blush of shame to those who love justice, religion and the fatherland".[8] Most Protestant preachers gave the expedition the same unqualified support, and cheerfully sent the Christian soldiers off to war.

The Queen's Jubilee, 1887

Queen Victoria's golden jubilee in June 1887 afforded another occasion to celebrate the inseparability of piety and patriotism. The governor, Lord Carrington, called for services of thanksgiving in the churches of the colony for the mercies vouchsafed to the Queen during her long reign. Too much should not be made of his formal recognition of religion, but churchmen greeted his request enthusiastically. Their patriotic utterances and extravagant eulogies were only to be expected. Recent events, however, gave more of a cutting edge to what they had to say about the place of religion in political and social life. The riots in the Town Hall, led by republicans and secularists, had shocked many people, and Parkes's closure of theatres against opponents of the monarchy and Christianity emphasized the bond between religion and the State. The "Mount Rennie Outrage" of 1886, a pack rape case, had also shocked colonial society.[9] Some began to wonder it this was the fruit of growing secularism.

Preachers could be relied on to draw the moral. Canon Kemmis, preaching at the jubilee service in St Andrew's Cathedral, condemned the insignificant and contemptible minority whose motto was "Republicanism and Mount Rennie". Piety and patriotism, he affirmed, could never be separated without evil results, as the excesses of the French Revolution showed. Similarly, at St. Thomas's Anglican Church, North Sydney, the Reverend G. North Ash asserted that disloyalty to law and order was the inevitable outcome of the atheism and infidelity that had been making such strides in Australia, as elsewhere. Atheism was a disintegrating principle, George Martin, a Wesleyan preacher, declared at a united Protestant jubilee service at Petersham. Religion and politics were more closely interwoven than many recognized "for it was the religious sentiment which existed among the English people that had made constitutional Government so splendidly possible among them". The fiery Particular Baptist preacher, Pastor David Allen, delivered an outright attack on "the lawless mobs of seditious persons" who stifled free speech in the Town Hall and had "blasphemed God and our Queen in our theatres and parks for years". Bible and throne, he asserted, were indivisibly linked; no one could rebel against one without rebelling against the other.[10]

Cardinal Moran* made a more restrained plea for loyalty to constituted authority at the jubilee church parade for Catholic troops, in St Mary's Cathedral. There was, he explained, no conflict between loyalty to God and loyalty to the throne. Not only did the Bible teach this, but the very nature of civil society required that "laws of order, authority and obedience" be upheld. Without them, "the human family would lapse into barbarism and savagery". So he charged the soldiers before him to be assert their loyalty, to make their "very lives a bulwark, a rampart around the throne".[11] Thus churchmen used the jubilee celebrations to assert that religion promoted social

*He became a cardinal late in 1885.

and political stability. If they harped on it, it was because they feared that men in the political world might forget it, if they had not already done so.

The Centenary Celebrations, 1888

This concern about the status of religion in colonial society was most conspicuous in the preparations for the celebration of the centenary of New South Wales. Dr. Jefferis made the issue the cornerstone of his proposals for a religious celebration in a paper he read to the Congregational Union in October 1886. In it he developed the idea he had asserted in his sermons on religious education two years earlier, that voluntaryism did not necessarily imply secularism. While "the union between one Church and the State" had been broken in Australia, "the true God-made union between Church and State has not been severed, and never must be." Australia was still a Christian nation, he affirmed, and it would be disgraceful if there were no "national acknowledgement of divine help" on the occasion of the colony's centenary. He proposed a united service of thanksgiving, led by Bishop Barry, which would demonstrate the fundamental unity of the churches; this, he suggested, might be a lesson "to our legislators, who are apt to think that Parliament is the only power in the State".[12]

Jefferis took up the same theme the next year in his address as Chairman of the Congregational Union in which he asserted that "the Church" ought to be "in closest union with the State, not as a State institution ... but as a spiritual power, impelling, directing, purifying", and so countering the tendency to secularize political life. The great voluntaryist himself had become one of the most eloquent champions of the religious State, after having advocated from the same chair in 1878 "the complete secularization of Australain politics".[13]

For all that Jefferis complained about the "legislators", the proposal for a religious celebration of the centenary seems to have come from Sir Henry Parkes in the first place. He included it among his suggestions for the centenary celebrations in a letter to the premier, Sir Patrick Jennings, in August 1886. Parkes thought that "a united Service of Thanksgiving and Prayer for Australia" would add to "the moral grandeur of the events". Jennings included "special and appropriate services" by the religious denominations in his proposals for the celebration of the centenary made to Parliament later the same month.[14]

The *Australian Christian World* then took the matter up circularizing representative Protestant ministers to gauge what support there might be for a united service which would proclaim to all that "the Christianity of Australia has largely made it what it is today". Responses were on the whole encouraging, although the high church Bishop of Grafton and Armidale, Dr Turner, was opposed to any religious celebration of the occasion, presumably because of the compromise of church principles he would have to make with both schismatics and the apostate State. But this extreme view was not shared by many. Bishop Barry and the Sydney Ministers' Union welcomed the proposals and in November 1887 Barry called a conference to consider how best to add religious character to the celebrations. Representatives of the six Protestant denominations at the conference agreed to a programme much along the lines Jefferis had suggested, including both local services of thanksgiving on a nominated day and a united service in the Exhibition Building in January 1888. It was expected that churches in suburban and country districts would do likewise. The celebrations would conclude with a Sunday school demonstration in February.[15]

Meanwhile, the Catholic Church was also making its own plans for the religious celebration of the centenary, determined, as the *Freeman's Journal* expressed it, that the recently elected Parkes government should not have everything its own way in the celebrations. It seems that Catholics were not invited to cooperate in united celebrations, perhaps because so many similar approaches in the past had been refused. But the *Freeman's Journal* claimed that Cardinal Moran had planned a programme to interest not only Catholics, but the whole colony and Australia at large. There would be a Provincial Synod with all the Australian hierarchy present; they would organize a start to the completion of the chancel of St Mary's Cathedral as a centenary memorial, lay various foundations stones, bless extensions and open new Catholic institutions. At special services they would commemorate the founding and growth of Roman Catholicism in the southern hemisphere.[16] Thus Moran proposed a mammoth demonstration of the might of the Catholic Church that would upstage the united Protestant celebrations.

The religious celebration of the centenary began with separate services in the churches on Sunday 22 January before the official celebrations had begun. Bishop Barry found this significant in that it implied Christianity was relevant to the whole system of social and political life; with that sentiment, he believed, "substantially all agreed". And Dr Jefferis told his congregation that it would have been "a burning shame and an evil omen" if the second century had begun in the same way as their fathers began the first. Unlike their "American brothers" whose "history began with thanksgiving and prayer upon that Plymouth Rock", Australians had "to remember and mourn" that their own history began with "no becoming act of religion, but with a military parade and honours to the earthly sovereign". The second century was making a better start, for this time the Christian people as one recognized their "dependence upon God", and commended themselves "and the generations yet unborn to his favour and help".

Other preachers also dwelt on the place of religion in national life, and, as well, most sermons conveyed a sense of divine providence and destiny. Bishop Barry contrasted the prosperous colony and its stately cathedrals and churches with the rude beginnings of religious life in Australia, and in St. Stephen's Presbyterian Church Dr Steel contemplated how Providence had in due course overruled the view of Australia as a dumping ground for criminal exiles, and turned it into a land of promise and plenty. But he did not take too harsh a view of the convicts, many of whom, particularly political transportees, were "a blessing to the colony by their intelligence, integrity, and even piety". Protestant preachers claimed a share in the mission of the British peoples. Australia was "a young growing scion of the old English tree", said Barry, and Steel claimed that the Australian colonists had made "a new Britannia in another world", complete with all its virtues. [17]

This theme was most elaborately developed by Dr Jefferis in his sermon on "Australia's Mission and Opportunity". Australia's mission, he declared, being largely that of the Anglo-Saxon race, was not to found great empires by conquest or to enrich the world with knowledge and philosophy: it was the less ambitious, but not the less commendable mission "to understand and explain and employ the great forces of the universe for the comfort and benefit of humanity". This justified the expansion of British people into the unexplored and underdeveloped parts of the world. They took with them all the noble hallmarks of democracy and proved "in a thousand settlements, that equality, justice, and unfettered freedom are the divine appointment for human life". Above all, it was a Protestant mission, for the British shared with Lutheran Germany the task of restoring "the direct contact of humanity with God". Australia's unique vocation was to carry Britain's mission forward to conclusions that Britain could not reach, hindered as she was in some points by "traditionalism and feudalism". It was for Australia to show that she could solve the problems of poverty and social injustice and degradation, and to use her wealth and resources responsibly. Although Jefferis attested the superiority of the Anglo-Saxons he did not envisage a "white" Australia. Despite the anti-Chinese sentiment of the day, he looked forward to "the construc-

tion of a great Commonwealth . . . a mingling of the best charac-
teristics of Asiatic and European [races], with our own civilisation
supreme: a commonwealth welded together in the strength of an
empire which realises the Divine ideal of justice and freedom".[18]

Similar sentiments were expressed at the United National
Thanksgiving held in the Exhibition Building the following Sunday
afternoon; about eight thousand people filled the building and
"several thousands" formed an overflow congregation outside,
where a group of ministers addressed them from an open air platform. Governor Carrington attended, with Lord and Lady Carnar-
von representing the imperial government, and the governors of
Victoria, Tasmania, New Zealand, and the ex-governor of Fiji in the
vice-regal party. The service was also a church parade for the colony's permanent and voluntary defence forces. Some seven
hundred troops marched behind their bands to the Exhibition Building, a contingent of Catholic soldiers breaking off at St. Mary's
Cathedral. The remainder filled the gallery with a splash of scarlet
and blue. A massed choir of 300 voices, conducted by P.D. McCor-
mick, composer of "Advance, Australia Fair", occupied a terraced
stand behind the party of officiating ministers. Only half the
congregation in the building could hear what was said, but they
could all sing and the combined sound of choir and congregation
singing the "Old Hundredth" and the national anthem carried far
and loud to those in the park outside.

Nothing like it had been seen or heard before in the colony.
United services were held annually by Orangemen to celebrate the
Twelfth of July, the anniversary of the Battle of the Boyne, but they
were unofficial and not nearly so well attended; bishops and other
church leaders did not participate in them. This was one of the first
official united services; others were held in suburbs and in some
larger country towns such as Bathurst, and also in Newcastle, but
there the Anglicans did not unite with others. Some Anglicans
denounced bishops and clergy who cooperated in united services as
schismatics themselves. The *Church of England Guardian*
emphatically rejected this narrow attitude, while with less charity,
Zachary Barry's *Protestant Standard* gloated over the implicit rebuke
to high church Anglicans in the primate's participation in the United
National Thanksgiving in Sydney. Caught up in the euphoria of the
occasion, Bishop Barry told the vast congregation that "the frost-
work of division" was "quelled as by a glorious flame" on such
great national occasions. The event also impressed others, and the
Sydney Morning Herald sanguinely observed that there was nothing
now to keep the churches apart save the "memory of old traditions
and differences of opinion as to doctrine and polity".[19] But the

United National Thanksgiving did demonstrate that the Protestant denominations were as one in their perceptions of the character of their society and of the relation of religion to it.

This "free outburst of prayer and thanksgiving", Bishop Barry claimed, grew out of the deep and instinctive desire of people to offer themselves and their country to God in a common gesture during the celebration. He thought that, like the depths of the ocean, the belief that the life of the nation was inspired and guided by God remained undisturbed by the surface turbulence of their age. Dr Steel reviewed once more the ways of Providence in Australia's history and thought it significant that the rise of modern missions was coeval with the founding of the colony; Sydney had become the depot for mission ships serving "already 300 isles of the Pacific owning Christ". Dr Kelynack, the Wesleyan representative, also claimed that God had chosen the Anglo-Saxons to settle Australia and among their greatest achievements there was the system of state education. But it was not enough to remove "the curse of ignorance"; religion was needed to enlighten conscience and purify social life. To secure the great future of the land Christianity had to become "the royal force to which all other forces must bow."

Likewise Dr Jefferis acknowledged the potential of the nation, but he also told the congregation that serious social problems had to be solved, above all "how to create wealth without creating poverty". If Australian democracy could not solve this problem and contemporary trends continued, he predicted a class war within 100 years. He also mourned the jealousy and rivalry that existed between the various colonies, warning of the need for an early federation before they drifted further apart. But he did not look to democracy and federation alone to fulfil Australia's destiny. His solution was the same as Kelynack's: in the end "everything depended on Christianity".[20]

This great Protestant service ended with the "Hallelujah Chorus" and the hymn "God Bless Our Native Land". But the grandeur of the Catholic celebrations overshadowed it, as the *Freeman's Journal* readily boasted.[21] It was an impressive company of prelates and priests from the Church in Australia which processed into St Mary's Cathedral, gorgeously decorated with flowers and crimson and yellow drapes, for the opening of the Provincial Synod on Sunday 22 January. A choir of 100 voices with professional soloists and orchestral accompaniment performed a new Mass for the occasion. The preacher was Archbishop Carr of Melbourne and his theme the progress of the Catholic Church in Australia. The temporal blessings and material progress of Australia he would leave to other speakers and more appropriate occasions. He declared that their imposing

William Kelynack, silver-tongued orator of Methodism and President of Newington College (1890-91). (From *The Illustrated History of Methodism* by J. Colwell [Sydney: William Brooks and Co., 1904]. Photo courtesy of La Trobe University Library, Melbourne.)

ceremony was itself a tribute to the Church's "steady and stately" progress in the colony "within the narrow span of 100 years".[22]

The next Sunday, when Protestants were proclaiming the civilizing mission of the Anglo-Saxon race, Cardinal Moran exulted in the religious mission of the Irish Celts. He did speak of the wealth and resources of Australia and the hardy intelligent races who developed it, in whom he discerned "the fair features of a great nation". But the blessings of Christian civilization had been brought to Australia by the sons of St Patrick. The Irish had renewed the mission of earlier times to carry the faith to different lands, wherever the flag of British conquest had been raised. As Protestants rejoiced in their missionary expansion in the Pacific, so Moran hailed the work of Catholics in the South Seas, recognizing that it was largely the work of Catholics of nationalities other than the Irish. But without "the apostolate of the Irish race", he claimed without much exaggeration, the Catholic Church would have been "little better than an empty name throughout Australia".[23]

It was a different culture and faith he celebrated, but there were points of contact between Catholic and Protestant utterances on this occasion. Barry or Jefferis would have agreed with Moran's prayer that it might "ever be Australia's destiny to be a bulwark of true Christian civilization, a home of freedom, a centre of intellectual light and a sanctuary of piety"; and Protestants could hardly disagree with his statement that only the Christian religion, of which the Southern Cross was a symbol, could "make nations truly happy, truly great". It was not the assertion that religion was necessary to the well-being of society that separated Catholic and Protestant, but the understanding and definition of religion. Yet in each case there was the same undertone, that society in general, and statesmen in particular, should recognize that they could not do without God and his representatives.

The Centennial State Banquet, however, seemed to exhibit the tendency of statesmen to forget the lesson the churchmen would have them learn. The banquet began without anyone "saying grace", although a primate, a cardinal and other churchmen were in attendance. These little public religious acts were important to churchmen as tokens of their country's Christianity, and they all deplored the omission. But who was to say it? Cardinal Moran, in an interview, claimed the prerogative "as the first ecclesiastical dignitary of any church", but he thought it would be better for the governor to say grace on such occasions. Bishop Barry submitted that he might have some claim by weight of numbers, although not by law, but he would not press for it; he thought that the chairman should have said grace, or even that the whole assembly should have sung it, as was the custom at large banquets in England. Both prelates suggested a way around the touchy question of ecclesiastical precedency, on which Cardinal Moran was particularly sensitive. Rather than play second fiddle to Bishop Barry he had declined invitations to Government House on previous occasions, and during the centenary celebrations he sent three suffragan bishops to the unveiling of Queen Victoria's statue, instead of attending himself. Nevertheless, he attended the Centennial State Banquet, even though Barry was accorded precedence over him. But both enjoyed precedence over other church leaders, to the irritation of the non-episcopal Protestants. Nevertheless, they recognized Barry as a leader of the Christian community and Jefferis stated publicly that it was the primate's prerogative to say grace on such occasions, not only because he was head of the largest denomination, but also because his "catholicity of thought, courtesy as well as right" marked him out as "*primus inter pares*".[24]

It would have suited Protestants to have Bishop Barry officiate at the banquet but it certainly would not have suited Cardinal Moran; he would most probably have stayed away in protest had Barry been invited to say grace. So it is understandable why the organizers of the banquet preferred to leave the matter well alone, if indeed they thought of it all. The colony had long since learned to do without these religious formalities on state occasions. The difficulty of finding a form acceptable to both Protestant and Catholic had led to the exclusion of prayers from Parliament early in the colony's history, and in these matters, at least, governments wished to avoid offending any religious group — "an exaggerated fear of a so-called religious difficulty", observed Bishop Barry in reviewing the centenary celebrations at synod in April. He regretted that such religious divisions played "into the hands of godlessness", but thought that the United National Thanksgiving had demonstrated the vitality and underlying unity of the churches in a very memorable way.

The omission of grace at the banquet gave Barry occasion to lament the exclusion of prayers from Parliament and public schools. If "the great American Republic" could allow prayers in Congress he did not see why they should be excluded in Australia.[25] The general threat of secularism and attacks on the Christian institutions of Sunday and marriage invested these religious formalities with some significance for churchmen, although there had always been a minority which regretted the absence of prayers from Parliament. They had a moment of triumph in 1862 when the Legislative Assembly adopted a prayer, proposed by a Congregationalist, Thomas Holt. But after three days the decision was rescinded on the motion of the Catholic Member for Yass, Peter Faucett, who had remained outside with David Buchanan and others while the prayer was read. But most voluntaryists in that Parliament who had voted for the abolition of state aid to religion, such as John Dunmore Lang, supported prayers in Parliament. The voluntaryist principal of Camden Congregational College, the Reverend S.C. Kent, disappointed at the abandonment of this pious ceremony, asked why it seemed there could be "no public admission by our rulers of the existence and government of God", just because there was no "State

Church''. That was the opinion of most Protestants in the 1880s, in Victoria as well as in New South Wales.[26]

In Victoria the forthcoming Centennial International Exhibition, opened in August 1888, aroused in churchmen the same concern for the recognition of God: would the Exhibition open with a religious ceremony? The *Church of England Messenger* pleaded that the occasion should ''not be lowered to the level of a Secularists' Demonstration''. Dismissing the argument that denominational divisions made a common religious ceremony impossible, it declared that it was the desire of most of the denominations that ''all our national institutions and enterprises should . . . be opened in the name of God, and that his blessing should be invoked upon them''. There could be no choice between the alternatives of slighting God as a nation and offending the prejudices of a minority. The Catholic difficulty, it asserted, had caused enough trouble in the banishment of religion from the state schools; their difficulty ''must not be allowed to unchristianise the nation''.[27]

The Congregationalist, Alexander Gosman, also argued for a religious ceremony in an article in the *Victorian Independent* in May 1888. Developing the idea that the State ought to be religious, he dismissed the objection that there could be no religious ceremony because there was no state church. Congregationalists, he claimed, were ''opposed to all forms of State churchism'', but of the need for state religion they were ''firmly convinced''. ''State religion is not only desirable, but necessary'', he contended; ''it is in harmony with the word of God, the teachings of history, and the principles of human nature, and by no means opposed to a liberal and enlightened nonconformity.'' Gosman advocated ''some simple and comprehensive religious ceremony'' to open the Exhibition in which the representatives of the churches would ''act for the time being as the high priests of the nation''; or, if the churches could not agree to cooperate, he suggested a chaplain appointed by the government rather than no ceremony at all.[28] A few Congregationalists dissented from Gosman's argument for a religious state, but the majority supported his views, as probably did most in the larger Protestant denominations.

Melbourne's Centennial Exhibition did open with a religious ceremony. The prayer, devised by the bishop of Melbourne, with the concurrence of the other Protestant denominations, was read by Sir James MacBain, president of the Exhibition commission. But in New South Wales churchmen's efforts had been less successful in securing the recognition of God. There was no acknowledgement of religion in any of the civil ceremonies marking the centenary in New South Wales, which was hardly surprising in view of an attempt made the previous year to revive daily prayer in the legislature. Parkes claimed to express no opinion on the matter, although it was he who put the proposal to the Speaker on behalf of "a number of gentlemen representative of our common Christanity", (most probably the Sydney Ministers' Union). There were also petitions from the Presbyterian General Assembly, the Sydney Women's Prayer Union and others, all decrying the absence of homage to God in Parliamentary procedure. The petitioners believed that good would come from the "wholesome custom" of opening each sitting of Parliament with prayer. The matter was referred to the Standing Orders Committee, but it declined to recommend any change. Many members were probably aware of the opposition to such proposals in the past.[29]

The question came up in the Legislative Assembly three years later when a Salvationist, E.W. Turner, Member for Gunnedah, introduced a resolution for daily prayers. A few thought such an observance would be appropriate recognition of God, but the Quaker Alfred Allen and W.H. Traill, formerly an editor of the Sydney *Bulletin*, both argued against formal and public prayer on the grounds of Christ's teaching on prayer in the Sermon on the Mount. It was probably foolish of Turner to remind the House of the unfortunate experience of prayers in the Legislative Assembly in 1862 for the majority, apparently persuaded that prayers promoted discord rather then harmony, defeated the motion solidly. But churchmen had not accepted defeat and the *Presbyterian* expected the question to come up again.[30] The public recognition of God did become a significant issue in the 1890s, but in a different context. What churchmen could not obtain from a colonial parliament they now sought in federation.

Churchmen and the Campaign for Federation

The unity of the Australian colonies was implicit in much that Protestant and Catholic churchmen said during the centenary celebrations in 1888 and they forecast that the day would come in the new century when Australia would no longer be "a number of rival and jealous little states, but a great confederation of nations".[31] Among them were seasoned campaigners for federation, especially some Presbyterians and Congregationalists. The former denomination thought that a federated Australia would protect the Pacific, where it had extensive missionary interests, from the dominance of Catholic France. The Victorian government was more sympathetic to the Presbyterians' demands for federation and the annexation of the

New Hebrides than New South Wales, but many churchmen in the older colony supported the Victorian campaign.[32]

One of the most consistent contenders for federation in New South Wales was Dr Jefferis. He had advocated union of the Australian colonies almost from the day of his arrival in the country, and during the 1870s wrote a number of leading articles on the question for the Adelaide *Advertiser*. He sought to advance the cause in public lectures before distinguished audiences in Adelaide in 1880 and Sydney in 1883, and his last two public lectures in Sydney in December 1889 were on federation, with Parkes presiding at the first and Dr Andrew Garran at the second. His interest in federation was not narrowly religious, but he advocated it with religious zeal. Only through federation would Australia's "true destiny be accomplished" and her civilizing mission be fulfilled.[33]

Catholics could not be expected to sympathize with the mainly Presbyterian demands for annexation in the 1880s. During the New Hebrides crisis in 1886 the *Freeman's Journal* sneered that that "little insignificant Protestant denomination" had "tasted the sweets of oil and bêche de mer" and thought that this made them "the arbiters of the destiny of a great people". But there was support for federation among Catholics, especially from Cardinal Moran. He took up the cause during the centenary year and called on Catholics to support "a federation combining all the highest and most endearing sentiments of true charity and true mercy, and based upon the principles and feelings of Christianity.[34]

Here was not only a call for federation, but a plea for the recognition of religion by the new nation. To get Christianity acknowledged by a federal government was Cardinal Moran's special interest over the next decade. In this he was on common ground with most Protestant churchmen interested in the movement. In June 1890 the *Presbyterian* ventured the opinion that federation might help to pull New South Wales into line with the other colonies in the matter of Sunday observance.[35] So both Protestant and Catholic churchmen looked to federation to assert the religious character of Australian society, which they feared was weakening or had been lost altogether.

The social and economic crises of the early 1890s undoubtedly quickened the churchmen's sense of the importance of religion to social well-being, but these crises do not account for those who sought recognition of God in the Commonwealth Constitution, as Richard Ely has suggested is the case.[36] The source of this movement can be traced back at least to the 1880s. It was then that the challenge from secularism was felt most intensely and churchmen began to long for some recognition of Christianity from the State.

As with the great river system in south-east Australia, streams that had their sources in New South Wales, and some from Victoria, flowed together in the federation campaign in the 1890s, like a river in full flood. Catholic as well as Protestant concern poured into it for the first time. Hitherto, Catholics had objected on grounds of conscience to prayers in Parliament and religious ceremonies on public occasions. Now they had come to think that any recognition of religion was better than none at all.

The first move for the formal recognition of God in the federal sphere was made at the People's Federal Convention at Bathurst late in 1896. That seasoned contender for the religious State, Alexander Gosman, moved to acknowledge "the existence of a widespread belief in the government of the world by Divine Providence" and to invoke "the Supreme Ruler . . . so to guide and direct the course of events that Australian unity may rest upon an enlightened public opinion and on a solid foundation of righteousness, the only guarantee for the creation and continuance of national prosperity and peace". The verboseness, if not the theology, was too much and Gosman ultimately withdrew his motion. But before the convention disbanded a simpler resolution was carried. "Acknowledging the Government of the World by Divine Providence," it commended "the cause of Federation" to all who desired "not only the material, but also the moral and social advancement of the people of Australia".[37]

The next step was to have this acknowledgement of God accepted by the framers of the Constitution who were to meet in a Federal Convention in Adelaide in March 1897. Cardinal Moran had this in view when he stood as a candidate for election to the convention. He announced that he would seek to include a statement in the preamble of the federal Constitution that "religion is the basis of our Australian Commonwealth and of its laws", although with full recognition of the right to liberty of conscience and freedom of worship, "so far as may be consistent with public order and morality". Moran confidently hoped that people of all religions would support him. "In matters of religion", he acknowledged, Australians were "a mixed community", but they were not atheists. They believed in "the Creator and Sovereign Lord of all, the Divine arbiter of our destinies, the source whence comes the authority for making laws, and the duty and sanction of their observance". But Moran's attempt to get into the politics of federation proved to be a serious miscalculation. His candidature provoked division rather than unity. Some Protestants actually campaigned against him, and although the Anglicans did not, few would have been content to leave religious interests in his hands. Generally, he aroused more fear than hope.

While he did not poll disastrously, he was defeated and virtually retired from the campaign for federation after that.[38] He might have done more for the movement had he not stood for the convention.

With the approach of the Federal Convention in Adelaide the New South Wales Council of Churches drew up a petition asking that God be recognized in the preamble of the Constitution as "the Supreme Ruler of the World and the ultimate source of all law and authority in nations". The petition also requested the institution of daily prayers in both Houses of the federal Parliament, and that the governor general be empowered "to appoint days of national thanksgiving and humiliation". Similar petitions came from many sources: the Councils of Churches in other colonies and their member denominations and local congregations, the Salvation Army, Christian Endeavour Societies and the Woman's Christian Temperance Union. There was also a petition from the Catholic hierarchy in South Australia,[39] for Cardinal Moran's defeat had not entirely dampened Catholic enthusiasm for the cause. All in all, there seemed to be a substantial body of opinion in favour of some recognition of God in the Constitution.

There was also some opposition. It came, not from avowed secularists as might have been the case had the campaign been mounted in the 1880s, but from Seventh Day Adventists, recently established in Australia. They organized counter-petitions against any religious declaration in the Constitution. Religious legislation, they submitted, was "subversive of good government"; being "contrary to the principles of sound religion" it could only result in religious persecution. It was the same "secularism" that Baptists and Congregationalists, and even Catholics in Australia, had once professed. Now this anxious minority looked for a guarantee of religious freedom in the form of a declaration "that neither the Federal Government nor any State Parliament shall make any law respecting religion or prohibiting the free exercise thereof".[40]

The Seventh Day Adventists' fears were based partly on American experience. In 1892 the United States Supreme Court handed down a judgment that America was "a Christian nation" and in the same year Congress made Sunday closing a condition of its financial grant to the Chicago World Fair. There had also been pressure in America for federal laws on Sunday observance and for a religious declaration in the United States Constitution. Some Presbyterians in Australia hoped that federation would lead to uniformly strict Sunday laws throughout their country, but Seventh Day Adventists imagined what this would mean for them. Several of them had been prosecuted for labouring on Sunday in 1894, and although the conviction was quashed on appeal, the harassment was bad enough.[41] Their opposition to the recognition of God in the federal Constitution was entrenched.

Two attempts in the Adelaide convention to have some recognition of God inserted in the draft failed. The Seventh Day Adventists must have been reassured, but some churchmen were full of indignation. The refusal amounted to "a perfectly gratuitous denial of God in our national affairs", according to Professor Andrew Harper of Ormond College, Melbourne, who called on all Australian Christians to rally to the cause. The *Australian Christian World* lamented that "our Federationists seem unable to acknowledge that God is the Supreme Ruler of all Nations, not to speak of framing a Constitution with the union of Church and State as one of its planks." Harper did not go quite that far. He accepted the separation of Church and State, but argued that this did not mean that the State had no religious duties, as official religious observances in the separate colonies demonstrated. He found it ironical that "the very men who are refusing to acknowledge God have appointed a day of prayer to Him" for the relief of drought.[42] (A day of Humiliation and Prayer was proclaimed in both New South Wales and Victoria in April 1897.)

Disappointed by the recent failures but not defeated, churchmen now looked to the colonial parliaments, each of which was to debate the Adelaide draft of the Constitution. The New South Wales Council of Churches organized fresh petitions asking its colonial legislators to insist on the recognition of God in the draft. Similar petitions flowed into other colonial parliaments, especially in Victoria, including one there from the Catholic hierarchy. In Sydney the Council of Churches held a public meeting at which the mayor presided, to win support for the demand. Among the speakers were Rabbi Davis, Sir W.P. Manning, a Catholic, and J.C. Neild, the champion of divorce law reform. They declared that the people of New South Wales would not rest content until God was recognized in the Constitution. It was not a sectarian question, Manning protested, (although counter-petitions were organized by the Seventh Day Adventists). Fervent were the hopes that the solemn chorus from the major religious bodies would prevail with the legislators. The *Australian Christian World* challenged them to defy "such a definite demand . . . made by all classes and creeds". The legislators and convention delegates could "only refuse the petition if they [meant] boldly and openly to hoist the Atheist flag".[43]

The churchmen's fears were allayed in August 1897 when the New South Wales Legislative Assembly agreed, with little debate, to include in the preamble of the draft constitution the words proposed by the Council of Churches — "duly acknowledging Almighty God as the supreme ruler of the universe, and the source of all true government''. The *Australian Christian World* purred with satisfaction, trusting that other parliaments would follow ''the good example'' set by New South Wales. All did, except the Tasmanian Legislative Council. There was some dissent in the South Australian Parliament, but, like New South Wales, the Victorian Legislative Assembly agreed to an amendment for recognition with little discussion, but in a different phrase — ''in reliance upon the blessing of Almighty God''.[44]

It seemed that the tide had turned. The *Australian Christian World* was confident that the next convention in Melbourne would vote for recognition, because four of the New South Wales delegates had declared a change of mind. Fewer petitions for recognition were presented to the Melbourne convention, but this in itself was evidence of the churchmen's confidence that their campaign was succeeding. Nevertheless, the Christian Endeavour Council of New South Wales reminded the convention that ''no scheme of federation will be acceptable ... which does not recognise Almighty God as the Supreme Ruler of Nations and Fountain of all Law and Authority''.[45] The matter was finally resolved on 2 March 1898, when the convention agreed to include in the preamble the words ''humbly relying upon the blessing of Almighty God'' — a variation on the phrase adopted by Victoria, and considered by the Drafting Committee to be the most acceptable form of words.[46]

The amendment was moved by Patrick McMahon Glynn, an Adelaide barrister who had attempted unsuccessfully to have some recognition of God included in the Adelaide draft of the Constitution. A Catholic of some culture but not impeccably orthodox, Glynn hoped that ''faith may find a recommendation and doubt discover no offence'' in his ''simple and unsectarian'' amendment, by which they might fix the ''stamp of the Eternal'' in the Constitution. There were two formidable opponents to the amendment. Edmund Barton, the future prime minister, thought any reference to God inappropriate in a political constitution. Henry Bourne Higgins, a Victorian lawyer and future High Court judge, had become the spokesman for the Seventh Day Adventists. He could not support the amendment without ''a sufficient safeguard against the passing of religious laws by the Commonwealth''. Most delegates did not take this point seriously and were in favour of, or at least ready to acquiesce in, the recognition of God.[47]

It was a political rather than a religious decision for most of the delegates, although some like Dr John Quick, the Victorian lawyer, were moved by religious feelings. The New South Wales delegate, William Lyne, was perfectly frank about his chief reason for supporting the amendment: he was convinced that it would influence a large number of votes in favour of federation. Nevertheless, the Anglican *Churchman* saw the decision as evidence of a "latent Christianity" among politicians.[48] Be that as it may, the passing of the amendment did testify to the strength of the churches as a pressure group on matters which touched them deeply.

Why this particular matter should be of such importance to churchmen deserves further investigation. When Professor Harper attacked the initial refusal to acknowledge God, he denied that the decision would bring "any special divine displeasure". Nor would he make any connection between the convention's denying attitude and the drought that assailed the country. It is significant that he felt it necessary to say that much. At least one other minister did make the connection. Religious men of that age generally believed in the overruling providence of God, and some churchmen did not hesitate to link the drought, depression and social unrest of the early 1890s with man's neglect of God.[49] Governments did proclaim days of humiliation and prayer for rain, although these proclamations were probably issued as much to please churchmen as to placate the Deity. Of course the more theologically liberal churchmen rationalized these events to suit their acceptance of a scientific world view, but even that view allowed for the extraordinary intervention of the Almighty. In any case this belief in divine providence was sufficiently strong for religious people to expect some blessing from God on their nation, or at least to be genuinely concerned at a refusal to acknowledge his might.

It was the specific refusal by the convention to recognize the Almighty that made the question matter more. After New South Wales had voted for recognition the *Australian Christian World* acknowledged that recognition in the Constitution would not of itself make Australia "a godly Commonwealth", but it would save it from the peril of formally denying God and his "authority over Nations". Australians of the future, who it hoped would "be more Christian than we are", would look back in gratitude to the generation that did what it could to remind people of "the Supreme Mind and Will".[50]

But there was more than this to the churchmen's campaign for the recognition of God. As Ely argues, they were motivated by anxiety over their status in society. Their repeated assertions of the necessity of religion to social well-being were in effect cries for their recognition as God's representatives. Gosman put it this way, as early as 1887: "If the State is religious, the existence of the Churches cannot be ignored, and if the Churches cannot be ignored, we cannot be ignored."[51] Concern for public status, however, does not fully explain the intensity with which churchmen pursued their goal. For all their vanity, they were basically men of religion and religion was their primary concern. When they sought to influence politics on Sunday observance, divorce, gambling or temperance reform, politics was a means to an end — the endorsement of religious values and moral standards. It was the authority that religion should wield rather than their status as men of religion that concerned them most. At a time when their "internal" authority over their congregations was weakening they looked to the State to buttress it by upholding laws or passing statutes that enshrined Christian values. At that time too the relevance of religion to social questions was disputed, so they looked to the State to recognize God. The State ought to do something to maintain Christianity, Bishop Barry argued in a sermon during the general election in January 1889. The Christian statesman could help to make the State pro-Christian rather than anti-Christian by safeguarding the sanctity of the Lord's Day and the hallowing of great public acts with prayer.[52] This is the essence of what lay behind the campaign for the recognition of God; in the federal sphere it was an attempt to make the Commonwealth not a promoter of parsons, but an ally of religion.

It may be questioned how successful they were in the campaign in view of Section 116, which states:

> The Commonwealth shall not make any law for establishing any religion, or for imposing any religious observance, or for prohibiting the free exercise of any religion, and no religious test shall be required as a qualification for any office or public trust under the Commonwealth.

The persistence of Higgins led to its adoption. He had attempted unsuccessfully to have something along these lines adopted before the convention adopted the recognition of God, but the convention rejected any such clause. But on the day it passed Glynn's amendment Higgins tried again. Most delegates were prepared to support a prohibition of religious tests, but regarded the clause Higgins proposed as unnecessary. They took religious freedom and equality for granted. The separation of Church and State was "an unwritten law of the Constitution", according to the South Australian delegate J.H. Symon. But Higgins argued that religious powers might be inferred from the preamble to the Constitution. While not sharing this opinion, several delegates thought that the clause might be adopted to allay such fears and thus commend the Constitution to those opposed to the recognition of God for those reasons. So Higgins's clause was adopted, but not unanimously.[53]

But did it detract from the recognition accorded to God in the preamble? Quick and Garran, in a comment in the *Annotated Consti-*

tution, did not think so. They offered this interpretation of Section 116:

> By the establishment of religion is meant the erection and recognition of a State Church, or the concession of special favours, titles, and advantages to one church which are denied to others. It is not intended to prohibit the Federal Government from recognizing religion or religious worship. The Christian religion is, in most English speaking countries, recognized as a part of the common law.[54]

Ely regards this interpretation as "on the evidence indefensible", and argues that the clause should be interpreted in a "strict separationist" sense, rather than the "non-preferential" sense in which Quick and Garran understand it. Furthermore, he sees the adoption of Section 116 as a blow to the hope churchmen had of securing a degree of support for religion from the emerging Commonwealth. However, a careful reading of the *Convention Debates* and other evidence does not suggest that Quick and Garran's interpretation is in conflict with the outlook of the convention delegates, in so far as that can be discerned.[55] A strict separationist view of Church-State relations on the grounds of Section 116 can no more be ascribed to them than to credit them with a fervent faith for recognizing God in the preamble of the Constitution. They passed both measures mostly to please persistent petitioners, no doubt regarding them as proper and, on the whole, harmless provisions.

Most churchmen seemed to see Section 116 in the same light as Quick and Garran — that it did not prevent the Commonwealth from recognizing religion. Some embraced the new clause wholeheartedly. The South Australian Council of Churches' message commending the Constitution in the 1898 referendum mentioned as well as its recognition of God its provision "for the most perfect religious freedom". Dr Jefferis, then in Adelaide, had drafted it. He elaborated on the theme in his sermon marking the inauguration of the Commonwealth in January 1901. "In religion the prospect is most cheering", he announced. "At last the unholy compact between Caesar and [the] priest who claimed the sole authority to represent God has been repudiated and put away. A liberal press and a generous people have demanded and obtained a free church in a free State. There is no dominant sect."[56] Jefferis's utterance provoked an Anglican clergyman opposed to Section 116, J.W. Owen, to lament that "the church being abolished nothing is left but sects — not one of them dominant, and all equally impotent for any lasting good." If this was so, Higgins's clause had not caused it, as Bishop Broughton, the first Anglican bishop in Australia, could have told Owen. The *Australian Christian World* dismissed this Anglo-

Catholic view with disdain. It defended Section 116 as "clear and fair" and certainly not antagonistic to religion.[57] As far as most churchmen were concerned the recognition of God had made the Commonwealth friendly to religion, and for that much they were grateful.

But they had asked for more than the recognition of God. They wanted the governor general to have the authority to proclaim days of humiliation and prayer. This was an unwritten right of the state governors, and it might have been considered within the governor general's capacity had churchmen not pressed for it to be specifically provided for. It was never denied, although Section 116 seems to have been read as prohibiting it; at least no governor general has proclaimed such a day. Even so, state governors continued to do so after federation, for the states' rights in religion remained unaffected by this section of the Commonwealth Constitution.

Prayers in Parliament was the other matter that concerned the churchmen, and they did not consider that anything decided in the conventions had made that impossible. Once the referendums were passed churchmen took steps to ensure that the Commonwealth would be inaugurated with a religious ceremony and to advocate that there be prayers in the new Parliament. The New South Wales Council of Churches began its campaign for these measures in August 1900 and secured the support of the Anglican General Synod which was meeting that month. The synod authorized the primate, Archbishop Saumerez Smith, to take up the question with the New South Wales government, which had the responsibility of organizing the ceremony. The Council of Churches supported the primate and their counterparts in other colonies also backed the campaign. Smith and the Reverend James Fordyce, secretary of the council, approached the government, which agreed to their proposal and charged them with arranging an appropriate religious service. The premier, Sir William Lyne, also invited the churches to conduct watchnight services on 31 December, the eve of the new century, to pray for "the Empire, the Commonwealth and the States", and to observe Sunday 6 January as Commonwealth Sunday.[58]

All this pleased the Protestants, but Cardinal Moran declined to take part in the religious ceremony. Instead, he proposed to read his own prayer before or after the official religious ceremony. Lyne would not agree to this, and prevented Moran from arranging with Government House to read his prayer before the ceremony. This rebuff, and confusion over ecclesiastical precedence led to Moran's withdrawal from the official ceremony altogether. The Cardinal, however, sat in state upon the steps of St Mary's Cathedral surrounded by vested clergy and 2,000 schoolchildren, to review the

William Saumerez Smith, Anglican Bishop of Sydney (1890-97), and First Archbishop (1897-1909). From portrait in Chapter House, St. Andrew's Cathedral, Sydney by Howard Barron, date unknown. (Photo courtesy of Anglican Information Service, Sydney.)

inaugural procession. The governor general's carriage paused as it passed to hear the children sing "A Song of the Commonwealth", composed by a Catholic musician.[59] So Cardinal Moran also had his hour.

Presbyterians and Wesleyans were also put out by the precedency arrangements which gave special distinction to the two prelates over the heads of other denominations. When they failed to secure a change which would have grouped all the heads of churches together but ranked in order of numerical strength, thus placing the Protestant primate ahead of the Catholic cardinal, they also stayed out of the inaugural procession in protest. But the heads of the smaller denominations and the Jewish rabbis took their assigned places.[60]

The primate was the only clergyman on the platform at the inaugural ceremony in Centennial Park. Yet, for all their disputes over precedency, his presence there gratified other Protestant churchmen. He was there, not only as the Primate of the Church of England in Australia, the *Australian Christian World* pointed out, but also "as the chosen representative of the Protestant Churches of Australia", conducting a service devised by the Council of Churches, although Smith, no doubt, had most say in its content. It was plainly a Christian service. The prayers included the invocation of Jesus Christ and the service concluded with the ancient creedal canticle, the *Te Deum,* and the trinitarian benediction. "In the view of some", the *Christian World* taunted, "a nation that has no Established Church has no way of acknowledging God. . . . That this is not so was publicly demonstrated in the Centennial Park on Tuesday last." It thought that this service was a logical consequence of the recognition of God in the Constitution. So whatever the Constitution might say against "establishing any religion", the new Commonweath had tacitly recognized Christianity as the national religion — and the government gave the clergy a picnic the following Saturday![61]

Commonwealth Sunday coincided with the feast of the Epiphany and churchmen hailed the manifestation of the new nation to the world. The patriotic rhetoric of the occasion recalled the sermons at the centenary celebrations in 1888, although there was not the same mighty demonstration of Protestant unity in 1901. Both the Presbyterian Moderator and the recently-formed Evangelical Council (of which Anglicans were not members) arranged separate services for the Sunday afternoon. The state government assisted the Evangelical Council in organizing its service in Hyde Park and some Members of Parliament were among the large congregation that attended. But the governor general (a Presbyterian himself) and a handful of civil dignitaries attended the moderator's "National Thanksgiving Service" in the Town Hall, with a large number of Presbyterian ministers. The presence of the primate, who pronounced the benediction, gave it the appearance of a united service. The morning service in St Andrew's Cathedral, however, "largely took the form of a State function". The governor general, Prime Minister Barton and ministers of state, the judiciary, the military and the great of the land were there. The shadow of the old establishment lingered on.[62]

Churchmen saw to it that prayers were included in the opening of the first federal Parliament in Melbourne on 9 May 1901. But this time the governor general, not the primate read the prayers, at the suggestion of the Council of Churches, presumably to avoid any dispute between the Anglican and Catholic prelates, for while both Catholic and Protestant now agreed as to the desirability of prayers in Parliament, Catholics would not cooperate in a religious ceremony with Protestant ministers. Even so, yet another slight led to Cardinal Moran's absence from the ceremony. Like the inaugural ceremony in January, the religious opening was clearly Christian. It was further cause for congratulation that so far "Australia has formally and at every stage of its progress acknowledged God's hand in this matter of the Commonwealth".[63]But churchmen were wondering whether prayers would become a regular part of the procedure in federal Parliament.

The New South Wales Council of Churches appointed the primate to convey their wishes to the government that Parliament should adopt daily prayers. But as Melbourne was the temporary federal capital it rested with the Victorian Council of Churches to press the matter on Parliament. The council found sponsors who in June moved the introduction of daily prayers in the House of Representatives and the Senate, to be read by the Speaker and the President respectively. As in the convention debates, there were some who doubed the propriety of this step. Barton was one of them, but he would not oppose the motion; in fact he seems to have voted for it. To adopt the proposal was, he said, "the course . . . least offensive to the religious susceptibilities of the public". So the motion was carried easily in both Houses. The form adopted was based on the prayer composed by Lord Tennyson, governor of South Australia, which was read at the opening of the federal Parliament, but it was shorter and without the invocation of Jesus Christ. It also included the Lord's Prayer, from the Authorized or King James Version, according to Protestant usage.[64]But it was not as overtly Christian as the prayers offered at the opening of Parliament.

Yet the form was not acceptable to everyone. Barton had wanted no more than the Lord's Prayer, which was presumably acceptable to Unitarian and Jew. And the Catholic Archbishop of Melbourne, Dr Carr, thought that Tennyson's prayer was unworthy of the occasion and objected to the form of the Lord's prayer adopted.[65]Still, Protestants were pleased. In spite of "our 'unhappy divisions' ", the *Australian Christian World* rejoiced, "it has yet been possible for us to make the public worship of Almighty God an essential element in the life of the new Commonwealth". Relieved that the prime minister had not opposed the introduction of prayers, it took peculiar pleasure in his reminder "that the Great Master had emphasized the spiritual secret nature of prayer". What then of formal public prayers? "In weighing the worth of this recognition of God", the *Christian World* acknowledged that familiarity might breed contempt, but it hoped that prayer would "silently and subtly leaven" the proceedings, so that "the legislation of the Commonwealth may do the will of God". It might have reflected on Dr Dale's comment on the yearning of Australian churchmen to have public acts hallowed with prayer, that the "bowing out" of the Bible and the chaplain after the prayer in the House of Commons was "the most significant part of the ceremony".[66]

Probably not many Members expected the prayers to make any difference to their deliberations. They had adopted them more to please the persistent churchmen than to honour God. So churchmen could at times exert a powerful influence on political life, even if only at a superficial level. In the early months of the Commonwealth's history they basked in the glow of success upon success. If they had not achieved all they set out to accomplish they did not complain too much. They had obtained that public recognition of God that they had craved since the 1880s. The custom of one half-century's standing in New South Wales and other colonies was now reversed. They might have foreseen that the state parliaments would follow the federal Parliament's example in due course. It seemed to them that the dark clouds of secularism that had been gathering for so long had been dispersed. A new century had a new era in Australia seemed to promise better days for religion. But it was an Indian summer for Christianity in Australia, or a least for Protestant Christianity.

10

The Legacy of the 1880s

The twentieth century dawned with new hope for Australian churchmen, now confident that they would "win Australia for God and His Christ". They looked forward "to a broader, deeper, purer, and higher life" in the nation "that would make our Commonwealth the praise of the whole earth". But the national regeneration they envisaged was rather circumscribed; it was determined largely by the last two decades of the nineteenth century, when religion had seemed to be fighting for survival. Looking ahead from the threshold of the new century, the *Australian Christian World* imagined a more vital religious life in Australia with more agreement in "our ideas about Law, Marriage, Divorce, Sunday, Temperance, Gambling and the like". In a similar vein, the Anglican *Church Standard* looked forward to national regeneration through an attack on "the sins of sensuality, infidelity, impurity, dishonesty and indifferentism" and, above all, a crusade against drink and gambling. The topics chosen by the Balmain Ministers' Association for their series of meetings to commemorate the birth of the Commonwealth display the same preoccupations. "Righteousness exalteth a Nation" was the theme of the series; but righteousness was narrowly defined under these headings: Sin and Salvation; Gambling; Temperance; Men Only, with Dr Arthur.[1] Justice, equality of opportunity, better living conditions and similar topics were conspicuously absent from their agendas.

All this presents a very different picture of Protestantism at the turn of the century from that given by J.D. Bollen: he is impressed "most by its closeness to Australian life". It also makes his claim that there was a narrowing of Protestant social concern from 1910 onwards unconvincing. "Resistance", he argues, "has been a main theme of Protestant history ever since".[2] But the features which he delineates as marks of resistance, the campaign to "keep Australia Christian" and attempts to counter new trends in leisure time activities, were evident in the 1880s and the 1890s. When Protestant churchmen in early years after World War I worried about the effect of the cinema and the motor car on churchgoing and on morals, they were behaving in much the same way as their predecessors of the

1880s, who condemned Sunday trains and harbour cruises as well as Sunday concerts and other forms of entertainment. The Central Methodist Mission was already pointing the way to the institutional church catering for social and recreational as well as religious life, only suburban churches adopted the pattern to hold their youth rather than to attract the working classes. And if Protestant churchmen in the twentieth century have been defensive about the rights of religion in a Christian country, resisting the liberalization of laws supposed to uphold Christian standards, they were only taking similar stands to the churchmen in the 1880s. Indeed, it is the similarity, not the difference, in the stance of Protestantism towards society in the late nineteenth century and the greater part of this century, at least up to the 1960s, that is most striking.

Of course there were changes, and some of these were already apparent in the 1880s, especially in theology. After some initial resistance the majority of Australian churchmen came to terms with modern science and higher criticism. There is little substance in the belief that science caused many people to lose their faith. There were still pockets of fundamentalism, particularly in Sydney, but generally theological liberalism prevailed in Protestantism. There were also changes in attitudes to sexual morality. At the beginning of the twentieth century most Australian churchmen were opposed to contraception, but in the interwar period Protestants came to accept it as proper within marriage.[3] This far they accommodated themselves to changing mores, but the old obsession with "sins of the flesh" prevailed up to about the 1950s. Apart from the Anglicans, Protestants generally came to terms with new divorce laws, and remarried divorced persons. The traditional evangelical doctrine of social reform through individual regeneration, beginning to weaken in the 1880s, was modified as churchmen recognized the need for some legislative regulation in industrial relations and of state action in social welfare. Some churchmen espoused a more social Christianity and others tried to wean Protestantism from the Liberal party to a position of political independence. After World War I repentant clergy preached pacifism. These developments are largely uncharted, but that many churchmen thought differently on these questions from their predecessors at the turn of the century is indisputable.

But the more radical attitudes on social justice were confined to a distinguished minority. The Protestant consensus on social questions remained essentially conservative, and attached to the attitudes of the 1880s. This was especially the case with questions such as temperance, gambling and Sunday observance, as indicated in the statements of churchmen greeting the dawn of the new century. Although most churchmen adoped a liberal theology, they retained the old attitudes in these areas. Furthermore, they continued to employ fundamentalist evangelists to revive religion in their congregations, and these evangelists reinforced Puritan morality in their opposition to the theatre, dancing, card-playing and the novel. They also underpinned the Protestant attitudes to drink, to gambling and to Sunday recreation.

Dr Chapman, for example, greatly stimulated the mounting temperance campaign in the years before World War I, with his absolute and uncompromising hostility to drink. He drew several bursts of applause in Sydney in 1909, when he delivered his standard sermon on prohibition. Arguing from the same premises as the temperance campaigners of the 1880s, he announced that the time had come for every patriotic and decent man "to stand against the whisky business". The liquor trade was so evil and "so marked by destruction and despair" that no man who had anything to do with it had "a right to call himself a Christian". Moreover, anyone who was "not out and out for temperance, and in the thick of the fight", he told his audience, should write to his minister immediately "and ask him to take [his] name off the church books."[4] Next to drink, Chapman placed gambling as one of the greatest causes of poverty and degradation. In another sermon in Sydney in 1909 he held an American "dollar bill" before his audience, telling them that on the back someone had written these words: "This is the last of 50,000 dollars. I had a wife and child and a beautiful home, but strong drink and gambling caused the loss of them all. This is the last dollar."[5] This kind of preaching drew large numbers of "converts" to the front at his meetings. He gave an additional boost to these views on his second visit to Australia in 1912, by which time the campaign for the early closing of liquor bars had begun.

"Six o'clock closing" of hotel bars came to south-east Australia in 1916, and was regarded by many as a temporary wartime measure. Nevertheless, it arose out of the temperance crusade that had been gathering momentum since the 1880s. Important as the patriotic motive might have been, the success of the campaign cannot be explained apart from forty years of temperance education, and the agitation for complete local option and prohibition during the first decade of this century.[6] The victory was exhilarating for churchmen, who saw it as the last campaign before the final battle for prohibition. That sanguine hope remained unfulfilled, and six o'clock closing became, instead of the last staging camp in the war against drink, a position to be defended, along with the Sunday laws and the Christian status of the country.

The Catholic Church did not share most of these Protestant concerns, except for the defence of the Christian character of Australia. But it had its own concerns in opposition to easier divorce and birth control, looking to the law to uphold Catholic moral values.[7] Catholics and Protestants were both concerned about indecent literature and the relaxing of moral standards in society, but as in the 1880s they rarely cooperated in these causes. One notable exception was the social purity campaign in South Australia in the 1880s. Parliament was prepared to raise the age of consent to fifteen, but the Social Purity Society demanded sixteen. As the government was adamant, the society organized a rally, preceded by a torchlight procession led by the Salvation Army to the Adelaide Town Hall. It was a Catholic, Bishop Reynolds, seconded by the Anglican Dean of Adelaide, who moved that the age of consent should be raised to sixteen. It was a remarkable demonstration of Christian unity, and Parliament capitulated to it.[8] The other important instance of Catholic-Protestant unanimity was in the campaign for the recognition of God in the Constitution, when once more the politicians gave in to religious pressure. The ecumenical Christian might wish that there had been more of this unity in the past. Australia may have been more overtly Christian, its laws more reflective of Christian morality and government policy more supportive of religion than has been the case. But the contemplation of this might well cause those who love liberty to be glad that sectarianism prevented a united front from forming too frequently.

Nevertheless, churchmen won further victories in their campaign for the recognition of Christianity, notably in the introduction of religious instruction into state schools in those states which had excluded it in the nineteenth century. But the campaign in New South Wales in 1964 in opposition to the new syllabus of general religious teaching, which would have deprived Christianity of its primacy, was one of the last occasions when churchmen united to force their will on the government. Premier J.B. Renshaw took the unprecedented step of meeting the primate and the Protestant churchmen at Bishopscourt, and their demands were largely conceded.[9]

So it seemed that Protestant churchmen were still a force in the land. But they were losing their militancy. In opposition to the new syllabus the Reverend Alan Walker, superintendent of the Central Methodist Mission, had asserted that the 95 per cent of Christian parents were being sacrificed to the 5 per cent non-Christian minority.[10] Yet, almost overnight, some leading churchmen began to see themselves as representatives of a religious minority in a secular society.

This changed attitude was most evident on the Sunday question.

In August 1965 the chief secretary of New South Wales, Eric Willis, circularized the churches, seeking their attitudes to proposed changes in the Sunday entertainment laws. He claimed in Parliament the next year that only the Baptist Union, the Churches of Christ and the Salvation Army expressed any outright opposition to a relaxation of the Sunday observance laws. Willis understated the opposition. A deputation from the New South Wales Council of Churches, led by Canon D.B. Knox, principal of Moore College, Sydney, had waited on him in November 1965 to oppose any liberalization of the laws. Protestant churchmen in Sydney generally did not show any enthusiasm for a freer Sunday with "commercialised sport" and entertainment. But they did not campaign as actively against liberalization of the laws as they had done in the past, probably because the unanimity of old was missing. Cardinal Gilroy and the Greek Orthodox Archbishop, Ezekiel Tsoukalas, supported the reform of the laws, but that was to be expected. The surprise came from the Anglican primate, Archbishop Gough, whom Willis quoted as saying that he fully recognized "the fact that the Churches represent only a minority of the population and have no right to enforce their principles upon the majority who do not hold them".[11]

Gough's attitude to the Sunday question did not please the militant Evangelicals in his diocese, however most of the bishops in New South Wales apparently supported him,[12] and other Australian churchmen shared his attitude. In Tasmania in 1967 the Reverend B.D. Prewer, a representative of the Tasmanian Methodist Assembly, told the Board of Inquiry on Sunday observance that it was "impossible and undesirable to attempt to enforce on the community at large a Christian approach to Sunday". While he wished to see some protection afforded to Sunday morning services, he did not object to spectator sports or public entertainments after 1 p.m. Commissioner P.D. Phillips concluded that the Anglican Bishop, Dr R.E. Davies, and the Catholic Archbishop, Dr Guilford Young, concurred with this "liberal" Methodist view, which the commissioner thought contained "the most acceptable description of the role of the State and of the law in relation to Sunday observance". Furthermore, these three denominations represented among them "in excess of two-thirds of the population.[13] So Phillips discounted the views of the Council of Churches and the smaller denominations which took the traditional stand on Sunday observance.

It was much the same in Victoria where a small sample of Protestant ministers in 1967 showed themselves in favour of liberalization of the law. Similarly, an inquiry conducted in the Australian Capital Territory in 1971 found most churchmen ready for reform. One of them told the inquiry: "We see the Christian church today as a minority group within the community. We also see that the situation has changed from what it has been in previous generations when the church more or less looked to the community [sic] to impose its standards upon the community and expected the community to accept them".[14] Had the situation really changed so much, or had churchmen learned the lesson at last? At any rate, this changed attitude enabled state governments to liberalize their Sunday observance laws along the same lines as New South Wales, without too much opposition from the churches.

Protestants abandoned another stronghold in the 1960s — "six o'clock closing" — which they had defended so tenaciously for fifty years. It was abolished after a referendum in New South Wales in 1954, in which 10 o'clock won narrowly. But churchmen and officials of the Temperance Alliance had defended it uncompromisingly before a Royal Commission in 1954; and opinion in Victoria and South Australia was still firmly behind the earlier closing hour in the 1950s. Sixty percent of Victorian voters opposed a change to ten o'clock in a referendum in April 1956, before the Olympic Games in Melbourne.[15]

Victorian churchmen were still defending six o'clock closing when the Victorian Royal Commission on the liquor industry met in 1964. The Reverend John Westerman, a Methodist, represented the Social Questions Secretariat of the Protestant Churches before the commission, and at his initial appearance argued for the retention of the restrictive hotel trading-hours. But after consultation with the social questions committees of most of the Protestant denominations, he abandoned his defence of six o'clock closing and adopted "a position of neutrality" on hotel hours. He conceded that there was "no significant relationship between the hours of trading in hotel bars and sociological consequences from the consumption of liquor".[16]

The smaller denominations of Baptists, Churches of Christ and the Salvation Army did not support these major changes in Protestant policy, and wherever conservative evangelical theology held sway the old attitudes mostly still prevailed. But the principal Protestant denominations relinquished the legacy of the 1880s during the 1960s, and adopted a different stance towards society.

One reason for these changes was that churchmen were coming to terms with the standards accepted by the members of their congregations, many of whom must have been forced to live in bad faith with their churches over social questions. A number of Methodists, for example, attended dances before the Methodist General Conference decided in 1954 to allow dancing, within limits, on

Methodist Church property.[17]It had been apparent from the 1880s that many churchgoers were not sabbatarians, and by 1960 a good number in the congregation had rejected teetotalism. Wowserism was on the wane.

New theological emphases from overseas also contributed to the change of attitude. Through a spate of critical books and articles in the early 1960s many Australian churchmen were caught up in the religious crisis that was troubling western Christendom. Assumptions that held good for generations were now being questioned. It was argued that modern Christians were living in a post-Christian age, and that the model for the Church in the twentieth century was in early Christianity, before Constantine, when Christians were a minority in a pagan society. Dr John Robinson, then Bishop of Woolwich, helped to popularize this "new theology" in his sensational book, *Honest to God,* published in 1963. "I would see much more hope for the Church", wrote Robinson, "if it was organized not to defend the interests of religion against the inroads of the state . . . but to equip Christians . . . to enter with their 'secret discipline' into all the exhilarating, and dangerous secular strivings of our day . . ."[18] This literature helped to induce a new awareness among churchmen of the estrangement between churchgoing Christians and their fellow men in society at large.

The Second Vatican Council (1962-65) added to the ferment among Christians, although the new ecumenism opened the way for the first time for a common Catholic-Protestant front in society. It was not likely, however, to be formed in the interests of the narrower defence of religion that had preoccupied Protestants for so long, since both Catholic and Protestant were already reappraising their relationship to the world as well as to one another. Some on both sides resisted the new trends, but the 1960s were a watershed in the relationship of the churches to society in Australia; the stands and policies formulated in the 1880s were now virtually abandoned.

Most of them deserved to be abandoned. The tragedy is that they were held to and defended for so long. The churchmen of the 1880s had left to their successors a legacy of largely negative attitudes towards society. Their anxiety about the status of Australia as a Christian country, and their place in it, clouded their vision and led them on a fruitless quest for the public recognition of religion. They did not heed Dr Dale's warning that political life remains secular while men think that "exceptional political acts", such as prayers in Parliament, "are necessary to consecrate it".[19] Contrary to the optimistic prophecies uttered at the beginning of this century, Australia did not become more Christian or more righteous in the sense in which churchmen understood that term. Protestantism, in fact, lost some support,[20] and this might be partly because of the wowserism so much associated with it.

But there is another side to the tale of the 1880's. Churchmen in that decade did not resist on every front. They also adapted to their age and sacrificed some things to the progress of the times. They coped creditably with the challenge of suburban expansion in Sydney and other large cities; and there were some changes in worship and forms of church organization. But their response to the challenge to modern science and higher criticism of the Bible is perhaps the most striking aspect of their adaptability. Admittedly, they followed a pattern similar to that observed in churchmen overseas, but, by the same token, they must have agreed that an obscurantist position on these questions would not have helped their cause. The theological changes enabled some to stay within the fold who might otherwise have been forced out. Recent times chronicle a similar story. Modern churchmen have abandoned the old standards and attitudes that have since become liabilities for the Church in society and have begun to look again at ways of reaching those outside their aegis.

Churchmen have always hoped to influence their society and to shape the future. This impulse lay behind their anxious defence of the Christian character of Australia in the late nineteenth century. Modern churchmen have abandoned the legacy of the 1880s, but their reasons for doing so are not too far removed from the motives that underlay the behaviour of their sterner predecessors. The latter thought that to shape the future they had to resist much in their society. That might have been true, but they often fought the wrong battles. Modern churchmen have accommodated themselves to much in contemporary society. This new attitude may involve risky compromises, but it may also be more realistic for being more humble. Be that as it may, the history of the 1880s, together with that of more recent times, does suggest at least that the churches in Australia have a capacity to survive, whether or not it is a Christian country.

Abbreviations

ACW	*Australian Christian World* (Sydney)
DT	*Daily Telegraph* (Sydney)
JRAHS	*Royal Australian Historical Society Journal and Proceedings*
JRH	*Journal of Religious History*
MPGA	*Minutes of the Proceedings of the General Assembly of the Presbyterian Church of New South Wales*
MSDB	*Minutes of the Synod of the [Anglican] Diocese of Bathurst*
MWC	*Minutes of the New South Wales and Queensland Annual Conference of the Australasian Wesleyan Methodist Church*
NSW	New South Wales
PD	*Parliamentary Debates*
PSDG	*Minutes of the Proceedings of the Synod of the [Anglican] Diocese of Goulburn*
PSDG&A	*Report of the Proceedings of the Synod of the [Anglican] Diocese of Grafton and Armidale*
PSDN	*Report of the Proceedings of the Synod of the [Anglican] Diocese of Newcastle*
PSDS	*Votes and Proceedings of the Synod of the [Anglican] Diocese of Sydney*
S.A.	South Australia
SMH	*Sydney Morning Herald*
Vic	Victoria
V&PLA	*Votes and Proceedings of the Legislative Assembly*

Notes

1. The Churches in a Challenging Decade

1. See "Order" for *Opening of the First Parliament of the Commonwealth of Australia,* Parliamentary Library, Parliament House, Canberra.
2. R.B. Walker, "The Later History of the Church and School Lands", *JRAHS* 47, no. 4 (1961): 234-45; *PD* (NSW), 1st ser., 3: 2246-3143, 3193.
3. *Christian Advocate and Wesleyan Record* (Sydney), 20 December 1864.
4. Archdeacon King at the revival of the Lord's Day Observance Society, *SMH,* 12 October 1880.
5. *SMH*, 27, 28 November 1889.
6. For a fuller discussion of the religious composition of the colony, see W. Phillips, "Religious Profession and Practice in New South Wales, 1850-1901: The Statistical Evidence". *Historical Studies* 15 (1972-73): 378-400.
7. *PSDS*, 1881, p. 23. See also ibid., 1889, p. 23. Cowper was Dean of Sydney 1858-1902.
8. (Barry) *PSDS*, 1887, pp. 24-27; *SMH*, 28 August 1885; (Pearson) *PSDN*, 1882, pp. 18-20; ibid., 1886, pp. 84-89; *PSDS*, 1890, p. 18 and Ross Border, *Church and State in Australia, 1788-1872* (London: S.P.C.K., 1962), pp. 251, 272.
9. W. Moore White, *Presbyterian* (Sydney), 20 May 1882. See also R.B. Walker, "Presbyterian Church and People in the Colony of New South Wales in the late Nineteenth Century", *JRH* 2 (1962-63): 56.
10. Dr. Robert Steel, "We are not Dissenters", *Presbyterian*, 21 November 1885. See also ibid., 15 May 1880; "Progress", ibid., 2 September 1882; R. Walker, "Congregationalism in South Australia, 1837-1900", *Proceedings of the Royal Geographical Society of Australasia, South Australian Branch* 69 (1968): 17; *Australasian Independent* (Sydney), 15 March 1898.
11. Renate Howe, "Social Composition of the Wesleyan Church in Victoria During the Nineteenth Century", *JRH* 4 (1966-67): 206-17. Although there is no comparative study for New South Wales, an analysis of the correlation of occupation and religion in the Census of 1901 suggests that the situation was much the same. See W.W. Phillips, "Christianity and its defence in New South Wales circa 1880 to 1890" (Ph.D. thesis, Australian National University, 1969), pp. 30-33, 443-44.
12. J.E. Carruthers, *Memories of an Australian Ministry, 1868-1921* (London: Epworth Press, 1922), pp. 316-22.
13. *SMH*, 21 January 1885, 2 February 1883; *Weekly Advocate* (Sydney), 5 March 1881, 21 January 1888, 10 May 1890. Wesleyan Methodists increased at a greater rate than the general population increase between 1861 and 1891. T.A. Coghlan, *General Report on the Eleventh Census of New South Wales* (Sydney, 1894), pp. 213-19. I am indebted to my colleague, Dr. John Barrett, for information on the Methodist union movement.
14. *New South Wales Congregational Year Book*, 1881, pp. 48-58; 1883, p. 88. *Report*

of the Intercolonial Conference held in Pitt Street Congregational Church, Sydney, May 15th to May 23rd 1883 . . . to celebrate the Jubilee of the Introduction of Congregationalism to Australia (Sydney, 1883), pp. 230-31 (hereafter cited as Report, Intercolonial Congregational Conference, Sydney, 1883).

15. New South Wales Baptist (Sydney), 4 March 1887; H.E. Hughes, Our First Hundred Years: The Baptist Church in South Australia (Adelaide: South Australian Baptist Union, 1937), pp. 38-39, 63.

16. Alan C. Prior, Some Fell on Good Ground (Sydney: Baptist Union of New South Wales, 1966), pp. 93-98. The government statistician, T.A. Coghlan, also assumed that the Baptist Union comprised General Baptists. See Coghlan, General Report, p. 215.

17. F.J. Wilkin, Baptists in Victoria: Our First Hundred Years, 1838-1938 (Melbourne: Baptist Union of Victoria, 1939), p. 46; Prior, Some Fell on Good Ground, pp. 110, 125; Banner of Truth (Sydney), 5 May 1881. See also J.D. Bollen, Australian Baptists: A Religious Minority (London: The Baptist Historical Society, 1975), p. 22.

18. W.J. Rose, "Alfred Barry, Bishop of Sydney", Sydney Quarterly Magazine 5 (1888): 233-37; Crockford's Clerical Directory (1908) p. 82.

19. Church of England Guardian (Sydney), 28 April 1888; Freeman's Journal (Sydney), 31 July 1886.

20. SMH, 2 May 1884; DT, 19 May 1884.

21. Jefferis to J.F. Conigrave, 22 February 1884, State Library of South Australia Archives (SRG 95/51); DT, 19 May 1884.

22. Congregational Year Book, 1887, p. 87; New South Wales Independent (Sydney), 15 July 1884; see also A. Gosman, "The Religion of the State", Victorian Independent (Melbourne), May 1888, pp. 97-101.

23. SMH, 7 March 1888.

24. Weekly Advocate, 22 November 1884.

25. R.E.N. Twopeny, Town Life in Australia (London: Elliott Stock, 1883), pp. 112-17.

26. See A.D. Gilbert, Religion and Society in Industrial England: Church, Chapel and Social Change (London: Longman, 1976), chap. 6 esp. pp. 142-45, and K.J. Cable, "Protestant Problems in the Mid-Nineteenth Century", JRH 3 (1964-65): 119-36. For discussion of the term denomination in relation to church and sect see D.A. Martin, "The Denomination", British Journal of Sociology 13 (1962): 1-14; and Bryan Wilson, Religion in Secular Society (London: C.A. Watts, 1966), pp. 119-220.

29. Pastoral Letter of the Archbishops and Bishops of Australia assembled in Second Plenary Council to the Clergy and Laity of their Charge, 1895 [Sydney, 1895] p. 9 (hereafter cited as Pastoral, Second Plenary Council, 1895).

28. P.F. Moran, "Sermon Preached at the Close of the First Plenary Council of Australasia on the First Sunday in Advent, 1885", pp. 11-12. Quoted in P. O'Farrell, ed., Documents in Australian Catholic History, 2 vols. (London: Geoffrey Chapman, 1969). 2: 33; Cardinal Moran and the Federal Convention [Sydney, 1897], pp. 6, 14-15.

29. SMH, 28 April 1888.

30. P.F. Moran, "The Reunion of Christendom" (Sydney, 1895), p. 6; Freeman's Journal (Sydney), 31 May 1884, 20 November 1886; J. Tighe Ryan, The Attitude of the Catholic Church: A Special Interview with His Eminence Cardinal Moran (Sydney, 1894), pp. 34-44. Quoted in O'Farrell, Documents, 2: 176; Pastoral, Second Plenary Council, 1895, pp. 4-5.

31. Herbert M. Moran, Viewless Winds (London: Peter Davies, 1939), p. 10, quoted in O'Farrell, Documents, 2: 23.

32. P.F. Moran, "The Mission Field of the Nineteenth Century" (Sydney, 1895); Moran's story had its origin in a report in the *Freeman's Journal* in 1880, but the report was retracted shortly afterwards. See *Freeman's Journal*, 22, 27 March, 17 April 1880, and also P. Ford, *Cardinal Moran and the A.L.P.* (Melbourne: Melbourne University Press, 1966), p. 208.

33. *Australian Catholic Hymn Book*, 5th ed. (Sydney, n.d.) [1st ed. 1884], p. 92.

34. See *Pastoral Letter of the Archbishop and Bishops of New South Wales*, (Sydney, 1879).

35. Suggestions for Australian Synod of 1885, Dunne to Moran, 24 October 1884, Moran Papers, St. Mary's Cathedral Archives, Sydney.

36. See James Waldersee, *Catholic Society in New South Wales, 1788-1860* (Sydney: Sydney University Press, 1974), pp. 71-73.

37. See Phillips, "Christianity and its defence", pp. 9-40, 440-44, for a discussion of the occupational and regional distributions of the various denominations, with tables. See also H.N. Birt, *Benedectine Pioneers*, 2 vols. (London: Herbert and Daniel, 1911), 2: 336-37; *Freeman's Journal*, 29 January 1887, 31 March 1888.

38. B.R. Wise, "Plain Speaking on Great Questions", *Centennial Magazine* 2 (1889): 81-88; F.B. Freehill, "Colonial Know-Nothingism: A Reply to Mr. B.R. Wise", ibid., pp. 226-31; *Freeman's Journal*, 6 July 1889.

39. *Pastoral Letter of the Archbishops and Bishops of Australasia in Plenary Council Assembled to the Clergy and Laity of their Charge, Sydney, 29 November 1885*, pp. 16-18 (hereafter cited as *Pastoral, Plenary Council, 1885.)*

40. H.M. Moran, *Viewless Winds*, Chaps. 1-3; *Freeman's Journal*, 12 May 1888.

41. *Leaves from Australian Forests: The Poetical Works of Henry Kendall.* (Hawthorn: Lloyd O'Neil, 1970), p. 317.

42. *Freeman's Journal*, 14 June 1884.

43. Ibid., 16 April 1881.

44. Hobart Wesleyan Leaders' Meeting, Minute Books, 1830-1852 (4 August 1830). Information supplied by Dr. John Barrett. See also H.R. Jackson, "Aspects of Congregationalism in South-Eastern Australia circa 1880 to 1930" (Ph.D. thesis, Australian National University, 1978), pp. 28-29.

45. *Presbyterian*, 12 November 1880; *Jubilee of Congregationalism in South Australia. Report of the Intercolonial Conference held in Adelaide, September 1887* (Adelaide: W.R. Thomas and Co., 1887), p. 49 (hereafter cited as *Report, Intercolonial Congregational Conference, Adelaide, 1887).*

46. See R.B. Walker, "Religious Changes in Liverpool in the Nineteenth Century", *Journal of Ecclesiastical History* 19 (1968): 195-211; *Presbyterian*, 25 February 1882.

47. *Congregational Year Book 1882,*, pp. 43-44. The calculation of percentages are my own. Church attendance figures included those attending services in school buildings, court houses etc. which were not included in accommodation figures.

48. Sunday school attendances rose from 39 to 49 per cent of the eligible population (between five and fifteen years) during the 1880s, but they were around 40 per cent in 1900. See Phillips, "Religious Profession and Practice", pp. 396-98.

49. See F.K. Crowley, "The British Contribution to the Australian Population: 1860-1919", *University Studies in History and Economics* 2, no. 2 (1954): 76; see also K.S. Inglis, *Churches and the Working Classes in Victorian England* (London: Routledge and Kegan Paul, 1963), pp. 1-20; *Presbyterian*, 13 June 1885.

50. *SMH*, 28 August 1885.

51. *Report, Intercolonial Congregational Conference, Sydney, 1883,* pp. 99-100.

2. An Honourable Rivalry

1. Address to Church Society Conference, 27 August 1885 reported in *SMH*, 28 August 1885.

2. Ibid., 10 April 1888; *PD* (NSW) 7: 233; *Presbyterian*, 18 September 1880; *Weekly Advocate*, 15 October 1881; *Congregational Year Book*, 1882, p. 46.

3. *MPGA*, 1886, p. 81; *SMH*, 14 March 1890; W.J. Green, "Congregationalism in New South Wales", *NSW Independent*, 15 August 1881. For a recent comment on the importance of distance, see R. Currie, A. Gilbert and L. Horsley, *Churches and Churchgoers* (Oxford: Clarendon Press, 1977), p. 117.

4. *SMH*, 28 August 1885; *Presbyterian*, 16 October 1886. See also A.D. Gilbert, *Religion and Society in Industrial England: Church, Chapel and Social Change* (London: Longman, 1976) pp. 168-72 and Renate Howe, "The Response of the Protestant Churches to Urbanization in Melbourne and Chicago, 1875-1914" (Ph.D. thesis, University of Melbourne, 1972), p. 423.

5. Polding to Goold in P.F. Moran, *History of the Catholic Church in Australasia* (Sydney: Frank Coffee and Co., [1895]), pp. 768-69; Barker to Rev. Earnest Hawkins, 30 November 1867, in Ruth Teale, "By Hook and By Crook: The Anglican Diocese of Bathurst, 1870-1911" (M.A. thesis, University of Sydney, 1967), p. 33.

6. *PSDS*, 1881, pp. 18-19; *The Presbyterian Church of New South Wales: A Paper prepared by the Church Extension Committee for the General Presbyterian Council...* (Sydney, 1877), pp. 7-8; *Presbyterian*, 27 January, 10 March 1883; *MPGA*, 1883, pp. 14-15. On Victoria see Howe, "The Response of the Protestant Churches", chap. 8. See also M. French, "Churches and Society in South Australia, 1890-1900: An Exercise in Reassurance" (M.A. thesis, Flinders University, 1969), chap. 1.

7. W.S. Fielden to W.J. Green, 14 December 1882 in Correspondence, Church Extension Society, Congregational Union Papers, Mitchell Library; *NSW Independent*, 15 February, 15 March 1882; *Report, Intercolonial Congregational Conference, Sydney, 1883*, pp. 226-31.

8. *SMH*, 3 March 1883.

9. There was little mission work among Aborigines in the second half of the nineteenth century, apart from two missions in the Riverina, the Maloga Mission on the Murray near Moama and the Warangesda Mission on the Murrumbidgee. Founded in 1879 as a non-sectarian mission, Warangesda came under the diocese of Goulburn early in the 1880s. It also received some financial aid from the Sydney Church Society.

10. A.P. Elkin, *The Diocese of Newcastle*, (Glebe: Australian Medical Publishing Company, 1955), pp. 229, 486.

11. *Blue Book* (NSW), 1880, pp. 142-44: *PSDN*, 1881, appendix 2: 71-72. On the introduction and abolition of state aid to the various denominations, see John Barrett, *That Better Country* (Melbourne: Melbourne University Press, 1966), pp. 29-44 and Naomi Turner, *Sinews of Sectarian Warfare? State Aid in New South Wales 1836-1862* (Canberra: Australian National University Press, 1972), chaps. 8-11.

12. In 1856 the government had guaranteed an annual income of £2,000 to the bishop of Sydney until the Bishopsthorpe Estate should reach that amount. While this arrangement continued the revenues of Bishopsthorpe were paid into the treasury. By 1880 the bishop's income came entirely from the estate and the item shown in the *Blue Book* was no more than a book entry. Information supplied by Associate Professor K.J. Cable of Sydney University.

13. H.B. Callachor to Father Gillett, 13 September 1880, in Detached Parishes, St.

Mary's Cathedral Archives, Sydney; Thomas to Barker, 6 January 1880 in Barbara Thorn, ed., *Letters from Goulburn* (Canberra: Diocese of Canberra and Goulburn, 1964) pp. 60-61.

14. *PSDN*, 1881, p. 8. A number of grants of land were made subsequently in fulfilment of promises made before 11 May 1880. See *V & PLA* (NSW), 1883-84, 1: 565.

15. *SMH*, 10 April 1888; *PSDN*, 1886, p. 24; see also *PSDG*, 1881, p. 24; ibid., 1884, pp. 5-6; *PSDN*, appendix 7: 79-80; Elkin, *Diocese of Newcastle*, pp. 395-404.

16. Bourke's Church Act, 7 William IV No. 3; see also English Church Temporalities Act, 8 William IV No. 8; Barrett, *That Better Country*, p. 65. I am also indebted to comments of Associate Professor Cable on this point.

17. *PSDN*, 1885, pp. 82-83; *PSDS*, 1882, pt. 2, pp. 7-9, 1886, p. 38; Suggestions for Australian Synod of 1885, Dunne to Moran, 24 October 1884, Moran Papers, St. Mary's Cathedral Archives, Sydney; *NSW Independent*, 15 October 1880; J.S. Austin, *Missionary Enterprise and Home Mission Service* (Sydney, n.d.) p. 295.

18. *SMH*, 11 April 1882.

19. Ibid., 11, 15 April 1882.

20. *NSW Independent*, 15 May 1882; *SMH*, 10 May 1882. The figure of £4000 is an estimate based on information supplied by the archivist of St. Thomas's Church, Mrs. Daphne Dobbyn. For report on the Catholic 'Fayre' see "Modern 'Fayres' and 'Bazaars' " in R.B. Vaughan, *Christ's Divinity . . . in Six Lectures, Lent 1882* (Sydney, 1882), p. 286.

21. *PSDS*, 1887, p. 103; *PSDG*, 1881, p. 5; *PSDN*, 1887, p. 11; *Presbyterian*, 3 June 1882; *Report, Intercolonial Congregational Conference, Sydney, 1883*, pp. 108-9.

22. Ibid., pp. 105-28; *SMH*, 7 August 1885; *NSW Independent*, 15 November 1886; *MPGA*, 1886, pp. 77-78, 91-92. See also C.A. White, *The Challenge of the Years: A History of the Presbyterian Church of Australia in the State of New South Wales* (Sydney: Angus and Robertson, 1951), pp. 34-36; *NSW Baptist*, September 1886; Alan C. Prior, *Some Fell on Good Ground* (Sydney: Baptist Union of New South Wales, 1966), pp. 121-23.

23. *MWC*, 1888, pp. 80-82; 1889, pp. 80-81, 89. Minutes, Wesleyan Centennial Thanksgiving Fund Committee, 13 February 1895, Mitchell Library. I am indebted to the secretary of the former Australasian Methodist Historical Society, the Rev. W. Tredennick, for information on the distribution of the fund.

24. *PSDS*, 1888, pp. 31-32; *PSDN*, 1890, pp. 17-18. See also "Report of the Diocese Council . . . 1889-90", ibid., Appendix 1:51. Circulars of the Diocese of Sydney, 1842-95, no. 157, Archives of the Anglican Archdiocese of Sydney; First Annual Report of the Executive Committee of the Centennial Church Extension Fund, Diocese of Sydney, 1889 in *PSDS*, 1889, Appendix 19: 127-38; *Centennial Fund Annual Report, Year Ending June 30th 1897* (Sydney, 1897) pp. 16-17.

25. *MSDB*, 1875, p. 7, 1890, pp. 17-18; *PSDS*, 1888, p. 30, 1890, Appendix, 19: 110-11.

26. *PSDN*, 1886, 11: 86.

27. Ibid., 1886, p. 15, 1892, p. 18.

28. J.T. Warlow Davies, "Church Finance", *NSW Independent*, 15 June 1881.

29. *Reports of the Church Society of the Diocese of Sydney*, 1880 to 1890; Ransome T. Wyatt, *The History of the Diocese of Goulburn* (Sydney: E. Bragg, 1937), pp. 112-13; *PSDN*, 1886, p. 14, 18-20. See also Elkin, *Diocese of Newcastle*, pp. 486-87.

30. R.W. Dale, *Impressions on Australia* (London: Hodder and Stoughton, 1889), p. 228.

31. Ecclesiastical Return, *Statistical Register* (NSW), 1870, 1880, 1890, 1901; (Vic), 1870, 1800, 1890, 1900. The Return for New South Wales probably includes some Union Churches, modest wood and iron buildings, shared by two or three denominations in remote districts. Sometimes they are indicated, but their number is not known. For an alternative estimate of the number of church buildings, see W. Phillips, "Christianity and its defence in New South Wales circa 1880 to 1890" (Ph.D. thesis, Australian National University, 1969) pp. 93-96, 449-50.

32. The numbers of churches are estimated as far as possible from denominational sources. See ibid.

33. *SMH*, 24 August 1885, 4 March 1891; *MPGA*, 1890, p. 150. The number of Presbyterian "preaching centres" includes church buildings as well as other places, such as schools and halls, where religious services were held.

34. *Weekly Advocate*, 1 September 1888. See also letter, "J.H.W.", ibid., 13 October 1883; *SMH*, 28 January 1885. See also "Early methodism at Bourke", *Journal and Proceedings of the Australasian Methodist Historical Society, Sydney*, no. 89 (1969), pp. 1228-89 and White, *Challenge of the Years*, p. 268.

35. J.E. Carruthers, *Memories of an Australian Ministry, 1868-1921* (London: Epworth Press, 1922), p. 85; F.W. Bourne, *The Bible Christians* (London: Bible Christian Bookroom, 1905), p. 354.

36. According to the "General Returns of the United Church in New South Wales — 1902" there were sixty-nine Primitive Methodist churches and ten United Methodist Free churches. The *Statistical Register* for 1980 lists eighty-one Primitive Methodist churches. Unfortunately the Primitive Methodist records for the 1880s have not survived although a newspaper report of the Annual Assembly in 1889 states that there were seventy-eight churches in the colony and new churches were under construction, thus the *Statistical Register* figure for 1890 seems accurate enough. I have found no explanation for the lower figure recorded in 1902. See F.H. McGowan, "Jubilee of Australasian Methodist Church Union", *Journal and Proceedings of the Australasian Methodist Historical Society, Sydney*, no. 623 (1952), p. 851; *ACW*, 21 February 1889.

37. *NSW Baptist*, January, March 1887; *NSW Independent*, 15 May 1887; *MWC*, 1891, pp. 114-15.

38. W. Phillips, "Religious Profession and Practice in New South Wales: The Statistical Evidence", *Historical Studies* 15 (1972-73): 390.

39. *Freeman's Journal*, 4 June 1887. See also *Nation* (Sydney), 23 January 1890.

40. Gilbert, *Religion and Society*, pp. 161-62.

41. *Presbyterian*, 28 November 1885; *ACW*, 18 June 1886; *Wesleyan Chronicle* (Melbourne), February 1867, p. 51, quoted in Renate Howe, "The Wesleyan Church in Victoria, 1855-1901: Its Ministry and Membership" (M.A. thesis, University of Melbourne, 1965), p. 9; *DT*, 19 October 1885.

42. *Presbyterian*, 6 August 1881; David Moore, ibid., 9 October 1880; *Weekly Advocate*, 8 April 1882; S.M. Johnstone, *The Book of St. Andrew's Cathedral*, rev. ed. (Sydney: Angus and Robertson, 1968), p. 29; R. Sutherland, *The Presbyterian Church of Victoria* (London: James Nisbet and Co., 1877), p. 352. See also J. Cameron, *Centenary History of the Presbyterian Church in New South Wales* (Sydney: Angus and Robertson, 1905), pp. 125-27.

43. *SMH*, 20 January 1885, *NSW Baptist*, 4 October 1888; Crown Street Primitive Methodist Church, Sydney, 1st Quarterly Meeting, Minute Book, 1873-1893, 13 March 1893, Uniting Church in Australia, New South Wales Synod, Records and Historical Society.

44. *Australian Churchman* (Sydney), 10 July 1884; *PSDS*, 1885, p. 19; W.M. Cowper, *The Autobiography and Reminiscences of William Macquarie Cowper, Dean. of Sydney* (Sydney: Angus and Robertson, 1902), pp. 196-97.

45. K.J. Cable, "Training for the Ministry in the Mid-Nineteenth Century", in John Garrett and L.W. Farr, *Camden College: A Centenary History*, (Glebe: Camden College, 1964), pp. 63-67; K.T. Livingston, *The Emergence of an Australian Catholic Priesthood, 1835-1915* (Sydney: Catholic Theological Faculty, 1977), esp. chaps. 1-3 and pp. 253-58.

46. For an account of the beginning of the denominational theological institutions in New South Wales, see J. Colwell, *The Illustrated History of Methodism* (Sydney: William Brooks & Co., 1904), pp. 599-604; Garrett and Farr, *Camden College pp. 63-67;* Prior, *Some Fell on Good Ground*, pp. 228-33; White, *Challenge of the Years*, pp. 197-98. On Victoria see D. Chambers, "A Sketch of the Institutional Framework of Victorian Protestant Theological Education from 1860 to the Present", *Journal of the Australian and New Zealand History of Education Society* 7, no. 1 (1978): 36-59. See also W. Phillips, "An Idea that Gave Rise to a University: The Story of Union College, Adelaide, 1872-1886", *Australian Congregationalist* (Sydney), July 1972, pp. 9-10.

47. *PSDS*, 1881, pp. 23-24; *Presbyterian*, 25 November 1890; P.F. Moran, *Pastoral Letter . . . to the Clergy of the Archdiocese, 1885*, (Sydney [1885]); *PSDN*, 1891, p. 12.

48. *PSDS*, 1887, pp. 102-3; *PSDN*, 1886, p. 24.

49. *SMH*, 29 May 1888; W. Jackson, ibid., 1 June 1888.

50. See Report, Sustentation Fund Committee, 1892, *MPGA*, 1893, pp. 97-100; for 1900, ibid., 1901, pp. 126-28. Anglican stipends were published in the *Sydney Diocesan Directory*. See also H.R. Jackson, "Aspects of Congregationalism in South-Eastern Australia circa 1880 to 1930" (Ph.D. thesis, Australian National University, 1978), p. 221; *Presbyterian*, 29 January 1881. For a discussion of wages in the 1880s, see T.A. Coghlan, *Labour and Industry from the First Settlement to the Establishment of the Commonwealth in 1901*, 4 vols. (Oxford: Oxford University Press, 1918), 3: 1425-1590; P.G. McCarthy, "Wages in Australia, 1891-1914", *Australian Economic History Review* 10 (1970): 56-76.

51. *SMH*, 24 January 1883; *MWC*, 1885, 22-23.

52. Alfred Allen, "Helps and Hindrances to Lay Preachers", *NSW Independent*, 15 January 1880; *MWC*, 1885, p. 66, 1886, p. 76. The Protestant denominations challenged this "illiberal" proscription. The ban was lifted in 1911. *MWC*, 1880, pp. 52-53, and *Minutes, Wesleyan General Conference*, 1890, p. 44; *Congregational Year Book*, 1890, p. 88; *PSDN*, 1884, pp. 29-30. On the status and disabilities of state school teachers as public servants, see B. Mitchell, *Teachers, Education and Politics* (St. Lucia: University of Queensland Press, 1975), pp.4-8, 30-32.

53. *Proceedings, Provincial Synod of NSW*, 1879, p. 19; *PSDS*, 1883, p. 23; *SMH*, 15 July 1884.

54. *St. James' Kalendar and Monthly Record* (Sydney), February 1889, pp. 302-3; Chambers, "Victorian Protestant Theological Education", pp. 40-41; Livingston, *Australian Catholic Priesthood*, p. 83.

55. White, *Challenge of the Years*, pp. 197-98; W.E. Bennett, "The History of Leigh College", *Journal and Proceedings Australasian Methodist Historical Society* 6 (1937): 263-67; C. Irving Benson, ed., *A Century of Victorian Methodism* (Melbourne: Spectator Publishing Co., 1935), pp. 270-79. On the New South Wales conference and Sugden, see *SMH*, 24 January 1885.

56. *PSDN*, 1886, pp. 22-23; *Presbyterian*, 10 September 1881; *MPGA*, 1875, p. 13; J. Jefferis, "A Plea for an Educated Ministry", (Sydney [1877]); *Report, Intercolonial Congregational Conference, Sydney, 1883*, pp. 130-35.

57. *The Presbyterian Church of New South Wales: A Paper Prepared by the Church Extension Committee . . . 1877*, p. 6. *Presbyterian*, 11 February 1898. The numbers of graduates in the various denominations in New South Wales are based

on denomination lists, the Return of Ministers registered to celebrate marriages in *Government Gazette* (NSW) 25 January 1890, and Teale, "By Hook and By Crook", p. 104. For Victoria, see *Year Book of the Diocese of Melbourne*, 1899-1900, pp. 30-35; *Year Book of the Presbyterian Church of Victoria for 1900*, pp. 64-73; Martin Dyson, ed., *Australasian Methodist Ministerial General Index* (Melbourne: Mason, Firth and McCutcheon, 1889).

58. *SMH*, 7 February 1884; Bishop Thomas, "To the Church Wardens & Others in Adelong District", 4 November 1879, in Thorn, ed., *Letters from Goulburn*, pp. 57-58; *PSDS*, 1883, p. 23; *PSDN*, 1886, pp. 22-23.

59. *Report, Intercolonial Congregational Conference, Sydney, 1883*, pp. 141-42; *MWC*, 1885, p. 56; Howe, "Wesleyan Church in Victoria", p. 183.

60. "Report of Committee on the subject of Candidates for Holy Orders", *PSDS*, 1887, 169-80; "R", *Presbyterian*, 30 December 1882; W.S. Fielden to W.J. Green, 28 August 1883, Congregational Union Papers, Mitchell Library. See also P. O'Farrell, *The Catholic Church and Community in Australia: A History* (Melbourne: Nelson, 1977), pp. 354-58.

61. Elkin, *Diocese of Newcastle*, pp. 166-67. I am also indebted to Associate Professor K.J. Cable for information supplied on Anglican clergy in the colony. For Gilchrist, *SMH*, 17 December 1896. See also Carruthers, *Memories*. On scientist clergymen, see *Presbyterian*, 14 April 1883.

62. *Express* (Sydney), 1 July 1882; O'Farrell, *Catholic Church and Community*, pp. 357-58.

63. *Sydney Diocesan Directory*; Teale, "By Hook and By Crook", p. 95; some information also supplied by K.J. Cable.

64. *Presbyterian Church in New South Wales: Paper Presented by the Church Extension Committee . . . 1877*; *MPGA*, 1890, pp. 49-52. For the origins of Presbyterian ministers inducted into charges in the 1880s, see Ministers' Roll, in White, *Challenge of the Years*, pp. 552-92.

65. Origins of Wesleyan ministers compiled from stationing lists 1880 and 1890, excluding Queensland, and from G. Kingston Daws, ed., *Methodist Ministerial Index for Australasia* (Melbourne: Methodist General Conference, 1962), pp. 180-207. For Victoria, see Howe, "The Wesleyan Church in Victoria", p. 138. On Congregationalists, *Congregational Year Book*, 1880, pp. 88-91; 1890, pp. 180-84. See also Chairman's Address, ibid., 1890, p. 71. For Baptists, see Prior, *Some Fell on Good Ground*, p. 226.

66. Cowper's comment is in Circulars of the Diocese of Sydney, 1842-1895, Circulars of the Diocese of Sydney, No. 251 (11 February 1890).

67. "R.K.", *Presbyterian*, 20 January 1883; John Fraser, ibid., 11 November 1882; *ACW*, 1 August 1890. For beginning of the Bush Brotherhood see C.H.S. Matthews, *A Parson in the Australian Bush*, rev. ed. (Adelaide: Rigby, 1973), esp. chaps. 7-10.

68. *SMH*, 24 June 1888; G. Grimm, *A Concise History of Australia* (Sydney: Angus and Robertson [1891]), p. 74.

3. Waves of Revival

1. *Presbyterian*, 21 January 1882. Walker entered the ministry after his arrival in Australia.

2. George Smith, *A Modern Apostle, Alexander N. Somerville, D.D., 1813-1889* (London: John Murray, 1890), esp. pp. 162-64.

3. For a description of "California" Taylor's mission in Sydney and Melbourne, see J.S. Austin, *Missionary Enterprise and Home Mission Service* (Sydney, n.d.),

pp. 52-55; W.L. Blamires and J.B. Smith, *The Early Story of the Wesleyan Methodist Church in Victoria* (Melbourne: Wesleyan Book Depot, 1886), pp. 97-99; J. Bickford, *An Autobiography of Christian Labour...* (London: Charles Kelly, 1890), pp. 181-82, 232-33; J. Colwell, *The Illustrated History of Methodism* (Sydney: William Brooks & Co., 1904), pp. 408-9. See also Renate Howe, "The Wesleyan Church in Victoria, 1855-1901: Its Ministry and Membership" (M.A. thesis, University of Melbourne, 1965), pp. 13-14.

4. Smith, *A Modern Apostle*, p. 171. On Moody and Sankey, see W.G. McLoughlin, Jr., *Modern Revivalism, Charles Grandison Finney to Billy Graham* (New York: The Ronald Press Company, 1959), chap. 4; J. Kent, *Holding the Fort: Studies in Victorian Revivalism* (London: Epworth Press, 1978), chaps. 3-5.

5. *SMH*, 10 September 1877; *Evening News* (Sydney), 11 September 1877.

6. *SMH*, 17, 18, 25 September 1877; *Evening News*, 18 September 1877. The full text of Somerville's sermon, "The Fiery Furnace", is included in Smith, *A Modern Apostle*, pp. 402-14. See also ibid., p. 174.

7. *SMH*, 28 September 1877; *Evening News*, 29 September 1877; Smith, *A Modern Apostle*, p. 177.

8. *SMH*, 6 October 1877.

9. J.T. Massey, *The YMCA in Australia* (Melbourne: Cheshire, 1950), p. 508. On the YMCA and evangelism, see also McLoughlin, *Modern Revivalism*, p. 222.

10. *Presbyterian*, 27 May 1882; *Weekly Advocate*, 22 July 1882.

11. See *SMH*, 24 January 1882, 15 April 1885; *DT*, 11 February 1884.

12. *S.A. Register*, 23 July, 2 August 1883.

13. *SMH*, 1, 18, 24 September, 23 October 1883.

14. *S.A. Advertiser* 23 July 1883. See also *S.A. Register*, 23 July 1883; *Echo* (Sydney), 17 September 1883; *Weekly Advocate*, 22 September 1883.

15. *SMH*, 24 September, 20 October (Religious Announcements), 23 October 1883; *S.A. Register*, 2 August 1883.

16. *NSW Independent*, 15 May 1887.

17. *S.A. Register*, 2 August 1883. See also B.H. Harrison, *Drink and the Victorians: The Temperance Question in England, 1815-1872* (London: Faber and Faber, 1971), chap. 8; M. Roe, *Quest for Authority in Eastern Australia, 1825-1851* (Melbourne: Melbourne University Press, 1965), chap. 8; McLoughlin, *Modern Revivalism*, pp. 232-33.

18. *SMH*, 13, 14 July, 5 September 1882.

19. Ibid., 7-10, 13 May 1884, 29 December 1886.

20. *DT*, 3, 8 July 1886; *ACW*, 9, 16 July 1886.

21. Blamires and Smith, *Wesleyan Methodist Church*, pp. 95-97; C. Irving Benson ed., *A Century of Victorian Methodism* (Melbourne: Spectator Publishing Co., 1935), pp. 129-30; *S.A. Register*, 10 April, 17 May 1880, and letter, M. Burnett, ibid., 17 April 1880; *SMH*, 15 July 1889.

22. *S.A. Register*, 10 May 1880 (see also Religious notices, April and May); *SMH*, 13 July 1889 (Religious Announcements), 15, 16, 18 July 1889.

23. *S.A. Register*, 26 April 1880; *SMH*, 15, 23 July 1889.

24. *SMH*, 31 May 1884.

25. C.W. Mackintosh, *Dr. Harry Guinness: The Life Story of Henry Grattan Guinness* (London: Regions Beyond Missionary Union, 1916), p. 22.

26. *SMH*, 26 June 1886; *ACW*, 2, 7 July 1886; *DT*, 7 July 1886; Mackintosh, *Dr. Harry Guinness*, pp. 22-28, 34. See also H. Grattan Guinness, "Men in Relation to the Social Evil" in *Public Morals* ed. J. Marchant (London [1902]), pp. 135-46.

27. Varley returned to England in 1910 and preached chiefly in the Glynn Vivian Miners' Mission Hall at Brighton almost until his death on 30 March 1912. See

Henry Varley Junior, *Henry Varley's Life-Story* (London: Alfred Holness, [1916]).

28.　*ACW*, 26 September 1889.

29.　Only two per cent of the cases of insanity in 1886 were attributed to sexual "intemperance", "self abuse" or venereal disease, and the latter accounted for around 0.3-0.4 per cent of deaths in the period 1876-85. Illegitimate births, however, while lower than in England, were increasing in New South Wales — from 7.13 per cent of births in 1871-75 to 13.61 per cent in 1886. T.A. Coghlan, *The Wealth and Progress of New South Wales, 1886-87* (Sydney, 1887) pp. 163-66, 187-88; *Thirteenth Annual Report from the Registrar General on Vital Statistics [for the year 1885]*, p. 11, in *V&PLA* (NSW), 1887, 5: 257-313.

30.　*ACW* 26 September 1889. See also Henry Varley, "Lecture to Men (Containing invaluable information for young men and all who are married)", 4th ed. (London [1884]); "Private Address to Boys and Youths on an Important Subject" (Melbourne, 1893).

31.　*ACW*, 19 September 1889. *The Dead Bird*, later *Bird O' Freedom* then the *Arrow*, began publication in 1889. See James Murray, *Larrikins, 19th Century Outrage* (Melbourne: Lansdowne Press, 1973).

32.　*ACW*, 26 September, 3 October, 21 November 1889; *Echo*, 24 September 1889. See also Henry Varley, *Five Addresses on the Second Coming of our Lord and the Subsequent Events* (Melbourne, 1878).

33.　*ACW*, 28 November 1889.

34.　*Echo*, 28 September 1889; *SMH*, 26 September (Religious Announcements), 27, 28 September 1889. There were references to an Evangelical Alliance in Sydney before 1889 but it does not seem to have been officially constituted before this date.

35.　*Church of England Guardian*, 7 December 1889.

36.　Canon [A.D.] Soares, "Parochial Missions", *Questions of the Day: A Series of Papers . . . read at a Clerical Conference held at Bishopsthorpe, Goulburn, N.S.W., 5, 6 and 7 October 1881* (Sydney, 1882), p. 55.

37.　*SMH*, 2 February 1880; *MWC*, 1885, pp. 11, 75; *MPGA*, 1884, pp. 27, 32. See also Report, Committee on Religion and Morals, 1883 in ibid., p. 48.

38.　*Congregational Year Book*, 1883, p. 76.

39.　*Weekly Advocate*, 23 December 1882; *SMH*, 19 January 1887, 27 January 1885, 2 February 1883; Austin, *Missionary Enterprise*, pp. 281-82, 309-10.

40.　*SMH*, 4 February 1885; *Presbyterian*, 7 March 1885.

41.　*SMH*, 20 April, 15, 19 June 1885; *PSDS*, 1885, pp. 19-20.

42.　*Proceedings of the General Synod of the [Anglican] Dioceses in Australia and Tasmania*, 1886, p. 18 (hereafter cited as *Proceedings, General Synod*).

43.　*ACW*, 28 May 1886. See chapter 4 for Barry's attempt to introduce the Church Army into his diocese.

44.　*Presbyterian*, 10 July 1886; Report, Committee on Religion and Morals, 1885, *MPGA*, 1886, pp. 49-50; *Presbyterian*, 12 June 1886. Criticisms were also made at the Presbytery of Sydney in May. See ibid., 22 May 1886.

45.　See Report, Committee on Religion and Morals, 1888, *MPGA*, 1889, p. 52. On John MacNeil, see C.A. White, *Challenge of the Years: A History of the Presbyterian Church of Australia in the State of New South Wales* (Sydney: Angus and Robertson, 1951), pp. 37-38, 561, and Hannah MacNeil, *John MacNeil: Late Evangelist in Australia and Author of "The Spirit-Filled Life"* (London: Marshall Brothers, 1897).

46.　*ACW*, 8, 15, 22 January 1886; *Weekly Advocate*, 18 April 1885. See also Bowring's reports to the conference; *SMH*, 4 February 1886, 7 February 1887.

47.　E.C. Pritchard, *Under the Southern Cross* (London: W.A. Hammond, 1914), pp. 119-27.

48. *DT*, 26 January 1885; *Weekly Advocate*, 31 January 1885; J.E. Carruthers, *Memories of an Australian Ministry, 1868-1921* (London: Epworth Press, 1922), p. 99.

49. *Weekly Advocate*, 13 April 1889; *SMH*, 11 November 1889.

50. *Baptist*, 1 May 1889.

51. *MWC*, 1880, p. 60. For a discussion of Wesley's doctrine of Sanctification, see C.W. Williams, *John Wesley's Theology Today* (London: Epworth Press, 1960), chap. 9. On holiness revivalism, see Kent, *Holding the Fort*, pp. 310-24.

52. *Proceedings of the United Methodist Convention for the Spread of Scriptural Holiness* (Sydney, 1886), p. 8.

53. *Weekly Advocate*, 21 May 1881; Austin, *Missionary Enterprise*, pp. 271-72; "X", *Presbyterian*, 28 May 1881, 11 June 1881.

54. *Proceedings, United Methodist Convention*, pp. 3, 38, 75.

55. *ACW*, 8 June 1886.

56. Austin, *Missionary Enterprise*, pp. 308-9.

57. Alan C. Prior, *Some Fell on Good Ground* (Sydney: Baptist Union of New South Wales, 1966), p. 243; Carruthers, *Memories*, p. 95; Austin, *Missionary Enterprise*, pp. 296-97.

58. *Pastoral Plenary Council, 1885*, p. 4; *Decrees of the Diocesan Synod of Sydney, 1891* (Sydney, 1891) Decree 32. On Redemptorists, see *DT*, 5 May 1884. See also P. O'Farrell, *The Catholic Church and Community in Australia: A History* (Melbourne: Nelson, 1977), pp. 211-12, 245.

59. Carruthers, *Memories*, p. 99; W.G. Taylor, *The Life Story of An Australian Evangelist* (London: Epworth Press, 1920), pp. 174-76; Austin, *Missionary Enterprise*, pp. 281-82, 311-12.

60. William Walkwary, *ACW*, 26 November 1886.

61. See M. Argyle and B. Beit-Hallahmi, *The Social Psychology of Religion* (London and Boston: Routledge and Kegan Paul, 1975, first published as *Religious Behaviour*, 1958), p. 42.

62. Austin, *Missionary Enterprise*, pp. 293-94, 310; *SMH*, 28 January 1882.

63. ACW, 2 April 1886.

64. Argyle and Beit-Hallahmi, *Social Psychology of Religion*, pp. 59-61.

65. Quoted in McLoughlin, *Modern Revivalism*, p. 232.

66. *Report, Intercolonial Congregational Conference, Sydney, 1883*, p. 186; *MPGA*, 1880, p. 36; *Presbyterian*, 19 June 1880.

67. *Minutes, Wesleyan General Conference*, 1875, p. 28; *MWC*, 1876, p. 26; 1881, p. 52.

68. See W. Phillips, "Religious Profession and Practice in New South Wales, 1850-1901: The Statistical Evidence", *Historical Studies* 15 (1972-73): 394-98, and R. Currie, A. Gilbert and L. Horsley, *Churches and Churchgoers* (Oxford: Clarendon Press, 1977), pp. 79-80, 86-87.

69. *Weekly Advocate*, 12 November 1881; J. Hill, "Evangelistic Enterprise", *Congregational Year Book*, 1885, p. 103; *Presbyterian*, 8 October 1887.

70. Austin, *Missionary Enterprise*, p. 294; *MPGA*, 1886, p. 48.

71. See McLoughlin, *Modern Revivalism*, p. 281 and passim; S.D. Clark, *Church and Sect in Canada* (Toronto: University of Toronto Press, 1948), esp. pp. 354, 401.

72. *ACW*, 26 November 1886.

73. The late Miss G.A. Roseby told the author this story in an interview in November 1966, when she was 94 years of age. For discussion of theological changes in the period, see chapter 5.

74. J.F. Hogan, *The Sister Dominions: Through Canada to Australia by the New Imperial Highway* (Sydney: Ward & Downey, 1896), pp. 135-36.

75. McLoughlin, *Modern Revivalism*, p. 377.

76. See Richard Broome, *Treasure in Earthen Vessels: Protestant Christianity in New*

South Wales, 1900-1914 (St. Lucia: University of Queensland Press, 1980) chap. 4; Renate Howe, "The Response of the Protestant Churches to Urbanization in Melbourne and Chicago, 1875-1914" (Ph.D. thesis, University of Melbourne, 1972), pp. 290-96; McLoughlin, *Modern Revivalism,* p. 378.

4. Worship for the Working Classes

1. *SMH,* 12 May 1888. The adult population in this case includes those aged fifteen and over. See W. Phillips, "Religious Profession and Practice in New South Wales, 1850-1901: The Statistical Evidence", *Historical Studies* 15 (1972-73): 387-89.
2. *NSW Independent,* 15 October 1884. See also J. Kent, *Holding the Fort: Studies in Victorian Revivalism* (London: Epworth Press, 1978), pp. 360-62.
3. See letters, *SMH,* 2, 4, 9, 17, 19, 22, 25, 29 May 1888.
4. Changes in worship in colonial churches around the 1880s are fully discussed in W.W. Phillips, "Christianity and its defence in New South Wales circa 1880 to 1890" (Ph.D. thesis, Australian National University, 1969), pp. 128-49.
5. See K.S. Inglis, *Churches and the Working Classes in Victorian England* (London: Routledge and Kegan Paul, 1963), esp. pp. 1-20.
6. *Freeman's Journal,* 2 June 1888. See also Jefferis's sermon "The Alienation of the Working Classes", *DT,* 12 November 1889.
7. See J. Rickard, *Class and Politics: New South Wales, Victoria and the Early Commonwealth, 1890-1910* (Canberra: Australian National University Press, 1976), pp. 288-89 and S. Macintyre, "The Making of the Australian Working Class: An Historiographical Survey", *Historical Studies* 18 (1978-79): 233-53.
8. *Congregational Year Book,* 1882, p. 45; *DT,* 12 November 1889. Twopeny comments that "The working-classes . . . can afford to be better dressed than at home". R.E.N. Twopeny, *Town Life in Australia* (London: Elliot Stock, 1883), p. 81. See also Rickard, *Class and Politics,* pp. 290-93.
9. *Presbyterian,* 14 September 1889; *Weekly Advocate,* 23 June 1888.
10. *SMH,* 9 May 1888.
11. Ibid.; Bourke's Church Act of 1836 (or An Act to promote the Building of Churches and Chapels and to provide for the maintenance of Ministers of Religion in New South Wales) 7 William IV, No. 3 and the English Church Temporalities Act of 1837, 8 William IV, No. 8. On the custom of pew-renting in England, see Owen Chadwick, *The Victorian Church,* 2 vols. (London: Adam and Charles Black, 1966 and 1970), 1: 329-31.
12. *PSDN,* 1882, pp. 28-29, 1885, p. 17; "One of the Visitors", *NSW Independent,* 15 May 1890.
13. Mary Gilmore, *Old Days, Old Ways* (Sydney: Angus and Robertson, 1934), pp. 69-70; *Weekly Advocate,* 15 August 1885. See also "A Stranger and Ye took me not in", *SMH,* 17 February 1880; "A Methodist", *Weekly Advocate,* 31 May 1890; "Another Old Methodist", ibid., 14 June 1890.
14. *Australian Churchman* (Sydney), 14 October, 4 November 1880; *MSDB,* 1882, pp. 11-12.
15. R. Whitycombe, "Church of England Attitudes to Social Questions in the Diocese of Sydney c. 1856-1866", *JRAHS* 47, no. 2 (1961): 106. On the campaign for free and open churches in Britain, see Inglis, *Churches and Working Classes,* pp. 48-57.
16. *PSDN,* 1884, pp. 22-25.
17. *Proceedings, Provincial Synod,* 1884, pp. 11-12; A. Barry, *A Charge delivered at his*

Primary Visitation of the Diocese, pp. 11-12; *PSDS*, 1886, p. 81. For pew-rents at St. James's, see Ecclesiastical Returns, *PSDS*, 1886, 1891.

18. *PSDN*, 1884, p. 25.
19. *MPGA*, 1881, p. 87; *MWC*, 1877, p. 17, 1894, p. 63.
20. *Weekly Advocate*, 17 May 1884; J.S. Austin, *Missionary Enterprise and Home Mission Service* (Sydney, n.d.), p. 323; *PSDN*, 1884, pp. 22-25, 1885, p. 17. See also the *Australian Churchman*, 14 October and 9 December 1880.
21. *SMH*, 8 May 1884; *PSDN*, 1884, p. 26.
22. *Proceedings, Provincial Synod*, 1884, pp. 11-12, 1887, pp. 15-16; *Church of England Guardian*, 14 April 1888.
23. See *Proceedings, Provincial Synod*, 1872, pp. 8-9, 1875, pp. 22, 26; *PSDG*, 1868, pp. 16, 20-21, 1871, p. 31.
24. *Proceedings, Provincial Synod*, 1879, p. 33, 1887, p. 27; *PSDS*, 1883, p. 41, 1884, p. 57.
25. *PSDS*, (Special synod, December 1888), pp. 19-20. See also *Proceedings, Provincial Synod*, 1892, Appendix 23: 161-74.
26. *Proceedings, Provincial Synod*, 1895, p. 45; Church Acts Repealing Act, 1897, Act No. 16. On the inclusion of married women in the definition of "Occupiers of seats", see *Proceedings, Provincial Synod*, 1901, p. 80, 1904, pp. 37-38, 69.
27. *PSDS*, 1889, p. 61. See also *PSDN*, 1884, pp. 22-25.
28. *MPGA*, 1890, p. 103, 1901, pp. 124-25; *Year Book of the Congregational Church, Pitt Street, Sydney*, 1879-80, p. 7; *Report, Intercolonial Congregational Conference, Sydney, 1883*, pp. 181-84.
29. *Year Book*, Woollahra (Point Piper Road) Congregational Church, 1880, p. 114; Renate Howe, "The Wesleyan Church in Victoria, 1855-1901: Its Ministry and Membership" (M.A. thesis, University of Melbourne, 1965), pp. 106-7.
30. *Age* (Melbourne), 3 October 1979.
31. Z. Barry, *SMH*, 29 May 1888; Inglis, *Churches and Working Classes*, pp. 56-57.
32. S. Meacham, "The Church in the Victorian City", *Victorian Studies* 2 (1967-68): 361.
33. *PSDS*, 1881, p. 19.
34. On Pigeon, see *Australian Dictionary of Biography* 2:333. On Goold, see Minutes, Committee of the City Mission in Connection with the Congregational Church, Pitt Street, Sydney, 10 October 1849 and subsequently, Congregational Union Papers, Mitchell Library.
35. *Year Book, Congregational Church, Pitt Street, Sydney*, 1879-80, p. 6; *ACW*, 26 February 1886. See also *Pitt Street Congregational Church Manual,* 1890, pp. 28-29.
36. On Short, see the Sydney City Mission's brochure, *Ten Decades: A History of Sydney City Mission* (Sydney 1962).
37. *SMH*, 24 January 1883.
38. *Presbyterian*, 17 February 1883.
39. J.W.C. Wand, *Anglicanism in History and Today* (London: Weidenfeld and Nicolson, 1961), pp. 180-81.
40. *PSDS*, 1885, pp. 26-29; *Church of England Record* (Sydney), 15 August 1884.
41. *SMH*, 26 October 1885.
42. "Ultimo", *Australian Churchman*, 29 October 1885, "Anglicanus", ibid., 5 November 1885; ibid., 24 December 1885.
43. See *PSDS*, 1885, pp. 28, 62, 128-31. The question of sisterhoods or deaconesses generated some debate among Anglicans in the 1880s and in 1891 the General Synod decided in favour of both sisterhoods and deaconesses. *Proceedings, General Synod*, 1891, p. 60. See also Laura Mary Allen, *A History of Christ Church S. Laurence*, (Sydney, [1939]), p. 58.

44. *Australian Churchman*, 24 December 1885, 8 January 1886.
45. *PSDS*, 1886, pp. 25-26; *ACW*, 28 May 1886; Allen, *Christ Church S. Laurence*, pp. 57-58.
46. See J.S. Cowland, *Mine Eyes have seen the Glory* (Newcastle, 1946), and A.W. Batley, *Soldiers of the Cross: The Story of the Church Army in Australia*, rev. ed. (Newcastle, 1959). See also Renate Howe, "The Response of the Protestant Churches to Urbanization in Melbourne and Chicago, 1875-1914" (Ph.D. thesis, University of Melbourne, 1972), p.456. Nothing seems to have been known of this abortive attempt to establish the Church Army in Sydney in 1885.
47. J. Colwell, *The Illustrated History of Methodism* (Sydney: William Brooks & Co., 1904), pp. 292-96, 531; J.E. Carruthers, "A Half-Century's Retrospect", cuttings from a journal [1921], in Mitchell Library, pp. 37-38. For the origin of Ichabod, see Old Testament, 1 Sam. 4:21-22.
48. *SMH*, 28 January 1882, 31 January 1883; *Weekly Advocate*, 12 August, 16 September 1882.
49. W.G. Taylor, *The Life Story of an Australian Evangelist* (London: Epworth Press, 1920), pp. 131-32; Colwell, *History of Methodism*, pp. 531-32.
50. Taylor, *Australian Evangelist*, pp. 136-37. See also J.E. Carruthers, *Memories of an Australian Ministry, 1886-1921* (London: Epworth Press, 1922), p. 135.
51. See Inglis, *Churches and Working Classes*, pp. 91-93 and N. Hicks, "The Establishment of a Central Methodist Mission in Adelaide", (B.A. Hons. thesis, University of Adelaide, 1966), pp. 5-10.
52. Taylor, *Australian Evangelist*, p. 139. In 1908 the mission took over the Lyceum Theatre, given by Ebenezer Vickery, MLC. Ibid., and chap. 22.
53. Ibid., pp. 285-87.
54. *SMH*, 3 February 1888.
55. *Weekly Advocate*, 23 June 1889.
56. *MWC*, 1889, pp. 12, 104-5, 1890, p. 12.
57. *Weekly Advocate*, 9 August 1890; Taylor, *Australian Evangelist*, pp. 195-212.
58. See Inglis, *Churches and Working Classes*, pp. 79-85 and J.D. Bollen, *Protestantism and Social Reform in New South Wales, 1890-1910* (Melbourne: Melbourne University Press, 1972), passim.
59. Taylor, *Australian Evangelist*, p. 179. See also Colwell, *History of Methodism*, pp. 535-44.
60. Howe, "Response of the Protestant Churches", pp. 231-33; see also Hicks, "The Establishment of a Central Methodist Mission in Adelaide".
61. (Primitive Methodists) *SMH*, 11 February 1889; *ACW*, 30 January 1890; (Clarke) *SMH*, 19 January 1889 and also *NSW Baptist*, February, March, April, August 1889.
62. Minutes, Church Meeting, Pitt Street Congregational Church, 5 September 1889 (held by Pitt Street Congregational Church).
63. See *Congregational Year Book*, 1883, p. 74; *Presbyterian*, 17 February 1883; *SMH*, 19 January 1887; *PSDS*, 1886, pp. 25-26.
64. According to Dr. Howe this was the case with the P.S.A. in Melbourne. Dr Bollen tells us what was said at the Sydney P.S.A., but not who heard it. Howe, "Wesleyan Church in Victoria", pp. 120-21; Bollen, *Protestantism and Social Reform*, p. 165.
65. Taylor, *Australian Evangelist*, p. 165.

5. Defending the Faith

1. See F.B. Smith, "Spiritualism in Victoria in the Nineteenth Century", *JRH* 3 (1964-65): 246-60, and "Religion and Freethought in Melbourne, 1870-1890 (M.A. thesis, University of Melbourne, 1960).

2. C. Bright, "Rationalism versus Dogma: Two Lectures delivered at the Theatre Royal, Sydney, in Review of Archbishop Vaughan's Lenten Discourses" (Sydney, 1879), pp. 9-10.

3. Quoted in *ACW*, 18 June 1886.

4. *Evening News,* 24 October 1883.

5. These titles appear in advertisements for lectures and sermons in the *Evening News,* September-December 1883.

6. *Bulletin* (Sydney), 24 July 1880, quoted in *Bulletin,* 30 July 1966.

7. R.W.B. Vaughan, "Hidden Springs; or, the Perils of the Future and how to Meet Them" (Sydney, 1876), pp. 36, 59; "A Suggestion for Lent: A Pastoral Letter to the Clergy and Laity of the Archdiocese of Sydney" (Sydney, 1881).

8. J. Jefferis, Pastoral Report, *Year Book of the Congregational Church, Pitt Street, Sydney,* 1879-80, pp. 5-7.

9. R.W.B. Vaughan, "Arguments for Christianity" (Sydney, 1879), esp. advertisement and p. 2; *Christ's Divinity . . . in Six Lectures, Lent 1882* (Sydney, 1882).

10. *Protestant Standard,* 25 August 1883; Bright, "Rationalism versus Dogma", p. 9.

11. *PSDS,* 1880, pp. 24-25.

12. *SMH,* 28, 30 January 1882.

13. *Presbyterian,* 28 June 1884, 28 January 1882.

14. Z. Barry, "Christian Free-Thought Sermons" (Sydney, 1876); C. Perry, "Science and the Bible" (Melbourne, 1869). See also C.C. Gillispie, *Genesis and Geology* (Massachusetts: Harper, 1951), p. 224.

15. The best known and most loathed of the German writers in the English-speaking world was David Strauss, whose *Life of Jesus* ([1835] trans. George Eliot, 1846) postulated that the gospels of the New Testament were mythological compilations dating from the second century. W.B. Boyce, *Six Lectures on Higher Criticism Upon the New Testament* (Sydney, 1878). See also W.B. Glover, *Evangelical Nonconformists and Higher Criticism in the Nineteenth Century* (London: Independent Press, 1954).

16. Canon Scott "Modern Objections to Christianity", *Questions of the Day: A Series of Papers . . . read at a Clerical Conference held at Bishopsthorpe, Goulburn, N.S.W., 5, 6 and 7 October 1881* (Sydney, 1882), p.25.

17. *SMH,* 30 August 1880. See also J. Jefferis, "The Highest Teachings of Astronomy", *Sydney Quarterly Magazine* 1 (1884): 234-46. See also William Paley, *Natural Theology Selections,* ed. Frederick Ferre (New York: Bobbs Merrill, 1963) and D.L. Le Mahieu, *The Mind of William Paley* (Lincoln: University of Nebraska Press, 1976).

18. G. Higinbotham, "Science and Religion, or the Relations of Modern Science with the Christian Churches" (Melbourne, 1883), esp. pp. 14-18.

19. *Weekly Advocate,* 5 August 1882; E. Merrick, "Charles Darwin", *Sydney University Review,* no. 3 (July 1882), pp. 244-53; T. Jeffrey Parker, "Charles Darwin", *Victorian Review* 6 (1882-83): 387-403; *SMH,* 30 October 1882.

20. *SMH,* 18 August 1880.

21. A. Renwick, "The Realm of Knowledge and the Realm of Faith, A Lecture delivered . . . to the Young Men's Christian Association on Monday, 10th July 1882" (Sydney, 1882), p. 26.

22. Josiah Mullens (1826-1915) was a member of the Royal Geographical Society and was elected a Fellow of the Royal Society of New South Wales in 1877. In addition to his religious and archaeological interests he was an art lover and for some years vice-president of the National Art Gallery. Obituary, *SMH*, 22 October 1915. The author is grateful to Mr F.H. Mullens, of Mullens and Company, Sydney, for supplying information on his great-grandfather.

23. J. Mullens, "Some Elucidations of Old Testament History from the Records of Assyria and Egypt . . . a Lecture delivered before the Young Men's Christian Association . . . 15 July 1884. (For Private Circulation)" (Sydney, n.d.); *Presbyterian*, 3 December 1881. See also Mullens's review of the Revised Version of the New Testament, *NSW Independent*, 15 August 1881.

24. *Presbyterian*, 8 July 1882.

25. *SMH*, 12-15, 21 July 1882. See also ibid., 22 July 1882 (Religious Announcements).

26. *Presbyterian*, 12 August 1882.

27. E.C. Spicer, "The Harmony Between Geology and Genesis: A Lecture given in reply to Mr Denton's Lecture on 'Science and the Bible' " (Sydney, 1883).

28. C. Bright and E.C. Spicer, "Are the Statements of Science and Genesis Contradictory?" (Sydney, 1883).

29. *Protestant Standard*, 25 August 1883 (a comment on the publication of the debate); *Presbyterian*, 26 May 1883; *Weekly Advocate*, 2 June 1883.

30. J.B. Pearson, "The Duty of the Church of England in Reference to Unbelief", *Papers read at the Church Congress Melbourne, 1882*, (Melbourne, 1882), 48-55.

31. "A Letter for Sunday on the Book called Genesis", *Echo*, 2 June 1883; "A Letter for Sunday on the Use of the Bible", ibid., 9 June 1883.

32. "A Letter for Sunday on the Study of the Book of Genesis, and certain other Practical Matters", ibid., 16 June 1883.

33. On Bishop Moorhouse, see Jill Roe, "Challenge and Response: Religious Life in Melbourne, 1876-1886", *JRH* 5 (1968-69): 149-66.

34. *Weekly Advocate*, 2 June 1883.

35. *SMH*, 17 January 1883. See also reports of the annual meeting, *DT*, 21 April 1884 and *Protestant Standard*, 31 May 1884.

36. *Presbyterian*, 20 January 1883.

37. *Protestant Standard*, 10 February 1883.

38. Ibid., 24 May 1884.

39. *Evening News*, 2 October 1883.

40. *Weekly Advocate*, 13 October 1883.

41. *Evening News*, 6 October 1883. On Ernest Waters, editor of the *Evening News*, see R.B. Walker, *The Newspaper Press in New South Wales, 1803-1920* (Sydney: Sydney University Press, 1976), p. 83.

42. See Progress Report of the Committee on Christian Evidences, *SMH*, 16 September 1884. The committee's activities seem to have received little publicity.

43. *Protestant Standard*, 31 May 1884.

44. The following are Barry's published lectures on apologetics: "What is Natural Theology?" (1877); "Manifold Witness for Christ" (1880); "Some Lights of Science on the Christian Faith" (1892). He was also Hulsean Lecturer in 1894. See *Dictionary of Natural Biography*, Supplement, 1 (1901-11): 103-5.

45. *SMH*, 16 September 1884.

46. Ibid., 18 October 1884.

47. Quoted in *Weekly Advocate*, 11 April 1885.

48. *SMH*, 19 November 1884; *Freeman's Journal*, 20 September 1884; *Weekly Advocate*, 25 October, 29 November 1884.

49. *SMH*, 19 November 1884.

50. Ibid.

51. Ibid., 16 May 1885.
52. C. Loring Brace, *Gesta Christi; or, A History of Humane Progress under Christianity* (London: Hodder and Stoughton, 1882). A New Englander, Brace expounded the liberal free trade creed and also exhibited a liberal theological outlook. Profoundly Protestant and Anglo-Saxon in outlook, he displayed a complacent confidence in the progress of human society towards perfection.
53. A. Barry, "Christian Evidence and Christian Faith", *Witness for Christ: Lectures delivered in connection with the Christian Evidence Society of New South Wales in 1884* [actually 1885] (Sydney, 1886), pp. 3-16; *Presbyterian,* 23 May 1885.
54. All the lectures in this series were published in *Witness for Christ.*
55. Canon [W.H.] Sharp, "How Does the Theory of Evolution Bear Upon Religious Belief?", *Witness for Christ,* pp. 99-112. On English churchmen and evolution, see Owen Chadwick, *The Victorian Church,* 2 vols. (London: Adam and Charles Black, 1966 and 1970), 2: 26.
56. See Annual Report, *SMH,* 10 April 1886; *Weekly Advocate,* 27 March 1886; *ACW,* 28 May 1886; *Protestant Standard,* 28 July 1886.
57. See T. Woolmington Hawkins, "The Secularists' Religion and Christianity", *Protestant Standard,* 12 March 1887, and W.J. McCloskie, "Sydney Secularism Exploded", ibid., 19 March 1887. See also ibid., 1 February 1890 and *ACW,* 11 February 1887.
58. W.G. Taylor, *The Life Story of An Australian Evangelist* (London: Epworth Press, 1920), pp. 174-76; J.S. Austin, *Missionary Enterprise and Home Mission Service* (Sydney, n.d.), pp. 311-12. See also report of sermon preached by G. Preston, *DT,* 21 April 1884 and reports of "infidel death-bed scenes", *Presbyterian,* 3 April 1886.
59. *Protestant Standard,* 19 March 1887; Bradlaugh's letter, ibid., 18 June 1887.
60. *SMH,* 10 April, 6 July 1886; *MSDB,* 1891, pp. 12-13. See also A. Richardson, "The Rise of Modern Biblical Scholarship, and Recent Discussion of the Authority of the Bible", *The Cambridge History of the Bible,* ed. S.L. Greenslade (Cambridge: Cambridge University Press, 1963), 3: 313-14.
61. *SMH,* 17 August 1886; G. Clarke, "Inspiration Not the Ground of our Faith: A Sermon" ([Hobart], 1885), p. 9. On Jowett, see B.M.G. Reardon, ed., *Religious Thought in the Nineteenth Century* (Cambridge: Cambridge University Press, 1966), pp. 321-22.
62. *SMH,* 20 April 1888, 9 April 1889.
63. *SMH,* 20 April 1888, 9 April 1889; H.L. Jackson, "The Church and Modern Thought", *Papers Read at the Church Congress, Sydney, 1889* (Sydney, 1889), pp. 112-21.
64. G. Clarke, "Our Theology in its Present Aspects", *Report, Intercolonial Congregational Conference, Adelaide, 1887,* pp. 64-71; *SMH,* 7 March 1888, 5, 6 March 1890.
65. Ibid., 20 June 1888, 6 March 1889.
66. T. Roseby, "The Genetic Unity of Nature Viewed in a Theistic and Christian Light", Livingstone Lectures, 1888, *NSW Independent,* Supplement, 15 July 1888.
67. *Presbyterian,* 6 September 1890; Roseby, "Genetic Unity of Nature", p. 12n. See also A. Gosman, review of Drummond, *Victorian Review* 11 (1884-85): 276-96/and J.C.C.[orlette], " 'Natural Law in the Spiritual World' by Henry Drummond, F.R.S.E., F.G.S.", *Sydney Quarterly Magazine* 7 (1890): 121-39. On Drummond's visit to Australia, see G.A. Smith, *The Life of Henry Drummond,* 10th ed. (London: Hodder and Stoughton, 1908), pp. 370-71. Drummond refused the press admission to his meetings.
68. *Weekly Advocate,* 14 January 1888; *Presbyterian,* 19 July 1890.
69. *SMH,* 15 June 1887, 4 February 1885.

70. W.R. Fletcher, "Modern Aspects of the Fight for Faith and the Higher Criticism of the Bible in the Light of Modern Discoveries" (Sydney, 1892) and "The Popular Difficulties of Higher Criticism", *Australian Independent*, 15 June 1893; G. MacInnes, "The Death of the Verbal Theory and the Unveiling of Christ: or the Bible as a 'sufficient witness' to the 'self-evidencing Christ' " (Sydney, 1894); G. Grimm, "The Plenary Inspiration of the Bible, a Defence and Reply" (Sydney, 1894).

71. See W. Phillips, "The Defence of Christian Belief in Australia 1875-1914: TheR Rsponses to Evolution and Higher Criticism", *JRH* 9 (1976-77): 402-33. On Britain, see Chadwick, *Victorian Church* 2: 97-111; Glover, *Evangelical Nonconformists*.

72. J.B. Walker, *Prelude to Federation (1884-1898): Extracts from the Journal of James Backhouse Walker, F.R.G.S.*, ed. P.D. Walker (Hobart: O.B.M. Publishing Company, 1976), pp. 46-47, 189.

73. Ibid., p. 47.

74. Jackson, "Church and Modern Thought", p. 115.

75. T.J. Hebblewhite, "The Ordeal of Faith", *Centennial Magazine* 2 (1889-90): 855.

76. T.J. Hebblewhite, "Artisan-Scepticism and Empty Churches", ibid., 2 (1889-90): 161-67. See also Jackson's reply, H.L. Jackson, "The Church and Modern Thought", ibid., pp. 353-62.

77. S.B. Holt, "The Church in Relation to the Various Grades of Society", *Papers, Church Congress Sydney, 1889,* esp. p. 282.

6. Applying the Gospel

1. P.J. O'Farrell, "The History of the New South Wales Labor Movement, 1880-1910: A Religious Interpretation", *JRH* 2 (1962-63): 138-39. O'Farrell also quotes from G.C. Percival, "Methodism: Past and Pesent", *Australasian Methodist Historical Journal and Proceedings* 2, no. 1 (October 1933): 72.

2. J. Jefferis, "The Enfranchisement of Labour" (Sydney [1878]), pp. 21-23.

3. J. Jefferis, "The Chinese and the Seamen's Strike" (Sydney [1878]); *Presbyterian,* 14 April 1888.

4. *Banner of Truth* (Sydney), 5 May 1880; J.E. Carruthers, *Memories of an Australian Ministry, 1868-1921* (London: Epworth Press, 1922), pp. 316-22; *Pastoral, Plenary Council, 1885,* pp. 9, 18. See also Cardinal Moran at Goulburn, *Freeman's Journal,* 21 May 1887.

5. *ACW,* 19 February 1886; *Presbyterian,* 30 August 1890.

6. See B. Dickey, "Charity in New South Wales, 1850-1914: Outdoor Relief to the Aged and Destitute", *JRAHS* 52 (1966) 9-32, and, by the same author, "Charity in New South Wales 1850-1914: A Study in Private, Public and State Provisions for the Poor" (Ph.D. thesis, Australian National University, 1966). See also J.D. Bollen, *Protestantism and Social Reform in New South Wales, 1890-1910* (Melbourne: Melbourne University Press, 1972), chap. 3.

7. J. Jefferis, "Australia Christianised: a lecture delivered ... in the Town Hall, Adelaide, on 19 June 1880", in Jefferis, ed., *Historical Records of the North Adelaide Congregational Church* (Adelaide, 1909), pp. 38-62, and Jefferis, "Pauperism in New South Wales", *Sydney University Review*, no. 3 (1882), pp. 254-76; E.G. Hodgson, "The Christian Aspect of our Worldly Calling", *Australian Churchman,* 16 October 1879. On Mrs Marian Jefferis and the boarding-out system, see Dickey, "Charity in New South Wales" (thesis), pp. 240-52.

8. Although Protestant and Catholic clergy largely provided the leadership for the

temperature movement in early colonial Australia, the denominations were not committed to the movement in the way that they were later in the nineteenth century. See paper on the history of the movement in New South Wales, read by G.D. Clark at the Centennial Temperance Congress in Sydney in 1888. *SMH*, 15 May 1888. See also M. Roe, *Quest for Authority in Eastern Australia, 1825-1851* (Melbourne: Melbourne University Press, 1965), chap. 8, and B.H. Harrison, *Drink and the Victorians: The Temperance Question in England, 1815-1872* (London: Faber and Faber, 1971), chap. 8.

9. A. Hyslop, "Temperance, Christianity and Feminism: The Woman's Christian Temperance Union of Victoria, 1887-97", *Historical Studies* 17 (1976-77): 27-49.

10. *SMH*, 25 September 1884; *Pastoral, Plenary Council, 1885,* pp. 8-9.

11. *SMH*, 25 September 1884. See also P. O'Farrell, *The Catholic Church and Community in Australia: A History* (Melbourne: Nelson, 1977), p. 283.

12. *International Temperance Conference, Melbourne, 1880. Papers, Debates and General Proceedings* (Melbourne, 1880), p. 5. On James Munro, see M. Cannon, *The Land Boomers*, rev. ed. (Melbourne: Nelson, 1976), pp. 180-89.

13. *Papers, Church Congress, Melbourne, 1882,* pp. 111-16; *Papers, Church Congress, Sydney, 1889,* pp. 225-31; *Report [First Part] of the Intoxicating Drink Inquiry Commission together with Minutes of Evidence and Appendices* (Sydney, 1887), Minutes, pp. 201-10, 215-27, 245-50, in *V&PLA* (NSW), 1887-88, 7: 1-678.

14. *International Temperance Conference, Melbourne, 1880, Papers,* p. 55.

15. *Report, Intoxicating Drink Inquiry,* Minutes, pp. 1, 150-57, 167-73; *Report of the Inspector General of Police, 1885,* pp. 2-3, in *V&PLA* (NSW), 1885-86, 4: 919-27; *Report of the Registrar-General on Vital Statistics [for the year 1885],* p. 11, in *V&PLA* (NSW), 1887, 5: 257-313; T.A. Coghlan, *The Wealth and Progress of New South Wales, 1886-87* (Sydney, 1887), p. 186.

16. C. Booth, *Life and Labour of the People in London,* 1st ser., rev. ed., (London: Macmillan, 1902), 1: 146-49. Booth, however, conceded that drink might be a "contributory cause . . . with a much larger proportion" of poverty. See also Harrison, *Drink and the Victorians,* p. 404.

17. *SMH*, 19 September 1884; Coghlan, *Wealth and Progress, 1886-87,* pp. 501-3; ibid., *1889-90,* pp. 387-92; *Victorian Year Book,* 1889-90, p. 331, 1895-98, p. 941; *Report, Intoxicating Drink Inquiry,* Minutes, pp. 5, 88, 171, 202, 255.

18. *SMH*, 16 May 1888; *Report, Intoxicating Drink Inquiry,* pp. 64-68, 108, Minutes, pp. 88-90, 219-22, 268, 270. There were some 500 public houses in the city of Sydney. The commission recommended a ratio of one to every eighty persons, which would have reduced the number by 100. On the building of hotels in the 1870s and 1880s, see J.M. Freeland, *The Australian Pub* (Melbourne: Melbourne University Press, 1966), pp 141-44, 152-55, and Appendix B: 204-5.

19. Jefferis, "Enfranchisement of Labour", pp. 16-18.

20. Ibid., pp. 4, 15-16, 19-22.

21. *Presbyterian,* 12 June 1880; *NSW Independent,* 15 December 1882.

22. Ibid., 15 February 1886.

23. *ACW* 22 January 1886. (This weekly was known as the *Intercolonial Christian Messenger* at this time. It changed its name in April 1886.)

24. *Weekly Advocate,* 16 December 1882.

25. *DT,* 11 February 1884.

26. *Official Report of the Sixth Intercolonial Trades and Labour Union Congress held in Hobart . . . February 1889* (Hobart, 1889), p. 51; R.A. Gollan, *Radical and Working Class Politics: A Study of Eastern Australia, 1850-1910* (Melbourne: Melbourne University Press, 1960), pp. 71-76.

27. *SMH*, 9 December 1885, 26 April 1888: *Minutes, Wesleyan General Conference, 1888,* p. 48; *ACW,* 23 January 1890. See also Bollen, *Protestantism and Social*

Reform, passim; and T.A. Coghlan, *Labour and Industry in Australia from the First Settlement in 1788 to the Establishment of the Commonwealth in 1901,* 4 vols. (Oxford: Oxford University Press, 1918), 4: 2087-97.

28. R.A. Gollan, *The Coalminers of New South Wales* (Melbourne: Melbourne University Press, 1963), pp. 73-77.

29. *SMH,* 20 August 1888.

30. *Nation,* 17 August 1888; *Weekly Advocate,* 18 August 1888; *Presbyterian,* 18 August 1888; *NSW Independent,* 15 September 1888.

31. *SMH,* 17 July 1888; *Report, Sixth Trades and Labour Congress,* pp. 52-55. See also J. Rickard, *Class and Politics: New South Wales, Victoria and the Early Commonwealth, 1890-1910* (Canberra: Australian National University Press, 1976), pp. 9-17.

32. *SMH,* 16, 18, 22-24 September 1888. See also Gollan, *Coalminers,* pp. 77-78.

33. *SMH,* 9 September 1889.

34. *Presbyterian,* 14 September 1889; *NSW Independent,* 15 September 1889.

35. *ACW,* 7 May 1886; *Freeman's Journal,* 30 October 1886.

36. *DT,* 6 September 1886. See also A. Barry, *Lectures on Socialism and Christianity* (London, 1890).

37. J. Jefferis, "Socialism in Germany" (Sydney [1878]; *DT,* 4, 11, 18, 25 October, 1, 8, 15 November 1886. See also A. Gosman, "Socialism in the Light of Right Conduct and Religion" (Melbourne, 1891) and E. Harris, "Socialism and the Church" (Sydney, 1890).

38. *Victorian Independent,* November 1886, pp. 174-75; T. Roseby, "The Labour Problem from a Christian Standpoint", in *Jubilee Volume of Victorian Congregationalism, 1888* (Melbourne, 1888), pp. 197-204; *Congregational Year Book,* 1891, pp. 96-109; *ACW,* 30 January 1890.

39. *Report of the Royal Commission on Strikes* (Sydney, 1891), p. 172; Roseby, "The Labour Problem" p. 203. See also Bollen, *Protestantism and Social Reform,* pp. 62-63.

40. *ACW,* 30 November 1890. See also, *Victorian Independent,* November 1886; *Report, Royal Commission on Strikes,* pp. 172-73. On Henry George in Australia, see Gollan, *Radical and Working Class Politics,* pp. 120-21.

41. *ACW,* 30 January 1890 and *Congregational Year Book,* 1891, pp. 106-8.

42. *DT,* 14 November 1890; *Banner and Anglo-Catholic Review* (Sydney), 1 November 1890. See also A.R. Vidler, *F.D. Maurice and Company* (London: S.C.M. Press, 1966), pp. 260-61.

43. *PSDS,* 1890, p. 44. The *Australian Record* is quoted without date in *Australian Workman* (Sydney), 29 November 1890.

44. O'Farrell, *Catholic Church and Community,* p. 286; T.J. Hebblewhite, "Artisan-Scepticism and Empty Churches", *Centennial Magazine* 2 (1889-90): 161-67.

45. *NSW Independent,* 15 January 1890.

46. *ACW,* 6, 27 March 1890; "A Man of Business", ibid., 3 April 1890. On E.J. Rodd, see Bollen, *Protestantism and Social Reform,* p. 91.

47. *ACW,* 3, 24 July 1890.

48. *Weekly Advocate,* 30 May, 12 July 1890. For an account of McMillan's speech, see Bollen, *Protestantism and Social Reform,* p. 55.

49. For a discussion of Maritime Strike and an interpretation of the conflict, see Rickard, *Class and Politics,* chap. 1.

50. *Weekly Advocate,* 30 August 1890; *DT,* 25 August 1890.

51. *Presbyterian,* 30 August, 6, 27 September 1890; *Weekly Advocate,* 30 August 1890; *NSW Independent,* 15 September 1890; *ACW,* 28 August 1890.

52. *DT,* 29 September 1890; *Report, Royal Commission on Strikes,* p. 172.

53. *SMH,* 11 September 1890; *Presbyterian,* 13 September 1890; *Freeman's Journal,* 20 September 1890; *ACW,* 11 September 1890.

54. *Official Report and Balance Sheet of the New South Wales Labour Defence Committee,* pp. 13-17, in *Select Documents in Australian History, 1851-1900* ed. C.M.H. Clark (Sydney: Angus and Robertson, 1955), pp. 772-76.

55. See J. Murtagh, *Australia: The Catholic Chapter* (Sydney: Angus and Robertson, 1959), chap. 8.

56. *Freeman's Journal,* 6 September, 4 October 1890. See also P. Ford, *Cardinal Moran and the A.L.P.* (Melbourne: Melbourne University Press, 1966), pp. 81-82.

57. K.S. Inglis, *Churches and the Working Classes in Victorian England* (London: Routledge and Kegan Paul, 1963), p. 314. Quotations from *Rerum Novarum* are taken from W.J. Gibbons, ed., *Seven Great Encyclicals* (New York: Paulist Press, 1963), pp. 1-30.

58. *Freeman's Journal,* 18 July 1891; Inglis, *Churches and the Working Classes,* p. 315.

59. *DT,* 18, 21 August 1891. See also Ford, *Cardinal Moran,* pp. 97-104.

60. Bollen, *Protestantism and Social Reform,* pp. 103-9.

61. T. Roseby, "Social Unrest — Labour: A Paper read at the Australasian Congregational Union Meetings, Melbourne, 28th October 1904" (Melbourne, 1904), p. 10.

62. Bollen, *Protestantism and Social Reform,* pp. 88-91.

63. *Weekly Advocate,* 16 August 1890; *Proceedings, General Synod,* 1891, p. 18.

64. On Evangelicalism and social reform, see Inglis, *Churches and Working Classes,* pp. 304-8; Bollen, *Protestantism and Social Reform,* pp. 43-44.

65. See Roseby's sermon on Sunday observance, *DT,* 25 February 1890.

66. *ACW,* 16 July 1886; *SMH,* 15-17 May 1888.

67. See Harrison, *Drink and the Victorians,* p. 405; N. Longmate, *The Waterdrinkers: A History of Temperance* (London: Hamish Hamilton, 1968), p. 247. F. Anstey, *Monopoly and Democracy* (Melbourne, 1906), p. 52; Richard Broome, *Treasure in Earthen Vessels: Protestant Christianity in New South Wales, 1900-1914* (St Lucia: University of Queensland Press, 1980), pp. 148-49.

68. According to J.D. Bollen, temperance became "*the* Protestant reform" around 1900, largely because of sectarianism and particular developments in New South Wales early in the twentieth century. But it had already become the major item on Protestant programmes of social reform before 1900. It was much the same in other Australian colonies as in the rest of the Anglo-Saxon Protestant world. Bollen, *Protestantism and Social Reform,* p. 151. See also Ann M. Mitchell, "Temperance and the Liquor Question in Later Nineteenth Century Victoria" (M.A. thesis, University of Melbourne, 1966); Renate Howe, "Protestantism, social Christianity and the Ecology of Melbourne, 1890-1900", *Historical Studies* 19 (April 1980): 59-73; Harrison, *Drink and the Victorians,* esp. chap. 8; S.D. Clark, *Church and Sect in Canada* (Toronto: University of Toronto Press, 1948) pp. 253-59, 266; W.G. McLoughlin, Jr., *Modern Revivalism, Charles Grandison Finney to Billy Graham* (New York: The Ronald Press Company, 1959), esp. chaps. 6-8.

7. Defending Christian Institutions

1. *SMH,* 26 August 1885.

2. *PD* (NSW), 1st ser., 11: 1265.

3. The Sunday Observance Acts were not specifically binding on the Crown, but G.H. Cox told the Legislative Council in 1884 that it was anomalous for the Crown to prosecute humble people for petty offences under the 1677 Act while the government employed hundreds of people on Sundays without being prosecuted. Ibid., 1260.

4. Great Britain, *Public General Statutes,* 29 Car. II, c.7 and 21 Geo. III, c.49. The Australian Courts Act of 1828 (*NSW Statutes* 9 Geo. IV, c.83, s.24) removed doubts concerning the application of British statutes up to that date in the colony. On prosecutions for Sunday trading etc., see *PD* (NSW), 18: 692-94, 1201, 29: 1584-86, 1595 and Report on 'Sunday Trading', *V&PLA* (NSW), 1891-92, 8: 1099.

5. Stanley's biographers have ignored his attitude to Sunday observance, but see his liberal exposition of the fourth commandment. A.P. Stanley, *Christian Institutions* (London, 1881), pp. 341-43. On the Sunday Freedom League, see M.G. Glazebrook in J. Hastings, ed., *Encyclopedia of Religion and Ethics* (Edinburgh, 1908), 7: 109. A Sunday Liberation Society was formed in Melbourne in 1883, with the Reverend Charles Strong among its supporters. See F.B. Smith, "The Sunday Observance Controversy in Melbourne, 1874-1910" (B.A. Hons. essay, Department of History, University of Melbourne, 1956).

6. *SMH,* 27 March, 6 April, 1878; *V&PLA* (NSW), 1877-78, 2: 697-724.

7. *SMH,* 11 August 1880.

8. Ibid., 6 September 1880. See also W. Phillips, "The Churches and the Sunday Question in Sydney in the 1880s", *JRH* 6 (1970-71): esp. 48-50.

9. *SMH,* 6 September 1880; *Presbyterian,* 11 September 1880; *Church of England Record,* October 1880.

10. *SMH,* 7 September 1880. See also Parkes's letter, ibid., 11 September 1880. Wisdom's opinion was tabled along with others in June 1887. See *V&PLA* (NSW), 1887, 5: 1157. For Parkes's previous attempt to control the use of theatres, see *PD* (NSW), 3: 2593-94.

11. *SMH,* 28 September, 5, 12, October 1880. On the original formation of the Lord's Day Observance Society, see Phillips, "Churches and the Sunday Question", p. 41.

12. *SMH,* 29 March 1881. See also sermons on Sunday observance, *DT,* 24 February 1890 and W.M. Cowper, "The Lord's Day Viewed in Three Lights, Religious, Moral and Social" (Sydney, 1880).

13. *SMH,* 12 October 1880, 29 March 1881.

14. Ibid., 12 October 1880.

15. Papers by H.B. Macartney, Canon Bromby and Dr W.H. Embling on "The Proper Attitude of the Church of England towards the Question of Sunday Observance", *Papers, Church Congress, Melbourne, 1882,* pp. 122-43.

16. See Barry's "Second Visitation Charge", *SMH,* 13 April 1888. Barry also contributed an article on the "Lord's Day" in Smith's *Dictionary of Christian Antiquities,* 2 vols. (London, 1875-1880) in which he refuted the sabbatarian argument. On Jackson, see *SMH,* 24 August 1885 and *Weekly Advocate,* 5 September 1885; *Presbyterian,* 29 August 1885.

17. *PD* (NSW), 7: 197-99: "Clericus", *Freeman's Journal,* 12 March 1881; *Pastoral, Plenary Council, 1885,* p. 14; *Rerum Novarum,* in W.J. Gibbons, ed., *Seven Great Encyclicals* (New York: Paulist Press, 1963), pp. 19-20; P.F. Moran, "The Reunion of Christendom" (Sydney, 1895) pp. 6-7. See also P. O'Farrell, *The Catholic Church and Community in Australia: A History* (Melbourne: Nelson, 1977), p. 282.

18. *PD* (NSW), 7: 230; *SMH,* 14 October 1882; Wm. McCreadie, Ibid., 17 April 1888.

19. See Barry's "Second Visitation Charge", and letter, Samuel Fox, ibid., 14 April 1888 and *Weekly Advocate,* 21 April 1888. Information on Dr Roseby's views gained from interview with the late J.R. Firth of Strathfield in November 1966, when he was 90 years of age. See also J.S. Austin, *Missionary Enterprise and Home Mission Service* (Sydney, n.d.) p. 367 and *Progress Report of the New*

South Wales Society for Promoting the Observance of the Lord's Day, 1883-4 (Sydney, 1884).

20. *SMH*, 29 March 1881; *PD* (NSW), 4: 1219. See also Smith, "Sunday Observance Controversy".

21. *V&PLA* (NSW), 1881, 5: 1135; see *PD* (NSW), 5: 1073-86; ibid., 7: 186-193.

22. Ibid., pp. 229-36. For petitions for and against Sunday-opening, see *V&PLA* (NSW), 1882, 2: 925, 4: 1599-1609.

23. *PD* (NSW), 7: 205.

24. *SMH*, 26 May 1883.

25. *SMH*, 19, 22 July 1884.

26. "XX", *SMH*, 17 April 1888. Information on the concerts is derived from advertisements in the amusement notices of the Saturday issues of the *SMH*. On Melbourne, see Smith, "Sunday Observance Controversy". The Catholic Church began to hold concerts in aid of the Cathdral Building Fund in 1885. This made it difficult to effect legal action against the Sunday concerts.

27. *V&PLA* (NSW), 8: 1156; *ACW*, 23 July 1886.

28. *SMH*, 3 November, 4 December 1886. See also *Presbyterian*, 6 November, 13 November 1886; *NSW Law Reports*, 5 (1884): 411.

29. *SMH*, 3 March 1887. See also Barry's "Second Visitation Charge".

30. *SMH*, 11 June 1887.

31. Ibid. See also B. Mansfield. "The Background to Radical Republicanism in New South Wales in the Eighteen-Eighties", *Historical Studies* 5 (1951-53): 338-48.

32. *SMH*, 13 June 1887.

33. Ibid., 14, 18, 20 June 1887. See also *Protestant Standard*, 18 June 1887.

34. Cartoon, *Bulletin*, 18 June 1887; *SMH*, 13 June 1887; Bishop Barry's "Second Visitation Charge".

35. *PD* (NSW), 27: 2101, 2124, 2128-31; *V&PLA* (NSW), 1887, 5: 1157, 1159; James Balfour to Parkes, 9 July 1887, Parkes Correspondence, 4: 138-41 (Mitchell Library).

36. *SMH*, 27 June 1887; *PD* (NSW), 27: 2269.

37. *SMH*, 10 March 1888. See also *Weekly Advocate*, 29 May 1886, 7 April 1886. On Sunday newspapers in Victoria, see Smith, "Sunday Observance Controversy".

38. *SMH*, 13 April 1888. See also *MWC*, 1886, p. 75; *MPGA*, 1885, p. 35; *Congregational Year Book*, 1889, pp. 59-61.

39. *ACW*, 12 January 1888, 3 October 1889; *SMH*, 20 September 1889; "R.K.S.", ibid., 26 September 1889. See also Smith, "Sunday Observance Controversy".

40. *MPGA*, 1889, p. 23. An account of the formation of the Council of Churches is given in Report, Committee on Religion and Morals, 1889, ibid., 1890, p. 58.

41. *PSDS*, 1889, p. 22; R.L. King, "Observance of the Lord's Day", *Papers, Church Congress, Sydney, 1889*, p. 132.

42. Kemmis's and Roseby's sermons are reported with others in *DT*, 24, 25 February 1890 respectively.

43. *SMH*, 26 May 1890; Advertisements, *SMH*, 5, 26 October 1889.

44. See Phillips, "Churches and the Sunday Question", p. 56.

45. *SMH*, 23 May 1890.

46. *DT*, 2 June 1890; *Presbyterian*, 7 June 1890; *Church of England Guardian*, 7, 28 June 1890.

47. *SMH*, 23 May 1890; *PD* (NSW), 46: 2276, 2440. See also *NSW Statutes*, 54 Vic., No. 8. On the British legislation, see Great Britain, *Public General Statutes*, 38 and 39 Vic., c.8.

48. The concert on the S.S. *Invincible* was technically free, but admission was charged to board the steamer. See Advertisements, *SMH*, 24, 31 May 1890, 24 January, 7 February 1891.

49. *SMH,* 6 August, 27 November 1890; *Protestant Standard,* 20 September 1890; *Presbyterian,* 21 June 1890.
50. *V&PLA* (NSW), 1890, 8: 761-85; *SMH,* 14 October 1890.
51. Report, Committee on Religion and Morals, 1890, *MPGA,* 1891, p. 62; *SMH,* 25 June 1909. See also Phillips, "Churches and the Sunday Question", pp. 58-59 and Richard Broome, *Treasure in Earthen Vessels: Protestant Christianity in New South Wales, 1900-1914* (St Lucia: University of Queensland Press, 1980), chap. 7.
52. I am much indebted in this section to Mrs Martha Campbell (formerly Martha Rutledge) who kindly allowed me to consult her thesis, "Sir Alfred Stephen and Divorce Law Reform in New South Wales, 1886-1892" (M.A. thesis, Australian National University, 1966). She has dealt most capably with the movement for divorce law reform in all its aspects.
53. Rutledge, "Sir Alfred Stephen", pp. 39-44. See also W. Latey, *The Tide of Divorce* (London: Longman, 1970), chap. 11 (on Britain); *NSW Statutes,* 36 Vic., No.9, 44 Vic. No.31.
54. See P. O'Farrell, ed., *Documents in Australian Catholic History,* 2 vols. (London: Geoffrey Chapman, 1969), 1: 195, 420.
55. Latey, *Tide of Divorce,* pp. 127-28. Latey dates the introduction of the law as 1889, but see Rutledge, "Sir Alfred Stephen", pp. 44-45.
56. *PD* (NSW), 15: 5454.
57. *PD* (NSW), 1: 303-14, 13: 4137-39. See also Latey, *Tide of Divorce,* p. 91.
58. F.B. Boyce, *SMH,* 27 April 1886; *PD* (NSW), 18: 703.
59. *SMH,* 27 March 1886.
60. "Alfred Sydney", ibid., 8 April 1886.
61. Rutledge, "Sir Alfred Stephen", p. 105; *PD* (NSW), 56: 4925.
62. P.F. Moran, *Pastoral Letter* [17 April 1886], pp. 7-11; *SMH,* 10 May 1886; *Freeman's Journal,* 3 April 1886.
63. Zachary Barry, *SMH,* 1 May 1886; "Anglo-Catholic", ibid., 27 June 1888.
64. *PSDN,* 1886, pp. 29-31; Rutledge, "Sir Alfred Stephen", p. 125.
65. *SMH,* 12, 17 April 1886.
66. *V&PLA* (NSW), 1885-86, 8: 1165.
67. *SMH,* 5 May 1886; Arthur E. Selwyn, ibid., 12 April 1887; H. Tennent Donaldson, ibid., 26 June 1888.
68. *PD* (NSW), 20: 2033-35 (Knox), 21: 4037(O'Sullivan), 23: 5096 (O'Connor), 5102 (Melville). See also O'Sullivan's letter, *SMH,* 14 August 1891, where he uses the same argument against divorce law reform.
69. *PSDS,* 1886, p. 31; *SMH,* 21 April 1888 (Stephen), 6 April 1887 (Darley).
70. *PD* (NSW), 21: 4034 (Neild), 23: 5099-5101 (Parkes). Luther allowed three main grounds for divorce; viz., impotence, adultery, refusal of conjugal rights and possibly plots against life of the spouse and desertion. Melanchthon, although reputedly more lenient than Luther, only allowed adultery, desertion, plots against life and cruelty. See J. McCabe, *The Influence of the Church on Marriage and Divorce* (London: Watts & Co., 1916), pp. 154-55. I am indebted to the Reverend Maurice Schild of Luther Seminary, Adelaide, and to Professor Kingston Braybrooke of La Trobe University for advice on the teaching of the Reformers on divorce.
71. Sir Alfred Stephen, "To the Right Reverend and Bishops and Clergy of the Anglican Church Synod, meeting lately in Sydney", *SMH,* 31 March 1887. On the *Reformatio Legum Ecclesiasticarum,* see Latey, *Tide of Divorce,* pp. 37-38.
72. R.L. King, *SMH,* 1 April 1887; see also F.W. Bode, ibid., 19 April 1887; George Spencer, Bega, ibid., 12 April 1887. On the frequency of divorce in the second half of the sixteenth century, see Latey, *Tide of Divorce,* pp. 38-40.

73. "Reply to the Address of the Most Reverend the Primate, by Sir Alfred Stephen, M.L.C.", *SMH*, 21 April 1888; "Beta", East Maitland, ibid., 19 April 1887.

74. Rutledge, "Sir Alfred Stephen", p. 141; *ACW*, 11, 25 June 1886; *V&PLA* (NSW), 1885-6, 8: 1179; *MPGA*, 1887, p. 33.

75. *Weekly Advocate*, 10, 24 April 1886; *SMH*, 11 February, 22 May 1890; *Minutes, Wesleyan General Conference*, 1890, p. 45.

76. *Congregational Year Book*, 1889, p. 83; *SMH*, 17 May 1886, 13 June 1888; *NSW Independent*, 15 April 1886; *PD* (NSW), 23: 5098.

77. "The Divorce Bill: The Rev. Charles Bright's View", *Echo*, 28 April 1886; *ACW*, 14 May 1886; "Nova Cambria", *SMH*, 30 April 1887. (Garran wrote under this pseudonym, Rutledge, "Sir Alfred Stephen", pp. 145-46.)

78. J. Palmer, *SMH*, 17 June 1890.

79. *ACW*, 23 April 1886; Rutledge, "Sir Alfred Stephen", p. 111; *PD* (NSW), 21: 4033.

80. *PSDS*, 1887, pp. 22-23; Rutledge, "Sir Alfred Stephen", p. 156.

81. The bishop of Sydney to the secretary of state for the colonies, 6 June 1887, C.O. 201/607, pp. 615-21, quoted in Rutledge, "Sir Alfred Stephen", pp. 157-61. See also ibid., pp. 159-62, 165-69; *PD* (NSW), 33: 5485-99, 5634-40.

82. Arthur E. Selwyn, *SMH*, 28 June 1890. For petitions, see *V&PLA* (NSW), 1890, 8: 753-54. See also Rutledge, "Sir Alfred Stephen", pp. 224-26 and "Table of Divorce Bills . . . 1886-1892", ibid., Appendix 4: xxxiv-vii.

83. J.S. Gregory, *Church and State: Changing Government Policies towards Religion in Australia; with particular reference to Victoria* (Melbourne: Cassell Australia, 1973), pp. 156-61; Rutledge, "Sir Alfred Stephen", pp. 195-202. The priority of the movement in New South Wales and the support opposing parties in both colonies received from one another deserve more recognition than Professor Gregory gives them.

84. Ibid., pp. 219-20; Zachary Barry, *SMH*, 15 May 1890; *Proceedings, General Synod*, 1891, p. 56; *SMH*, 26 September 1891.

85. *SMH*, 26 July 1891; Rutledge, "Sir Alfred Stephen", p. 237.

86. See F.B. Suttor, *PD* (NSW) 44: 442-43. For similar argument in Victoria, see Gregory, *Church and State*, pp. 158-59.

87. Zachary Barry, *SMH*, 18 April 1887.

88. Rev. Robert Potter, "On the Relation of the State to the Ecclesiastical Bodies in Victoria", *Melbourne Review* 1 (1876): 12-13. See also H. Richard Niebuhr, *The Kingdom of God in America* (New York: Harper, 1959), p. 184.

8. Reinforcing Religion in the Schools

1. See P. O'Farrell, *The Catholic Church in Australia: A Short History: 1788-1967* (Melbourne: Nelson, 1968), p. 127 (but see also the same author, *The Catholic Church and Community in Australia. A History* (Melbourne: Nelson, 1977), p. 188; R. Fogarty, *Catholic Education in Australia*, 2 vols. (Melbourne: Melbourne University Press, 1957), 1: esp. 157-60; J. Murtagh, *Australia: The Catholic Chapter* (Sydney: Angus and Robertson, 1959), pp. 94-104. A recent publication in this area perpetuates the view of the Act of 1880 as a "secularist" measure: G. Haines, *Lay Catholics and the Education Question in Nineteenth Century New South Wales* (Sydney: Catholic Theological Faculty, 1976).

2. A.G. Austin, *Australian Education, 1788-1900* (Melbourne: Pitman, 1961), pp. 267 ff. A. Barcan, *A Short History of Education in New South Wales* (Sydney: Martindale Press, 1965), p. 150. See also A.R. Crane, "The New South Wales

Public Schools League, 1874-1879'', *Melbourne Studies in Education*, 1964: 198-229.

3. *NSW Statutes*, 43 Vic. No. 23, Clauses 7 and 17. See also K. Elford, ''Church, State, Education and Society: An Analysis of Aspects of Eastern Australian Society, 1856-1872'' (Ph.D. thesis, Sydney University, 1971), pp. 229-33; J.S. Gregory, *Church and State: Changing Government Policies towards Religion in Australia; with particular reference to Victoria* (Melbourne: Cassell Australia, 1973), chap. 4.

4. *Scripture Lessons for the Use of Schools*, (Sydney, [1849]), Old Testament, no. 1, p. 6n, New Testament, no. 1, pp. 12n, 36n. For other examples, see John Barrett, *That Better Country* (Melbourne: Melbourne University Press, 1966), pp. 137-38. See also *Report of the Minister of Public Instruction, 1882*, pp. 116-17 in *V&PLA* (NSW), 1883-84, 7: 587-762.

5. ''An Old Teacher'', *Weekly Advocate*, 9 March 1889; ''Iona'', *Presbyterian*, 6 January 1894. On religious affiliations of state school teachers, see B. Mitchell, *Teachers, Education and Politics* (St Lucia: University of Queensland Press, 1975), pp. 16, 223 31n.

6. See Gregory, *Church and State*, pp. 172-74. See also S.G. Firth, ''Social Values in the New South Wales Primary School 1880-1914: An Analysis of School Texts'', *Melbourne Studies in Education*, 1970: 123-49, esp. 126-28.

7. *Manifesto of the Public Schools League of New South Wales* (Sydney, 1874) Mitchell Library; *Congregational Year Book*, 1880, pp. 51-55, 76-79; *MPGA*, 1879, p. 23; *V&PLA* (NSW), 1879-80, 3: 387.

8. R.B. Vaughan, *Pastorals and Speeches on Education* (Sydney, 1880), pp. 11, 84. See also Vaughan, ''Hidden Springs'', pp. 66-67.

9. *PD* (NSW), 1st ser. 1: 604.

10. Ibid., p. 276; p. 445-47; 2: 1116.

11. Ibid., 1: 268, 274. It will be seen that Brother Ronald Fogarty misrepresents Parkes's position in introducing the Public Instruction Bill of 1879. See Fogarty, *Catholic Education*, 1: 158-60 and W. Phillips, ''Australian Catholic Historiography: Some Recent Issues'', *Historical Studies* 14 (1971-72): 607.

12. Bishop Thornton of Ballarat to Parkes, 8 March 1880, Parkes Correspondence A & B, A919, pp. 922-23; *Freeman's Journal*, 6 November 1880. See also Pastoral Letter to be read on 7 September 1879 in Vaughan, *Pastorals and Speeches* (not paginated consecutively).

13. W. Wilkins, Memorandum to Inspector, Albury District, 18 September 1879, NSW State Archives (no. 79 14269 in Box P 4059); Letters and Memoranda regarding the use of the Collins Australian School Series and the retention of the Irish National Reading Book, 1880-81 Bundle in Ibid.

14. Gregory, *Church and State*, p. 172; *Freeman's Journal*, 18 September 1880.

15. Letters and Memoranda.

16. Ibid.

17. White reported the outcome of his correspondence in a letter *SMH*, 2 July 1884; see also *PD* (NSW), 4: 275.

18. *SMH*, 14 November 1883; *MPGA*, 1884, pp. 22-23; *Presbyterian*, 15 March 1884.

19. *Weekly Advocate*, 1, 29 March 1884; *PD* (NSW), 12: 2420-32; *Protestant Standard*, 31 May 1884.

20. A Return showing the number of times the Clergymen . . . of the various Denominations attended the Public and Denominational Schools for the purpose of giving religious instruction, for each month of the years 1879 and 1880. *V&PLA* (NSW), 1881, 2: 1071-98.

21. Return showing the number of visits of Clergymen to certain Public Schools, for the purpose of imparting special religious instruction, from the 1st January,

1877 to the present time [15 December 1879] *V&PLA* (NSW), 1879-80, 3: 355-57. Visits in 1879 calculated by comparison with subsequent table for 1879 and 1880. See above.

22. *PD* (NSW), 2: 1113. On Fitzpatrick and the Catholic Church, see Haines, *Lay Catholics and Education,* pp. 176-78.

23. *PSDN,* 1875, pp. 14-15; *PSDS,* 1875, pp. 40-41, 44; *SMH,* 27, 28 April, 18 August 1875; *Proceedings, Provincial Synod,* 1875,Appendix 3:36.

24. *PSDS,* 1878, pp. 36-37; Report of the Religious Instruction Committee, ibid., 1879, Appendix 6: 59-63 and resolutions, pp. 23-39, passim; Report of the Religious Instruction Committee, 1880, ibid., Appendix 13: 99-115. See also K.J. Cable, "The Church of England and its Policy towards Education" (M.A. thesis, University of Sydney, 1952), esp. 1: 122.

25. *PSDS,* 1880, p. 16; *PSDN,* 1880, p. 14; *SMH,* 13 August 1880.

26. Ibid., 17 August 1880 and letters, ibid., 14, 19, 20 August 1880. See also *Statistical Register NSW,* 1870, p. 17; 1880, p. 20.

27. *PSDN,* 1885, p. 14.

28. Allan W. Webb, *SMH,* 5 June 1875; J.K. Black, ibid., 8 November 1884; *PSDG,* 1879, p. 13.

29. *PSDN,* 1882, pp. 29-30.

30. *PSDS,* 1880, p. 16; *SMH,* 13 August 1880.

31. "Scrutator", *Protestant Standard,* 26 July 1879; *Weekly Advocate,* 3 December 1880; *MWC,* 1881, p. 48; *SMH,* 28 January 1882.

32. *Presbyterian,* 11, 25 December 1880, David Brown, ibid., 25 February 1882; *MPGA,* 1881, pp. 27-28; *SMH,* 10 February 1882.

33. See W. Phillips, "Religious Profession and Practice in New South Wales, 1850-1901: The Statistical Evidence", *Historical Studies* 15 (1972-73): 396-98.

34. *Presbyterian,* 25 December 1880; *SMH,* 19 August 1883.

35. Ibid., 14, 19 February; *Echo,* 15 February 1883.

36. See letter, *SMH,* 3 July 1884.

37. *SMH,* 2 May 1884. See also A. Barry, *Three Sermons on Religious Education* (Sydney, 1884), Sermon 1, p. 11.

38. *DT,* 19 May 1884.

39. See *SMH,* 20 May 1884; *DT,* 7 July 1884, and J. Jefferis, "Reply to The Joint Pastoral of the Roman Catholic Archbishop and Bishops of New South Wales" (Sydney 1879).

40. *DT,* 19 May 1884. The full value of each subject varied from grade to grade, but in the fourth class, for example, reading, grammar and arithmetic were valued at 100 marks each, writing and dictation at 50 marks each, geography and history 60 marks each. Scripture counted for 30 marks in the junior grades and 40 in the senior until 1884 when it was raised to 60. Regulations under the Public Instruction Act of 1880, 12 November 1885, *V&PLA* (NSW), 1885-86, 4: 215-28.

41. *DT,* 20 May 1884.

42. Ibid., 26 May 1884.

43. *DT,* 26 May 1884. See also Dorothea Berger, *Jean Paul Friedrich Richter* (New York: Twayne Publishers, 1972), esp. pp. 25-27.

44. *Australian Churchman,* 26 June 1884; *SMH,* 25 June 1884.

45. Ibid., 26 June 1884.

46. Letters, ibid., 27, 28 June 1884.

47. *DT,* 9 June 1884; *Protestant Standard,* 12 July 1884; *Weekly Advocate,* 5 July 1884.

48. *SMH,* 27 June 1884; *Bulletin,* 5 July 1884.

49. *SMH,* 27, 28 June 1884; *Freeman's Journal,* 21 June 1884.

50. *SMH,* 28 June 1884.

51. Letter, ibid., 7 June 1884.
52. Ibid., 28 June 1884, 24, 25 July, 1 August 1891. The legal difficulty was removed by the amendment to the Public Instruction Act in 1961, following the "Wyndham Report" on Secondary Education. Secondary schools were now included in the definition of a public school under the Act of 1880 hence the religious clauses now applied to them also. The Wyndham Report recommended religious education as a core subject in the curriculum and also suggested a form of corporate worship in the secondary schools. See *Report of the Committee Appointed to Survey Secondary Education in New South Wales* (Sydney: Government Printer, 1957), esp. pp. 50, 66 and *NSW Statutes,* No. 47, 1961.
53. *DT,* 28 May 1884; *SMH,* 1, 4 July 1884. See also Jefferis's letter, ibid., 28 June 1884.
54. A. Barry, ibid., 3 July 1884; *DT,* 7 July 1884.
55. "Presbuteros", *Freeman's Journal,* 5 July 1884; see also ibid., 21 June 1884.
56. Ibid., 31 May 1884.
57. Ibid., 21 June, 5 July 1884; *Australian Churchman,* 26 June 1884.
58. "Catholics", *SMH,* 17 July 1884; E. Jane Whately, ed., *The Life and Letters of Richard Whately* 2 vols. (London, 1866), 2: 46-47, 232-35, 243-45. See also *The Second Annual Report of the Catholic Association for the Promotion of Religion and Education in the Archdiocese of Sydney* (1869); Fogarty, *Catholic Education,* 1: 177. Ironically, the High Churchman Thomas Kemmis objected to the public schools in New South Wales on the grounds that the *Scripture Lessons* "taught Roman Catholic doctrine". *SMH,* 27 April 1878.
59. There is a breakdown of percentages of Catholic children enrolled in public schools in Haines, *Lay Catholics and Education,* Appendix.
60. *DT,* 14 July 1884; see also ibid., 4 August 1884; *SMH,* 27 June 1884; "Comas", *Freeman's Journal,* 28 June 1884.
61. Complaints of the Protestant bias of history taught in the public schools were aired in *Freeman's Journal,* 23, 30 May, 6 June 1885; *Express,* 3 February 1883. See also D. O'Donnell, "Sectarian Differences and the Inclusion of History in the Curriculum of NSW Public Schools", *JRAHS* 54 (1968): 283-98.
62. C.P.F. Collingridge, *SMH,* 26 June 1884.
63. *SMH,* 9, 13 September, 27 October 1884.
64. Ibid., 29 October 1884, 8 November 1884.
65. Ibid., 2, 3 July 1884.
66. Ibid., 21, 24 July 1884.
67. *Bulletin,* 12 July 1884; *SMH,* 28 July 1884.
68. Ibid., 11, 12 July, 20 October 1884.
69. *Congregational Year Book,* 1885, pp. 77-82. See also "Sentio", *NSW Independent,* 15 October 1884. On the Baptists, see Bishop Barry's comment, *PSDS,* 1885, pp. 55-56.
70. *Presbyterian,* 1 November 1884; *SMH,* 25 October 1884.
71. *DT,* 3 November 1884.
72. *Presbyterian,* 24 May, 1 November 1884, 7 March 1885; *SMH,* 4 February 1885.
73. *SMH,* 21 January 1885; "Gyges", *DT,* 30 January 1885; *Weekly Advocate,* 12 September 1885.
74. See *PSDS,* 1885, p. 56.
75. T.A. Coghlan, *The Wealth and Progress of New South Wales 1886-87* (Sydney, 1887) p. 438; *SMH,* 12 February 1889; Reports and Returns on Religious Instruction, *PSDS,* 1885, Appendix 18: 123-25; 1891, Appendix 16: after p. 100. See also *Official Year Book of NSW,* 1904-5, p. 546.
76. *SMH,* 31 July 1885, 14 October 1884.
77. Letter, J. Oram, *Weekly Advocate,* 23 February 1889. See also *MWC,* 1885, pp. 73-74, 1887, p. 69, 1888, p. 72.

78. Report of the Sabbath Schools and Religious Instruction Committee 1892, *MPGA*, 1893, p. 19 and Report, Statistics Committee, ibid., 1901, pp. 124-25. *Official Year Book of NSW*, 1904-5, p. 546.

79. See advertisement for the Wesleyan Ladies College, *ACW*, 12 January 1888. See also Barcan, *Education in New South Wales*, pp. 187-88.

80. Rev. J. Sheridan to Department of Public Instruction, 31 January 1888, NSW State Archives (1759 Bundle 6/31 Box P 245). On numbers of Catholic children in state schools, see *Report of the Minister of Public Instruction*, 1884, p. 47, 1890, p. 78 in *V&PLA* (NSW), 1885, 1: 397-593, 1892, 3: 1-320. See also Haines, *Lay Catholics and Education*, Appendix 1.

81. *Pastoral, Plenary Council, 1885,* p. 25; P.F. Moran, *Pastoral Letter to the Clergy . . . Feast of Corpus Christi, 1885,* p. 6; *SMH* 16 March 1888. See also O'Farrell, *Catholic Church and Community,* p. 242.

82. *SMH*, 25 November 1889; *Freeman's Journal*, 30 November 1889.

83. *SMH*, 3 July, 6 August 1891.

84. *S.A. Register,* 18 April 1901; see also M. French, "Churches and Society in South Australia, 1890-1900" (M.A. thesis, Flinders University, 1969), chap. 2.

85. See Gregory, *Church and State*, pp. 214-17. South Australia amended its Education Act in 1940 to allow the churches to give religious instruction in the schools.

86. *PD* (NSW) 41: 4638. Parkes spoke in similar terms in his electorate in December 1891. *SMH*, 18 December 1891; ibid., 27, 28, 31 August 1964, 3, 4 December 1964. Since 1964 Protestant churchmen have shown themselves more receptive to broader based studies of religion in schools.

9. Public Recognition for God

1. R.W. Dale, *Impressions of Australia* (London: Hodder and Stoughton, 1889), pp. 261-62.

2. A. Gosman, "Imperial Federation and Congregationalism", *Report, Intercolonial Congregational Conference, Adelaide, 1887*, pp. 83-85.

3. Parkes's protest is generally wrongly dismissed as sour grapes. See *SMH*, 14 February 1885; C.E. Lyne, *Life of Sir Henry Parkes* (Sydney: G. Robertson, 1896), pp. 329-31. On Jefferis, see *DT*, 20 April 1885. See also B.R. Penny, "The Age of Empire: An Australian Episode" *Historical Studies* 11 (1962-63): 32-42 and W.A. Wood, "The Sudan Contingent of 1885 and the Anti-War Movement" *Labour History*, no. 3 (1962), pp. 52-69.

4. *Protestant Standard*, 28 February 1885; *Presbyterian*, 21 February 1885.

5. Ibid., 28 February 1885. See also *Freeman's Journal*, 21 February 1885; *Weekly Advocate*, 28 February 1885; P.F. Moran, *History of the Catholic Church in Australasia* (Sydney: Frank Coffee and Co, [1895]), pp. 962-63.

6. Moran, Diary, 26, 28 February 1885, Moran Papers, St Mary's Cathedral Archives, Sydney; *SMH*, 2 March 1885; *Presbyterian*, 7 March 1885.

7. *SMH*, 2 March 1885. The government account of the expedition by Hutchinson and Myers, misrepresents Bishop Barry's position as one of unqualified support. Careful comparison with the press account will show that what purports to be a verbatim report in the official history is in fact distorted paraphrase. F. Hutchinson and F. Myers, *The Australian Contingent* (Sydney: Government Printer, 1885), pp. 37-38.

8. *SMH*, 2 March 1885.

9. On the Mount Rennie Outrage, see P.W. Grabosky, *Sydney in Ferment: Crime, Dissent and Official Reaction 1788-1973* (Canberra: Australian National Uni-

versity Press, 1977), pp. 20, 81, 92, and C.M.H. Clark, *A History of Australia*, 4 vols. (Melbourne: Melbourne University Press, 1962-78), 4: 362.

10. All the jubilee sermons are reported to *SMH*, 20 June 1887.
11. Ibid.
12. *Congregational Year Book*, 1887, pp. 87-90. This paper was also published as "The Religious Celebration of the Centenary of Australasia" (Sydney, 1886).
13. *Congregational Year Book*, 1888, p. 123; J. Jefferis, "A Free Church in a Free State" (Sydney [1878]), p. 23. Note, however, that as early as 1871 Jefferis had acknowledged that Church and State "cannot be completely separated as long as we continue a Christian people". See J. Jefferis, "The Relation of Christianity to the Civil Government", *South Australian Independent* (Adelaide), June 1871, pp. 61-62.
14. Parkes to Jennings, 7 August 1886, Parkes Correspondence 46: 51-58; *PD* (NSW), 1st ser., 22: 4403.
15. *ACW*, 1, 8 October 1886; *Presbyterian*, 4 December 1886; *SMH*, 30 November 1887.
16. *Freeman's Journal*, 5 November 1887; see also Moran, *History of the Catholic Church*, p. 701.
17. *SMH*, 23 January 1888.
18. Ibid. This sermon was also published under the same title in the *Centennial Magazine* 1 (1888): 102-4.
19. See "Zoilus", *DT*, 20 January 1888; *Church of England Guardian*, 28 January 1888; *Protestant Standard*, 4 February 1888; *SMH*, 30 January 1888.
20. Ibid.
21. *Freeman's Journal*, 4 February 1888.
22. *SMH*, 23 January 1888.
23. Ibid., 30 January 1888.
24. See interviews with the three churchmen, *Evening News*, 2, 4, 7 February 1888. For a report of the unveiling of the Queen's statue, see *SMH*, 25 January 1888.
25. *PSDS*, 1888, p. 28. See also J.S. Gregory, *Church and State: Changing Government Policies towards Religion in Australia; with particular reference to Victoria* (Melbourne: Cassell Australia, 1973), pp. 45-46, 66, 75-76, and Frances O'Kane, *A Path is Set* (Melbourne: Melbourne University Press, 1976), pp. 65-66.
26. *SMH*, 25, 28 June 1862; Samuel Chambers Kent, ibid., 30 June 1862.
27. *Church of England Messenger* (Melbourne), 10 April 1888.
28. A. Gosman, "The Religion of the State", *Victorian Independent*, May 1888.
29. *Argus* (Melbourne), 2 August 1888, Supplement; *PD* (NSW), 25: 240, 260-62. Standing Orders Committee Report and Petitions, *V&PLA* (NSW), 1887, 1: 479, 481-85.
30. *PD* (NSW), 45: 1727-34 (Division, Ayes 11 Noes 32); *Presbyterian*, 5 July 1890. See also letters in favour of prayers in Parliament, *SMH*, 11, 13 July 1891.
31. The Rev. E. Price, Baptist, at the united centenary thanksgiving service in Bathurst, *Bathurst Daily Times* (Bathurst), 23 January 1888.
32. G. Serle, "The Victorian Government's Campaign for Federation, 1883-1889" in *Essays in Australian Federation*, ed. A.W. Martin (Melbourne: Melbourne University Press, 1969), pp. 1-56.
33. *SMH*, 17 December 1889. See also ibid., 10 August 1883, 4 December 1889.
34. *Freeman's Journal*, 11 February 1888.
35. *Presbyterian*, 7, 21 June 1890.
36. R. Ely, *Unto God and Caesar: Religious Issues in the Emerging Commonwealth, 1891-1906* (Melbourne: Melbourne University Press, 1976), pp. 4-6.
37. Ibid., pp. 9-12.
38. *Cardinal Moran and the Federal Convention* (Sydney, 1897); *The Cardinal's Mani-*

festo to the Electors of New South Wales (Sydney [1897]). See also Ely, *God and Caesar*, chap. 2; P. Ford, *Cardinal Moran and the A.L.P.* (Melbourne: Melbourne University Press, 1966), pp. 203-18; P. O'Farrell, *The Catholic Church and Community in Australia: A History* (Melbourne: Nelson, 1977), pp. 263-71.

39. *Official Report . . . Convention Debates, Adelaide, 1897* (Adelaide, 1897); see index, and for text of petition, pp. 142, 203. See also J.A. La Nauze, *The Making of the Constitution* (Melbourne: Melbourne University Press, 1972), pp. 224-25; Ely, *God and Caesar*, pp. 21-24.

40. Quoted in a Seventh Day Adventist publication, A.W. Anderson, *Religious Liberty in Australasia* (Warburton, Victoria, 1917), p. 12. See also Ely, *God and Caesar*, chapters 3, 6 and 8. The Seventh Day Adventists began their mission in New South Wales in 1885.

41. See J. Quick and R.R. Garran, *The Annotated Constitution of the Australian Commonwealth* (Sydney, 1901), pp. 288-90 and Ely, *God and Caesar*, pp. 27-28. For prosecution of Seventh Day Adventists, see *Evening News,* 9, 14 August 1894; *SMH,* 10 August 1894. The penalty under the Caroline Statute was a fine or the stocks; and Seventh Day Adventists asked for the latter. But they were not put in the stocks, as Ely implies. However failure to pay the fine could also lead to measures to obtain it by "levy and distress" on the offender's goods and property, the course taken by the Sydney magistrate before the conviction was quashed. See ibid., 8 May, 10 August 1894.

42. *Convention Debates, Adelaide, 1897,* pp. 1184-89. See also La Nauze, *Making of the Constitution,* pp. 128, 224-26; Ely, *God and Caesar,* pp. 31-35; *ACW,* 7, 30 May 1897. Harper's address was also published as a pamphlet. See A. Harper, "Australia Without God: An Appeal to the Churches of Australia to secure an Acknowledgement of God in the Australian Constitution" (Melbourne, [1897]).

43. *V&PLA* (NSW), 1897, 1: 457-61; *ACW,* 9, 16 July 1897. For petitions from other colonies see *V&PLA* (Vic), 1897, 1: see index. *Journal and Papers of the Parliament of Tasmania,* 1897, vol. 36: see Abstract of Petitions.

44. *ACW,* 13 August 1897; *PD* (NSW), 89: 2599-600; *PD* (Vic), 86: 1697.

45. *ACW,* 13 August 1897; *Official Record of the Debates of the . . . Convention . . . Melbourne, 1898* (Melbourne, 1898), p. 123.

46. Ibid., p. 1732.

47. Ibid., pp. 1734-41. On Glynn's religious belief, see G. O'Collins, *Patrick McMahon Glynn* (Melbourne: Melbourne University Press, 1965), pp. 189-94.

48. *Convention Debates, Melbourne, 1898,* p. 1739; *Churchman* (Sydney), 6 May 1898. (It was quoting Bishop Barry's description, ten years earlier, of the attitude of colonial politicians to religion.)

49. *ACW,* 7, 28 May 1897. See also pastoral letter of the Presbyterian General Assembly, written after disastrous floods in 1893. *MPGA,* 1893, p. 39; J.D. Bollen, *Protestantism and Social Reform in New South Wales, 1890-1910* (Melbourne: Melbourne University Press, 1972), pp. 56-57; G. Davison, *The Rise and Fall of Marvellous Melbourne* (Melbourne: Melbourne University Press, 1978), pp. 249-50.

50. *ACW,* 13 August 1897.

51. Ely, *God and Caesar,* pp. 6, 38-39; Gosman, "Imperial Federation", p. 85.

52. *DT,* 29 January 1889.

53. *Convention Debates, Melbourne, 1898,* pp. 1769-80. For discussion of the history of the religious freedom clause from 1891 to 1898, see La Nauze, *Making of the Constitution,* pp. 228-29, and Ely, *God and Caesar,* chaps. 9 and 11.

54. Quick and Garran, *Annotated Constitution,* pp. 951-52.

55. See Ely, *God and Caesar,* pp. 89-102. It must be pointed out to the reader that

Ely takes statements actually made by E. Barton and R.E. O'Connor in opposition to Higgins's amendment as if they were commentaries on the meaning of "no establishment" in the proposed new section. He also misrepresents Barton as saying in effect that this amendment "prohibited the Commonwealth from recognizing any religion as the religion of the State". Furthermore, he quoted very selectively from Bryce's *American Commonwealth,* on which he ultimately rests his case. Bryce elucidated the American doctrine of separation of Church and State, but he also acknowledged that Christianity received "a species of recognition inconsistent with the view that civil government should be absolutely neutral in religious matters", and that it was "understood to be, though not the legally established religion, yet the national religion". Compare *Convention Debates, Melbourne, 1898,* pp. 1770-2, 1778-80 with Ely, *God and Caesar,* p. 88; see also James Bryce, *The American Commonwealth,* 2 vols. new ed. (New York: Macmillan, 1917) 2: 769-70. For a recent discussion of church-state relations in the United States, see F.J. Sorauf, *The Wall of Separation: The Constitutional Politics of Church and State* (Princeton: Princeton University Press, 1976).

56. *S.A. Register,* 2 January 1901. The draft of the Council of Churches' resolution is in the Jefferis Papers, currently in the present writer's custody. See also the Victorian Council of Churches' support for Section 116, Ely, *God and Caesar,* p. 106.

57. *ACW,* 11 January 1901. For Owen's earlier criticism of clause 116, see Ely, *God and Caesar,* pp. 104-5.

58. *ACW,* 28 September, 16 October, 30 November, 7 December 1900; *Methodist* (Sydney), 1 September, 6 October 1900; *SMH,* 25 October, 1, 3 December 1900; *Proceedings, General Synod,* 1900, p. 39.

59. *SMH,* 1, 2 January 1901; Ely, *God and Caesar,* pp. 112-16.

60. Ibid., 1, 2 January 1901. For a discussion of disputes over precedency, see Ely, *God and Caesar,* chap. 14.

61. *SMH,* 2, 7 January 1901; *ACW,* 7 December 1900, 4, 11 January 1901. For a lively account of the events on 1 January 1901, see G. Souter, *Lion and Kangaroo* (Sydney: Collins, 1976), chap. 2.

62. *Methodist,* 8 December 1900; *Presbyterian,* 20 December 1900; *DT,* 7 January 1901; *SMH,* 7 January 1901.

63. *ACW,* 10, 17 May 1901. On Cardinal Moran's reasons for not attending the ceremony, see Ely, *God and Caesar,* p. 121.

64. *ACW,* 10 May 1901; *PD* (Commonwealth), 1: 815-21 (House of Representatives), pp. 1136-40 (Senate). See also Ely, *God and Caesar,* pp. 122-24.

65. *PD* (Commonwealth), 1: 819; Ely, *God and Caesar,* p. 124.

66. *ACW,* 21, 28 June 1901; Dale, *Impressions,* p. 262.

10. The Legacy of the 1880s

1. *ACW,* 4 January 1901; *Church Standard* (Sydney), 1 December 1900, 19 January 1901.

2. J.D. Bollen, *Protestantism and Social Reform in New South Wales, 1890-1910* (Melbourne: Melbourne University Press, 1972), pp. 177, 180.

3. N. Hicks, *"This Sin and Scandal": Australia's Population Debate 1891-1911* (Canberra: Australian National University Press, 1978), chap. 4.

4. *SMH,* 28 June 1909. See also references to drink and intemperance in J. Wilbur Chapman, *Revival Addresses* (Melbourne, 1909), pp. 35-39, 107-8. For a discussion of Chapman's campaign against the liquor industry in America, see W.G.

McLoughlin, Jr., *Modern Revivalism, Charles Grandison Finney to Billy Graham* (New York: The Ronald Press Company, 1959), pp. 386-87.

5. *SMH*, 14 June 1909. Gambling became more prominent in the social concerns of Protestants in New South Wales at the turn of the century than it had been in the 1880s, partly because of the introduction of the totalizator. See Richard Broome, *Treasure in Earthen Vessels: Protestant Christianity in New South Wales, 1900-1914* (St Lucia: University of Queensland Press, 1980), chap. 7.

6. See W. Phillips, " 'Six O'clock Swill': The Introduction of Early Closing of Hotel Bars in Australia'', *Historical Studies*, 19 (October 1980): 76-92. See also, Bollen, *Protestantism and Social Reform*, chaps. 8-10.

7. See P. O'Farrell, *The Catholic Church and Community in Australia: A History* (Melbourne: Nelson, 1977), pp. 300, 318-19, 374-78.

8. *S.A. Register*, 22 September 1885.

9. *SMH*, 27, 28 August, 3, 4 December 1964.

10. Ibid., 14 August 1964.

11. *PD* (NSW), 3rd ser., 60: 3598-600. *Australian Church Record* (Sydney), 27 January 1966. See also letter from Willis and Knox's reply, ibid., 10 March 1966, and Presbyterian statement on the Sunday question in letter, Neil Macleod, ibid., 24 March 1966.

12. Only the bishop of Armidale opposed liberalization. Willis claimed that the other bishops supported amendment of the law. *Australian Church Record*, 27 January, 10 March 1966.

13. *Report of the Board of Inquiry on Sunday Observance in Tasmania* (1967) in *Journal and Printed Papers of the Parliament of Tasmania*, 1967, 177: esp. 21-26, 64-72.

14. Joint Committee on the Australian Capital Territory, *Report on Sunday Observance in the Australian Capital Territory* (Canbera: A.G.P.S., 1971), p. 3. See also *PD* (Vic.), 289: 2721.

15. *Year Book NSW*, 1955, p. 316. See also *Report of the Royal Commission . . . on Liquor Laws in New South Wales* (1954), pp. 75-88, in *Parliamentary Papers* (NSW), 1954, pp. 51-155; *Victorian Year Book* 1954-58, p. 264.

16. *Report of the Royal Commission into the Sale, Supply, Disposal or Consumption of Liquor in the State of Victoria* (1965), pt. 2, pp. 11-12, in *Parliamentary Papers* (Vic), 1964-65, 2: 1169-1219.

17. *Minutes, General Conference of the Methodist Church of Australasia*, 1953, pp. 133, 1957, pp. 97-98.

18. J.A.T. Robinson, *Honest to God* (London: S.C.M. Press, 1963), p. 139. For a summary of this literature, see A.R. Vidler, *The Church in an Age of Revolution*, rev. ed. (Penguin, 1971), chap. 24. See also E.R. Norman, *Church and Society in England 1770-1970: A Historical Study* (Oxford: Clarendon Press, 1976), chap. 10; N.W.H. Blaikie, *The Plight of the Australian Clergy: To Convert, Care or Challenge?* (St Lucia: University of Queensland Press, 1979), esp. chap. 1.

19. R.W. Dale, *Impressions of Australia* (London: Hodder and Stoughton, 1889), p. 263.

20. Protestants declined from 76.5 per cent of the Christian population in 1933 (the earliest reliable census for comparison with later figures) to 67.3 per cent in 1976. (The percentage of Christians fell from 86.4 per cent to 78.6 in the same period.) Of course migration since World War II has changed the distribution of the population among the various religious bodies. But an increasing proportion now specifically professes "no religion" — 0.8 per cent in 1966, 6.7 in 1971 and 8.3 in 1976, quite apart from the large number that does not reply to the question. The drop in the Protestant proportion of total church attendances is, however, significant — from 70 per cent in 1900 (when Protestants were about

the same percentage of the total population) to around 55 per cent in the 1960s. It has hardly changed since. See *Census of the Commonwealth of Australia,* 1933, 1961, 1966, 1971, 1976; W. Phillips, "Religious Profession and Practice in New South Wales, 1850-1901: The Statistical Evidence" *Historical Studies* 15 (1972-73): 385-94. See also AGE POLL, *Age,* 15 January 1979.

A Note on Sources

This book is based mainly on printed sources, viz., *Parliamentary Debates; Parliamentary Papers;* reports of proceedings of the various diocesan synods and denominational assemblies and conferences in New South Wales, and of the Anglican General Synod, the Wesleyan Methodist General Conference and other intercolonial conferences. Extensive use was also made of the daily press, especially the *Sydney Morning Herald* and *Sydney Daily Telegraph,* and the denominational weeklies and monthlies as well as the interdenominational weekly, the *Australian Christian World.* Other important printed sources were the *Pastoral Letters* of Archbishop R.B. Vaughan and Cardinal P.F. Moran, the *Pastoral Letters* of the First and Second Plenary Councils of the Catholic Church in Australia; and Circulars of the Diocese of Sydney, 1842 to 1895 (bound in one volume in Archives of the Anglican Archdiocese of Sydney). Space does not permit the listing of the many pamphlets, the clerical autobiographies and reminiscences and older denominational histories used in this work, but a number of these will be found in the notes. A full list will be found in the author's doctoral dissertation, "Christianity and its defence in New South Wales circa 1880 to 1890" (Ph.D. thesis, Australian National University, 1969).

The following manuscript sources were also consulted: Letters and Memoranda relating to religious instruction in public schools, Department of Public Instruction, (Box P4059, NSW State Archives); Parkes Correspondence, 1880-1890 (Mitchell Library, Public Library of New South Wales); Cardinal P.F. Moran's Diary and Papers; Archbishop Vaughan's Papers (St Mary's Cathedral Archives, Sydney); Congregational Union Papers, formerly collection of the Congregational Historical Committee (Mitchell Library, uncatalogued); Minute Books of various Primitive Methodist Churches in New South Wales (Uniting Church Records and Historical Society, Sydney); The Reverend James Jefferis's Papers (temporarily in the author's custody).

Select Bibliography

This bibliography is confined to modern works on religious history in Australia, mainly in the nineteenth century. Relevant works on British and American religious history are mentioned in the notes.

Books and Articles

General

Barrett, John. *That Better Country: The Religious Aspect of Life in Eastern Australia, 1835-1850*. (Melbourne: Melbourne University Press, 1966).

Bollen, J.D. "The Temperance Movement and the Liberal Party in New South Wales Politics, 1900-1914", *JRH* 1 (1960-61): 160-81.

——————— *Protestantism and Social Reform in New South Wales, 1890-1910* (Melbourne: Melbourne University Press, 1972).

Broome, Richard. *Treasure in Earthen Vessels: Protestant Christianity in New South Wales 1900-1914* (St Lucia: University of Queensland Press, 1980).

Cable, K.J. "Religious Controversies in New South Wales in the Mid-Nineteenth Century". 2 pts. *JRAHS* 49 (1963): 58-74, 136-48.

——————— "Protestant Problems in New South Wales in the Mid-Nineteenth Century". *JRH* 3: 119-36.

Davis, R.P. "Christian Socialism in Tasmania 1890-1920". *JRH* 7 (1972-73): 51-68.

Ely, Richard. "Andrew Inglis Clark and Church-State Separation". *JRH* 8 (1974-75): 271-89.

——————— *Unto God and Caesar: Religious Issues in the Emerging Commonwealth 1891-1906* (Melbourne: Melbourne University Press, 1976).

French, Maurice. "The Church Extension Crisis in South Australia: The Impact of Depression and Demographic Changes on Church Organization in the late Nineteenth Century". *JRH* 8 (1974-75): 390-405.

Gregory, J.S. *Church and State: Changing Government Policies towards Religion in Australia; with particular reference to Victoria since separation* (Melbourne: Cassell Australia, 1973).

Howe, Renate. "Protestantism, social Christianity and the ecology of Melbourne, 1890-1900". *Historical Studies* 19 (1980): 59-73.

Lawson, Ronald. "The Political Influence of the Churches in Brisbane in the 1890s". *JRH* 7 (1972-73): 144-62.

McKernan, Michael. "An Incident in Social Reform, Melbourne 1906". *JRH* 10 (1978-79): 70-85.

Mol, J.J. *Religion in Australia: A Sociological Investigation* (Melbourne: Nelson, 1971).

Mozley, Ann. "Evolution and the Climate of Opinion in Australia, 1840-1870". *Victorian Studies* 10 (1966-67): 411-30.

O'Farrell, P. "Writing the General History of Australian Religion". *JRH* 9 (1976-77): 85-92.

————— "Historians and Religious Convictions". *Historical Studies* 17 (1976-77): 279-98.

Phillips, Walter. "The Churches and the Sunday Question in Sydney in the 1880s". *JRH* 6 (1970-71): 41-61.

————— "Religious Profession and Practice in New South Wales, 1850-1901: The Statistical Evidence". *Historical Studies* 15 (1972-73): 378-400.

————— "The Defence of Christian Belief in Australia 1875-1914: The Responses to Evolution and Higher Criticism". *JRH* 9 (1976-77): 402-23.

Roe, Jill, "Challenge and Response: Religious Life in Melbourne, 1876-1886". *JRH* 5 (1968-69): 149-66.

Roe, M. *Quest for Authority in Eastern Australia, 1835-1851* (Melbourne: Melbourne University Press, in association with the Australian National University, 1965).

Sommers, Tess Van. *Religions in Australia: The Pix Series Extended to 41 Beliefs* (Adelaide: Rigby, 1966).

Suttor, T.L. "The Criticism of Religious Certitude in Australia, 1875-1900." *JRH* 1 (1960-61): 26-39.

Turner, Naomi. *Sinews of Sectarian Warfare? State Aid in New South Wales 1836-1862* (Canberra: Australian National University Press, 1972).

Walker, R.B. "The Later History of the Church and School Lands". *JRAHS* 47 (1961): 234-45.

Woolmington, Jean, ed. *Religion in Early Australia: The Problem of Church and State* (Melbourne: Cassell Australia, 1976).

Denominational

Anglican

Border, Ross. *Church and State in Australia 1788-1872: A Constitutional Study of the Church of England in Australia* (London: S.P.C.K., 1962).

Brown, Judith. *Augustus Short, D.D., Bishop of Adelaide* (Adelaide: Hodge Publishing House, 1973).

Daw, E.D. "Synodical Government for the Church of England in NSW: The First Attempt", *JRH* 6 (1970-71): 151-76.

Elkin, A.P. *The Diocese of Newcastle* (Glebe: Australian Medical Publishing Company, 1955).

Giles, R.A. *The Constitutional History of the Australian Church* (London: Skeffington and Son Ltd, 1929).

Meaney, N.K. "The Church of England in 'the Paradise of Dissent': A Problem of Assimilation". *JRH* 3 (1964-65): 137-57.

Rowland, E.C. *A Century of the English Church in New South Wales* (Sydney and London: Angus and Robertson, 1948).

Shaw, G.P. *Patriarch and Patriot: William Grant Broughton, 1788-1853, Colonial Statesman and Ecclesiastic* (Melbourne: Melbourne University Press, 1978).

Teale, Ruth. "A Brave New World in the Australian Bush: The Anglican Diocese of Bathurst and its First Bishop, Samuel Edward Marsden". *JRAHS* 53 (1967): 139-57.

Thorn, Barbara, ed. *Letters From Goulburn: A Selection of Letters from Mesac Thomas, First Bishop of Goulburn, 1863-1892* (Canberra: Diocese of Canberra and Goulburn, 1964).

Withycombe, Robert. "Church of England Attitudes to Social Questions in the Diocese of Sydney, c.1856-1866". *JRAHS* 47 (1966): 94-121.

Wyatt, Ransome T. *The History of the Diocese of Goulburn* (Sydney: E. Bragg, 1937).

Yarwood, A.T. *Samuel Marsden: The Great Survivor* (Melbourne: Melbourne University Press, 1977).

Baptist

Bollen, J.D. *Australian Baptists: A Religious Minority* (London: The Baptist Historical Society, 1975).
Hughes, H. Estcourt. *Our First Hundred Years: The Baptist Church of South Australia* (Adelaide: South Australian Baptist Union, 1937).
Prior, Alan C. *Some Fell on Good Ground: A History of the Beginnings and Development of the Baptist Church in New South Wales, Australia, 1831-1965* (Sydney: Baptist Union of New South Wales, 1966).
Wilkin, F.J. *Baptists in Victoria: Our First Hundred Years, 1838-1938* (Melbourne: Baptist Union of Victoria, 1939).

Catholic

Fogarty, Ronald. *Catholic Education in Australia, 1806-1950.* 2 vols (Melbourne: Melbourne University Press, 1959).
Ford, Patrick. *Cardinal Moran and the A.L.P.* (Melbourne: Melbourne University Press, 1966).
Haines, Gregory. *Lay Catholics and the Education Question in Nineteenth Century New South Wales: The Shaping of a Decision* (Sydney: Catholic Theological Faculty, 1976).
Livingston, K.T. *The Emergence of an Australian Catholic Priesthood 1835-1915* (Sydney: Catholic Theological Faculty, 1977).
Molony, John N. *The Roman Mould of the Australian Catholic Church* (Melbourne: Melbourne University Press, 1969).
Murtagh, James G. *Australia: The Catholic Chapter.* Australian Edition (Sydney: Angus and Robertson, 1959). First published New York, 1946.
O'Brien, Eris. "Cardinal Moran's Part in Public Affairs", *JRAHS* 28 (1942): 1-28.
O'Farrell, Patrick. ed. *Documents in Australian Catholic History.* 2 vols (London: Geoffrey Chapman, 1969).
————— *The Catholic Church and Community in Australia: A History* (Melbourne: Nelson, 1977) (A new, revised and expanded edition of *The Catholic Church in Australia: A Short History 1788-1967,* published 1968).
O'Kane, Frances. *A Path is Set: The Catholic Church in the Port Phillip District and Victoria 1839-1862* (Melbourne: Melbourne University Press, 1976).
Suttor, T.L. *Hierarchy and Democracy in Australia 1788-1870: The Formation of Australian Catholicism* (Melbourne: Melbourne University Press, 1965).
Waldersee, James. *Catholic Society in New South Wales 1788-1860* (Sydney: Sydney University Press, 1974).

Congregationalist

Garrett, John and Farr, L.W. *Camden College: A Centenary History* (Sydney: Camden College, 1964).
Jackson, Hugh. "Moving house and changing churches: the case of the Melbourne Congregationalists". *Historical Studies* 19 (1980): 74-85.
Kiek, E.S. *An Apostle in Australia: The Life and Reminiscences of Joseph Coles Kirby, Christian Pioneer and Social Reformer* (London: Independent Press, 1927).
Walker, R. "Congregationalism in South Australia 1837-1900". *Proceedings of the Royal Geographical Society of Australasia* 69 (1967-68): 12-28.

Methodist

Benson, C. Irving, ed. A Century of Victorian Methodism (Melbourne: Spectator Publishing Co., n.d.).

Bollen, J.D. "A Time of Small Things — the Methodist Mission in New South Wales, 1815-1836". *JRH* 7 (1972-73): 225-47.

Colwell, James. *The Illustrated History of Methodism. Australia: 1812-1855. New South Wales and Polynesia: 1856 to 1902* (Sydney: William Brook and Co. Ltd, 1904).

Howe, Renate. "Social Composition of the Wesleyan Church in Victoria During the Nineteenth Century". *JRH* 4 (1966-67): 206-17.

Walker, R.B. "Methodism in the 'Paradise of Dissent', 1837-1900". *JRH* 5 (1968-69): 331-47.

_____ "The Growth and Typology of the Wesleyan Methodist Church in New South Wales, 1812-1901", *JRH* 6 (1970-71): 331-47.

Presbyterian

Macdonald, A. *One Hundred Years of Presbyterianism in Victoria.* Centenary History issued by the authority of the General Assembly of the Presbyterian Church of Victoria (Melbourne: Robertson and Mullens, 1937).

Robinson, J. Campbell. *The Free Presbyterian Church of Australia* (Melbourne: W.A. Hamer, 1947).

Walker, R.B. "Presbyterian Church and People in the Colony of New South Wales in the Late Nineteenth Century". *JRH* 2 (1962-63): 49-65.

White, C.A. *The Challenge of the Years: A History of the Presbyterian Church of Australia in the State of New South Wales* (Sydney: Angus and Robertson, 1951).

Salvation Army

Dale, Percival. *Salvation Chariot: A Review of the First Seventy-One Years of the Salvation Army in Australia, 1880-1951* (Melbourne: Salvation Army Press, 1952).

Howe, Renate. " 'Five Conquering Years': The leadership of Commandant and Mrs W. Booth of the Salvation Army in Victoria, 1896 to 1901". *JRH* 6 (1970-71) 177-97.

Unpublished Theses

Cable, K.J. "The Church of England in New South Wales and its Policy towards Education prior to 1880". M.A. thesis. University of Sydney, 1952.

Elford, K. "Church, State, Education and Society: An Analysis of Aspects of Eastern Australian Society 1856-1872". Ph.D. thesis, University of Sydney, 1971.

French, Maurice. "Churches and Society in South Australia, 1890-1900: An Exercise in Reassurance". M.A. thesis, Flinders University, 1969.

Howe, Renate. "The Wesleyan Church in Victoria, 1855-1901: Its Ministry and Membership". M.A. thesis, University of Melbourne, 1965.

_____ "The Response of the Protestant Churches to Urbanization in Melbourne and Chicago, 1875-1914". Ph.D. thesis, University of Melbourne, 1972.

Jackson, H.R. "Aspects of Congregationalism in South-Eastern Australia circa 1880 to 1930". Ph.D. thesis, Australian National University, 1978.

Lyons, Mark. "Aspects of Sectarianism in New South Wales, circa 1865 to 1880". Ph.D. thesis, Australian National University, 1972.

Smith, F.B. "The Sunday Observance Controversy in Melbourne, 1874-1910". B.A. Honours essay, Department of History, University of Melbourne, 1956.

_____ "Religion and Freethought in Melbourne, 1870-1890". M.A. thesis, University of Melbourne, 1960.

Teale, Ruth. "By Hook and By Crook: The Anglican Diocese of Bathurst, 1870-1911". M.A. thesis, University of Sydney, 1967.

Index